Air Fryer

Cookbook for Beginners

800

Quick and Delicious Air Fryer Recipes with Only 5 Ingredients Or Less for the Smart People 2022 Edition

Debbi Holford

CONTENTS

Introduction..12

Chapter 1. Cooking with Your Air Fryer..**13**

Seeing the Benefits of Air Frying............................ 13   Simple Food You Can Make in the Air Fryer.................... 14

5 Ways to Prevent Air Frying Your Food to a Crisp......... 13   Tips and Tricks for Using the Air Fryer....................15

Air Fryer Safety Tips..................................16

Chapter 2. Bread And Breakfast...**17**

1......Sausage Solo..17
2......Mediterranean Egg Sandwich....................... 17
3......Bunless Breakfast Turkey Burgers...................17
4......Bacon & Hot Dogs Omelet.........................17
5......Not-so-english Muffins.............................17
6......Tomatoes Frittata....................................17
7......Taj Tofu...18
8......Simple Egg Soufflé.................................. 18
9......Easy Egg Bites.......................................18
10....Parmesan Garlic Naan...............................18
11....Almond Oatmeal......................................18
12....Egg Muffins..18
13....Breakfast Quiche.....................................19
14....Green Scramble.......................................19
15....All-in-one Breakfast Toast..........................19
16....English Muffin Sandwiches..........................19
17....Zucchini And Spring Onions Cakes..................19
18....Creamy Parsley Soufflé.............................19
19....Puffed Egg Tarts.....................................19
20....Grilled Bbq Sausages................................20
21....Strawberry Bread.....................................20
22....Banana Baked Oatmeal..............................20
23....Chocolate Almond Crescent Rolls...................20
24....Inside-out Cheeseburgers............................20
25....Hashbrown Potatoes Lyonnaise......................21
26....Smoked Salmon Croissant Sandwich................21
27....Scones...21
28....Spinach-bacon Rollups...............................21
29....Seasoned Herbed Sourdough Croutons..............21
30....Cheddar Soufflés.....................................22
31....Eggs Salad..22
32....Whole-grain Cornbread...............................22
33....Very Berry Breakfast Puffs..........................22
34....Perfect Burgers.......................................22
35....Avocado Tempura......................................22
36....Mini Pita Breads.....................................23
37....Pigs In A Blanket....................................23
38....Bacon Puff Pastry Pinwheels........................23
39....Mini Bagels...23

40....Garlic-cheese Biscuits...............................24
41....Flaky Cinnamon Rolls...............................24
42....Medium Rare Simple Salt And Pepper Steak.............24
43....Strawberry Pastry....................................24
44....Spinach Omelet.......................................24
45....Breakfast Bake..25
46....Sausage Bacon Fandango.............................25
47....Mini Bacon Egg Quiches.............................25
48....Bacon And Cheese Quiche............................25
49....Hole In One..25
50....Coconut Eggs Mix....................................25
51....Garlic Bread Knots...................................25
52....Hard-"boiled" Eggs...................................26
53....Cinnamon Rolls.......................................26
54....Country Gravy..26
55....Chocolate-hazelnut Bear Claws.......................26
56....Jalapeño Egg Cups...................................26
57....French Toast Sticks..................................27
58....Cheese Eggs And Leeks..............................27
59....Meaty Omelet...27
60....Jalapeño And Bacon Breakfast Pizza.................27
61....Roasted Golden Mini Potatoes.......................27
62....Chocolate Chip Scones...............................27
63....Banana-nut Muffins..................................28
64....Peppered Maple Bacon Knots.........................28
65....Green Onion Pancakes...............................28
66....Mini Tomato Quiche.................................28
67....Scrambled Eggs.......................................28
68....Cheesy Mustard Toasts..............................29
69....Strawberry Toast.....................................29
70....Egg White Frittata...................................29
71....Crunchy Falafel Balls................................29
72....Bacon Eggs...29
73....Coconut Pudding......................................29
74....English Breakfast....................................29
75....Onion Marinated Skirt Steak........................30
76....Cheese Pie..30
77....Egg In A Hole..30
78....Sausage Egg Muffins................................30

79....Black's Bangin' Casserole..................30
80....Bacon, Egg, And Cheese Calzones..................30
81....Baked Eggs..................31
82....Ham And Egg Toast Cups..................31
83....Spinach Eggs And Cheese..................31
84....Brown Sugar Grapefruit..................31
85....Sweet Potato-cinnamon Toast..................31
86....Pizza Eggs..................31
87....Greek-style Frittata..................32
88....Oregano And Coconut Scramble..................32
89....Maple-bacon Doughnuts..................32

90....Crust-less Quiche..................32
91....Parsley Egg Scramble With Cottage Cheese..............32
92....Tuscan Toast..................32
93....Sausage-crusted Egg Cups..................32
94....Cheesy Bell Pepper Eggs..................33
95....Breakfast Chimichangas..................33
96....Blueberry Muffins..................33
97....Buttery Scallops..................33
98....Chocolate Chip Muffins..................33
99....Bacon Cups..................34
100..Bagels..................34

Chapter 3. Appetizers And Snacks..................34

101..Potato Skins..................34
102..Greek Street Tacos..................34
103..Cheese Crackers..................34
104..Parmesan Pizza Nuggets..................35
105..Grilled Cheese Sandwich Deluxe..................35
106..Wrapped Shrimp Bites..................35
107..Homemade French Fries..................35
108..Mozzarella Sticks..................35
109..Buttery Spiced Pecans..................36
110..Carrot Chips..................36
111..Three Cheese Dip..................36
112..Plantain Chips..................36
113..Fried Pickles..................36
114..Homemade Pretzel Bites..................36
115..Crispy Ravioli Bites..................37
116..Bacon Candy..................37
117..Bacon-wrapped Cabbage Bites..................37
118..Pita Chips..................37
119..Bacon Butter..................38
120..Veggie Chips..................38
121..Thyme Sweet Potato Chips..................38
122..Fried Ranch Pickles..................38
123..Blue Cheesy Potato Wedges..................38
124..Parmesan Zucchini Fries..................38
125..Roasted Chickpeas..................39
126..Sugar-glazed Walnuts..................39
127..Cauliflower "tater" Tots..................39
128..Bacon-wrapped Goat Cheese Poppers..................39
129..Apple Rollups..................39
130..Buffalo Cauliflower Bites..................40
131..Roasted Peppers..................40
132..Sweet Apple Fries..................40
133..Beer-battered Onion Rings..................40
134..Green Olive And Mushroom Tapenade..................40
135..Bacon-wrapped Jalapeño Poppers..................41
136..Roasted Red Pepper Dip..................41

137..Sweet Potato Chips..................41
138..Okra Chips..................41
139..Cinnamon Pita Chips..................41
140..Chili Kale Chips..................41
141..Fried Olives..................42
142..Charred Shishito Peppers..................42
143..Croutons..................42
144..Bbq Chicken Wings..................42
145..Cheddar Cheese Lumpia Rolls..................42
146..Fiery Bacon-wrapped Dates..................42
147..Sausage And Cheese Rolls..................43
148..Taquito Quesadillas..................43
149..Home-style Taro Chips..................43
150..Spicy Turkey Meatballs..................43
151..Kale Chips..................43
152..Mini Greek Meatballs..................43
153..Mexican Muffins..................44
154..Savory Ranch Chicken Bites..................44
155..Avocado Fries..................44
156..Crispy Prawns..................44
157..Korean-style Wings..................44
158..Italian-style Fried Olives..................44
159..Roasted Red Salsa..................45
160..Ham And Cheese Sliders..................45
161..Garlic–cream Cheese Wontons..................45
162..Roasted Carrots..................45
163..Italian Dip..................45
164..Sweet-and-salty Pretzels..................45
165..Thick-crust Pepperoni Pizza..................46
166..Chocolate Bacon Bites..................46
167..Bacon-wrapped Mozzarella Sticks..................46
168..Bacon & Blue Cheese Tartlets..................46
169..Grilled Cheese Sandwiches..................46
170..Buffalo Chicken Dip..................46
171..Wrapped Smokies In Bacon..................46
172..Chives Meatballs..................47

173..Air Fry Bacon.....................................47	187..Cheesy Pigs In A Blanket.....................49
174..Fried Goat Cheese.............................47	188..Za'atar Garbanzo Beans.......................49
175..Pepperoni Rolls.................................47	189..Onion Ring Nachos............................50
176..Broccoli And Carrot Bites...................47	190..Tomato & Garlic Roasted Potatoes........50
177..Roasted Peanuts...............................47	191..Pickled Chips..................................50
178..Warm And Salty Edamame.................48	192..Fried Mozzarella Sticks.....................50
179..Fried Dill Pickle Chips......................48	193..Bacon-y Cauliflower Skewers..............50
180..Garlic Parmesan Kale Chips...............48	194..Crispy Salami Roll-ups......................51
181..Pork Egg Rolls................................48	195..Easy Crispy Prawns..........................51
182..Skinny Fries...................................48	196..Pepperoni Chips...............................51
183..Potato Chips...................................49	197..Zucchini Chips.................................51
184..Italian Bruschetta With Mushrooms & Cheese..........49	198..Buffalo Cauliflower Wings..................51
185..Herbed Cheese Brittle.......................49	199..Eggplant Fries.................................51
186..Bacon-wrapped Onion Rings...............49	200..Honey Tater Tots With Bacon...............52

Chapter 4. Beef , pork & Lamb Recipes...52

201..Honey-sriracha Pork Ribs....................52	233..Bacon With Shallot And Greens.............58
202..Pork Belly Marinated In Onion-coconut Cream....52	234..Air Fried Steak.................................58
203..Marinated Steak Kebabs.....................52	235..Spinach And Provolone Steak Rolls........58
204..Rosemary Lamb Chops......................52	236..Venison Backstrap............................58
205..Mustard Pork..................................53	237..Pork Chops....................................58
206..Chicken-fried Steak..........................53	238..Parmesan-crusted Pork Chops..............59
207..Barbecue-style Beef Cube Steak...........53	239..Easy Garlic Butter Steak.....................59
208..London Broil..................................53	240..Bacon Wrapped Filets Mignons............59
209..Crispy Pork Pork Escalopes................53	241..Cheddar Bacon Ranch Pinwheels..........59
210..Delicious Cheeseburgers....................53	242..Lamb Chops...................................59
211..Mustard And Rosemary Pork Tenderloin With Fried Apples.....54	243..Air Fried Grilled Steak.......................59
212..Baby Back Ribs...............................54	244..Empanadas.....................................60
213..Stuffed Peppers...............................54	245..Roast Beef.....................................60
214..Bourbon-bbq Sauce Marinated Beef Bbq....54	246..Air Fried Thyme Garlic Lamb Chops......60
215..City "chicken".................................55	247..Boneless Ribeyes.............................60
216..Garlic And Oregano Lamb Chops..........55	248..Crouton-breaded Pork Chops...............60
217..Cheeseburgers.................................55	249..Friday Night Cheeseburgers.................61
218..Peppered Steak Bites.........................55	250..Extra Crispy Country-style Pork Riblets...61
219..Simple Pork Chops...........................55	251..Ground Beef...................................61
220..Champagne-vinegar Marinated Skirt Steak....56	252..Herbed Beef Roast............................61
221..Beef & Mushrooms...........................56	253..Lamb Burgers..................................61
222..Canadian-style Rib Eye Steak..............56	254..Buttery Pork Chops...........................61
223..Teriyaki Country-style Pork Ribs..........56	255..Pepperoni Pockets............................62
224..Salty Lamb Chops............................56	256..Mozzarella-stuffed Meatloaf................62
225..Tasty Filet Mignon............................56	257..Meatloaf.......................................62
226..Orange And Brown Sugar–glazed Ham....56	258..Lemon-butter Veal Cutlets..................62
227..Cheese-stuffed Steak Burgers...............57	259..Easy & The Traditional Beef Roast Recipe....62
228..Barbecue-style London Broil.................57	260..Mustard Beef Mix.............................62
229..Rib Eye Steak.................................57	261..Egg Stuffed Pork Meatballs.................63
230..Sweet And Spicy Spare Ribs................57	262..Beef Al Carbon (street Taco Meat).........63
231..Wasabi-coated Pork Loin Chops............57	263..Bacon And Blue Cheese Burgers...........63
232..Mexican-style Shredded Beef...............58	264..Stress-free Beef Patties......................63
	265..Honey Mesquite Pork Chops................63

266..Bacon-wrapped Pork Tenderloin.................................. 63
267..Steak Bites And Spicy Dipping Sauce......................64
268..Mustard-crusted Rib-eye......................................64
269..Salted Porterhouse With Sage 'n Thyme Medley........64
270..Simple Beef..64
271..Mustard Herb Pork Tenderloin............................. 64
272..Sweet Potato–crusted Pork Rib Chops......................64
273..Marinated Rib Eye... 65
274..Maple'n Soy Marinated Beef..............................65
275..Simple Air Fryer Steak.....................................65
276..Almond And Sun-dried Tomato Crusted Pork Chops. 65
277..Fajita Flank Steak Rolls.................................... 65
278..Bjorn's Beef Steak...66
279..Perfect Strip Steaks....................................... 66
280..Mccornick Pork Chops......................................66
281..Smokehouse-style Beef Ribs................................66
282..German-style Pork Patties...............................66
283..Crispy Five-spice Pork Belly.............................. 66

284..Tonkatsu.. 67
285..Provençal Grilled Rib-eye................................67
286..Corn Dogs... 67
287..Beef Short Ribs.. 67
288..Steakhouse Filets Mignons............................... 67
289..Crispy Ham And Eggs.................................... 68
290..Crunchy Veal Cutlets..................................... 68
291..Pesto Coated Rack Of Lamb............................. 68
292..Steak Kebabs.. 68
293..Crispy Pierogi With Kielbasa And Onions............. 69
294..Salted 'n Peppered Scored Beef Chuck................. 69
295..Garlic Fillets.. 69
296..Jumbo Italian Meatballs................................. 69
297..Brown Sugar Mustard Pork Loin........................ 69
298..Sweet And Spicy Pork Ribs............................. 69
299..Spinach And Mushroom Steak Rolls.................... 70
300..Grilled Prosciutto Wrapped Fig......................... 70

Chapter 5. Poultry Recipes...70

301..Crispy Cajun Fried Chicken..............................70
302..Chicken Nuggets.. 70
303..Cajun-breaded Chicken Bites............................70
304..Bacon-wrapped Chicken.................................. 71
305..Tuscan Stuffed Chicken.................................. 71
306..Fried Chicken Halves..................................... 71
307..Hot Chicken Skin... 71
308..Roasted Chicken.. 71
309..Herb-marinated Chicken.................................. 71
310..Gingered Chicken Drumsticks........................... 72
311..Mustardy Chicken Bites.................................. 72
312..Jerk Chicken Kebabs..................................... 72
313..Pickle-brined Fried Chicken............................. 72
314..Chicken Wings.. 72
315..Crispy Tender Parmesan Chicken....................... 72
316..Spinach And Feta Stuffed Chicken Breasts............. 73
317..Buffalo Chicken Meatballs...............................73
318..Thyme Turkey Nuggets................................... 73
319..Parmesan Chicken Tenders............................... 73
320..Grilled Chicken Pesto.....................................73
321..Popcorn Chicken.. 74
322..Crunchy Chicken Strips................................... 74
323..Party Buffalo Chicken Drumettes........................ 74
324..Dill Pickle–ranch Wings.................................. 74
325..Fantasy Sweet Chili Chicken Strips..................... 74
326..Italian Chicken Thighs.................................... 74
327..Butter And Bacon Chicken............................... 75
328..Creamy Chicken Tenders................................. 75
329..Cinnamon Chicken Thighs................................75

330..Chipotle Drumsticks.....................................75
331..Blackened Chicken Tenders............................. 75
332..Spinach 'n Bacon Egg Cups............................. 75
333..15-minute Chicken...................................... 76
334..Barbecue Chicken Enchiladas.......................... 76
335..Family Chicken Fingers................................. 76
336..Pretzel-crusted Chicken.................................76
337..Chipotle Aioli Wings.................................... 76
338..Chicken Chunks... 76
339..Sticky Drumsticks....................................... 77
340..Pecan-crusted Chicken Tenders........................ 77
341..Chicken Parmesan Casserole........................... 77
342..Chicken Fajita Poppers..................................77
343..Sweet Lime 'n Chili Chicken Barbecue................. 77
344..Garlic Dill Wings.. 77
345..Salt And Pepper Wings.................................. 78
346..Lemon Sage Roast Chicken............................. 78
347..Shishito Pepper Rubbed Wings......................... 78
348..Creamy Onion Chicken.................................. 78
349..Basic Chicken Breasts................................... 78
350..Pulled Turkey Quesadillas.............................. 78
351..Bacon Chicken Mix...................................... 79
352..Barbecue Chicken Drumsticks.......................... 79
353..Air Fried Chicken Tenderloin........................... 79
354..Garlic Parmesan Drumsticks............................ 79
355..Easy & Crispy Chicken Wings.......................... 79
356..Chicken Tenders With Basil-strawberry Glaze.......... 79
357..Balsamic Duck And Cranberry Sauce................... 79
358..Turkey-hummus Wraps.................................. 80

359..Hasselback Alfredo Chicken....................80
360..Teriyaki Chicken Legs...........................80
361..Yummy Stuffed Chicken Breast..............80
362..Fried Herbed Chicken Wings..................80
363..Buffalo Chicken Wings...........................80
364..Crispy Italian Chicken Thighs.................81
365..Chicken & Pepperoni Pizza.....................81
366..Perfect Grill Chicken Breast....................81
367..Spice-rubbed Chicken Thighs..................81
368..Broccoli And Cheese–stuffed Chicken......81
369..Quick Chicken For Filling........................81
370..Crispy "fried" Chicken............................82
371..Zesty Ranch Chicken Drumsticks.............82
372..Ginger Turmeric Chicken Thighs.............82
373..Lemon Pepper Chicken Wings.................82
374..Chicken Pesto Pizzas..............................82
375..Cornish Hens With Honey-lime Glaze......82
376..Chicken Gruyere....................................83
377..Sweet Nutty Chicken Breasts...................83
378..Simple Salsa Chicken Thighs...................83
379..Peppery Lemon-chicken Breast...............83

380..Basic Chicken Breasts.............................83
381..Herb Seasoned Turkey Breast..................83
382..Buttermilk Brined Turkey Breast..............83
383..Air Fried Cheese Chicken........................84
384..Chicken Thighs In Salsa Verde................84
385..Quick 'n Easy Garlic Herb Wings............84
386..Spicy Pork Rind Fried Chicken................84
387..Baked Chicken Nachos...........................84
388..Buttermilk-fried Drumsticks....................84
389..Chicken Cordon Bleu.............................85
390..Italian Roasted Chicken Thighs...............85
391..Surprisingly Tasty Chicken......................85
392..Celery Chicken Mix................................85
393..Breaded Chicken Patties.........................85
394..Harissa Chicken Wings...........................85
395..Chicken Adobo......................................86
396..Yummy Shredded Chicken.....................86
397..Jerk Chicken Wings...............................86
398..Za'atar Chicken Drumsticks....................86
399..Garlic Ginger Chicken............................86
400..Tangy Mustard Wings............................86

Chapter 6. Fish And Seafood Recipes...87

401..Garlic Lemon Scallops............................87
402..Garlic-lemon Scallops.............................87
403..Crispy Smelts..87
404..French Clams...87
405..Teriyaki Salmon.....................................87
406..Great Cat Fish..87
407..Cajun Lobster Tails.................................88
408..Crunchy Coconut Shrimp.......................88
409..Easy Lobster Tail With Salted Butetr.........88
410..Ahi Tuna Steaks.....................................88
411..Shrimp Burgers......................................88
412..Ham Tilapia...88
413..Sesame Tuna Steak.................................88
414..Fish-in-chips...89
415..Timeless Garlic-lemon Scallops...............89
416..Crispy Sweet-and-sour Cod Fillets...........89
417..Crab-stuffed Avocado Boats....................89
418..Crunchy And Buttery Cod With Ritz Cracker Crust... 89
419..Potato-wrapped Salmon Fillets................90
420..Herbed Haddock....................................90
421..Honey-glazed Salmon.............................90
422..Super-simple Scallops.............................90
423..Cod Nuggets...90
424..Fish Taco Bowl......................................91
425..Garlic And Dill Salmon...........................91
426..Tuna Cakes...91

427..Simple Sesame Squid On The Grill...........91
428..Lemon And Thyme Sea Bass...................91
429..Miso Fish..91
430..Lime Flaming Halibut.............................91
431..Sardinas Fritas.......................................92
432..Fried Catfish Fillets................................92
433..Mediterranean-style Cod........................92
434..Simple Salmon Fillets.............................92
435..Shrimp Al Pesto.....................................92
436..Catalan Sardines With Romesco Sauce.....92
437..Lemon Butter Cod..................................92
438..Chili-lime Shrimp..................................93
439..Air Fried Cod With Basil Vinaigrette.........93
440..Lemon-roasted Salmon Fillets.................93
441..Better Fish Sticks...................................93
442..Very Easy Lime-garlic Shrimps................93
443..Seared Scallops In Beurre Blanc..............93
444..Sea Scallops...94
445..Italian Tuna Roast..................................94
446..Potato-crusted Cod................................94
447..Snapper Fillets With Thai Sauce..............94
448..Crab Cakes...94
449..Lemon Pepper–breaded Tilapia...............95
450..Italian Baked Cod..................................95
451..Nacho Chips Crusted Prawns..................95
452..Super Crunchy Flounder Fillets...............95

453..Horseradish-crusted Salmon Fillets..................95
454..Maple Butter Salmon...........................96
455..Tortilla-crusted With Lemon Filets..............96
456..Lemon-basil On Cod Filet.....................96
457..Lemon Shrimp And Zucchinis..................96
458..Salmon Patties................................96
459..Chili Blackened Shrimp.......................96
460..Coriander Cod And Green Beans...............96
461..Lemon Butter–dill Salmon.....................97
462..Beer-battered Cod............................97
463..Flounder Fillets..............................97
464..Tuna-stuffed Tomatoes........................97
465..Crab Rangoon................................97
466..Quick And Easy Shrimp.......................98
467..Fish Sticks For Kids..........................98
468..Thyme Scallops...............................98
469..Easy-peasy Shrimp............................98
470..Italian Shrimp................................98
471..Mahi-mahi "burrito" Fillets....................98
472..Simple Salmon................................98
473..Zesty Mahi Mahi..............................99
474..Bacon-wrapped Scallops.......................99
475..Coconut Shrimp...............................99
476..Tilapia Fish Fillets............................99

477..Tilapia Teriyaki...............................99
478..Catfish Nuggets...............................100
479..Coconut Jerk Shrimp..........................100
480..Lemon Butter Scallops.........................100
481..Air Fried Catfish..............................100
482..Smoked Halibut And Eggs In Brioche............100
483..Fried Oysters.................................101
484..Panko-breaded Cod Fillets.....................101
485..Perfect Soft-shelled Crabs.....................101
486..Southern-style Catfish.........................101
487..Spicy Mackerel...............................101
488..Crispy Parmesan Lobster Tails..................102
489..Outrageous Crispy Fried Salmon Skin............102
490..Maple Balsamic Glazed Salmon.................102
491..Spicy Prawns.................................102
492..Cajun Flounder Fillets.........................102
493..Restaurant-style Flounder Cutlets...............102
494..Miso-rubbed Salmon Fillets....................103
495..Buttery Lobster Tails..........................103
496..Stevia Cod...................................103
497..Fish Fillet Sandwich...........................103
498..Lime Bay Scallops............................103
499..Air Fried Calamari............................104
500..Sweet Potato–wrapped Shrimp..................104

Chapter 7. Vegetable Side Dishes Recipes...104

501..Bacon-balsamic Brussels Sprouts...............104
502..Honey-mustard Asparagus Puffs................104
503..Savory Roasted Carrots........................104
504..Fingerling Potatoes............................104
505..Zucchini Bites................................105
506..Crispy Herbed Potatoes........................105
507..Perfect Broccoli...............................105
508..Roasted Salsa.................................105
509..Spicy Fries...................................105
510..Lemon Tempeh.................................105
511..Grilled Lime Scallions..........................106
512..Lemon And Butter Artichokes...................106
513..Steak Fries...................................106
514..Buttery Mushrooms............................106
515..Fried Mashed Potato Balls......................106
516..Brussels Sprout And Ham Salad.................106
517..Taco Okra....................................107
518..Mini Hasselback Potatoes......................107
519..Beet Fries....................................107
520..Mouth-watering Provençal Mushrooms..........107
521..Cauliflower...................................107
522..Parmesan Herb Radishes.......................107
523..Perfect Asparagus.............................107

524..Cheesy Vegetarian Lasagna.....................108
525..Dinner Rolls..................................108
526..Polenta.......................................108
527..Balsamic Green Beans With Bacon..............108
528..Blistered Green Beans..........................108
529..Home Fries...................................109
530..Sweet Roasted Pumpkin Rounds.................109
531..Grits Again...................................109
532..Sage Hasselback Potatoes......................109
533..Hasselbacks..................................109
534..Garlic-parmesan French Fries...................109
535..Roasted Peppers With Balsamic Vinegar And Basil.110
536..Mashed Potato Pancakes.......................110
537..Garlic Knots..................................110
538..Macaroni And Cheese.........................110
539..Cheesy Baked Asparagus.......................110
540..Roasted Yellow Squash And Onions.............111
541..Onions.......................................111
542..Simple Roasted Sweet Potatoes.................111
543..Smashed Fried Baby Potatoes...................111
544..Asparagus Wrapped In Pancetta................111
545..Honey-roasted Parsnips........................112
546..Potato Wedges...............................112

547..Mediterranean Zucchini Boats.....................112
548..Twice-baked Potatoes With Pancetta.....................112
549..Roasted Fennel Salad.....................112
550..Roasted Broccoli Salad.....................112
551..Foil Packet Lemon Butter Asparagus.....................113
552..Corn Muffins.....................113
553..Mushrooms, Sautéed.....................113
554..Okra.....................113
555..Tomato Salad.....................113
556..Yellow Squash And Zucchinis Dish.....................113
557..Sweet Butternut Squash.....................114
558..Roasted Brussels Sprouts.....................114
559..Turmeric Cauliflower Rice.....................114
560..French Fries.....................114
561..Crunchy Green Beans.....................114
562..Asparagus Fries.....................114
563..Roman Artichokes.....................114
564..Grilled Cheese.....................115
565..Buttermilk Biscuits.....................115
566..Savory Brussels Sprouts.....................115
567..Rich Baked Sweet Potatoes.....................115
568..Fried Corn On The Cob.....................115
569..Easy Parmesan Asparagus.....................116
570..Green Beans And Tomatoes Recipe.....................116
571..Buttered Brussels Sprouts.....................116
572..Turmeric Cabbage Mix.....................116
573..Parmesan Asparagus.....................116

574..Cheesy Garlic Bread.....................116
575..Cauliflower Rice Balls.....................117
576..Rosemary New Potatoes.....................117
577..Dijon Roast Cabbage.....................117
578..Simple Taro Fries.....................117
579..Sweet Potato Fries.....................117
580..Yellow Squash.....................117
581..Sea Salt Radishes.....................118
582..Brussels Sprouts.....................118
583..Simple Zucchini Ribbons.....................118
584..Mexican-style Frittata.....................118
585..Chipotle Chickpea Tacos.....................118
586..Green Beans And Potatoes Recipe.....................118
587..Almond Green Beans.....................119
588..Shoestring Butternut Squash Fries.....................119
589..Corn On The Cob.....................119
590..Spicy Fried Green Beans.....................119
591..Cheesy Loaded Broccoli.....................119
592..Crispy Brussels Sprouts.....................119
593..Shallots Almonds Green Beans.....................120
594..Crispy Green Beans.....................120
595..Hot Okra Wedges.....................120
596..Simple Peppared Carrot Chips.....................120
597..Glazed Carrots.....................120
598..Roasted Brussels Sprouts With Bacon.....................120
599..Pancetta Mushroom & Onion Sautée.....................120
600..Green Peas With Mint.....................121

Chapter 8. Vegetarians Recipes.....................121

601..Crispy Apple Fries With Caramel Sauce.....................121
602..Breadcrumbs Stuffed Mushrooms.....................121
603..Crispy Cabbage Steaks.....................121
604..Roasted Vegetable Pita Pizza.....................121
605..Savory Herb Cloud Eggs.....................122
606..Spaghetti Squash.....................122
607..Easy Baked Root Veggies.....................122
608..Vegetable Nuggets.....................122
609..Portobello Mini Pizzas.....................122
610..Cheese And Bean Enchiladas.....................122
611..Broccoli With Olives.....................123
612..Avocado Rolls.....................123
613..Garden Fresh Green Beans.....................123
614..Crispy Wings With Lemony Old Bay Spice.....................123
615..Cheesy Broccoli Sticks.....................123
616..Sweet Pepper Nachos.....................123
617..Chewy Glazed Parsnips.....................124
618..Almond Flour Battered Wings.....................124
619..Green Bean Sautée.....................124
620..Almond Asparagus.....................124

621..Twice-baked Broccoli-cheddar Potatoes.....................124
622..Buttered Broccoli.....................124
623..Roasted Vegetable Grilled Cheese.....................125
624..Caprese Eggplant Stacks.....................125
625..Sweet And Sour Brussel Sprouts.....................125
626..Spicy Celery Sticks.....................125
627..Pizza Dough.....................125
628..Cheese & Bean Burgers.....................125
629..Lemony Green Beans.....................126
630..Caribbean-style Fried Plantains.....................126
631..Two-cheese Grilled Sandwiches.....................126
632..Parmesan Artichokes.....................126
633..Broccoli With Cauliflower.....................126
634..Pesto Spinach Flatbread.....................126
635..Cauliflower Steaks Gratin.....................126
636..Garlic Okra Chips.....................127
637..Wine Infused Mushrooms.....................127
638..Brussels Sprouts With Balsamic Oil.....................127
639..Lemon Caper Cauliflower Steaks.....................127
640..Stuffed Mushrooms.....................127

641..Thyme Lentil Patties.. 127

642..Tortilla Pizza Margherita... 128

643..Pepper-pineapple With Butter-sugar Glaze.............. 128

644..Bell Peppers Cups.. 128

645..Layered Ravioli Bake.. 128

646..Pesto Vegetable Kebabs... 128

647..Crispy Eggplant Rounds.. 128

648..Sweet Roasted Carrots... 129

649..Curried Eggplant... 129

650..Black Bean And Rice Burrito Filling....................... 129

651..Caramelized Carrots.. 129

652..Effortless Mac 'n' Cheese.. 129

653..Spinach Pesto Flatbread... 129

654..Stuffed Portobellos... 129

655..Basil Tomatoes.. 130

656..Eggplant Parmesan... 130

657..Cool Mini Zucchini's.. 130

658..Alfredo Eggplant Stacks.. 130

659..Broccoli & Parmesan Dish.. 130

660..Falafels... 130

661..Cottage And Mayonnaise Stuffed Peppers.............. 130

662..Roasted Spaghetti Squash.. 131

663..Toasted Ravioli.. 131

664..Broccoli Salad... 131

665..Gourmet Wasabi Popcorn.. 131

666..Easy Glazed Carrots... 131

667..Roasted Cauliflower... 131

668..Grilled 'n Glazed Strawberries................................. 131

669..Spicy Roasted Cashew Nuts...................................... 132

670..Cauliflower Rice–stuffed Peppers............................ 132

671..Cheesy Cauliflower Crust Pizza................................ 132

672..Home-style Cinnamon Rolls...................................... 132

673..Gorgeous Jalapeño Poppers....................................... 132

674..Cauliflower Pizza Crust.. 132

675..Mediterranean Pan Pizza.. 133

676..Garlicky Roasted Mushrooms.................................... 133

677..Sesame Seeds Bok Choy.. 133

678..Honey Pear Chips.. 133

679..Zucchini Fritters.. 133

680..Italian Seasoned Easy Pasta Chips............................ 134

681..Sweet And Spicy Barbecue Tofu.............................. 134

682..Spinach And Feta Pinwheels..................................... 134

683..Spinach And Artichoke–stuffed Peppers.................. 134

684..Cauliflower Steak With Thick Sauce........................ 134

685..Sautéed Spinach.. 134

686..Zucchini Gratin.. 135

687..Baked Polenta With Chili-cheese.............................. 135

688..Pesto Vegetable Skewers.. 135

689..Cinnamon Sugar Tortilla Chips................................. 135

690..Healthy Apple-licious Chips...................................... 135

691..White Cheddar And Mushroom Soufflés................... 135

692..Caramelized Brussels Sprout..................................... 135

693..Skewered Corn In Air Fryer...................................... 136

694..Vegetable Burgers... 136

695..Zucchini Topped With Coconut Cream 'n Bacon..... 136

696..Turmeric Crispy Chickpeas.. 136

697..Tacos... 136

698..Crustless Spinach And Cheese Frittata..................... 136

699..Colorful Vegetable Medley.. 137

700..Crispy Shawarma Broccoli.. 137

Chapter 9. Desserts And Sweets..137

701..Apple Pie... 137

702..Fried Cannoli Wontons... 137

703..Apple Dumplings... 137

704..Pineapple Sticks.. 138

705..Shortbread Fingers.. 138

706..Dark Chocolate Cake.. 138

707..Chocolate Brownie.. 138

708..Brown Sugar Baked Apples....................................... 138

709..Cherry Cheesecake Rolls... 139

710..Easy Mug Brownie.. 139

711..Easy Keto Danish.. 139

712..Fried Banana S'mores... 139

713..Grilled Banana Boats.. 139

714..Cranberries Pudding.. 139

715..Cinnamon Canned Biscuit Donuts............................ 140

716..Banana And Rice Pudding.. 140

717..Orange Marmalade.. 140

718..Toasted Coconut Flakes.. 140

719..Grape Stew... 140

720..Fruit Turnovers.. 140

721..Keto Butter Balls... 140

722..Brownies For Two... 140

723..Fiesta Pastries.. 141

724..Glazed Donuts... 141

725..Chilled Strawberry Pie... 141

726..Lemon Iced Donut Balls... 141

727..Chocolate-covered Maple Bacon.............................. 141

728..Pumpkin Cake.. 141

729..Cocoa Bombs... 142

730..Monkey Bread.. 142

731..Roasted Pecan Clusters... 142

732..Raspberry Empanada... 142

733..Fried Snickers Bars... 142

734..S'mores Pockets... 143

735..Brownies...143
736..Coconut Macaroons.....................................143
737..Brown Sugar Cookies..................................143
738..Honey-roasted Mixed Nuts............................143
739..Cocoa Spread...144
740..Dark Chocolate Peanut Butter S'mores.............144
741..Baked Apple..144
742..Pumpkin Pie..144
743..No Flour Lime Muffins.................................144
744..Party S´mores..144
745..Sweet Potato Pie Rolls.................................145
746..Marshmallow Pastries..................................145
747..Merengues...145
748..Almond Shortbread Cookies..........................145
749..Molten Lava Cakes......................................145
750..Crème Brulee..146
751..Nutty Fudge Muffins...................................146
752..Ricotta Lemon Cake....................................146
753..Creamy Pudding...146
754..Chocolate Chip Cookie Cake.........................146
755..Oreo-coated Peanut Butter Cups....................146
756..Moon Pie..147
757..Tortilla Fried Pies.......................................147
758..Ricotta Stuffed Apples.................................147
759..Lemon Berries Stew.....................................147
760..Cream Cheese Shortbread Cookies..................147
761..Hearty Banana Pastry...................................147
762..Chocolate Doughnut Holes............................147
763..Cinnamon Pretzels......................................148
764..Mini Crustless Peanut Butter Cheesecake..........148
765..Cranberry Jam..148
766..Lemon Mousse...148
767..Peanut Butter S'mores..................................148

768..Custard..149
769..Chocolate Soufflés......................................149
770..Sage Cream...149
771..Hot Coconut 'n Cocoa Buns..........................149
772..Cinnamon-sugar Pretzel Bites........................149
773..Nutella And Banana Pastries..........................150
774..Fried Oreos...150
775..Lime Bars...150
776..Easy Churros...150
777..Glazed Chocolate Doughnut Holes..................150
778..Coconut Rice Cake......................................151
779..Pumpkin Pie–spiced Pork Rinds......................151
780..Peanut Butter Cookies..................................151
781..Olive Oil Cake...151
782..Delicious Vanilla Custard..............................151
783..Fried Pineapple Chunks................................151
784..Delicious Spiced Apples................................152
785..Peanut Cookies...152
786..Midnight Nutella Banana Sandwich..................152
787..Fried Twinkies...152
788..Kiwi Pastry Bites..152
789..Pecan Snowball Cookies...............................152
790..Strawberry Shortcake...................................153
791..Strawberry Cups...153
792..Coconut Flour Cake.....................................153
793..Chocolate Macaroons...................................153
794..Coconut And Berries Cream..........................153
795..Apple Pie Crumble......................................153
796..Roasted Pumpkin Seeds & Cinnamon...............154
797..Cream Cups...154
798..Banana Chips With Chocolate Glaze................154
799..Chocolate Lava Cakes..................................154
800..Cinnamon Apple Chips.................................154

INDEX..**155**

Introduction

The Air Fryer—the first truly new appliance introduced to home cooks in decades—is a wonderful piece of kitchen equipment! It is. It literally fries foods using hot dry air—not oil—that circulates around each piece, sealing in the flavor and creating a crust with a fabulous crunch. Yes, crunch.

Believe it or not, this technique is similar to deep-fat frying, also a dry-heat cooking method. When you deep-fry foods, the hot oil instantly removes the water from foods and cooks each piece quickly.

While an air fryer may seem like a specialized kitchen appliance, it's not one that will sit and gather dust in your pantry. In addition to creating healthy "fried" foods, you can also bake, grill, roast, steam, and stir-fry using this delightful invention. In fact, you likely will use it every day.

With this appliance you can re-create and enjoy those deep-fried foods you may have given up—donuts, French fries, fried chicken—and take this concept a step further. If you want to cook foods that are not just better for you than deep-fried foods, but also actually healthy, good-for-you foods in and of themselves, this book can help you do just that.

I have always loved fried foods. Growing up, for our birthday dinners, we were allowed to choose our favorite meal. Mine was grilled steak served with homemade French fries that were (gulp) fried in an entire can of solid shortening. That is not a meal I choose today, but, using the air fryer, I can have similar foods that taste even better and that are actually good for me!

When I first ventured into cooking healthy foods in the air fryer, I was committed to learning to cook food with less fat and better nutrition. Like you, I'm sure, I also wanted it to taste good and be quick and easy. I love to try new appliances, and this sounded simple. However, I admit I was slightly skeptical at first—would shrimp toast made with whole-wheat-breaded veggies taste good? Could I possibly create a donut hole that was healthy yet still yummy? Yes—the answer is yes. And the most surprising thing of all? Foods cooked with just hot air can be as crisp and flavorful as those cooked in fat. What's not to love?

In this book, you'll find 800 recipes that don't just claim to be healthy, but that are truly healthy. You'll also find tips for using your air fryer, information on how recipes were selected for inclusion in this book. Let's get started!

Chapter 1. Cooking with Your Air Fryer

Seeing the Benefits of Air Frying

Still wondering if you made the right decision when you purchased an air fryer? Wonder no more.

1. Air frying is better for your health. In fact, most recipes cook without any added fat. The recipes that do use oil use only a very small amount for flavor, usually just a few teaspoons. If there is too much oil on the food, it will melt off, and the appliance may emit smoke.
2. It's very safe, even for beginning cooks. The system is completely closed, unlike deep-frying in a pan on the stovetop. There's no danger of a pan full of hot oil falling off the stove. Because the machine is closed while it's cooking, you won't burn your fingers or be splattered with hot liquid as the food cooks.
3. Most air fryers have automatic cooking functions, so there's no guesswork. Depending on the model you choose, you can cook French fries, chicken fingers, tater tots, and other foods with just a press of a button. The machine controls the cooking times and cooking temperatures of these foods for you.
4. Cleanup is a breeze. Air fryers are made with nonstick material, so, to clean, you simply wash the basket and pan in the sink with soap and water, using a sponge that won't scratch. If any food is burned onto the basket, a quick soak will loosen it. The appliance itself can be cleaned with a damp paper towel or sponge. You don't have to worry about safely disposing of cups of oil.
5. Using only one appliance to prepare your food is extremely convenient. The cooking method is hands-free,so you can prepare a salad while your food cooks. If you have a small kitchen, this may be the only appliance you need.

5 Ways to Prevent Air Frying Your Food to a Crisp

When cooking certain foods at high temperatures, charring can occur. That charring produces a chemical called acrylamide. And acrylamide might be linked to an increased risk of cancer. It's important to note that, according to the American Cancer Society, "It's not yet clear if the levels of acrylamide in foods raise cancer risk. . . ." Still, you can take some steps to avoid frying foods to a crisp. Here's what we recommend:

1. Cook at lower temperatures for longer periods of time (instead of high temperatures for shorter periods). Turning the temperature knob down to 300 to 325 degrees and increasing the time to 10 or 20 minutes may prevent charred coffee cake and blackened fries.
2. Cover foods with foil. The air fryer works to cook your foods by circulating air throughout the basket, so you don't want to prevent that air flow. However, you can use foil to cover a chicken breast, for example, and place it in the basket to cook (low and slow). We also suggest using foil to cover cakes and egg dishes to prevent the top from cooking too quickly. Just be sure there is enough room between the foil and the top of the air fryer.
3. Don't overfill the basket. You may be tempted to throw the entire batch of beet chips or broccoli florets into the basket at once to save time, but that will result in uneven cooking and a few pieces getting burned to a crisp. Either invest in a larger fryer or cook in smaller batches to produce the perfect air-fried foods every time.
4. Use air-fryer-safe equipment. The key to producing bakery-perfect muffins or quick breads lies in making sure you're using the right equipment. Using the right equipment helps allow the air to circulate properly, leaving your air-fried foods crisp, crunchy, and evenly cooked.
5. Set timers and reminders. We all need to set alarms to remember important things, and air frying your foods is no different. Set timers not only on your air fryer but on your phone so you don't leave the foods cooking any longer than required.

Simple Food You Can Make in the Air Fryer

First, let's take a look at some super-simple foods you can make in the air fryer. Before you get into more advanced recipes, feel free to try out your air fryer on these simple classics. Trust us; make it once in the air fryer, and you'll never want to make it any other way.

1.   Make Easy Bacon in Seconds

Bacon is one of the easiest and tastiest things you can make in an air fryer. Simply place the bacon in the fryer basket at 375 degrees, and let it cook for 2-3 minutes. This way, there's no mess of standing in front of a greasy pan, laboriously cooking bacon a couple strips at a time.

2.   Hard-Boiled Eggs Are Great in An Air Fryer

Like bacon, hard-boiled eggs are another easy breakfast to whip up in the air fryer. Simply place your eggs in the basket, and preheat to 250 degrees. Cook for six minutes and boom! Perfect hard-boiled eggs every time. Doesn't that sound a lot easier than sitting around waiting for your water to boil?

3.   Veggies Are Great in An Air Fryer

Got a bunch of fresh veggies you aren't sure what to do with? Throw 'em in the air fryer! Air-fried vegetables are quick, easy, and a delicious way to get all those nutrients that veggies are jam-packed with. These vegetables will help spruce up any simple rice or pasta dish!

4.   Air Fryers Make Great Grilled Cheeses!

Do you remember when we said air fryers could cook almost anything? Well, we weren't lying. Think outside the box when it comes to the things your air fryer can do. To make a perfect air-fried grilled cheese, just spread a couple of pieces of bread with a thin layer of mayonnaise, preheat your air fryer to 360 degrees, and cook for 3-5 minutes. You'll never want to make a grilled cheese any other way!

Tips and Tricks for Using the Air Fryer

Air fryers can give you crispier foods that satisfy your cravings. Here are some great tips for you to get the most out of your air fryer!

1. Shake it!

Be sure to open the fryer and shake what you are cooking around as they "fry" in the basket. Smaller foods such as French fries and chips may compress. Even if a recipe does not mention to rotate, shake, or flip, for the best results, make sure to do so every 5-10 minutes.

2. Do not overcrowd.

Make sure you give foods lots of space for the hot air to circulate effectively around what you are cooking. This will give you the crispy results you crave! Also, it is best to work in small batches.

3. Spray foods.

Most recipes will tell you to do such, but if not, it is a good idea to lightly spray foods with a bit of oil, so they do not stick to the basket as they cook. I suggest investing in a kitchen spray bottle to put oil in. Much easier to spray foods, so you don't totally saturate them with this greasy stuff.

4. Keep dry.

Make sure you pat foods dry before adding them to air fryer basket. This helps to prevent splattering and excess smoking. So, let marinated foods drip a bit before adding and make sure to empty the fat from the bottom of the fryer when you are done cooking foods that are high in fat content.

5. Master other methods of cooking.

The air fryer is not just for frying! It is great for other methods of cooking, such as grilling, roasting, and even baking! It is my go-to appliance to get the best-tasting salmon!

6. Add water when cooking fatty foods.

Add water to the drawer underneath the basket will help to prevent the grease in fattier foods from becoming too hot and causing smoke to engulf your kitchen. Do this with burgers, sausage, and bacon especially.

7. Hold foods down with toothpicks.

On occasion, your air fryer will pick up foods that are light and blow them around the fryer. Secure foods you cook with toothpicks!

8. Open as often as you like.

One of the best benefits of cooking with an air fryer is that you do not have to worry about how often you open it up to check for doneness.

 If you are an anxious chef, this can give you peace of mind to create yummy meals and snacks every single time!

9. Take out basket before removing food.

If you go to invert the air fryer basket when it is still locked tightly in the drawer, you will dump all the fat that has rendered from your food.

10. Clean the drawer after each use.

The air fryer drawer is extremely easy to clean and quite hassle-free. But if you leave it unwashed, you can risk contaminating future food you cook, and you may have a nasty smell takeover your kitchen. Simply clean it after every use to prevent this.

11. Use the air dryer to dry the appliance out.

After you wash the basket and air fryer drawer, you can pop them back into the fryer and turn on the appliance for 2-3 minutes. This is a great way to thoroughly dry it for your next use!

Air Fryer Safety Tips

1. Turn off your Air fryer when it is not in use. This is pretty explanatory. Leaving your appliances on when they are not in use will just make them continue to consume power. Also, in case of a power surge, it could affect the items plugged into an outlet.
2. If your Air fryer packs up, don't try to fix it yourself. It is better you let a professional handle it. Also, the warranty on it may be voided if it is detected that a non-professional has worked on it. Most importantly, you could make the problem even worse.
3. Different foods cook best at different temperatures. So, don't just assume that the highest temperature will make your food cook faster.
4. You'll often get foods that are burnt, overcooked, or unevenly cooked. It is better to follow the temperature stipulated above.
5. Since the Air fryer is powered by electricity, it is not smart to operate it with wet hands. Even if you have just done anything that made your hands wet, wipe them dry before you operate your Air fryer. Water and electricity are never compatible.
6. Spray some oil on the baskets to prevent your food from sticking to them. That is why you should never submerge the appliance in water. Some of the components can be damaged by water.

It could be worse. There may be short circuits. So, you should only wipe the body of your Air fryer with a piece of cloth. In addition, we advise that you refer to the user manual of your Air fryer on the best way to clean i

Chapter 2. Bread And Breakfast

Sausage Solo

Servings:4
Cooking Time:22 Minutes
Ingredients:
- 6 eggs
- 4 cooked sausages, sliced
- 2 bread slices, cut into sticks
- ½ cup mozzarella cheese, grated
- ½ cup cream

Directions:
1. Preheat the Air fryer to 355°F and grease 4 ramekins lightly.
2. Whisk together eggs and cream in a bowl and beat well.
3. Transfer the egg mixture into ramekins and arrange the bread sticks and sausage slices around the edges.
4. Top with mozzarella cheese evenly and place the ramekins in Air fryer basket.
5. Cook for about 22 minutes and dish out to serve warm.

Mediterranean Egg Sandwich

Servings: 1
Cooking Time: 8 Minutes
Ingredients:
- 1 large egg
- 5 baby spinach leaves, chopped
- 1 tablespoon roasted bell pepper, chopped
- 1 English muffin
- 1 thin slice prosciutto or Canadian bacon

Directions:
1. Spray a ramekin with cooking spray or brush the inside with extra-virgin olive oil.
2. In a small bowl, whisk together the egg, baby spinach, and bell pepper.
3. Split the English muffin in half and spray the inside lightly with cooking spray or brush with extra-virgin olive oil.
4. Preheat the air fryer to 350°F for 2 minutes. Place the egg ramekin and open English muffin into the air fryer basket, and cook at 350°F for 5 minutes. Open the air fryer drawer and add the prosciutto or bacon; cook for an additional 1 minute.
5. To assemble the sandwich, place the egg on one half of the English muffin, top with prosciutto or bacon, and place the remaining piece of English muffin on top.

Bunless Breakfast Turkey Burgers

Servings:4
Cooking Time: 15 Minutes
Ingredients:
- 1 pound ground turkey breakfast sausage
- ½ teaspoon salt
- ¼ teaspoon ground black pepper
- ¼ cup seeded and chopped green bell pepper
- 2 tablespoons mayonnaise
- 1 medium avocado, peeled, pitted, and sliced

Directions:
1. In a large bowl, mix sausage with salt, black pepper, bell pepper, and mayonnaise. Form meat into four patties.
2. Place patties into ungreased air fryer basket. Adjust the temperature to 370°F and set the timer for 15 minutes, turning patties halfway through cooking. Burgers will be done when dark brown and they have an internal temperature of at least 165°F.
3. Serve burgers topped with avocado slices on four medium plates.

Bacon & Hot Dogs Omelet

Servings:2
Cooking Time: 10 Minutes
Ingredients:
- 4 eggs
- 1 bacon slice, chopped
- 2 hot dogs, chopped
- 2 small onions, chopped

Directions:
1. Set the temperature of Air Fryer to 320°F.
2. In an Air Fryer baking pan, crack the eggs and beat them well.
3. Now, add in the remaining ingredients and gently, stir to combine.
4. Air Fry for about 10 minutes.
5. Serve hot.

Not-so-english Muffins

Servings: 4
Cooking Time: 10 Minutes
Ingredients:
- 2 strips turkey bacon, cut in half crosswise
- 2 whole-grain English muffins, split
- 1 cup fresh baby spinach, long stems removed
- ¼ ripe pear, peeled and thinly sliced
- 4 slices Provolone cheese

Directions:
1. Place bacon strips in air fryer basket and cook for 2 minutes. Check and separate strips if necessary so they cook evenly. Cook for 4 more minutes, until crispy. Remove and drain on paper towels.
2. Place split muffin halves in air fryer basket and cook at 390°F for 2 minutes, just until lightly browned.
3. Open air fryer and top each muffin with a quarter of the baby spinach, several pear slices, a strip of bacon, and a slice of cheese.
4. Cook at 360°F for 2 minutes, until cheese completely melts.

Tomatoes Frittata

Servings: 4
Cooking Time: 20 Minutes
Ingredients:
- 4 eggs, whisked
- 1 pound cherry tomatoes, halved
- 1 tablespoon parsley, chopped
- Cooking spray
- 1 tablespoon cheddar, grated
- Salt and black pepper to the taste

Directions:
1. Put the tomatoes in the air fryer's basket, cook at 360°F for 5 minutes and transfer them to the baking pan that fits the machine greased with cooking spray. In a bowl, mix the eggs

with the remaining ingredients, whisk, pour over the tomatoes an cook at 360°F for 15 minutes. Serve right away for breakfast.

Taj Tofu

Servings: 4
Cooking Time: 40 Minutes
Ingredients:
- 1 block firm tofu, pressed and cut into 1-inch thick cubes
- 2 tbsp. soy sauce
- 2 tsp. sesame seeds, toasted
- 1 tsp. rice vinegar
- 1 tbsp. cornstarch

Directions:
1. Set your Air Fryer at 400°F to warm.
2. Add the tofu, soy sauce, sesame seeds and rice vinegar in a bowl together and mix well to coat the tofu cubes. Then cover the tofu in cornstarch and put it in the basket of your fryer.
3. Cook for 25 minutes, giving the basket a shake at five-minute intervals to ensure the tofu cooks evenly.

Simple Egg Soufflé

Servings: 2
Cooking Time: 8 Minutes
Ingredients:
- 2 eggs
- 1/4 tsp chili pepper
- 2 tbsp heavy cream
- 1/4 tsp pepper
- 1 tbsp parsley, chopped
- Salt

Directions:
1. In a bowl, whisk eggs with remaining gradients.
2. Spray two ramekins with cooking spray.
3. Pour egg mixture into the prepared ramekins and place into the air fryer basket.
4. Cook soufflé at 390°F for 8 minutes.
5. Serve and enjoy.

Easy Egg Bites

Servings:2
Cooking Time: 9 Minutes
Ingredients:
- 2 large eggs
- ¼ cup full-fat cottage cheese
- ¼ cup shredded sharp Cheddar cheese
- ¼ teaspoon salt
- ⅛ teaspoon ground black pepper
- 6 tablespoons diced cooked ham

Directions:
1. Preheat the air fryer to 300°F. Spray six silicone muffin cups with cooking spray.
2. In a blender, place eggs, cottage cheese, Cheddar, salt, and pepper. Pulse five times until smooth and frothy.
3. Place 1 tablespoon ham in the bottom of each prepared baking cup, then divide egg mixture among cups.
4. Place in the air fryer basket and cook 9 minutes until egg bites are firm in the center. Carefully remove cups from air fryer basket and cool 3 minutes before serving. Serve warm.

Parmesan Garlic Naan

Servings: 6
Cooking Time: 4 Minutes

Ingredients:
- 1 cup bread flour
- 1 teaspoon baking powder
- ⅛ teaspoon salt
- 1 teaspoon garlic powder
- 2 tablespoon shredded parmesan cheese
- 1 cup plain 2% fat Greek yogurt
- 1 tablespoon extra-virgin olive oil

Directions:
1. Preheat the air fryer to 400°F.
2. In a medium bowl, mix the flour, baking powder, salt, garlic powder, and cheese. Mix the yogurt into the flour, using your hands to combine if necessary.
3. On a flat surface covered with flour, divide the dough into 6 equal balls and roll each out into a 4-inch-diameter circle.
4. Lightly brush both sides of each naan with olive oil and place one naan at a time into the basket. Cook for 3 to 4 minutes. Remove and repeat for the remaining breads.
5. Serve warm.

Almond Oatmeal

Servings: 4
Cooking Time: 15 Minutes
Ingredients:
- 2 cups almond milk
- 1 cup coconut, shredded
- 2 teaspoons stevia
- 2 teaspoons vanilla extract

Directions:
1. In a pan that fits your air fryer, mix all the ingredients, stir well, introduce the pan in the machine and cook at 360°F for 15 minutes. Divide into bowls and serve for breakfast.

Egg Muffins

Servings: 4
Cooking Time: 11 Minutes
Ingredients:
- 4 eggs
- salt and pepper
- olive oil
- 4 English muffins, split
- 1 cup shredded Colby Jack cheese
- 4 slices ham or Canadian bacon

Directions:
1. Preheat air fryer to 390°F.
2. Beat together eggs and add salt and pepper to taste. Spray air fryer baking pan lightly with oil and add eggs. Cook for 2minutes, stir, and continue cooking for 4minutes, stirring every minute, until eggs are scrambled to your preference. Remove pan from air fryer.
3. Place bottom halves of English muffins in air fryer basket. Take half of the shredded cheese and divide it among the muffins. Top each with a slice of ham and one-quarter of the eggs. Sprinkle remaining cheese on top of the eggs. Use a fork to press the cheese into the egg a little so it doesn't slip off before it melts.
4. Cook at 360°F for 1 minute. Add English muffin tops and cook for 4minutes to heat through and toast the muffins.

Breakfast Quiche

Servings:4
Cooking Time: 18 Minutes
Ingredients:
- 1 refrigerated piecrust
- 2 large eggs
- ¼ cup heavy cream
- ½ teaspoon salt
- ¼ teaspoon ground black pepper
- ½ cup shredded Cheddar cheese
- 2 slices bacon, cooked and crumbled

Directions:
1. Preheat the air fryer to 325°F. Spray a 6" pie pan with cooking spray. Trim piecrust to fit the pan.
2. In a medium bowl, whisk together eggs, cream, salt, and pepper. Stir in Cheddar and bacon.
3. Pour egg mixture into crust and cook 18 minutes until firm, brown, and a knife inserted into the center comes out clean. Serve warm.

Green Scramble

Servings: 4
Cooking Time: 20 Minutes
Ingredients:
- 1 tablespoon olive oil
- ½ teaspoon smoked paprika
- 12 eggs, whisked
- 3 cups baby spinach
- Salt and black pepper to the taste

Directions:
1. In a bowl, mix all the ingredients except the oil and whisk them well. Heat up your air fryer at 360°F, add the oil, heat it up, add the eggs and spinach mix, cover, cook for 20 minutes, divide between plates and serve.

All-in-one Breakfast Toast

Servings: 1
Cooking Time: 10 Minutes
Ingredients:
- 1 strip of bacon, diced
- 1 slice of 1-inch thick bread (such as Texas Toast or hand-sliced bread)
- 1 tablespoon softened butter (optional)
- 1 egg
- salt and freshly ground black pepper
- ¼ cup grated Colby or Jack cheese

Directions:
1. Preheat the air fryer to 400°F.
2. Air-fry the bacon for 3 minutes, shaking the basket once or twice while it cooks. Remove the bacon to a paper towel lined plate and set aside.
3. Use a sharp paring knife to score a large circle in the middle of the slice of bread, cutting halfway through, but not all the way through to the cutting board. Press down on the circle in the center of the bread slice to create an indentation. If using, spread the softened butter on the edges and in the hole of the bread.
4. Transfer the slice of bread, hole side up, to the air fryer basket. Crack the egg into the center of the bread, and season with salt and pepper.
5. Air-fry at 380°F for 5 minutes. Sprinkle the grated cheese around the edges of the bread leaving the center of the yolk uncovered, and top with the cooked bacon. Press the cheese and bacon into the bread lightly to help anchor it to the bread and prevent it from blowing around in the air fryer.
6. Air-fry for one or two more minutes, just to melt the cheese and finish cooking the egg. Serve immediately.

English Muffin Sandwiches

Servings: 4
Cooking Time: 15 Minutes
Ingredients:
- 4 English muffins
- 8 pepperoni slices
- 4 cheddar cheese slices
- 1 tomato, sliced

Directions:
1. Preheat air fryer to 370°F. Split open the English muffins along the crease. On the bottom half of the muffin, layer 2 slices of pepperoni and one slice of the cheese and tomato. Place the top half of the English muffin to finish the sandwich. Lightly spray with cooking oil. Place the muffin sandwiches in the air fryer. Bake for 8 minutes, flipping once. Let cool slightly before serving.

Zucchini And Spring Onions Cakes

Servings: 4
Cooking Time: 8 Minutes
Ingredients:
- 8 ounces zucchinis, chopped
- 2 spring onions, chopped
- 2 eggs, whisked
- Salt and black pepper to the taste
- ¼ teaspoon sweet paprika, chopped
- Cooking spray

Directions:
1. In a bowl, mix all the ingredients except the cooking spray, stir well and shape medium fritters out of this mix. Put the basket in the Air Fryer, add the fritters inside, grease them with cooking spray and cook at 400°F for 8 minutes. Divide the fritters between plates and serve for breakfast.

Creamy Parsley Soufflé

Servings:2
Cooking Time:10 Minutes
Ingredients:
- 2 eggs
- 1 tablespoon fresh parsley, chopped
- 1 fresh red chili pepper, chopped
- 2 tablespoons light cream
- Salt, to taste

Directions:
1. Preheat the Air fryer to 390°F and grease 2 soufflé dishes.
2. Mix together all the ingredients in a bowl until well combined.
3. Transfer the mixture into prepared soufflé dishes and place in the Air fryer.
4. Cook for about 10 minutes and dish out to serve warm.

Puffed Egg Tarts

Servings:4
Cooking Time:42 Minutes
Ingredients:

- 1 sheet frozen puff pastry half, thawed and cut into 4 squares
- ¾ cup Monterey Jack cheese, shredded and divided
- 4 large eggs
- 1 tablespoon fresh parsley, minced
- 1 tablespoon olive oil

Directions:
1. Preheat the Air fryer to 390°F
2. Place 2 pastry squares in the air fryer basket and cook for about 10 minutes.
3. Remove Air fryer basket from the Air fryer and press each square gently with a metal tablespoon to form an indentation.
4. Place 3 tablespoons of cheese in each hole and top with 1 egg each.
5. Return Air fryer basket to Air fryer and cook for about 11 minutes.
6. Remove tarts from the Air fryer basket and sprinkle with half the parsley.
7. Repeat with remaining pastry squares, cheese and eggs.
8. Dish out and serve warm.

Grilled Bbq Sausages

Servings:3
Cooking Time: 30 Minutes
Ingredients:
- 6 sausage links
- ½ cup prepared BBQ sauce

Directions:
1. Preheat the air fryer at 390°F.
2. Place the grill pan accessory in the air fryer.
3. Place the sausage links and grill for 30 minutes.
4. Flip halfway through the cooking time.
5. Before serving brush with prepared BBQ sauce.

Strawberry Bread

Servings: 6
Cooking Time: 28 Minutes
Ingredients:
- ½ cup frozen strawberries in juice, completely thawed (do not drain)
- 1 cup flour
- ½ cup sugar
- 1 teaspoon cinnamon
- ½ teaspoon baking soda
- ⅛ teaspoon salt
- 1 egg, beaten
- ⅓ cup oil
- cooking spray

Directions:
1. Cut any large berries into smaller pieces no larger than ½ inch.
2. Preheat air fryer to 330°F.
3. In a large bowl, stir together the flour, sugar, cinnamon, soda, and salt.
4. In a small bowl, mix together the egg, oil, and strawberries. Add to dry ingredients and stir together gently.
5. Spray 6 x 6-inch baking pan with cooking spray.
6. Pour batter into prepared pan and cook at 330°F for 28 minutes.
7. When bread is done, let cool for 10minutes before removing from pan.

Banana Baked Oatmeal

Servings:2
Cooking Time:10 Minutes
Ingredients:
- 1 cup quick-cooking oats
- 1 cup whole milk
- 2 tablespoons unsalted butter, melted
- 1 medium banana, peeled and mashed
- 2 tablespoons brown sugar
- ½ teaspoon vanilla extract
- ½ teaspoon salt

Directions:
1. Preheat the air fryer to 360°F.
2. In a 6" round pan, add oats. Pour in milk and butter.
3. In a medium bowl, mix banana, brown sugar, vanilla, and salt until combined. Add to pan and mix until well combined.
4. Place in the air fryer and cook 10 minutes until the top is brown and oats feel firm to the touch. Serve warm.

Chocolate Almond Crescent Rolls

Servings: 4
Cooking Time: 8 Minutes
Ingredients:
- 1 tube of crescent roll dough
- ⅔ cup semi-sweet or bittersweet chocolate chunks
- 1 egg white, lightly beaten
- ¼ cup sliced almonds
- powdered sugar, for dusting
- butter or oil

Directions:
1. Preheat the air fryer to 350°F.
2. Unwrap the crescent roll dough and separate it into triangles with the points facing away from you. Place a row of chocolate chunks along the bottom edge of the dough. Roll the dough up around the chocolate and then place another row of chunks on the dough. Roll again and finish with one or two chocolate chunks. Be sure to leave the end free of chocolate so that it can adhere to the rest of the roll.
3. Brush the tops of the crescent rolls with the lightly beaten egg white and sprinkle the almonds on top, pressing them into the crescent dough so they adhere.
4. Brush the bottom of the air fryer basket with butter or oil and transfer the crescent rolls to the basket. Air-fry at 350°F for 8 minutes. Remove and let the crescent rolls cool before dusting with powdered sugar and serving.

Inside-out Cheeseburgers

Servings: 3
Cooking Time: 9-11 Minutes
Ingredients:
- 1 pound 2 ounces 90% lean ground beef
- ¾ teaspoon Dried oregano
- ¾ teaspoon Table salt
- ¾ teaspoon Ground black pepper
- ¼ teaspoon Garlic powder
- 6 tablespoons Shredded Cheddar, Swiss, or other semi-firm cheese, or a purchased blend of shredded cheeses
- 3 Hamburger buns (gluten-free, if a concern), split open

Directions:
1. Preheat the air fryer to 375°F .

2. Gently mix the ground beef, oregano, salt, pepper, and garlic powder in a bowl until well combined without turning the mixture to mush. Form it into two 6-inch patties for the small batch, three for the medium, or four for the large.

3. Place 2 tablespoons of the shredded cheese in the center of each patty. With clean hands, fold the sides of the patty up to cover the cheese, then pick it up and roll it gently into a ball to seal the cheese inside. Gently press it back into a 5-inch burger without letting any cheese squish out. Continue filling and preparing more burgers, as needed.

4. Place the burgers in the basket in one layer and air-fry undisturbed for 8 minutes for medium or 10 minutes for well-done.

5. Use a nonstick-safe spatula, and perhaps a flatware fork for balance, to transfer the burgers to a cutting board. Set the buns cut side down in the basket in one layer and air-fry undisturbed for 1 minute, to toast a bit and warm up. Cool the burgers a few minutes more, then serve them warm in the buns.

Hashbrown Potatoes Lyonnaise

Servings: 4
Cooking Time: 33 Minutes
Ingredients:
- 1 Vidalia (or other sweet) onion, sliced
- 1 teaspoon butter, melted
- 1 teaspoon brown sugar
- 2 large russet potatoes, sliced ½-inch thick
- 1 tablespoon vegetable oil
- salt and freshly ground black pepper

Directions:
1. Preheat the air fryer to 370°F.
2. Toss the sliced onions, melted butter and brown sugar together in the air fryer basket. Air-fry for 8 minutes, shaking the basket occasionally to help the onions cook evenly.
3. While the onions are cooking, bring a 3-quart saucepan of salted water to a boil on the stovetop. Par-cook the potatoes in boiling water for 3 minutes. Drain the potatoes and pat them dry with a clean kitchen towel.
4. Add the potatoes to the onions in the air fryer basket and drizzle with vegetable oil. Toss to coat the potatoes with the oil and season with salt and freshly ground black pepper.
5. Increase the air fryer temperature to 400°F and air-fry for 22 minutes tossing the vegetables a few times during the cooking time to help the potatoes brown evenly. Season to taste again with salt and freshly ground black pepper and serve warm.

Smoked Salmon Croissant Sandwich

Servings: 1
Cooking Time: 30 Minutes
Ingredients:
- 1 croissant, halved
- 2 eggs
- 1 tbsp guacamole
- 1 smoked salmon slice
- Salt and pepper to taste

Directions:
1. Preheat air fryer to 360°F. Place the croissant, crusty side up, in the frying basket side by side. Whisk the eggs in a small ceramic dish until fluffy. Place in the air fryer. Bake for 10 minutes. Gently scramble the half-cooked egg in the baking dish with a fork. Flip the croissant and cook for another 10 minutes until the scrambled eggs are cooked, but still fluffy, and the croissant is toasted.

2. Place one croissant on a serving plate, then spread the guacamole on top. Scoop the scrambled eggs onto guacamole, then top with smoked salmon. Sprinkle with salt and pepper. Top with the second slice of toasted croissant, close sandwich, and serve hot.

Scones

Servings: 9
Cooking Time: 8 Minutes Per Batch
Ingredients:
- 2 cups self-rising flour, plus ¼ cup for kneading
- ⅓ cup granulated sugar
- ¼ cup butter, cold
- 1 cup milk

Directions:
1. Preheat air fryer at 360°F.
2. In large bowl, stir together flour and sugar.
3. Cut cold butter into tiny cubes, and stir into flour mixture with fork.
4. Stir in milk until soft dough forms.
5. Sprinkle ¼ cup of flour onto wax paper and place dough on top. Knead lightly by folding and turning the dough about 6 to 8 times.
6. Pat dough into a 6 x 6-inch square.
7. Cut into 9 equal squares.
8. Place all squares in air fryer basket or as many as will fit in a single layer, close together but not touching.
9. Cook at 360°F for 8minutes. When done, scones will be lightly browned on top and will spring back when pressed gently with a dull knife.
10. Repeat steps 8 and 9 to cook remaining scones.

Spinach-bacon Rollups

Servings: 4
Cooking Time: 9 Minutes
Ingredients:
- 4 flour tortillas
- 4 slices Swiss cheese
- 1 cup baby spinach leaves
- 4 slices turkey bacon

Directions:
1. Preheat air fryer to 390°F.
2. On each tortilla, place one slice of cheese and ¼ cup of spinach.
3. Roll up tortillas and wrap each with a strip of bacon. Secure each end with a toothpick.
4. Place rollups in air fryer basket, leaving a little space in between them.
5. Cook for 4minutes. Turn and rearrange rollups and cook for 5minutes longer, until bacon is crisp.

Seasoned Herbed Sourdough Croutons

Servings: 4
Cooking Time: 7 Minutes
Ingredients:
- 4 cups cubed sourdough bread, 1-inch cubes
- 1 tablespoon olive oil
- 1 teaspoon fresh thyme leaves
- ¼ – ½ teaspoon salt
- freshly ground black pepper

Directions:

1. Combine all ingredients in a bowl and taste to make sure it is seasoned to your liking.
2. Preheat the air fryer to 400°F.
3. Toss the bread cubes into the air fryer and air-fry for 7 minutes, shaking the basket once or twice while they cook.
4. Serve warm or store in an airtight container.

Cheddar Soufflés

Servings:4
Cooking Time: 12 Minutes
Ingredients:
- 3 large eggs, whites and yolks separated
- ¼ teaspoon cream of tartar
- ½ cup shredded sharp Cheddar cheese
- 3 ounces cream cheese, softened

Directions:
1. In a large bowl, beat egg whites together with cream of tartar until soft peaks form, about 2 minutes.
2. In a separate medium bowl, beat egg yolks, Cheddar, and cream cheese together until frothy, about 1 minute. Add egg yolk mixture to whites, gently folding until combined.
3. Pour mixture evenly into four 4" ramekins greased with cooking spray. Place ramekins into air fryer basket. Adjust the temperature to 350°F and set the timer for 12 minutes. Eggs will be browned on the top and firm in the center when done. Serve warm.

Eggs Salad

Servings: 4
Cooking Time: 10 Minutes
Ingredients:
- 1 tablespoon lime juice
- 4 eggs, hard boiled, peeled and sliced
- 2 cups baby spinach
- Salt and black pepper to the taste
- 3 tablespoons heavy cream
- 2 tablespoons olive oil

Directions:
1. In your Air Fryer, mix the spinach with cream, eggs, salt and pepper, cover and cook at 360°F for 6 minutes. Transfer this to a bowl, add the lime juice and oil, toss and serve for breakfast.

Whole-grain Cornbread

Servings: 6
Cooking Time: 25 Minutes
Ingredients:
- 1 cup stoneground cornmeal
- ½ cup brown rice flour
- 1 teaspoon sugar
- 2 teaspoons baking powder
- ¼ teaspoon salt
- 1 cup milk
- 2 tablespoons oil
- 2 eggs
- cooking spray

Directions:
1. Preheat the air fryer to 360°F.
2. In a medium mixing bowl, mix cornmeal, brown rice flour, sugar, baking powder, and salt together.
3. Add the remaining ingredients and beat with a spoon until batter is smooth.

4. Spray air fryer baking pan with nonstick cooking spray and add the cornbread batter.
5. Bake at 360°F for 25 minutes, until center is done.

Very Berry Breakfast Puffs

Servings:3
Cooking Time: 20 Minutes
Ingredients:
- 2 tbsp mashed strawberries
- 2 tbsp mashed raspberries
- ¼ tsp vanilla extract
- 2 cups cream cheese
- 1 tbsp honey

Directions:
1. Preheat the air fryer to 375°F. Divide the cream cheese between the dough sheets and spread it evenly. In a small bowl, combine the berries, honey and vanilla.
2. Divide the mixture between the pastry sheets. Pinch the ends of the sheets, to form puff. Place the puffs on a lined baking dish. Place the dish in the air fryer and cook for 15 minutes.

Perfect Burgers

Servings: 3
Cooking Time: 13 Minutes
Ingredients:
- 1 pound 2 ounces 90% lean ground beef
- 1½ tablespoons Worcestershire sauce (gluten-free, if a concern)
- ½ teaspoon Ground black pepper
- 3 Hamburger buns (gluten-free if a concern), split open

Directions:
1. Preheat the air fryer to 375°F .
2. Gently mix the ground beef, Worcestershire sauce, and pepper in a bowl until well combined but preserving as much of the meat's fibers as possible. Divide this mixture into two 5-inch patties for the small batch, three 5-inch patties for the medium, or four 5-inch patties for the large. Make a thumbprint indentation in the center of each patty, about halfway through the meat.
3. Set the patties in the basket in one layer with some space between them. Air-fry undisturbed for 10 minutes, or until an instant-read meat thermometer inserted into the center of a burger registers 160°F. You may need to add 2 minutes cooking time if the air fryer is at 360°F.
4. Use a nonstick-safe spatula, and perhaps a flatware fork for balance, to transfer the burgers to a cutting board. Set the buns cut side down in the basket in one layer and air-fry undisturbed for 1 minute, to toast a bit and warm up. Serve the burgers in the warm buns.

Avocado Tempura

Servings: 4
Cooking Time: 20 Minutes
Ingredients:
- ½ cup breadcrumbs
- ½ tsp. salt
- 1 Haas avocado, pitted, peeled and sliced
- Liquid from 1 can white beans or aquafaba

Directions:
1. Set your Air Fryer to 350°F and allow to warm.
2. Mix the breadcrumbs and salt in a shallow bowl until well-incorporated.

3. Dip the avocado slices in the bean/aquafaba juice, then into the breadcrumbs. Put the avocados in the fryer, taking care not to overlap any slices, and fry for 10 minutes, giving the basket a good shake at the halfway point.

Mini Pita Breads

Servings: 8
Cooking Time: 6 Minutes
Ingredients:
- 2 teaspoons active dry yeast
- 1 tablespoon sugar
- 1¼ to 1½ cups warm water
- 3¼ cups all-purpose flour
- 2 teaspoons salt
- 1 tablespoon olive oil, plus more for brushing
- kosher salt (optional)

Directions:
1. Dissolve the yeast, sugar and water in the bowl of a stand mixer. Let the mixture sit for 5 minutes to make sure the yeast is active – it should foam a little. Combine the flour and salt in a bowl, and add it to the water, along with the olive oil. Mix with the dough hook until combined. Add a little more flour if needed to get the dough to pull away from the sides of the mixing bowl, or add a little more water if the dough seems too dry.
2. Knead the dough until it is smooth and elastic. Transfer the dough to a lightly oiled bowl, cover and let it rise in a warm place until doubled in bulk. Divide the dough into 8 portions and roll each portion into a circle about 4-inches in diameter. Don't roll the balls too thin, or you won't get the pocket inside the pita.
3. Preheat the air fryer to 400°F.
4. Brush both sides of the dough with olive oil, and sprinkle with kosher salt if desired. Air-fry one at a time at 400°F for 6 minutes, flipping it over when there are two minutes left in the cooking time.

Pigs In A Blanket

Servings: 10
Cooking Time: 8 Minutes
Ingredients:
- 1 cup all-purpose flour, plus more for rolling
- 1 teaspoon baking powder
- ¼ cup salted butter, cut into small pieces
- ½ cup buttermilk
- 10 fully cooked breakfast sausage links

Directions:
1. In a large mixing bowl, whisk together the flour and baking powder. Using your fingers or a pastry blender, cut in the butter until you have small pea-size crumbles.
2. Using a rubber spatula, make a well in the center of the flour mixture. Pour the buttermilk into the well, and fold the mixture together until you form a dough ball.
3. Place the sticky dough onto a floured surface and, using a floured rolling pin, roll out until ½-inch thick. Using a round biscuit cutter, cut out 10 rounds, reshaping the dough and rolling out, as needed.
4. Place 1 fully cooked breakfast sausage link on the left edge of each biscuit and roll up, leaving the ends slightly exposed.
5. Using a pastry brush, brush the biscuits with the whisked eggs, and spray them with cooking spray.

6. Place the pigs in a blanket into the air fryer basket with at least 1 inch between each biscuit. Set the air fryer to 340°F and cook for 8 minutes.

Bacon Puff Pastry Pinwheels

Servings: 8
Cooking Time: 10 Minutes
Ingredients:
- 1 sheet of puff pastry
- 2 tablespoons maple syrup
- ¼ cup brown sugar
- 8 slices bacon (not thick cut)
- coarsely cracked black pepper
- vegetable oil

Directions:
1. On a lightly floured surface, roll the puff pastry out into a square that measures roughly 10 inches wide by however long your bacon strips are. Cut the pastry into eight even strips.
2. Brush the strips of pastry with the maple syrup and sprinkle the brown sugar on top, leaving 1 inch of dough exposed at the far end of each strip. Place a slice of bacon on each strip of puff pastry, letting 1/8-inch of the length of bacon hang over the edge of the pastry. Season generously with coarsely ground black pepper.
3. With the exposed end of the pastry strips away from you, roll the bacon and pastry strips up into pinwheels. Dab a little water on the exposed end of the pastry and pinch it to the pinwheel to seal the pastry shut.
4. Preheat the air fryer to 360°F.
5. Brush or spray the air fryer basket with a little vegetable oil. Place the pinwheels into the basket and air-fry at 360°F for 8 minutes. Turn the pinwheels over and air-fry for another 2 minutes to brown the bottom. Serve warm.

Mini Bagels

Servings:6
Cooking Time: 10 Minutes
Ingredients:
- 2 cups blanched finely ground almond flour
- 2 cups shredded mozzarella cheese
- 3 tablespoons salted butter, divided
- 1½ teaspoons baking powder
- 1 teaspoon apple cider vinegar
- 2 large eggs, divided

Directions:
1. In a large microwave-safe bowl, combine flour, mozzarella, and 1 tablespoon butter. Microwave on high 90 seconds, then form into a soft ball of dough.
2. Add baking powder, vinegar, and 1 egg to dough, stirring until fully combined.
3. Once dough is cool enough to work with your hands, about 2 minutes, divide evenly into six balls. Poke a hole in each ball of dough with your finger and gently stretch each ball out to be 2" in diameter.
4. In a small microwave-safe bowl, melt remaining butter in microwave on high 30 seconds, then let cool 1 minute. Whisk with remaining egg, then brush mixture over each bagel.
5. Line air fryer basket with parchment paper and place bagels onto ungreased parchment, working in batches if needed.
6. Adjust the temperature to 350°F and set the timer for 10 minutes. Halfway through, use tongs to flip bagels for even cooking.

7. Allow bagels to set and cool completely, about 15 minutes, before serving. Store leftovers in a sealed bag in the refrigerator up to 4 days.

Garlic-cheese Biscuits

Servings: 8
Cooking Time: 8 Minutes
Ingredients:
- 1 cup self-rising flour
- 1 teaspoon garlic powder
- 2 tablespoons butter, diced
- 2 ounces sharp Cheddar cheese, grated
- ½ cup milk
- cooking spray

Directions:
1. Preheat air fryer to 330°F.
2. Combine flour and garlic in a medium bowl and stir together.
3. Using a pastry blender or knives, cut butter into dry ingredients.
4. Stir in cheese.
5. Add milk and stir until stiff dough forms.
6. If dough is too sticky to handle, stir in 1 or 2 more tablespoons of self-rising flour before shaping. Biscuits should be firm enough to hold their shape. Otherwise, they'll stick to the air fryer basket.
7. Divide dough into 8 portions and shape into 2-inch biscuits about ¾-inch thick.
8. Spray air fryer basket with nonstick cooking spray.
9. Place all 8 biscuits in basket and cook at 330°F for 8 minutes.

Flaky Cinnamon Rolls

Servings:8
Cooking Time: 12 Minutes Per Batch
Ingredients:
- 1 sheet frozen puff pastry, thawed
- 6 tablespoons unsalted butter, melted
- ¾ cup granulated sugar
- 2 tablespoons ground cinnamon
- ½ cup confectioners' sugar
- 2 tablespoons heavy cream

Directions:
1. Preheat the air fryer to 320°F. Cut parchment paper to fit the air fryer basket.
2. Unroll puff pastry into a large rectangle. Brush with butter, then evenly sprinkle sugar and cinnamon around dough, coating as evenly as possible.
3. Starting at one of the long sides, roll dough into a log, then use a little water on your fingers to seal the edge.
4. Slice dough into eight rounds. Place on parchment in the air fryer basket, working in batches as necessary, and cook 12 minutes until golden brown and flaky. Let cool 5 minutes.
5. In a small bowl, whisk confectioners' sugar and cream together until smooth. Drizzle over cinnamon rolls and serve.

Medium Rare Simple Salt And Pepper Steak

Servings:3
Cooking Time: 30 Minutes
Ingredients:
- 1 ½ pounds skirt steak

- Salt and pepper to taste

Directions:
1. Preheat the air fryer at 390°F.
2. Place the grill pan accessory in the air fryer.
3. Season the skirt steak with salt and pepper.
4. Place on the grill pan and cook for 15 minutes per batch.
5. Flip the meat halfway through the cooking time.

Strawberry Pastry

Servings:8
Cooking Time: 15 Minutes Per Batch
Ingredients:
- 1 package refrigerated piecrust
- 1 cup strawberry jam
- 1 large egg, whisked
- ½ cup confectioners' sugar
- 2 tablespoons whole milk
- ½ teaspoon vanilla extract

Directions:
1. Preheat the air fryer to 320°F. Cut parchment paper to fit the air fryer basket.
2. On a lightly floured surface, lay piecrusts out flat. Cut each piecrust round into six 4" × 3" rectangles, reserving excess dough.
3. Form remaining dough into a ball, then roll out and cut four additional 4" × 3" rectangles, bringing the total to sixteen.
4. For each pastry, spread 2 tablespoons jam on a pastry rectangle, leaving a 1" border around the edges. Top with a second pastry rectangle and use a fork to gently press all four edges together. Repeat with remaining jam and pastry.
5. Brush tops of each pastry with egg and cut an X in the center of each to prevent excess steam from building up.
6. Place pastries on parchment in the air fryer basket, working in batches as necessary. Cook 12 minutes, then carefully flip and cook an additional 3 minutes until each side is golden brown. Let cool 10 minutes.
7. In a small bowl, whisk confectioners' sugar, milk, and vanilla. Brush each pastry with glaze, then place in the refrigerator 5 minutes to set before serving.

Spinach Omelet

Servings:2
Cooking Time: 12 Minutes
Ingredients:
- 4 large eggs
- 1½ cups chopped fresh spinach leaves
- 2 tablespoons peeled and chopped yellow onion
- 2 tablespoons salted butter, melted
- ½ cup shredded mild Cheddar cheese
- ¼ teaspoon salt

Directions:
1. In an ungreased 6" round nonstick baking dish, whisk eggs. Stir in spinach, onion, butter, Cheddar, and salt.
2. Place dish into air fryer basket. Adjust the temperature to 320°F and set the timer for 12 minutes. Omelet will be done when browned on the top and firm in the middle.
3. Slice in half and serve warm on two medium plates.

Breakfast Bake

Servings:4
Cooking Time: 15 Minutes
Ingredients:
- 6 large eggs
- 2 tablespoons heavy cream
- ½ teaspoon salt
- ¼ teaspoon ground black pepper
- ⅓ pound ground pork breakfast sausage, cooked and drained
- ½ cup shredded Cheddar cheese

Directions:
1. Preheat the air fryer to 320°F. Spray a 6" round cake pan with cooking spray.
2. In a large bowl, whisk eggs, cream, salt, and pepper until fully combined.
3. Arrange cooked sausage in the bottom of prepared pan. Pour egg mixture into pan on top of sausage. Sprinkle Cheddar on top.
4. Place in the air fryer basket and cook 15 minutes until the top begins to brown and the center is set. Let cool 5 minutes before serving. Serve warm.

Sausage Bacon Fandango

Servings:4
Cooking Time:20 Minutes
Ingredients:
- 8 bacon slices
- 8 chicken sausages
- 4 eggs
- Salt and black pepper, to taste

Directions:
1. Preheat the Air fryer to 320°F and grease 4 ramekins lightly.
2. Place bacon slices and sausages in the Air fryer basket.
3. Cook for about 10 minutes and crack 1 egg in each prepared ramekin.
4. Season with salt and black pepper and cook for about 10 more minutes.
5. Divide bacon slices and sausages in serving plates.
6. Place 1 egg in each plate and serve warm.

Mini Bacon Egg Quiches

Servings:6
Cooking Time: 30 Minutes
Ingredients:
- 3 eggs
- 2 tbsp heavy cream
- ¼ tsp Dijon mustard
- Salt and pepper to taste
- 3 oz cooked bacon, crumbled
- ¼ cup grated cheddar

Directions:
1. Preheat air fryer to 350ºF. Beat the eggs with salt and pepper in a bowl until fluffy. Stir in heavy cream, mustard, cooked bacon, and cheese. Divide the mixture between 6 greased muffin cups and place them in the frying basket. Bake for 8-10 minutes. Let cool slightly before serving.

Bacon And Cheese Quiche

Servings:2
Cooking Time: 12 Minutes

Ingredients:
- 3 large eggs
- 2 tablespoons heavy whipping cream
- ¼ teaspoon salt
- 4 slices cooked sugar-free bacon, crumbled
- ½ cup shredded mild Cheddar cheese

Directions:
1. In a large bowl, whisk eggs, cream, and salt together until combined. Mix in bacon and Cheddar.
2. Pour mixture evenly into two ungreased 4" ramekins. Place into air fryer basket. Adjust the temperature to 320°F and set the timer for 12 minutes. Quiche will be fluffy and set in the middle when done.
3. Let quiche cool in ramekins 5 minutes. Serve warm.

Hole In One

Servings: 1
Cooking Time: 7 Minutes
Ingredients:
- 1 slice bread
- 1 teaspoon soft butter
- 1 egg
- salt and pepper
- 1 tablespoon shredded Cheddar cheese
- 2 teaspoons diced ham

Directions:
1. Place a 6 x 6-inch baking dish inside air fryer basket and preheat fryer to 330°F.
2. Using a 2½-inch-diameter biscuit cutter, cut a hole in center of bread slice.
3. Spread softened butter on both sides of bread.
4. Lay bread slice in baking dish and crack egg into the hole. Sprinkle egg with salt and pepper to taste.
5. Cook for 5minutes.
6. Turn toast over and top it with shredded cheese and diced ham.
7. Cook for 2 more minutes or until yolk is done to your liking.

Coconut Eggs Mix

Servings: 4
Cooking Time: 8 Minutes
Ingredients:
- 1 tablespoon olive oil
- 1 and ½ cup coconut cream
- 8 eggs, whisked
- ½ cup mint, chopped
- Salt and black pepper to the taste

Directions:
1. In a bowl, mix the cream with salt, pepper, eggs and mint, whisk, pour into the air fryer greased with the oil, spread, cook at 350°F for 8 minutes, divide between plates and serve.

Garlic Bread Knots

Servings: 8
Cooking Time: 5 Minutes
Ingredients:
- ¼ cup melted butter
- 2 teaspoons garlic powder
- 1 teaspoon dried parsley
- 1 tube of refrigerated French bread dough

Directions:

1. Mix the melted butter, garlic powder and dried parsley in a small bowl and set it aside.
2. To make smaller knots, cut the long tube of bread dough into 16 slices. If you want to make bigger knots, slice the dough into 8 slices. Shape each slice into a long rope about 6 inches long by rolling it on a flat surface with the palm of your hands. Tie each rope into a knot and place them on a plate.
3. Preheat the air fryer to 350°F.
4. Transfer half of the bread knots into the air fryer basket, leaving space in between each knot. Brush each knot with the butter mixture using a pastry brush.
5. Air-fry for 5 minutes. Remove the baked knots and brush a little more of the garlic butter mixture on each. Repeat with the remaining bread knots and serve warm.

Hard-"boiled" Eggs

Servings:6
Cooking Time: 15 Minutes
Ingredients:
- 6 large eggs
Directions:
1. Preheat the air fryer to 280°F.
2. Place eggs in the air fryer basket and cook 15 minutes. Store cooked eggs in the refrigerator until ready to use, or peel and serve warm.

Cinnamon Rolls

Servings:12
Cooking Time: 20 Minutes
Ingredients:
- 2½ cups shredded mozzarella cheese
- 2 ounces cream cheese, softened
- 1 cup blanched finely ground almond flour
- ½ teaspoon vanilla extract
- ½ cup confectioners' erythritol
- 1 tablespoon ground cinnamon
Directions:
1. In a large microwave-safe bowl, combine mozzarella cheese, cream cheese, and flour. Microwave the mixture on high 90 seconds until cheese is melted.
2. Add vanilla extract and erythritol, and mix 2 minutes until a dough forms.
3. Once the dough is cool enough to work with your hands, about 2 minutes, spread it out into a 12" × 4" rectangle on ungreased parchment paper. Evenly sprinkle dough with cinnamon.
4. Starting at the long side of the dough, roll lengthwise to form a log. Slice the log into twelve even pieces.
5. Divide rolls between two ungreased 6" round nonstick baking dishes. Place one dish into air fryer basket. Adjust the temperature to 375°F and set the timer for 10 minutes.
6. Cinnamon rolls will be done when golden around the edges and mostly firm. Repeat with second dish. Allow rolls to cool in dishes 10 minutes before serving.

Country Gravy

Servings: 2
Cooking Time: 7 Minutes
Ingredients:
- ¼ pound pork sausage, casings removed
- 1 tablespoon butter
- 2 tablespoons flour
- 2 cups whole milk
- ½ teaspoon salt
- freshly ground black pepper
- 1 teaspoon fresh thyme leaves
Directions:
1. Preheat a saucepan over medium heat. Add and brown the sausage, crumbling it into small pieces as it cooks. Add the butter and flour, stirring well to combine. Continue to cook for 2 minutes, stirring constantly.
2. Slowly pour in the milk, whisking as you do, and bring the mixture to a boil to thicken. Season with salt and freshly ground black pepper, lower the heat and simmer until the sauce has thickened to your desired consistency – about 5 minutes. Stir in the fresh thyme, season to taste and serve hot.

Chocolate-hazelnut Bear Claws

Servings:4
Cooking Time: 10 Minutes
Ingredients:
- 1 sheet frozen puff pastry dough, thawed
- 1 large egg, beaten
- ½ cup chocolate-hazelnut spread
- 1 tablespoon confectioners' sugar
- 1 tablespoon sliced almonds
Directions:
1. Preheat the air fryer to 320°F.
2. Unfold puff pastry and cut into four equal squares.
3. Brush egg evenly over puff pastry.
4. To make each bear claw, spread 2 tablespoons chocolate-hazelnut spread over a pastry square. Fold square horizontally to form a triangle and cut four evenly spaced slits about halfway through the top of folded square. Repeat with remaining spread and pastry squares.
5. Sprinkle confectioners' sugar and almonds over bear claws and place directly in the air fryer basket. Cook 10 minutes until puffy and golden brown. Serve warm.

Jalapeño Egg Cups

Servings:4
Cooking Time: 14 Minutes
Ingredients:
- 4 large eggs
- ½ teaspoon salt
- ¼ teaspoon ground black pepper
- ¼ cup chopped pickled jalapeños
- 2 ounces cream cheese, softened
- ¼ teaspoon garlic powder
- ½ cup shredded sharp Cheddar cheese
Directions:
1. In a medium bowl, beat eggs together with salt and pepper, then pour evenly into four 4" ramekins greased with cooking spray.
2. In a separate large bowl, mix jalapeños, cream cheese, garlic powder, and Cheddar. Spoon ¼ of the mixture into the center of one ramekin. Repeat with remaining mixture and ramekins.
3. Place ramekins in air fryer basket. Adjust the temperature to 320°F and set the timer for 14 minutes. Eggs will be set when done. Serve warm.

French Toast Sticks

Servings:4
Cooking Time: 8 Minutes
Ingredients:

- 4 slices Texas toast, or other thick-sliced bread
- 2 large eggs
- ¼ cup heavy cream
- 4 tablespoons salted butter, melted
- ½ cup granulated sugar
- 1 ½ tablespoons ground cinnamon

Directions:
1. Preheat the air fryer to 350°F. Cut parchment paper to fit the air fryer basket.
2. Slice each piece of bread into four even sticks.
3. In a medium bowl, whisk together eggs and cream. Dip each bread stick into mixture and place on parchment in the air fryer basket.
4. Cook 5 minutes, then carefully turn over and cook an additional 3 minutes until golden brown on both sides.
5. Drizzle sticks with butter and toss to ensure they're covered on all sides.
6. In a medium bowl, mix sugar and cinnamon. Dip both sides of each stick into the mixture and shake off excess. Serve warm.

Cheese Eggs And Leeks

Servings: 2
Cooking Time: 7 Minutes
Ingredients:

- 2 leeks, chopped
- 4 eggs, whisked
- ¼ cup Cheddar cheese, shredded
- ½ cup Mozzarella cheese, shredded
- 1 teaspoon avocado oil

Directions:
1. Preheat the air fryer to 400°F. Then brush the air fryer basket with avocado oil and combine the eggs with the rest of the ingredients inside. Cook for 7 minutes and serve.

Meaty Omelet

Servings: 4
Cooking Time: 20 Minutes
Ingredients:

- 6 eggs
- ½ cup grated Swiss cheese
- 3 breakfast sausages, sliced
- 8 bacon strips, sliced
- Salt and pepper to taste

Directions:
1. Preheat air fryer to 360°F. In a bowl, beat the eggs and stir in Swiss cheese, sausages and bacon. Transfer the mixture to a baking dish and set in the fryer. Bake for 15 minutes or until golden and crisp. Season and serve.

Jalapeño And Bacon Breakfast Pizza

Servings:2
Cooking Time: 10 Minutes
Ingredients:

- 1 cup shredded mozzarella cheese
- 1 ounce cream cheese, broken into small pieces
- 4 slices cooked sugar-free bacon, chopped
- ¼ cup chopped pickled jalapeños
- 1 large egg, whisked
- ¼ teaspoon salt

Directions:
1. Place mozzarella in a single layer on the bottom of an ungreased 6" round nonstick baking dish. Scatter cream cheese pieces, bacon, and jalapeños over mozzarella, then pour egg evenly around baking dish.
2. Sprinkle with salt and place into air fryer basket. Adjust the temperature to 330°F and set the timer for 10 minutes. When cheese is brown and egg is set, pizza will be done.
3. Let cool on a large plate 5 minutes before serving.

Roasted Golden Mini Potatoes

Servings:4
Cooking Time: 22 Minutes
Ingredients:

- 6 cups water
- 1 pound baby Dutch yellow potatoes, quartered
- 2 tablespoons olive oil
- ½ teaspoon garlic powder
- ¾ teaspoon seasoned salt
- ¼ teaspoon salt
- ½ teaspoon ground black pepper

Directions:
1. In a medium saucepan over medium-high heat bring water to a boil. Add potatoes and boil 10 minutes until fork-tender, then drain and gently pat dry.
2. Preheat the air fryer to 400°F.
3. Drizzle oil over potatoes, then sprinkle with garlic powder, seasoned salt, salt, and pepper.
4. Place potatoes in the air fryer basket and cook 12 minutes, shaking the basket three times during cooking. Potatoes will be done when golden brown and edges are crisp. Serve warm.

Chocolate Chip Scones

Servings:8
Cooking Time:15 Minutes
Ingredients:

- ½ cup cold salted butter, divided
- 2 cups all-purpose flour
- ½ cup brown sugar
- ½ teaspoon baking powder
- 1 large egg
- ¾ cup buttermilk
- ½ cup semisweet chocolate chips

Directions:
1. Preheat the air fryer to 320°F. Cut parchment paper to fit the air fryer basket.
2. Chill 6 tablespoons butter in the freezer 10 minutes. In a small microwave-safe bowl, microwave remaining 2 tablespoons butter 30 seconds until melted, and set aside.
3. In a large bowl, mix flour, brown sugar, and baking powder.
4. Remove butter from freezer and grate into bowl. Use a wooden spoon to evenly distribute.
5. Add egg and buttermilk and stir gently until a soft, sticky dough forms. Gently fold in chocolate chips.
6. Turn dough out onto a lightly floured surface. Fold a couple of times and gently form into a 6" round. Cut into eight triangles.

7. Place scones on parchment in the air fryer basket, leaving at least 2" space between each, working in batches as necessary.
8. Brush each scone with melted butter. Cook 15 minutes until scones are dark golden brown and crispy on the edges, and a toothpick inserted into the center comes out clean. Serve warm.

Banana-nut Muffins

Servings:12
Cooking Time: 15 Minutes
Ingredients:
- 1 ½ cups all-purpose flour
- ½ cup granulated sugar
- 1 teaspoon baking powder
- ½ cup salted butter, melted
- 1 large egg
- 2 medium bananas, peeled and mashed
- ½ cup chopped pecans

Directions:
1. Preheat the air fryer to 300°F.
2. In a large bowl, whisk together flour, sugar, and baking powder.
3. Add butter, egg, and bananas to dry mixture. Stir until well combined. Batter will be thick.
4. Gently fold in pecans. Divide batter evenly among twelve silicone or aluminum muffin cups, filling cups about halfway full.
5. Place cups in the air fryer basket, working in batches as necessary. Cook 15 minutes until muffin edges are brown and a toothpick inserted into the center comes out clean. Let cool 5 minutes before serving.

Peppered Maple Bacon Knots

Servings: 6
Cooking Time: 8 Minutes
Ingredients:
- 1 pound maple smoked center-cut bacon
- ¼ cup maple syrup
- ¼ cup brown sugar
- coarsely cracked black peppercorns

Directions:
1. Tie each bacon strip in a loose knot and place them on a baking sheet.
2. Combine the maple syrup and brown sugar in a bowl. Brush each knot generously with this mixture and sprinkle with coarsely cracked black pepper.
3. Preheat the air fryer to 390°F.
4. Air-fry the bacon knots in batches. Place one layer of knots in the air fryer basket and air-fry for 5 minutes. Turn the bacon knots over and air-fry for an additional 3 minutes.
5. Serve warm.

Green Onion Pancakes

Servings: 4
Cooking Time: 8 Minutes
Ingredients:
- 2 cup all-purpose flour
- ½ teaspoon salt
- ¾ cup hot water
- 1 tablespoon vegetable oil
- 1 tablespoon butter, melted
- 2 cups finely chopped green onions

- 1 tablespoon black sesame seeds, for garnish

Directions:
1. In a large bowl, whisk together the flour and salt. Make a well in the center and pour in the hot water. Quickly stir the flour mixture together until a dough forms. Knead the dough for 5 minutes; then cover with a warm, wet towel and set aside for 30 minutes to rest.
2. In a small bowl, mix together the vegetable oil and melted butter.
3. On a floured surface, place the dough and cut it into 8 pieces. Working with 1 piece of dough at a time, use a rolling pin to roll out the dough until it's ¼ inch thick; then brush the surface with the oil and butter mixture and sprinkle with green onions. Next, fold the dough in half and then in half again. Roll out the dough again until it's ¼ inch thick and brush with the oil and butter mixture and green onions. Fold the dough in half and then in half again and roll out one last time until it's ¼ inch thick. Repeat this technique with all 8 pieces.
4. Meanwhile, preheat the air fryer to 400°F.
5. Place 1 or 2 pancakes into the air fryer basket, and cook for 2 minutes or until crispy and golden brown. Repeat until all the pancakes are cooked. Top with black sesame seeds for garnish, if desired.

Mini Tomato Quiche

Servings:2
Cooking Time:30 Minutes
Ingredients:
- 4 eggs
- ¼ cup onion, chopped
- ½ cup tomatoes, chopped
- ½ cup milk
- 1 cup Gouda cheese, shredded
- Salt, to taste

Directions:
1. Preheat the Air fryer to 340°F and grease a large ramekin with cooking spray.
2. Mix together all the ingredients in a ramekin and transfer into the air fryer basket.
3. Cook for about 30 minutes and dish out to serve hot.

Scrambled Eggs

Servings: 2
Cooking Time: 6 Minutes
Ingredients:
- 4 eggs
- 1/4 tsp garlic powder
- 1/4 tsp onion powder
- 1 tbsp parmesan cheese
- Pepper
- Salt

Directions:
1. Whisk eggs with garlic powder, onion powder, parmesan cheese, pepper, and salt.
2. Pour egg mixture into the air fryer baking dish.
3. Place dish in the air fryer and cook at 360°F for 2 minutes. Stir quickly and cook for 3-4 minutes more.
4. Stir well and serve.

Cheesy Mustard Toasts

Servings:4
Cooking Time: 15 Minutes
Ingredients:
- 4 bread slices
- 2 tablespoons cheddar cheese, shredded
- 2 eggs, whites and yolks, separated
- 1 tablespoon mustard
- 1 tablespoon paprika

Directions:
1. Set the temperature of Air Fryer to 355°F.
2. Place the bread slices in an Air fryer basket.
3. Air Fry for about 5 minutes or until toasted.
4. Add the egg whites in a clean glass bowl and beat until they form soft peaks.
5. In another bowl, mix together the cheese, egg yolks, mustard, and paprika.
6. Gently, fold in the egg whites.
7. Spread the mustard mixture over the toasted bread slices.
8. Air Fry for about 10 minutes.
9. Serve warm!

Strawberry Toast

Servings: 4
Cooking Time: 8 Minutes
Ingredients:
- 4 slices bread, ½-inch thick
- butter-flavored cooking spray
- 1 cup sliced strawberries
- 1 teaspoon sugar

Directions:
1. Spray one side of each bread slice with butter-flavored cooking spray. Lay slices sprayed side down.
2. Divide the strawberries among the bread slices.
3. Sprinkle evenly with the sugar and place in the air fryer basket in a single layer.
4. Cook at 390°F for 8minutes. The bottom should look brown and crisp and the top should look glazed.

Egg White Frittata

Servings:2
Cooking Time: 8 Minutes
Ingredients:
- 2 cups liquid egg whites
- ½ cup chopped fresh spinach
- ¼ cup chopped Roma tomato
- ½ teaspoon salt
- ¼ cup chopped white onion

Directions:
1. Preheat the air fryer to 320°F. Spray a 6" round baking dish with cooking spray.
2. In a large bowl, whisk egg whites until frothy. Mix in spinach, tomato, salt, and onion. Stir until combined.
3. Pour egg mixture into prepared dish.
4. Place in the air fryer basket and cook 8 minutes until the center is set. Serve warm.

Crunchy Falafel Balls

Servings: 8
Cooking Time: 16 Minutes
Ingredients:
- 2½ cups Drained and rinsed canned chickpeas

- ¼ cup Olive oil
- 3 tablespoons All-purpose flour
- 1½ teaspoons Dried oregano
- 1½ teaspoons Dried sage leaves
- 1½ teaspoons Dried thyme
- ¾ teaspoon Table salt
- Olive oil spray

Directions:
1. Preheat the air fryer to 400°F.
2. Place the chickpeas, olive oil, flour, oregano, sage, thyme, and salt in a food processor. Cover and process into a paste, stopping the machine at least once to scrape down the inside of the canister.
3. Scrape down and remove the blade. Using clean, wet hands, form 2 tablespoons of the paste into a ball, then continue making 9 more balls for a small batch, 15 more for a medium one, and 19 more for a large batch. Generously coat the balls in olive oil spray.
4. Set the balls in the basket in one layer with a little space between them and air-fry undisturbed for 16 minutes, or until well browned and crisp.
5. Dump the contents of the basket onto a wire rack. Cool for 5 minutes before serving.

Bacon Eggs

Servings: 2
Cooking Time: 5 Minutes
Ingredients:
- 2 eggs, hard-boiled, peeled
- 4 bacon slices
- ½ teaspoon avocado oil
- 1 teaspoon mustard

Directions:
1. Preheat the air fryer to 400°F. Then sprinkle the air fryer basket with avocado oil and place the bacon slices inside. Flatten them in one layer and cook for 2 minutes from each side. After this, cool the bacon to the room temperature. Wrap every egg into 2 bacon slices. Secure the eggs with toothpicks and place them in the air fryer. Cook the wrapped eggs for 1 minute at 400°F.

Coconut Pudding

Servings: 4
Cooking Time: 20 Minutes
Ingredients:
- 1 cup cauliflower rice
- ½ cup coconut, shredded
- 3 cups coconut milk
- 2 tablespoons stevia

Directions:
1. In a pan that fits the air fryer, combine all the ingredients and whisk well. Introduce the in your air fryer and cook at 360°F for 20 minutes. Divide into bowls and serve for breakfast.

English Breakfast

Servings: 2
Cooking Time: 30 Minutes
Ingredients:
- 6 bacon strips
- 1 cup cooked white beans
- 1 tbsp melted butter
- ½ tbsp flour

- Salt and pepper to taste
- 2 eggs

Directions:
1. Preheat air fryer to 360°F. In a second bowl, combine the beans, butter, flour, salt, and pepper. Mix well. Put the bacon in the frying basket and Air Fry for 10 minutes, flipping once. Remove the bacon and stir in the beans. Crack the eggs on top and cook for 10-12 minutes until the eggs are set. Serve with bacon.

Onion Marinated Skirt Steak

Servings:3
Cooking Time: 45 Minutes
Ingredients:
- 1 large red onion, grated or pureed
- 2 tablespoons brown sugar
- 1 tablespoon vinegar
- 1 ½ pounds skirt steak
- Salt and pepper to taste

Directions:
1. Place all ingredients in a Ziploc bag and allow to marinate in the fridge for at least 2 hours.
2. Preheat the air fryer at 390°F.
3. Place the grill pan accessory in the air fryer.
4. Grill for 15 minutes per batch.
5. Flip every 8 minutes for even grilling.

Cheese Pie

Servings: 4
Cooking Time: 16 Minutes
Ingredients:
- 8 eggs
- 1 1/2 cups heavy whipping cream
- 1 lb cheddar cheese, grated
- Pepper
- Salt

Directions:
1. Preheat the air fryer to 325°F.
2. In a bowl, whisk together cheese, eggs, whipping cream, pepper, and salt.
3. Spray air fryer baking dish with cooking spray.
4. Pour egg mixture into the prepared dish and place in the air fryer basket.
5. Cook for 16 minutes or until the egg is set.
6. Serve and enjoy.

Egg In A Hole

Servings: 4
Cooking Time: 10 Minutes
Ingredients:
- 4 slices white sandwich bread
- 4 large eggs
- ½ teaspoon salt
- ¼ teaspoon ground black pepper

Directions:
1. Preheat the air fryer to 350°F. Spray a 6" round cake pan with cooking spray.
2. Place as many pieces of bread as will fit in one layer in prepared pan, working in batches as necessary.
3. Using a small cup or cookie cutter, cut a circle out of the center of each bread slice. Crack an egg directly into each cutout and sprinkle eggs with salt and pepper.

4. Cook 5 minutes, then carefully turn and cook an additional 5 minutes or less, depending on your preference. Serve warm.

Sausage Egg Muffins

Servings: 4
Cooking Time: 30 Minutes
Ingredients:
- 6 oz Italian sausage
- 6 eggs
- 1/8 cup heavy cream
- 3 oz cheese

Directions:
1. Preheat the fryer to 350°F.
2. Grease a muffin pan.
3. Slice the sausage links and place them two to a tin.
4. Beat the eggs with the cream and season with salt and pepper.
5. Pour over the sausages in the tin.
6. Sprinkle with cheese and the remaining egg mixture.
7. Cook for 20 minutes or until the eggs are done and serve!

Black's Bangin' Casserole

Servings: 4
Cooking Time: 40 Minutes
Ingredients:
- 5 eggs
- 3 tbsp chunky tomato sauce
- 2 tbsp heavy cream
- 2 tbsp grated parmesan cheese

Directions:
1. Preheat your fryer to 350°F
2. Combine the eggs and cream in a bowl.
3. Mix in the tomato sauce and add the cheese.
4. Spread into a glass baking dish and bake for 25-35 minutes.
5. Top with extra cheese.
6. Enjoy!

Bacon, Egg, And Cheese Calzones

Servings:4
Cooking Time: 12 Minutes
Ingredients:
- 2 large eggs
- 1 cup blanched finely ground almond flour
- 2 cups shredded mozzarella cheese
- 2 ounces cream cheese, softened and broken into small pieces
- 4 slices cooked sugar-free bacon, crumbled

Directions:
1. Beat eggs in a small bowl. Pour into a medium nonstick skillet over medium heat and scramble. Set aside.
2. In a large microwave-safe bowl, mix flour and mozzarella. Add cream cheese to bowl.
3. Place bowl in microwave and cook 45 seconds on high to melt cheese, then stir with a fork until a soft dough ball forms.
4. Cut a piece of parchment to fit air fryer basket. Separate dough into two sections and press each out into an 8" round.
5. On half of each dough round, place half of the scrambled eggs and crumbled bacon. Fold the other side of the dough over and press to seal the edges.
6. Place calzones on ungreased parchment and into air fryer basket. Adjust the temperature to 350°F and set the timer for 12

minutes, turning calzones halfway through cooking. Crust will be golden and firm when done.

7. Let calzones cool on a cooking rack 5 minutes before serving.

Baked Eggs

Servings: 4
Cooking Time: 6 Minutes
Ingredients:
- 4 large eggs
- ⅛ teaspoon black pepper
- ⅛ teaspoon salt

Directions:
1. Preheat the air fryer to 330°F. Place 4 silicone muffin liners into the air fryer basket.
2. Crack 1 egg at a time into each silicone muffin liner. Sprinkle with black pepper and salt.
3. Bake for 6 minutes. Remove and let cool 2 minutes prior to serving.

Ham And Egg Toast Cups

Servings:2
Cooking Time:5 Minutes
Ingredients:
- 2 eggs
- 2 slices of ham
- 2 tablespoons butter
- Cheddar cheese, for topping
- Salt, to taste
- Black pepper, to taste

Directions:
1. Preheat the Air fryer to 400°F and grease both ramekins with melted butter.
2. Place each ham slice in the greased ramekins and crack each egg over ham slices.
3. Sprinkle with salt, black pepper and cheddar cheese and transfer into the Air fryer basket.
4. Cook for about 5 minutes and remove the ramekins from the basket.
5. Serve warm.

Spinach Eggs And Cheese

Servings: 2
Cooking Time: 40 Minutes
Ingredients:
- 3 whole eggs
- 3 oz cottage cheese
- 3-4 oz chopped spinach
- ¼ cup parmesan cheese
- ¼ cup of milk

Directions:
1. Preheat your fryer to 375°F.
2. In a large bowl, whisk the eggs, cottage cheese, the parmesan and the milk.
3. Mix in the spinach.
4. Transfer to a small, greased, fryer dish.
5. Sprinkle the cheese on top.
6. Bake for 25-30 minutes.
7. Let cool for 5 minutes and serve.

Brown Sugar Grapefruit

Servings: 2

Cooking Time: 4 Minutes
Ingredients:
- 1 grapefruit
- 2 to 4 teaspoons brown sugar

Directions:
1. Preheat the air fryer to 400°F.
2. While the air fryer is Preheating, cut the grapefruit in half horizontally (in other words not through the stem or blossom end of the grapefruit). Slice the bottom of the grapefruit to help it sit flat on the counter if necessary. Using a sharp paring knife (serrated is great), cut around the grapefruit between the flesh of the fruit and the peel. Then, cut each segment away from the membrane so that it is sitting freely in the fruit.
3. Sprinkle 1 to 2 teaspoons of brown sugar on each half of the prepared grapefruit. Set up a rack in the air fryer basket (use an air fryer rack or make your own rack with some crumpled up aluminum foil). You don't have to use a rack, but doing so will get the grapefruit closer to the element so that the brown sugar can caramelize a little better. Transfer the grapefruit half to the rack in the air fryer basket. Depending on how big your grapefruit are and what size air fryer you have, you may need to do each half separately to make sure they sit flat.
4. Air-fry at 400°F for 4 minutes.
5. Remove and let it cool for just a minute before enjoying.

Sweet Potato-cinnamon Toast

Servings: 6
Cooking Time: 8 Minutes
Ingredients:
- 1 small sweet potato, cut into ⅜-inch slices
- oil for misting
- ground cinnamon

Directions:
1. Preheat air fryer to 390°F.
2. Spray both sides of sweet potato slices with oil. Sprinkle both sides with cinnamon to taste.
3. Place potato slices in air fryer basket in a single layer.
4. Cook for 4minutes, turn, and cook for 4 more minutes or until potato slices are barely fork tender.

Pizza Eggs

Servings:2
Cooking Time: 10 Minutes
Ingredients:
- 1 cup shredded mozzarella cheese
- 7 slices pepperoni, chopped
- 1 large egg, whisked
- ¼ teaspoon dried oregano
- ¼ teaspoon dried parsley
- ¼ teaspoon garlic powder
- ¼ teaspoon salt

Directions:
1. Place mozzarella in a single layer on the bottom of an ungreased 6" round nonstick baking dish. Scatter pepperoni over cheese, then pour egg evenly around baking dish.
2. Sprinkle with remaining ingredients and place into air fryer basket. Adjust the temperature to 330°F and set the timer for 10 minutes. When cheese is brown and egg is set, dish will be done.
3. Let cool in dish 5 minutes before serving.

Greek-style Frittata

Servings:2
Cooking Time: 10 Minutes
Ingredients:
- 2 tbsp heavy cream
- 2 cups spinach, chopped
- 1 cup chopped mushrooms
- 3 oz feta cheese, crumbled
- A handful of fresh parsley, chopped
- Salt and black pepper

Directions:
1. Spray your air fryer basket with cooking spray. In a bowl, whisk eggs and until combined. Stir in spinach, mushrooms, feta, parsley, salt, and black pepper.
2. Pour into the basket and cook for 6 minutes at 350°F. Serve immediately with a touch of tomato relish.

Oregano And Coconut Scramble

Servings: 4
Cooking Time: 20 Minutes
Ingredients:
- 8 eggs, whisked
- 2 tablespoons oregano, chopped
- Salt and black pepper to the taste
- 2 tablespoons parmesan, grated
- ¼ cup coconut cream

Directions:
1. In a bowl, mix the eggs with all the ingredients and whisk. Pour this into a pan that fits your air fryer, introduce it in the preheated fryer and cook at 350°F for 20 minutes, stirring often. Divide the scramble between plates and serve for breakfast.

Maple-bacon Doughnuts

Servings:8
Cooking Time: 5 Minutes
Ingredients:
- 1 can refrigerated biscuit dough, separated
- 1 cup confectioners' sugar
- ¼ cup heavy cream
- 1 teaspoon maple extract
- 6 slices bacon, cooked and crumbled

Directions:
1. Preheat the air fryer to 350°F.
2. Place biscuits in the air fryer basket and cook 5 minutes, turning halfway through cooking time, until golden brown. Let cool 5 minutes.
3. In a medium bowl, whisk together confectioners' sugar, cream, and maple extract until smooth.
4. Dip top of each doughnut into glaze and set aside to set for 5 minutes. Top with crumbled bacon and serve immediately.

Crust-less Quiche

Servings:2
Cooking Time:30 Minutes
Ingredients:
- 4 eggs
- ¼ cup onion, chopped
- ½ cup tomatoes, chopped
- ½ cup milk
- 1 cup Gouda cheese, shredded
- Salt, to taste

Directions:
1. Preheat the Air fryer to 340°F and grease 2 ramekins lightly.
2. Mix together all the ingredients in a ramekin until well combined.
3. Place in the Air fryer and cook for about 30 minutes.
4. Dish out and serve.

Parsley Egg Scramble With Cottage Cheese

Servings:2
Cooking Time: 15 Minutes
Ingredients:
- 1 tbsp cottage cheese, crumbled
- 4 eggs
- Salt and pepper to taste
- 2 tsp heavy cream
- 1 tbsp chopped parsley

Directions:
1. Preheat air fryer to 400ºF. Grease a baking pan with olive oil. Beat the eggs, salt, and pepper in a bowl. Pour it into the pan, place the pan in the frying basket, and Air Fry for 5 minutes. Using a silicone spatula, stir in heavy cream, cottage cheese, and half of parsley and Air Fry for another 2 minutes. Scatter with parsley to serve.

Tuscan Toast

Servings: 4
Cooking Time: 5 Minutes
Ingredients:
- ¼ cup butter
- ½ teaspoon lemon juice
- ½ clove garlic
- ½ teaspoon dried parsley flakes
- 4 slices Italian bread, 1-inch thick

Directions:
1. Place butter, lemon juice, garlic, and parsley in a food processor. Process about 1 minute, or until garlic is pulverized and ingredients are well blended.
2. Spread garlic butter on both sides of bread slices.
3. Place bread slices upright in air fryer basket.
4. Cook at 390°F for 5 minutes or until toasty brown.

Sausage-crusted Egg Cups

Servings:6
Cooking Time: 15 Minutes
Ingredients:
- 12 ounces ground pork breakfast sausage
- 6 large eggs
- ½ teaspoon salt
- ¼ teaspoon ground black pepper
- ½ teaspoon crushed red pepper flakes

Directions:
1. Place sausage in six 4" ramekins greased with cooking oil. Press sausage down to cover bottom and about ½" up the sides of ramekins. Crack one egg into each ramekin and sprinkle evenly with salt, black pepper, and red pepper flakes.
2. Place ramekins into air fryer basket. Adjust the temperature to 350°F and set the timer for 15 minutes. Egg cups will be done when sausage is fully cooked to at least 145°F and the egg is firm. Serve warm.

Cheesy Bell Pepper Eggs

Servings:4
Cooking Time: 15 Minutes
Ingredients:
- 4 medium green bell peppers, tops removed, seeded
- 1 tablespoon coconut oil
- 3 ounces chopped cooked no-sugar-added ham
- ¼ cup peeled and chopped white onion
- 4 large eggs
- ½ teaspoon salt
- 1 cup shredded mild Cheddar cheese

Directions:
1. Place peppers upright into ungreased air fryer basket. Drizzle each pepper with coconut oil. Divide ham and onion evenly among peppers.
2. In a medium bowl, whisk eggs, then sprinkle with salt. Pour mixture evenly into each pepper. Top each with ¼ cup Cheddar.
3. Adjust the temperature to 320°F and set the timer for 15 minutes. Peppers will be tender and eggs will be firm when done.
4. Serve warm on four medium plates.

Breakfast Chimichangas

Servings: 4
Cooking Time: 8 Minutes
Ingredients:
- Four 8-inch flour tortillas
- ½ cup canned refried beans
- 1 cup scrambled eggs
- ½ cup grated cheddar or Monterey jack cheese
- 1 tablespoon vegetable oil
- 1 cup salsa

Directions:
1. Lay the flour tortillas out flat on a cutting board. In the center of each tortilla, spread 2 tablespoons refried beans. Next, add ¼ cup eggs and 2 tablespoons cheese to each tortilla.
2. To fold the tortillas, begin on the left side and fold to the center. Then fold the right side into the center. Next fold the bottom and top down and roll over to completely seal the chimichanga. Using a pastry brush or oil mister, brush the tops of the tortilla packages with oil.
3. Preheat the air fryer to 400°F for 4 minutes. Place the chimichangas into the air fryer basket, seam side down, and air fry for 4 minutes. Using tongs, turn over the chimichangas and cook for an additional 2 to 3 minutes or until light golden brown.

Blueberry Muffins

Servings:12
Cooking Time:15 Minutes
Ingredients:
- 1 cup all-purpose flour
- ½ cup granulated sugar
- 1 teaspoon baking powder
- ¼ cup salted butter, melted
- 1 large egg
- ½ cup whole milk
- 1 cup fresh blueberries

Directions:
1. Preheat the air fryer to 300°F.
2. In a large bowl, whisk together flour, sugar, and baking powder.
3. Add butter, egg, and milk to dry mixture. Stir until well combined.
4. Gently fold in blueberries. Divide batter evenly among twelve silicone or aluminum muffin cups, filling cups about halfway full.
5. Place cups in the air fryer basket, working in batches as necessary. Cook 15 minutes until muffins are brown at the edges and a toothpick inserted in the center comes out clean. Serve warm.

Buttery Scallops

Servings: 2
Cooking Time: 8 Minutes
Ingredients:
- 1 lb jumbo scallops
- 1 tbsp fresh lemon juice
- 2 tbsp butter, melted

Directions:
1. Preheat the air fryer to 400°F.
2. In a small bowl, mix together lemon juice and butter.
3. Brush scallops with lemon juice and butter mixture and place into the air fryer basket.
4. Cook scallops for 4 minutes. Turn halfway through.
5. Again brush scallops with lemon butter mixture and cook for 4 minutes more. Turn halfway through.
6. Serve and enjoy.

Chocolate Chip Muffins

Servings:6
Cooking Time: 15 Minutes
Ingredients:
- 1½ cups blanched finely ground almond flour
- ⅓ cup granular brown erythritol
- 4 tablespoons salted butter, melted
- 2 large eggs, whisked
- 1 tablespoon baking powder
- ½ cup low-carb chocolate chips

Directions:
1. In a large bowl, combine all ingredients. Evenly pour batter into six silicone muffin cups greased with cooking spray.
2. Place muffin cups into air fryer basket. Adjust the temperature to 320°F and set the timer for 15 minutes. Muffins will be golden brown when done.
3. Let muffins cool in cups 15 minutes to avoid crumbling. Serve warm.

Bacon Cups

Servings: 2
Cooking Time: 40 Minutes
Ingredients:
- 2 eggs
- 1 slice tomato
- 3 slices bacon
- 2 slices ham
- 2 tsp grated parmesan cheese

Directions:
1. Preheat your fryer to 375°F
2. Cook the bacon for half of the directed time.
3. Slice the bacon strips in half and line 2 greased muffin tins with 3 half-strips of bacon
4. Put one slice of ham and half slice of tomato in each muffin tin on top of the bacon
5. Crack one egg on top of the tomato in each muffin tin and sprinkle each with half a teaspoon of grated parmesan cheese.
6. Bake for 20 minutes.
7. Remove and let cool.
8. Serve!

Bagels

Servings:4
Cooking Time: 10 Minutes
Ingredients:
- 1 cup self-rising flour
- 1 cup plain full-fat Greek yogurt
- 2 tablespoons granulated sugar
- 1 large egg, whisked

Directions:
1. Preheat the air fryer to 320°F.
2. In a large bowl, mix flour, yogurt, and sugar together until a ball of dough forms.
3. Turn dough out onto a lightly floured surface. Knead dough for 3 minutes, then form into a smooth ball. Cut dough into four sections. Roll each piece into an 8" rope, then shape into a circular bagel shape. Brush top and bottom of each bagel with egg.
4. Place in the air fryer basket and cook 10 minutes, turning halfway through cooking time to ensure even browning. Let cool 5 minutes before serving.

Chapter 3. Appetizers And Snacks

Potato Skins

Servings:4
Cooking Time: 35 Minutes Per Batch
Ingredients:
- 4 large russet potatoes
- ½ cup shredded sharp Cheddar cheese
- 1 teaspoon salt
- ½ teaspoon ground black pepper
- ½ cup sour cream
- 1 medium green onion, sliced

Directions:
1. Preheat the air fryer to 400°F.
2. Using a fork, poke several holes in potatoes. Place potatoes in the air fryer basket and cook 30 minutes until fork tender.
3. Once potatoes are cool enough to handle, slice them in half lengthwise and scoop out the insides, being careful to maintain the structural integrity of the potato skins. Reserve potato flesh for another use.
4. Sprinkle insides of potato skins with Cheddar, salt, and pepper. Working in batches if needed, place back in the air fryer basket and cook 5 minutes until cheese is melted and bubbling.
5. Let cool 5 minutes, then top with sour cream and green onion. Serve.

Greek Street Tacos

Servings: 8
Cooking Time: 3 Minutes
Ingredients:
- 8 small flour tortillas

- 8 tablespoons hummus
- 4 tablespoons crumbled feta cheese
- 4 tablespoons chopped kalamata or other olives (optional)
- olive oil for misting

Directions:
1. Place 1 tablespoon of hummus or tapenade in the center of each tortilla. Top with 1 teaspoon of feta crumbles and 1 teaspoon of chopped olives, if using.
2. Using your finger or a small spoon, moisten the edges of the tortilla all around with water.
3. Fold tortilla over to make a half-moon shape. Press center gently. Then press the edges firmly to seal in the filling.
4. Mist both sides with olive oil.
5. Place in air fryer basket very close but try not to overlap.
6. Cook at 390°F for 3minutes, just until lightly browned and crispy.

Cheese Crackers

Servings:4
Cooking Time: 10 Minutes Per Batch
Ingredients:
- 4 ounces sharp Cheddar cheese, shredded
- ½ cup all-purpose flour
- 2 tablespoons salted butter, cubed
- ½ teaspoon salt
- 2 tablespoons cold water

Directions:
1. In a large bowl, using an electric hand mixer, mix all ingredients until dough forms. Pack dough together into a ball and wrap tightly in plastic wrap. Chill in the freezer 15 minutes.

2. Preheat the air fryer to 375°F. Cut parchment paper to fit the air fryer basket.

3. Spread a separate large sheet of parchment paper on a work surface. Remove dough from the freezer and roll out ¼" thick on parchment paper. Use a pizza cutter to cut dough into 1" squares.

4. Place crackers on precut parchment in the air fryer basket and cook 10 minutes, working in batches as necessary.

5. Allow crackers to cool at least 10 minutes before serving.

Parmesan Pizza Nuggets

Servings: 8
Cooking Time: 6 Minutes
Ingredients:
- ¾ cup warm filtered water
- 1 package fast-rising yeast
- ½ teaspoon salt
- 2 cups all-purpose flour
- ¼ cup finely grated Parmesan cheese
- 1 teaspoon Italian seasoning
- 2 tablespoon extra-virgin olive oil
- 1 teaspoon kosher salt

Directions:
1. Preheat the air fryer to 370°F.
2. In a large microwave-safe bowl, add the water. Heat for 40 seconds in the microwave. Remove and mix in the yeast and salt. Let sit 5 minutes.
3. Meanwhile, in a medium bowl, mix the flour with the Parmesan cheese and Italian seasoning. Set aside.
4. Using a stand mixer with a dough hook attachment, add the yeast liquid and then mix in the flour mixture ⅓ cup at a time until all the flour mixture is added and a dough is formed.
5. Remove the bowl from the stand, and then let the dough rise for 1 hour in a warm space, covered with a kitchen towel.
6. After the dough has doubled in size, remove it from the bowl and punch it down a few times on a lightly floured flat surface.
7. Divide the dough into 4 balls, and then roll each ball out into a long, skinny, sticklike shape.
8. Using a sharp knife, cut each dough stick into 6 pieces. Repeat for the remaining dough balls until you have about 24 nuggets formed.
9. Lightly brush the top of each bite with the egg whites and cover with a pinch of sea salt.
10. Spray the air fryer basket with olive oil spray and place the pizza nuggets on top. Cook for 6 minutes, or until lightly browned. Remove and keep warm.
11. Repeat until all the nuggets are cooked.
12. Serve warm.

Grilled Cheese Sandwich Deluxe

Servings: 4
Cooking Time: 6 Minutes
Ingredients:
- 8 ounces Brie
- 8 slices oat nut bread
- 1 large ripe pear, cored and cut into ½-inch-thick slices
- 2 tablespoons butter, melted

Directions:
1. Spread a quarter of the Brie on each of four slices of bread.
2. Top Brie with thick slices of pear, then the remaining 4 slices of bread.

3. Lightly brush both sides of each sandwich with melted butter.
4. Cooking 2 at a time, place sandwiches in air fryer basket and cook at 360°F for 6 minutes or until cheese melts and outside looks golden brown.

Wrapped Shrimp Bites

Servings: 4
Cooking Time: 15 Minutes
Ingredients:
- 2 jumbo shrimp, peeled
- 2 bacon strips, sliced
- 2 tbsp lemon juice
- ½ tsp chipotle powder
- ½ tsp garlic salt

Directions:
1. Preheat air fryer to 350°F. Wrap the bacon around the shrimp and place the shrimp in the foil-lined frying basket, seam side down. Drizzle with lemon juice, chipotle powder and garlic salt. Air Fry for 10 minutes, turning the shrimp once until cooked through and bacon is crispy. Serve hot.

Homemade French Fries

Servings: 2
Cooking Time: 25 Minutes
Ingredients:
- 2 to 3 russet potatoes, peeled and cut into ½-inch sticks
- 2 to 3 teaspoons olive or vegetable oil
- salt

Directions:
1. Bring a large saucepan of salted water to a boil on the stovetop while you peel and cut the potatoes. Blanch the potatoes in the boiling salted water for 4 minutes while you Preheat the air fryer to 400°F. Strain the potatoes and rinse them with cold water. Dry them well with a clean kitchen towel.
2. Toss the dried potato sticks gently with the oil and place them in the air fryer basket. Air-fry for 25 minutes, shaking the basket a few times while the fries cook to help them brown evenly. Season the fries with salt mid-way through cooking and serve them warm with tomato ketchup, Sriracha mayonnaise or a mix of lemon zest, Parmesan cheese and parsley.

Mozzarella Sticks

Servings: 4
Cooking Time: 5 Minutes
Ingredients:
- 1 egg
- 1 tablespoon water
- 8 eggroll wraps
- 8 mozzarella string cheese "sticks"
- sauce for dipping

Directions:
1. Beat together egg and water in a small bowl.
2. Lay out egg roll wraps and moisten edges with egg wash.
3. Place one piece of string cheese on each wrap near one end.
4. Fold in sides of egg roll wrap over ends of cheese, and then roll up.
5. Brush outside of wrap with egg wash and press gently to seal well.
6. Place in air fryer basket in single layer and cook 390°F for 5 minutes. Cook an additional 1 or 2minutes, if necessary, until they are golden brown and crispy.

7. Serve with your favorite dipping sauce.

Buttery Spiced Pecans

Servings: 6
Cooking Time: 4 Minutes
Ingredients:
- 2 cups (½ pound) Pecan halves
- 2 tablespoons Butter, melted
- 1 teaspoon Mild paprika
- ½ teaspoon Ground cumin
- Up to ½ teaspoon Cayenne
- ½ teaspoon Table salt

Directions:
1. Preheat the air fryer to 400°F.
2. Toss the pecans, butter, paprika, cumin, cayenne, and salt in a bowl until the nuts are evenly coated.
3. When the machine is at temperature, pour the nuts into the basket, spreading them into as close to one layer as you can. Air-fry for 4 minutes, tossing after every minute, and perhaps even more frequently for the last minute if the pecans are really browning, until the pecans are warm, dark brown in spots, and very aromatic.
4. Pour the contents of the basket onto a lipped baking sheet and spread the nuts into one layer. Cool for at least 5 minutes before serving. The nuts can be stored at room temperature in a sealed container for up to 1 week.

Carrot Chips

Servings: 4
Cooking Time: 10 Minutes
Ingredients:
- 1 pound carrots, thinly sliced
- 2 tablespoons extra-virgin olive oil
- ¼ teaspoon garlic powder
- ¼ teaspoon black pepper
- ½ teaspoon salt

Directions:
1. Preheat the air fryer to 390°F.
2. In a medium bowl, toss the carrot slices with the olive oil, garlic powder, pepper, and salt.
3. Liberally spray the air fryer basket with olive oil mist.
4. Place the carrot slices in the air fryer basket. To allow for even cooking, don't overlap the carrots; cook in batches if necessary.
5. Cook for 5 minutes, shake the basket, and cook another 5 minutes.
6. Remove from the basket and serve warm. Repeat with the remaining carrot slices until they're all cooked.

Three Cheese Dip

Servings:8
Cooking Time: 12 Minutes
Ingredients:
- 8 ounces cream cheese, softened
- ½ cup mayonnaise
- ¼ cup sour cream
- ½ cup shredded sharp Cheddar cheese
- ¼ cup shredded Monterey jack cheese

Directions:
1. In a large bowl, combine all ingredients. Scoop mixture into an ungreased 4-cup nonstick baking dish and place into air fryer basket.

2. Adjust the temperature to 375°F and set the timer for 12 minutes. Dip will be browned on top and bubbling when done. Serve warm.

Plantain Chips

Servings: 2
Cooking Time: 14 Minutes
Ingredients:
- 1 large green plantain
- 2½ cups filtered water, divided
- 2 teaspoons sea salt, divided
- Cooking spray

Directions:
1. Slice the plantain into 1-inch pieces. Place the plantains into a large bowl, cover with 2 cups water and 1 teaspoon salt. Soak the plantains for 30 minutes; then remove and pat dry.
2. Preheat the air fryer to 390°F.
3. Place the plantain pieces into the air fryer basket, leaving space between the plantain rounds. Cook the plantains for 5 minutes, and carefully remove them from the air fryer basket.
4. Add the remaining water to a small bowl.
5. Using a small drinking glass, dip the bottom of the glass into the water and mash the warm plantains until they're ¼-inch thick. Return the plantains to the air fryer basket, sprinkle with the remaining sea salt, and spray lightly with cooking spray.
6. Cook for another 6 to 8 minutes, or until lightly golden brown edges appear.

Fried Pickles

Servings: 2
Cooking Time: 15 Minutes
Ingredients:
- 1 egg
- 1 tablespoon milk
- ¼ teaspoon hot sauce
- 2 cups sliced dill pickles, well drained
- ¾ cup breadcrumbs
- oil for misting or cooking spray

Directions:
1. Preheat air fryer to 390°F.
2. Beat together egg, milk, and hot sauce in a bowl large enough to hold all the pickles.
3. Add pickles to the egg wash and stir well to coat.
4. Place breadcrumbs in a large plastic bag or container with lid.
5. Drain egg wash from pickles and place them in bag with breadcrumbs. Shake to coat.
6. Pile pickles into air fryer basket and spray with oil.
7. Cook for 5 minutes. Shake basket and spray with oil.
8. Cook 5 more minutes. Shake and spray again. Separate any pickles that have stuck together and mist any spots you've missed.
9. Cook for 5 minutes longer or until dark golden brown and crispy.

Homemade Pretzel Bites

Servings: 8
Cooking Time: 6 Minutes
Ingredients:
- 4¾ cups filtered water, divided
- 1 tablespoon butter
- 1 package fast-rising yeast

- ½ teaspoon salt
- 2⅓ cups bread flour
- 2 tablespoons baking soda
- 2 egg whites
- 1 teaspoon kosher salt

Directions:

1. Preheat the air fryer to 370°F.

2. In a large microwave-safe bowl, add ¾ cup of the water. Heat for 40 seconds in the microwave. Remove and whisk in the butter; then mix in the yeast and salt. Let sit 5 minutes.

3. Using a stand mixer with a dough hook attachment, add the yeast liquid and mix in the bread flour ⅓ cup at a time until all the flour is added and a dough is formed.

4. Remove the bowl from the stand; then let the dough rise 1 hour in a warm space, covered with a kitchen towel.

5. After the dough has doubled in size, remove from the bowl and punch down a few times on a lightly floured flat surface.

6. Divide the dough into 4 balls; then roll each ball out into a long, skinny, sticklike shape. Using a sharp knife, cut each dough stick into 6 pieces.

7. Repeat Step 6 for the remaining dough balls until you have about 24 bites formed.

8. Heat the remaining 4 cups of water over the stovetop in a medium pot with the baking soda stirred in.

9. Drop the pretzel bite dough into the hot water and let boil for 60 seconds, remove, and let slightly cool.

10. Lightly brush the top of each bite with the egg whites, and then cover with a pinch of kosher salt.

11. Spray the air fryer basket with olive oil spray and place the pretzel bites on top. Cook for 6 to 8 minutes, or until lightly browned. Remove and keep warm.

12. Repeat until all pretzel bites are cooked.

13. Serve warm.

Crispy Ravioli Bites

Servings: 5
Cooking Time: 7 Minutes
Ingredients:
- ⅓ cup All-purpose flour
- 1 Large egg(s), well beaten
- ⅔ cup Seasoned Italian-style dried bread crumbs
- 10 ounces Frozen mini ravioli, meat or cheese, thawed
- Olive oil spray

Directions:

1. Preheat the air fryer to 400°F.

2. Pour the flour into a medium bowl. Set up and fill two shallow soup plates or small pie plates on your counter: one with the beaten egg(s) and one with the bread crumbs.

3. Pour all the ravioli into the flour and toss well to coat. Pick up 1 ravioli, gently shake off any excess flour, and dip the ravioli in the egg(s), coating both sides. Let any excess egg slip back into the rest, then set the ravioli in the bread crumbs, turning it several times until lightly and evenly coated on all sides. Set aside on a cutting board and continue on with the remaining ravioli.

4. Lightly coat the ravioli on both sides with olive oil spray, then set them in the basket in as close to a single layer as you can. Some can lean up against the side of the basket. Air-fry for 7 minutes, tossing the basket at the 4-minute mark to rearrange the pieces, until brown and crisp.

5. Pour the contents of the basket onto a wire rack. Cool for 5 minutes before serving.

Bacon Candy

Servings: 6
Cooking Time: 6 Minutes
Ingredients:
- 1½ tablespoons Honey
- 1 teaspoon White wine vinegar
- 3 Extra thick–cut bacon strips, halved widthwise (gluten-free, if a concern)
- ½ teaspoon Ground black pepper

Directions:

1. Preheat the air fryer to 350°F .

2. Whisk the honey and vinegar in a small bowl until incorporated.

3. When the machine is at temperature, remove the basket. Lay the bacon strip halves in the basket in one layer. Brush the tops with the honey mixture; sprinkle each bacon strip evenly with black pepper.

4. Return the basket to the machine and air-fry undisturbed for 6 minutes, or until the bacon is crunchy. Or a little less time if you prefer bacon that's still pliable, an extra minute if you want the bacon super crunchy. Take care that the honey coating doesn't burn. Remove the basket from the machine and set aside for 5 minutes. Use kitchen tongs to transfer the bacon strips to a serving plate.

Bacon-wrapped Cabbage Bites

Servings:6
Cooking Time: 12 Minutes
Ingredients:
- 3 tablespoons sriracha hot chili sauce, divided
- 1 medium head cabbage, cored and cut into 12 bite-sized pieces
- 2 tablespoons coconut oil, melted
- ½ teaspoon salt
- 12 slices sugar-free bacon
- ½ cup mayonnaise
- ¼ teaspoon garlic powder

Directions:

1. Evenly brush 2 tablespoons sriracha onto cabbage pieces. Drizzle evenly with coconut oil, then sprinkle with salt.

2. Wrap each cabbage piece with bacon and secure with a toothpick. Place into ungreased air fryer basket. Adjust the temperature to 375°F and set the timer for 12 minutes, turning cabbage halfway through cooking. Bacon will be cooked and crispy when done.

3. In a small bowl, whisk together mayonnaise, garlic powder, and remaining sriracha. Use as a dipping sauce for cabbage bites.

Pita Chips

Servings: 4
Cooking Time: 10 Minutes
Ingredients:
- 2 rounds Pocketless pita bread
- Olive oil spray or any flavor spray you prefer, even coconut oil spray
- Up to 1 teaspoon Fine sea salt, garlic salt, onion salt, or other flavored salt

Directions:

1. Preheat the air fryer to 400°F.

2. Lightly coat the pita round(s) on both sides with olive oil spray, then lightly sprinkle each side with salt.

3. Cut each coated pita round into 8 even wedges. Lay these in the basket in as close to a single even layer as possible. Many will overlap or even be on top of each other, depending on the exact size of your machine.

4. Air-fry for 6 minutes, shaking the basket and rearranging the wedges at the 4-minute marks, until the wedges are crisp and brown. Turn them out onto a wire rack to cool a few minutes or to room temperature before digging in.

Bacon Butter

Servings:5
Cooking Time: 2 Minutes
Ingredients:
- ½ cup butter
- 3 oz bacon, chopped

Directions:
1. Preheat the air fryer to 400°F and put the bacon inside. Cook it for 8 minutes. Stir the bacon every 2 minutes. Meanwhile, soften the butter in the oven and put it in the butter mold. Add cooked bacon and churn the butter. Refrigerate the butter for 30 minutes.

Veggie Chips

Servings: X
Cooking Time: X
Ingredients:
- sweet potato
- large parsnip
- large carrot
- turnip
- large beet
- vegetable or canola oil, in a spray bottle
- salt

Directions:
1. You can do a medley of vegetable chips, or just select from the vegetables listed. Whatever you choose to do, scrub the vegetables well and then slice them paper-thin using a mandolin.
2. Preheat the air fryer to 400°F.
3. Air-fry the chips in batches, one type of vegetable at a time. Spray the chips lightly with oil and transfer them to the air fryer basket. The key is to NOT over-load the basket. You can overlap the chips a little, but don't pile them on top of each other. Doing so will make it much harder to get evenly browned and crispy chips. Air-fry at 400°F for the time indicated below, shaking the basket several times during the cooking process for even cooking.
4. Sweet Potato – 8 to 9 minutes
5. Parsnips – 5 minutes
6. Carrot – 7 minutes
7. Turnips – 8 minutes
8. Beets – 9 minutes
9. Season the chips with salt during the last couple of minutes of air-frying. Check the chips as they cook until they are done to your liking. Some will start to brown sooner than others.
10. You can enjoy the chips warm out of the air fryer or cool them to room temperature for crispier chips.

Thyme Sweet Potato Chips

Servings: 2
Cooking Time: 20 Minutes
Ingredients:
- 1 tbsp olive oil

- 1 sweet potato, sliced
- ¼ tsp dried thyme
- Salt to taste

Directions:
1. Preheat air fryer to 390°F. Spread the sweet potato slices in the greased basket and brush with olive oil. Air Fry for 6 minutes. Remove the basket, shake, and sprinkle with thyme and salt. Cook for 6 more minutes or until lightly browned. Serve warm and enjoy!

Fried Ranch Pickles

Servings:4
Cooking Time: 10 Minutes
Ingredients:
- 4 dill pickle spears, halved lengthwise
- ¼ cup ranch dressing
- ½ cup blanched finely ground almond flour
- ½ cup grated Parmesan cheese
- 2 tablespoons dry ranch seasoning

Directions:
1. Wrap spears in a kitchen towel 30 minutes to soak up excess pickle juice.
2. Pour ranch dressing into a medium bowl and add pickle spears. In a separate medium bowl, mix flour, Parmesan, and ranch seasoning.
3. Remove each spear from ranch dressing and shake off excess. Press gently into dry mixture to coat all sides. Place spears into ungreased air fryer basket. Adjust the temperature to 400°F and set the timer for 10 minutes, turning spears three times during cooking. Serve warm.

Blue Cheesy Potato Wedges

Servings: 4
Cooking Time: 20 Minutes
Ingredients:
- 2 Yukon Gold potatoes, peeled and cut into wedges
- 2 tablespoons ranch seasoning
- Kosher salt, to taste
- 1/2 cup blue cheese, crumbled

Directions:
1. Sprinkle the potato wedges with the ranch seasoning and salt. Grease generously the Air Fryer basket.
2. Place the potatoes in the cooking basket.
3. Roast in the preheated Air Fryer at 400 °F for 12 minutes. Top with the cheese and roast an additional 3 minutes or until cheese begins to melt. Bon appétit!

Parmesan Zucchini Fries

Servings:8
Cooking Time: 10 Minutes
Ingredients:
- 2 medium zucchini, ends removed, quartered lengthwise, and sliced into 3"-long fries
- ½ teaspoon salt
- ⅓ cup heavy whipping cream
- ½ cup blanched finely ground almond flour
- ¾ cup grated Parmesan cheese
- 1 teaspoon Italian seasoning

Directions:
1. Sprinkle zucchini with salt and wrap in a kitchen towel to draw out excess moisture. Let sit 2 hours.

2. Pour cream into a medium bowl. In a separate medium bowl, whisk together flour, Parmesan, and Italian seasoning.

3. Place each zucchini fry into cream, then gently shake off excess. Press each fry into dry mixture, coating each side, then place into ungreased air fryer basket. Adjust the temperature to 400°F and set the timer for 10 minutes, turning fries halfway through cooking. Fries will be golden and crispy when done. Place on clean parchment sheet to cool 5 minutes before serving.

Roasted Chickpeas

Servings: 1
Cooking Time: 15 Minutes
Ingredients:
- 1 15-ounce can chickpeas, drained
- 2 teaspoons curry powder
- ¼ teaspoon salt
- 1 tablespoon olive oil

Directions:
1. Drain chickpeas thoroughly and spread in a single layer on paper towels. Cover with another paper towel and press gently to remove extra moisture. Don't press too hard or you'll crush the chickpeas.
2. Mix curry powder and salt together.
3. Place chickpeas in a medium bowl and sprinkle with seasonings. Stir well to coat.
4. Add olive oil and stir again to distribute oil.
5. Cook at 390°F for 15 minutes, stopping to shake basket about halfway through cooking time.
6. Cool completely and store in airtight container.

Sugar-glazed Walnuts

Servings: 6
Cooking Time: 5 Minutes
Ingredients:
- 1 Large egg white(s)
- 2 tablespoons Granulated white sugar
- ⅛ teaspoon Table salt
- 2 cups Walnut halves

Directions:
1. Preheat the air fryer to 400°F.
2. Use a whisk to beat the egg white(s) in a large bowl until quite foamy, more so than just well combined but certainly not yet a meringue.
3. If you're working with the quantities for a small batch, remove half of the foamy egg white.
4. If you're working with the quantities for a large batch, remove a quarter of it. It's fine to eyeball the amounts.
5. You can store the removed egg white in a sealed container to save for another use.
6. Stir in the sugar and salt. Add the walnut halves and toss to coat evenly and well, including the nuts' crevasses.
7. When the machine is at temperature, use a slotted spoon to transfer the walnut halves to the basket, taking care not to dislodge any coating. Gently spread the nuts into as close to one layer as you can. Air-fry undisturbed for 2 minutes.
8. Break up any clumps, toss the walnuts gently but well, and air-fry for 3 minutes more, tossing after 1 minute, then every 30 seconds thereafter, until the nuts are browned in spots and very aromatic. Watch carefully so they don't burn.
9. Gently dump the nuts onto a lipped baking sheet and spread them into one layer. Cool for at least 10 minutes before serving, separating any that stick together. The walnuts can be stored in a sealed container at room temperature for up to 5 days.

Cauliflower "tater" Tots

Servings: 6
Cooking Time: 10 Minutes
Ingredients:
- 1 head of cauliflower
- 2 eggs
- ¼ cup all-purpose flour*
- ½ cup grated Parmesan cheese
- 1 teaspoon salt
- freshly ground black pepper
- vegetable or olive oil, in a spray bottle

Directions:
1. Grate the head of cauliflower with a box grater or finely chop it in a food processor. You should have about 3½ cups. Place the chopped cauliflower in the center of a clean kitchen towel and twist the towel tightly to squeeze all the water out of the cauliflower.
2. Place the squeezed cauliflower in a large bowl. Add the eggs, flour, Parmesan cheese, salt and freshly ground black pepper. Shape the cauliflower into small cylinders or "tater tot" shapes, rolling roughly one tablespoon of the mixture at a time. Place the tots on a cookie sheet lined with paper towel to absorb any residual moisture. Spray the cauliflower tots all over with oil.
3. Preheat the air fryer to 400°F.
4. Air-fry the tots at 400°F, one layer at a time for 10 minutes, turning them over for the last few minutes of the cooking process for even browning. Season with salt and black pepper. Serve hot with your favorite dipping sauce.

Bacon-wrapped Goat Cheese Poppers

Servings: 10
Cooking Time: 10 Minutes
Ingredients:
- 10 large jalapeño peppers
- 8 ounces goat cheese
- 10 slices bacon

Directions:
1. Preheat the air fryer to 380°F.
2. Slice the jalapeños in half. Carefully remove the veins and seeds of the jalapeños with a spoon.
3. Fill each jalapeño half with 2 teaspoons goat cheese.
4. Cut the bacon in half lengthwise to make long strips. Wrap the jalapeños with bacon, trying to cover the entire length of the jalapeño.
5. Place the bacon-wrapped jalapeños into the air fryer basket. Cook the stuffed jalapeños for 10 minutes or until bacon is crispy.

Apple Rollups

Servings: 8
Cooking Time: 5 Minutes
Ingredients:
- 8 slices whole wheat sandwich bread
- 4 ounces Colby Jack cheese, grated
- ½ small apple, chopped
- 2 tablespoons butter, melted

Directions:

1. Remove crusts from bread and flatten the slices with rolling pin. Don't be gentle. Press hard so that bread will be very thin.
2. Top bread slices with cheese and chopped apple, dividing the ingredients evenly.
3. Roll up each slice tightly and secure each with one or two toothpicks.
4. Brush outside of rolls with melted butter.
5. Place in air fryer basket and cook at 390°F for 5minutes, until outside is crisp and nicely browned.

Buffalo Cauliflower Bites

Servings:6
Cooking Time: 15 Minutes
Ingredients:
- 1 medium head cauliflower, leaves and core removed, cut into bite-sized pieces
- 4 tablespoons salted butter, melted
- ¼ cup dry ranch seasoning
- ⅓ cup buffalo sauce

Directions:
1. Place cauliflower pieces into a large bowl. Pour butter over cauliflower and toss to coat. Sprinkle in ranch seasoning and toss to coat.
2. Place cauliflower into ungreased air fryer basket. Adjust the temperature to 350°F and set the timer for 12 minutes, shaking the basket three times during cooking.
3. When timer beeps, place cooked cauliflower in a clean large bowl. Toss with buffalo sauce, then return to air fryer basket to cook another 3 minutes. Cauliflower bites will be darkened at the edges and tender when done. Serve warm.

Roasted Peppers

Servings: 4
Cooking Time: 40 Minutes
Ingredients:
- 12 medium bell peppers
- 1 sweet onion, small
- 1 tbsp. Maggi sauce
- 1 tbsp. extra virgin olive oil

Directions:
1. Warm up the olive oil and Maggi sauce in Air Fryer at 320°F.
2. Peel the onion, slice it into 1-inch pieces, and add it to the Air Fryer.
3. Wash and de-stem the peppers. Slice them into 1-inch pieces and remove all the seeds, with water if necessary.
4. Place the peppers in the Air Fryer.
5. Cook for about 25 minutes, or longer if desired. Serve hot.

Sweet Apple Fries

Servings: 3
Cooking Time: 8 Minutes
Ingredients:
- 2 Medium-size sweet apple(s), such as Gala or Fuji
- 1 Large egg white(s)
- 2 tablespoons Water
- 1½ cups Finely ground gingersnap crumbs (gluten-free, if a concern)
- Vegetable oil spray

Directions:
1. Preheat the air fryer to 375°F .

2. Peel and core an apple, then cut it into 12 slices. Repeat with more apples as necessary.
3. Whisk the egg white(s) and water in a medium bowl until foamy. Add the apple slices and toss well to coat.
4. Spread the gingersnap crumbs across a dinner plate. Using clean hands, pick up an apple slice, let any excess egg white mixture slip back into the rest, and dredge the slice in the crumbs, coating it lightly but evenly on all sides. Set it aside and continue coating the remaining apple slices.
5. Lightly coat the slices on all sides with vegetable oil spray, then set them curved side down in the basket in one layer. Air-fry undisturbed for 6 minutes, or until browned and crisp. You may need to air-fry the slices for 2 minutes longer if the temperature is at 360°F.
6. Use kitchen tongs to transfer the slices to a wire rack. Cool for 2 to 3 minutes before serving.

Beer-battered Onion Rings

Servings: 4
Cooking Time: 25 Minutes
Ingredients:
- 2 sliced onions, rings separated
- 1 cup flour
- Salt and pepper to taste
- 1 tsp garlic powder
- 1 cup beer

Directions:
1. Preheat air fryer to 350°F. In a mixing bowl, combine the flour, garlic powder, beer, salt, and black pepper. Dip the onion rings into the bowl and lay the coated rings in the frying basket. Air Fry for 15 minutes, shaking the basket several times during cooking to jostle the onion rings and ensure a good even fry. Once ready, the onions should be crispy and golden brown. Serve hot.

Green Olive And Mushroom Tapenade

Servings: 1
Cooking Time: 10 Minutes
Ingredients:
- ¾ pound Brown or Baby Bella mushrooms, sliced
- 1½ cups (about ½ pound) Pitted green olives
- 3 tablespoons Olive oil
- 1½ tablespoons Fresh oregano leaves, loosely packed
- ¼ teaspoon Ground black pepper

Directions:
1. Preheat the air fryer to 400°F.
2. When the machine is at temperature, arrange the mushroom slices in as close to an even layer as possible in the basket. They will overlap and even stack on top of each other.
3. Air-fry for 10 minutes, tossing the basket and rearranging the mushrooms every 2 minutes, until shriveled but with still-noticeable moisture.
4. Pour the mushrooms into a food processor. Add the olives, olive oil, oregano leaves, and pepper. Cover and process until grainy, not too much, just not fully smooth for better texture, stopping the machine at least once to scrape down the inside of the canister. Scrape the tapenade into a bowl and serve warm, or cover and refrigerate for up to 4 days.

Bacon-wrapped Jalapeño Poppers

Servings:4
Cooking Time: 12 Minutes
Ingredients:
- 3 ounces full-fat cream cheese
- ½ cup shredded sharp Cheddar cheese
- ¼ teaspoon garlic powder
- 6 jalapeño peppers, trimmed and halved lengthwise, seeded and membranes removed
- 12 slices bacon

Directions:
1. Preheat the air fryer to 400°F.
2. In a large microwave-safe bowl, place cream cheese, Cheddar, and garlic powder. Microwave 20 seconds until softened and stir. Spoon cheese mixture into hollow jalapeño halves.
3. Wrap a bacon slice around each jalapeño half, completely covering pepper.
4. Place in the air fryer basket and cook 12 minutes, turning halfway through cooking time. Serve warm.

Roasted Red Pepper Dip

Servings: 2
Cooking Time: 15 Minutes
Ingredients:
- 2 Medium-size red bell pepper(s)
- 1¾ cups Canned white beans, drained and rinsed
- 1 tablespoon Fresh oregano leaves, packed
- 3 tablespoons Olive oil
- 1 tablespoon Lemon juice
- ½ teaspoon Table salt
- ½ teaspoon Ground black pepper

Directions:
1. Preheat the air fryer to 400°F.
2. Set the pepper(s) in the basket and air-fry undisturbed for 15 minutes, until blistered and even blackened.
3. Use kitchen tongs to transfer the pepper(s) to a zip-closed plastic bag or small bowl. Seal the bag or cover the bowl with plastic wrap. Set aside for 20 minutes.
4. Peel each pepper, then stem it, cut it in half, and remove all its seeds and their white membranes.
5. Set the pieces of the pepper in a food processor. Add the beans, oregano, olive oil, lemon juice, salt, and pepper. Cover and process until smooth, stopping the machine at least once to scrape down the inside of the canister. Scrape the dip into a bowl and serve warm, or cover and refrigerate for up to 3 days.

Sweet Potato Chips

Servings: 4
Cooking Time: 10 Minutes
Ingredients:
- 2 medium sweet potatoes, washed
- 2 cups filtered water
- 1 tablespoon avocado oil
- 2 teaspoons brown sugar
- ½ teaspoon salt

Directions:
1. Using a mandolin, slice the potatoes into ⅛-inch pieces.
2. Add the water to a large bowl. Place the potatoes in the bowl, and soak for at least 30 minutes.
3. Preheat the air fryer to 350°F.

4. Drain the water and pat the chips dry with a paper towel or kitchen cloth. Toss the chips with the avocado oil, brown sugar, and salt. Liberally spray the air fryer basket with olive oil mist.
5. Set the chips inside the air fryer, separating them so they're not on top of each other. Cook for 5 minutes, shake the basket, and cook another 5 minutes, or until browned.
6. Remove and let cool a few minutes prior to serving. Repeat until all the chips are cooked.

Okra Chips

Servings: 4
Cooking Time: 16 Minutes
Ingredients:
- 1¼ pounds Thin fresh okra pods, cut into 1-inch pieces
- 1½ tablespoons Vegetable or canola oil
- ¾ teaspoon Coarse sea salt or kosher salt

Directions:
1. Preheat the air fryer to 400°F.
2. Toss the okra, oil, and salt in a large bowl until the pieces are well and evenly coated.
3. When the machine is at temperature, pour the contents of the bowl into the basket. Air-fry, tossing several times, for 16 minutes, or until crisp and quite brown.
4. Pour the contents of the basket onto a wire rack. Cool for a couple of minutes before serving.

Cinnamon Pita Chips

Servings: 4
Cooking Time: 6 Minutes
Ingredients:
- 2 tablespoons sugar
- 2 teaspoons cinnamon
- 2 whole 6-inch pitas, whole grain or white
- oil for misting or cooking spray

Directions:
1. Mix sugar and cinnamon together.
2. Cut each pita in half and each half into 4 wedges. Break apart each wedge at the fold.
3. Mist one side of pita wedges with oil or cooking spray. Sprinkle them all with half of the cinnamon sugar.
4. Turn the wedges over, mist the other side with oil or cooking spray, and sprinkle with the remaining cinnamon sugar.
5. Place pita wedges in air fryer basket and cook at 330°F for 2minutes.
6. Shake basket and cook 2 more minutes. Shake again, and if needed cook 2 more minutes, until crisp. Watch carefully because at this point they will cook very quickly.

Chili Kale Chips

Servings:4
Cooking Time: 5 Minutes
Ingredients:
- 1 teaspoon nutritional yeast
- 1 teaspoon salt
- 2 cups kale, chopped
- ½ teaspoon chili flakes
- 1 teaspoon sesame oil

Directions:
1. Mix up kale leaves with nutritional yeast, salt, chili flakes, and sesame oil. Shake the greens well. Preheat the air fryer to 400°F and put the kale leaves in the air fryer basket. Cook them

for 3 minutes and then give a good shake. Cook the kale leaves for 2 minutes more.

Fried Olives

Servings: 5
Cooking Time: 10 Minutes
Ingredients:
- ⅓ cup All-purpose flour or tapioca flour
- 1 Large egg white(s)
- 1 tablespoon Brine from the olive jar
- ⅔ cup Plain dried bread crumbs (gluten-free, if a concern)
- 15 Large pimiento-stuffed green olives
- Olive oil spray

Directions:
1. Preheat the air fryer to 400°F.
2. Pour the flour in a medium-size zip-closed plastic bag. Whisk the egg white and pickle brine in a medium bowl until foamy. Spread out the bread crumbs on a dinner plate.
3. Pour all the olives into the bag with the flour, seal, and shake to coat the olives. Remove a couple of olives, shake off any excess flour, and drop them into the egg white mixture. Toss gently but well to coat. Pick them up one at a time and roll each in the bread crumbs until well coated on all sides, even the ends. Set them aside on a cutting board as you finish the rest. When done, coat the olives with olive oil spray on all sides.
4. Place the olives in the basket in one layer. Air-fry for 8 minutes, gently shaking the basket once halfway through the cooking process to rearrange the olives, until lightly browned.
5. Gently pour the olives onto a wire rack and cool for at least 10 minutes before serving. Once cooled, the olives may be stored in a sealed container in the fridge for up to 2 days. To rewarm them, set them in the basket of a heated 400°F air fryer undisturbed for 2 minutes.

Charred Shishito Peppers

Servings: 4
Cooking Time: 5 Minutes
Ingredients:
- 20 shishito peppers
- 1 teaspoon vegetable oil
- coarse sea salt
- 1 lemon

Directions:
1. Preheat the air fryer to 390°F.
2. Toss the shishito peppers with the oil and salt. You can do this in a bowl or directly in the air fryer basket.
3. Air-fry at 390°F for 5 minutes, shaking the basket once or twice while they cook.
4. Turn the charred peppers out into a bowl. Squeeze some lemon juice over the top and season with coarse sea salt. These should be served as finger foods – pick the pepper up by the stem and eat the whole pepper, seeds and all.

Croutons

Servings:4
Cooking Time: 5 Minutes
Ingredients:
- 4 slices sourdough bread, diced into small cubes
- 2 tablespoons salted butter, melted
- 1 teaspoon chopped fresh parsley
- 2 tablespoons grated Parmesan cheese

Directions:

1. Preheat the air fryer to 400°F.
2. Place bread cubes in a large bowl.
3. Pour butter over bread cubes. Add parsley and Parmesan. Toss bread cubes until evenly coated.
4. Place bread cubes in the air fryer basket in a single layer. Cook 5 minutes until well toasted. Serve cooled for maximum crunch.

Bbq Chicken Wings

Servings: 4
Cooking Time: 15 Minutes
Ingredients:
- 1 lb chicken wings
- 1/2 cup BBQ sauce, sugar-free
- 1/4 tsp garlic powder
- Pepper

Directions:
1. Preheat the air fryer to 400 F.
2. Season chicken wings with garlic powder and pepper and place into the air fryer basket.
3. Cook chicken wings for 15 minutes. Shake basket 3-4 times while cooking.
4. Transfer cooked chicken wings in a large mixing bowl. Pour BBQ sauce over chicken wings and toss to coat.
5. Serve and enjoy.

Cheddar Cheese Lumpia Rolls

Servings: 5
Cooking Time: 20 Minutes
Ingredients:
- 5 ounces mature cheddar cheese, cut into 15 sticks
- 15 pieces spring roll lumpia wrappers
- 2 tablespoons sesame oil

Directions:
1. Wrap the cheese sticks in the lumpia wrappers. Transfer to the Air Fryer basket. Brush with sesame oil.
2. Bake in the preheated Air Fryer at 395°F for 10 minutes or until the lumpia wrappers turn golden brown. Work in batches.
3. Shake the Air Fryer basket occasionally to ensure even cooking. Bon appétit!

Fiery Bacon-wrapped Dates

Servings: 16
Cooking Time: 6 Minutes
Ingredients:
- 8 Thin-cut bacon strips, halved widthwise (gluten-free, if a concern)
- 16 Medium or large Medjool dates, pitted
- 3 tablespoons (about ¾ ounce) Shredded semi-firm mozzarella
- 32 Pickled jalapeño rings

Directions:
1. Preheat the air fryer to 400°F.
2. Lay a bacon strip half on a clean, dry work surface. Split one date lengthwise without cutting through it, so that it opens like a pocket. Set it on one end of the bacon strip and open it a bit. Place 1 teaspoon of the shredded cheese and 2 pickled jalapeño rings in the date, then gently squeeze it together without fully closing it. Roll up the date in the bacon strip and set it bacon seam side down on a cutting board. Repeat this process with the remaining bacon strip halves, dates, cheese, and jalapeño rings.

3. Place the bacon-wrapped dates bacon seam side down in the basket. Air-fry undisturbed for 6 minutes, or until crisp and brown.
4. Use kitchen tongs to gently transfer the wrapped dates to a wire rack or serving platter. Cool for a few minutes before serving.

Sausage And Cheese Rolls

Servings: 3
Cooking Time: 18 Minutes
Ingredients:
- 3 3- to 3½-ounce sweet or hot Italian sausage links
- 2 1-ounce string cheese stick(s), unwrapped and cut in half lengthwise
- Three quarters from one thawed sheet A 17.25-ounce box frozen puff pastry

Directions:
1. Preheat the air fryer to 400°F.
2. When the machine is at temperature, set the sausage links in the basket and air-fry undisturbed for 12 minutes, or until cooked through.
3. Use kitchen tongs to transfer the links to a wire rack. Cool for 15 minutes.
4. Cut the sausage links in half lengthwise. Sandwich half a string cheese stick between two sausage halves, trimming the ends so the cheese doesn't stick out beyond the meat.
5. Roll each piece of puff pastry into a 6 x 6-inch square on a clean, dry work surface. Set the sausage-cheese sandwich at one edge and roll it up in the dough. The ends will be open like a pig-in-a-blanket. Repeat with the remaining puff pastry, sausage, and cheese.
6. Set the rolls seam side down in the basket. Air-fry undisturbed for 6 minutes, or until puffed and golden brown.
7. Use a nonstick-safe spatula, and perhaps a flatware fork for balance, to transfer the rolls to a wire rack. Cool for at least 5 minutes before serving.

Taquito Quesadillas

Servings: 4
Cooking Time: 35 Minutes
Ingredients:
- 8 tbsp Mexican blend shredded cheese
- 8 soft corn tortillas
- 2 tsp olive oil
- ¼ cup chopped cilantro

Directions:
1. Preheat air fryer at 350ºF. Spread cheese and coriander over 4 tortillas; top each with the remaining tortillas and brush the tops lightly with oil. Place quesadillas in the frying basket and Air Fry for 6 minutes. Serve warm.

Home-style Taro Chips

Servings: 2
Cooking Time: 20 Minutes
Ingredients:
- 1 tbsp olive oil
- 1 cup thinly sliced taro
- Salt to taste
- ½ cup hummus

Directions:
1. Preheat air fryer to 325°F. Put the sliced taro in the greased frying basket, spread the pieces out, and drizzle with olive oil.

Air Fry for 10-12 minutes, shaking the basket twice. Sprinkle with salt and serve with hummus.

Spicy Turkey Meatballs

Servings:18
Cooking Time: 15 Minutes
Ingredients:
- 1 pound 85/15 ground turkey
- 1 large egg, whisked
- ¼ cup sriracha hot chili sauce
- ½ teaspoon salt
- ½ teaspoon paprika
- ¼ teaspoon ground black pepper

Directions:
1. Combine all ingredients in a large bowl. Roll mixture into eighteen meatballs, about 3 tablespoons each.
2. Place meatballs into ungreased air fryer basket. Adjust the temperature to 375°F and set the timer for 15 minutes, shaking the basket three times during cooking. Meatballs will be done when browned and internal temperature is at least 165°F. Serve warm.

Kale Chips

Servings: 2
Cooking Time: 5 Minutes
Ingredients:
- 4 Medium kale leaves, about 1 ounce each
- 2 teaspoons Olive oil
- 2 teaspoons Regular or low-sodium soy sauce or gluten-free tamari sauce

Directions:
1. Preheat the air fryer to 400°F.
2. Cut the stems from the leaves. Tear each leaf into three pieces. Put them in a large bowl.
3. Add the olive oil and soy or tamari sauce. Toss well to coat. You can even gently rub the leaves along the side of the bowl to get the liquids to stick to them.
4. When the machine is at temperature, put the leaf pieces in the basket in one layer. Air-fry for 5 minutes, turning and rearranging with kitchen tongs once halfway through, until the chips are dried out and crunchy. Watch carefully so they don't turn dark brown at the edges.
5. Gently pour the contents of the basket onto a wire rack. Cool for at least 5 minutes before serving. The chips can keep for up to 8 hours uncovered on the rack.

Mini Greek Meatballs

Servings:36
Cooking Time: 10 Minutes
Ingredients:
- 1 cup fresh spinach leaves
- ¼ cup peeled and diced red onion
- ½ cup crumbled feta cheese
- 1 pound 85/15 ground turkey
- ½ teaspoon salt
- ½ teaspoon ground cumin
- ¼ teaspoon ground black pepper

Directions:
1. Place spinach, onion, and feta in a food processor, and pulse ten times until spinach is chopped. Scoop into a large bowl.

2. Add turkey to bowl and sprinkle with salt, cumin, and pepper. Mix until fully combined. Roll mixture into thirty-six meatballs.

3. Place meatballs into ungreased air fryer basket, working in batches if needed. Adjust the temperature to 350°F and set the timer for 10 minutes, shaking basket twice during cooking. Meatballs will be browned and have an internal temperature of at least 165°F when done. Serve warm.

Mexican Muffins

Servings:4
Cooking Time: 15 Minutes
Ingredients:
- 1 cup ground beef
- 1 teaspoon taco seasonings
- 2 oz Mexican blend cheese, shredded
- 1 teaspoon keto tomato sauce
- Cooking spray

Directions:
1. Preheat the air fryer to 375°F. Meanwhile, in the mixing bowl mix up ground beef and taco seasonings. Spray the muffin molds with cooking spray. Then transfer the ground beef mixture in the muffin molds and top them with cheese and tomato sauce. Transfer the muffin molds in the preheated air fryer and cook them for 15 minutes.

Savory Ranch Chicken Bites

Servings:6
Cooking Time: 15 Minutes
Ingredients:
- 2 boneless, skinless chicken breasts, cut into 1" cubes
- 1 tablespoon coconut oil
- ½ teaspoon salt
- ¼ teaspoon ground black pepper
- ⅓ cup ranch dressing
- ½ cup shredded Colby cheese
- 4 slices cooked sugar-free bacon, crumbled

Directions:
1. Drizzle chicken with coconut oil. Sprinkle with salt and pepper, and place into an ungreased 6" round nonstick baking dish.
2. Place dish into air fryer basket. Adjust the temperature to 370°F and set the timer for 10 minutes, stirring chicken halfway through cooking.
3. When timer beeps, drizzle ranch dressing over chicken and top with Colby and bacon. Adjust the temperature to 400°F and set the timer for 5 minutes. When done, chicken will be browned and have an internal temperature of at least 165°F. Serve warm.

Avocado Fries

Servings: 4
Cooking Time: 20 Minutes
Ingredients:
- ½ cup panko
- ½ tsp. salt
- 1 whole avocado
- 1 oz. aquafaba

Directions:
1. In a shallow bowl, stir together the panko and salt.
2. In a separate shallow bowl, add the aquafaba.

3. Dip the avocado slices into the aquafaba, before coating each one in the panko.
4. Place the slices in your Air Fryer basket, taking care not to overlap any. Air fry for 10 minutes at 390°F.

Crispy Prawns

Servings:4
Cooking Time: 8 Minutes
Ingredients:
- 1 egg
- ½ pound nacho chips, crushed
- 18 prawns, peeled and deveined

Directions:
1. In a shallow dish, crack the egg, and beat well.
2. Put the crushed nacho chips in another dish.
3. Now, dip the prawn into beaten egg and then, coat with the nacho chips.
4. Set the temperature of Air Fryer to 355°F.
5. Place the prawns in an Air Fryer basket in a single layer.
6. Air Fry for about 8 minutes.
7. Serve hot.

Korean-style Wings

Servings: 4
Cooking Time: 10 Minutes
Ingredients:
- 1 pound chicken wings, drums and flats separated
- ½ teaspoon salt
- ¼ teaspoon ground black pepper
- ¼ cup gochujang sauce
- 2 tablespoons soy sauce
- 1 teaspoon ground ginger
- ¼ cup mayonnaise

Directions:
1. Preheat the air fryer to 350°F.
2. Sprinkle wings with salt and pepper. Place wings in the air fryer basket and cook 15 minutes, turning halfway through cooking time.
3. In a medium bowl, mix gochujang sauce, soy sauce, ginger, and mayonnaise.
4. Toss wings in sauce mixture and adjust the air fryer temperature to 400°F.
5. Place wings back in the air fryer basket and cook an additional 5 minutes until the internal temperature reaches at least 165°F. Serve warm.

Italian-style Fried Olives

Servings: 4
Cooking Time: 25 Minutes
Ingredients:
- 1 jar pitted green olives
- ½ cup all-purpose flour
- Salt and pepper to taste
- 1 tsp Italian seasoning
- ½ cup bread crumbs
- 1 egg

Directions:
1. Preheat air fryer to 400°F. Set out three small bowls. In the first, mix flour, Italian seasoning, salt and pepper. In the bowl, beat the egg. In the third bowl, add bread crumbs. Dip the olives in the flour, then the egg, then in the crumbs. When all of the olives are breaded, place them in the greased frying basket

and Air Fry for 6 minutes. Turn them and cook for another 2 minutes or until brown and crispy. Serve chilled.

Roasted Red Salsa

Servings: 4
Cooking Time: 10 Minutes
Ingredients:
- 10 medium Roma tomatoes, quartered
- 1 medium white onion, peeled and sliced
- 2 medium cloves garlic, peeled
- 2 tablespoons olive oil
- ¼ cup chopped fresh cilantro
- ½ teaspoon salt

Directions:
1. Preheat the air fryer to 340°F.
2. Place tomatoes, onion, and garlic into a 6" round baking dish. Drizzle with oil and toss to coat.
3. Place in the air fryer basket and cook 10 minutes, stirring twice during cooking, until vegetables start to turn dark brown and caramelize.
4. In a food processor, add roasted vegetables, cilantro, and salt. Pulse five times until vegetables are mostly broken down. Serve immediately.

Ham And Cheese Sliders

Servings:3
Cooking Time: 10 Minutes
Ingredients:
- 6 Hawaiian sweet rolls
- 12 slices thinly sliced Black Forest ham
- 6 slices sharp Cheddar cheese
- ⅓ cup salted butter, melted
- 1 ½ teaspoons minced garlic

Directions:
1. Preheat the air fryer to 350°F.
2. For each slider, slice horizontally through the center of a roll without fully separating the two halves. Place 2 slices ham and 2 slices cheese inside roll and close. Repeat with remaining rolls, ham, and cheese.
3. In a small bowl, mix butter and garlic and brush over all sides of rolls.
4. Place in the air fryer and cook 10 minutes until rolls are golden on top and cheese is melted. Serve warm.

Garlic–cream Cheese Wontons

Servings: 4
Cooking Time: 8 Minutes
Ingredients:
- 6 ounces full-fat cream cheese, softened
- 1 teaspoon garlic powder
- 12 wonton wrappers
- ¼ cup water

Directions:
1. Preheat the air fryer to 375°F.
2. In a medium bowl, mix cream cheese and garlic powder until smooth.
3. For each wonton, place 1 tablespoon cream cheese mixture in center of a wonton wrapper.
4. Brush edges of wonton with water to help it seal. Fold wonton to form a triangle. Spritz both sides with cooking spray. Repeat with remaining wontons and cream cheese mixture.

5. Place wontons in the air fryer basket. Cook 8 minutes, turning halfway through cooking time, until golden brown and crispy. Serve warm.

Roasted Carrots

Servings: 2
Cooking Time: 20 Minutes
Ingredients:
- 1 tbsp. olive oil
- 3 cups baby carrots or carrots, cut into large chunks
- 1 tbsp. honey
- Salt and pepper to taste

Directions:
1. In a bowl, coat the carrots with the honey and olive oil before sprinkling on some salt and pepper.
2. Place into the Air Fryer and cook at 390°F for 12 minutes. Serve hot.

Italian Dip

Servings:8
Cooking Time: 12 Minutes
Ingredients:
- 8 oz cream cheese, softened
- 1 cup mozzarella cheese, shredded
- 1/2 cup roasted red peppers
- 1/3 cup basil pesto
- 1/4 cup parmesan cheese, grated

Directions:
1. Add parmesan cheese and cream cheese into the food processor and process until smooth.
2. Transfer cheese mixture into the air fryer pan and spread evenly.
3. Pour basil pesto on top of cheese layer.
4. Sprinkle roasted pepper on top of basil pesto layer.
5. Sprinkle mozzarella cheese on top of pepper layer and place dish in air fryer basket.
6. Cook dip at 250°F for 12 minutes.
7. Serve and enjoy.

Sweet-and-salty Pretzels

Servings: 4
Cooking Time: 5 Minutes
Ingredients:
- 2 cups Plain pretzel nuggets
- 1 tablespoon Worcestershire sauce
- 2 teaspoons Granulated white sugar
- 1 teaspoon Mild smoked paprika
- ½ teaspoon Garlic or onion powder

Directions:
1. Preheat the air fryer to 350°F .
2. Put the pretzel nuggets, Worcestershire sauce, sugar, smoked paprika, and garlic or onion powder in a large bowl. Toss gently until the nuggets are well coated.
3. When the machine is at temperature, pour the nuggets into the basket, spreading them into as close to a single layer as possible. Air-fry, shaking the basket three or four times to rearrange the nuggets, for 5 minutes, or until the nuggets are toasted and aromatic. Although the coating will darken, don't let it burn, especially if the machine's temperature is 360°F.
4. Pour the nuggets onto a wire rack and gently spread them into one layer. Cool for 5 minutes before serving.

Thick-crust Pepperoni Pizza

Servings: 2
Cooking Time: 10 Minutes
Ingredients:
- 10 ounces Purchased fresh pizza dough (not a prebaked crust)
- Olive oil spray
- ¼ cup Purchased pizza sauce
- 10 slices Sliced pepperoni
- ⅓ cup Purchased shredded Italian 3- or 4-cheese blend

Directions:
1. Preheat the air fryer to 400°F.
2. Generously coat the inside of a 6-inch round cake pan for a small air fryer, a 7-inch round cake pan for a medium air fryer, or an 8-inch round cake pan for a large model with olive oil spray.
3. Set the dough in the pan and press it to fill the bottom in an even, thick layer. Spread the sauce over the dough, then top with the pepperoni and cheese.
4. When the machine is at temperature, set the pan in the basket and air-fry undisturbed for 10 minutes, or until puffed, brown, and bubbling.
5. Use kitchen tongs to transfer the cake pan to a wire rack. Cool for only a minute or so. Use a spatula to loosen the pizza from the pan and lift it out and onto the rack. Continue cooling for a few minutes before cutting into wedges to serve.

Chocolate Bacon Bites

Servings: 4
Cooking Time: 10 Minutes
Ingredients:
- 4 bacon slices, halved
- 1 cup dark chocolate, melted
- A pinch of pink salt

Directions:
1. Dip each bacon slice in some chocolate, sprinkle pink salt over them, put them in your air fryer's basket and cook at 350°F for 10 minutes. Serve as a snack.

Bacon-wrapped Mozzarella Sticks

Servings:6
Cooking Time: 12 Minutes
Ingredients:
- 6 sticks mozzarella string cheese
- 6 slices sugar-free bacon

Directions:
1. Place mozzarella sticks on a medium plate, cover, and place into freezer 1 hour until frozen solid.
2. Wrap each mozzarella stick in 1 piece of bacon and secure with a toothpick. Place into ungreased air fryer basket. Adjust the temperature to 400°F and set the timer for 12 minutes, turning sticks once during cooking. Bacon will be crispy when done. Serve warm.

Bacon & Blue Cheese Tartlets

Servings: 6
Cooking Time: 30 Minutes
Ingredients:
- 6 bacon slices
- 16 phyllo tartlet shells
- ½ cup diced blue cheese
- 3 tbsp apple jelly

Directions:
1. Preheat the air fryer to 400°F. Put the bacon in a single layer in the frying basket and Air Fry for 14 minutes, turning once halfway through. Remove and drain on paper towels, then crumble when cool. Wipe the fryer clean. Fill the tartlet shells with bacon and the blue cheese cubes and add a dab of apple jelly on top of the filling. Lower the temperature to 350°F, then put the shells in the frying basket. Air Fry until the cheese melts and the shells brown, about 5-6 minutes. Remove and serve.

Grilled Cheese Sandwiches

Servings:2
Cooking Time:5 Minutes
Ingredients:
- 4 white bread slices
- ½ cup melted butter, softened
- ½ cup sharp cheddar cheese, grated
- 1 tablespoon mayonnaise

Directions:
1. Preheat the Air fryer to 355°F and grease an Air fryer basket.
2. Spread the mayonnaise and melted butter over one side of each bread slice.
3. Sprinkle the cheddar cheese over the buttered side of the 2 slices.
4. Cover with the remaining slices of bread and transfer into the Air fryer basket.
5. Cook for about 5 minutes and dish out to serve warm.

Buffalo Chicken Dip

Servings: 6
Cooking Time: 25 Minutes
Ingredients:
- 4 ounces full-fat cream cheese, softened
- ½ teaspoon garlic powder
- ½ cup buffalo sauce
- 1 cup shredded Cheddar cheese, divided
- 2 cups cooked and shredded chicken breast

Directions:
1. Preheat the air fryer to 350°F.
2. In a large bowl, mix cream cheese, garlic powder, buffalo sauce, and ½ cup Cheddar until well combined. Fold in chicken until well coated.
3. Scrape mixture into a 6" round baking dish and top with remaining ½ cup Cheddar.
4. Place dish in the air fryer basket and cook 10 minutes until top is brown and edges are bubbling. Serve warm.

Wrapped Smokies In Bacon

Servings: 4
Cooking Time: 15 Minutes
Ingredients:
- 8 small smokies
- 8 bacon strips, sliced
- Salt and pepper to taste

Directions:
1. Preheat air fryer to 350°F. Wrap the bacon slices around smokies. Arrange the rolls, seam side down, on the greased frying basket. Sprinkle with salt and pepper and Air Fry for 5-8 minutes, turning once until the bacon is crisp and juicy around them. Serve and enjoy!

Chives Meatballs

Servings: 6
Cooking Time: 20 Minutes
Ingredients:

- 1 pound beef meat, ground
- 1 teaspoon onion powder
- 1 teaspoon garlic powder
- A pinch of salt and black pepper
- 2 tablespoons chives, chopped
- Cooking spray

Directions:

1. In a bowl, mix all the ingredients except the cooking spray, stir well and shape medium meatballs out of this mix. Pace them in your lined air fryer's basket, grease with cooking spray and cook at 360°F for 20 minutes. Serve as an appetizer.

Air Fry Bacon

Servings:11
Cooking Time: 10 Minutes
Ingredients:

- 11 bacon slices

Directions:

1. Place half bacon slices in air fryer basket.
2. Cook at 400°F for 10 minutes.
3. Cook remaining half bacon slices using same steps.
4. Serve and enjoy.

Fried Goat Cheese

Servings: 3
Cooking Time: 4 Minutes
Ingredients:

- 7 ounces 1- to 1½-inch-diameter goat cheese log
- 2 Large egg(s)
- 1¾ cups Plain dried bread crumbs (gluten-free, if a concern)
- Vegetable oil spray

Directions:

1. Slice the goat cheese log into ½-inch-thick rounds. Set these flat on a small cutting board, a small baking sheet, or a large plate. Freeze uncovered for 30 minutes.
2. Preheat the air fryer to 400°F.
3. Set up and fill two shallow soup plates or small pie plates on your counter: one in which you whisk the egg(s) until uniform and the other for the bread crumbs.
4. Take the goat cheese rounds out of the freezer. With clean, dry hands, dip one round in the egg(s) to coat it on all sides. Let the excess egg slip back into the rest, then dredge the round in the bread crumbs, turning it to coat all sides, even the edges. Repeat this process—egg, then bread crumbs—for a second coating. Coat both sides of the round and its edges with vegetable oil spray, then set it aside. Continue double-dipping, double-dredging, and spraying the remaining rounds.
5. Place the rounds in one layer in the basket. Air-fry undisturbed for 4 minutes, or until lightly browned and crunchy. Do not overcook. Some of the goat cheese may break through the crust. A few little breaks are fine but stop the cooking before the coating reaches structural failure.
6. Remove the basket from the machine and set aside for 3 minutes. Use a nonstick-safe spatula, and maybe a flatware fork for balance, to transfer the rounds to a wire rack. Cool for 5 minutes more before serving.

Pepperoni Rolls

Servings:12
Cooking Time: 8 Minutes
Ingredients:

- 2½ cups shredded mozzarella cheese
- 2 ounces cream cheese, softened
- 1 cup blanched finely ground almond flour
- 48 slices pepperoni
- 2 teaspoons Italian seasoning

Directions:

1. In a large microwave-safe bowl, combine mozzarella, cream cheese, and flour. Microwave on high 90 seconds until cheese is melted.
2. Using a wooden spoon, mix melted mixture 2 minutes until a dough forms.
3. Once dough is cool enough to work with your hands, about 2 minutes, spread it out into a 12" × 4" rectangle on ungreased parchment paper. Line dough with pepperoni, divided into four even rows. Sprinkle Italian seasoning evenly over pepperoni.
4. Starting at the long end of the dough, roll up until a log is formed. Slice the log into twelve even pieces.
5. Place pizza rolls in an ungreased 6" nonstick baking dish. Adjust the temperature to 375°F and set the timer for 8 minutes. Rolls will be golden and firm when done. Allow cooked rolls to cool 10 minutes before serving.

Broccoli And Carrot Bites

Servings:20
Cooking Time: 12 Minutes
Ingredients:

- 1 steamer bag broccoli, cooked according to package instructions
- ½ cup shredded sharp Cheddar cheese
- 2 tablespoons peeled and grated carrot
- ½ cup blanched finely ground almond flour
- 1 large egg, whisked
- ¼ teaspoon salt
- ¼ teaspoon ground black pepper

Directions:

1. Let cooked broccoli cool 5 minutes, then wring out excess moisture with a kitchen towel. In a large bowl, mix broccoli with Cheddar, carrot, flour, egg, salt, and pepper. Scoop 2 tablespoons of the mixture into a ball, then roll into a bite-sized piece. Repeat with remaining mixture to form twenty bites.
2. Cut a piece of parchment to fit into the bottom of air fryer basket. Place bites into a single layer on ungreased parchment. Adjust the temperature to 320°F and set the timer for 12 minutes, turning bites halfway through cooking. Bites will be golden brown when done. Serve warm.

Roasted Peanuts

Servings:10
Cooking Time: 14 Minutes
Ingredients:

- 2½ cups raw peanuts
- 1 tablespoon olive oil
- Salt, as required

Directions:

1. Set the temperature of Air Fryer to 320°F.
2. Add the peanuts in an Air Fryer basket in a single layer.
3. Air Fry for about 9 minutes, tossing twice.

4. Remove the peanuts from Air Fryer basket and transfer into a bowl.
5. Add the oil, and salt and toss to coat well.
6. Return the nuts mixture into Air Fryer basket.
7. Air Fry for about 5 minutes.
8. Once done, transfer the hot nuts in a glass or steel bowl and serve.

Warm And Salty Edamame

Servings: 4
Cooking Time: 10 Minutes
Ingredients:
- 1 pound Unshelled edamame
- Vegetable oil spray
- ¾ teaspoon Coarse sea salt or kosher salt

Directions:
1. Preheat the air fryer to 400°F.
2. Place the edamame in a large bowl and lightly coat them with vegetable oil spray. Toss well, spray again, and toss until they are evenly coated.
3. When the machine is at temperature, pour the edamame into the basket and air-fry, tossing the basket quite often to rearrange the edamame, for 7 minutes, or until warm and aromatic. Air-fry for 10 minutes if the edamame were frozen and not thawed.
4. Pour the edamame into a bowl and sprinkle the salt on top. Toss well, then set aside for a couple of minutes before serving with an empty bowl on the side for the pods.

Fried Dill Pickle Chips

Servings: 4
Cooking Time: 12 Minutes
Ingredients:
- 1 cup All-purpose flour or tapioca flour
- 1 Large egg white(s)
- 1 tablespoon Brine from a jar of dill pickles
- 1 cup Seasoned Italian-style dried bread crumbs (gluten-free, if a concern)
- 2 Large dill pickle(s), cut into ½-inch-thick rounds
- Vegetable oil spray

Directions:
1. Preheat the air fryer to 400°F.
2. Set up and fill three shallow soup plates or small pie plates on your counter: one for the flour, one for the egg white(s) whisked with the pickle brine, and one for the bread crumbs.
3. Set a pickle round in the flour and turn it to coat all sides, even the edge. Gently shake off the excess flour, then dip the round into the egg-white mixture and turn to coat both sides and the edge. Let any excess egg white mixture slip back into the rest, then set the round in the bread crumbs and turn it to coat both sides as well as the edge. Set aside on a cutting board and soldier on, dipping and coating the remaining rounds. Lightly coat the coated rounds on both sides with vegetable oil spray.
4. Set the pickle rounds in the basket in one layer. Air-fry undisturbed for 7 minutes, or until golden brown and crunchy. Cool in the basket for a few minutes before using kitchen tongs to transfer the rounds to a serving platter.

Garlic Parmesan Kale Chips

Servings: 2
Cooking Time: 6 Minutes
Ingredients:
- 16 large kale leaves, washed and thick stems removed
- 1 tablespoon avocado oil
- ½ teaspoon garlic powder
- 1 teaspoon soy sauce or tamari
- ¼ cup grated Parmesan cheese

Directions:
1. Preheat the air fryer to 370°F.
2. Make a stack of kale leaves and cut them into 4 pieces.
3. Place the kale pieces into a large bowl. Drizzle the avocado oil onto the kale and rub to coat. Add the garlic powder, soy sauce or tamari, and cheese, tossing to coat.
4. Pour the chips into the air fryer basket and cook for 3 minutes, shake the basket, and cook another 3 minutes, checking for crispness every minute. When done cooking, pour the kale chips onto paper towels and cool at least 5 minutes before serving.

Pork Egg Rolls

Servings: 4
Cooking Time: 17 Minutes
Ingredients:
- ½ pound 84% lean ground pork
- 3 tablespoons low-sodium soy sauce, divided
- ½ teaspoon salt
- 2 cups broccoli slaw
- ½ teaspoon ground ginger
- 8 egg roll wrappers

Directions:
1. In a medium skillet over medium heat, crumble ground pork and cook about 10 minutes until fully cooked and no pink remains. Drain fat and return meat to skillet.
2. Pour 2 tablespoons soy sauce over pork, then sprinkle with salt and stir. Reduce heat to low and cook 2 minutes.
3. Add broccoli slaw. Pour remaining soy sauce over broccoli slaw and sprinkle with ginger. Stir and continue cooking 5 minutes until slaw is tender.
4. Preheat the air fryer to 350°F.
5. For each egg roll, position a wrapper so that one corner is pointed toward you. Spoon 3 tablespoons pork mixture across the wrapper near the corner closest to you.
6. Roll the point closest to you over the filling. Fold the left and right corners toward the center, then roll the wrapper closed toward the far corner. Repeat with remaining wrappers and filling.
7. Place in the air fryer basket seam side down and cook 10 minutes, turning halfway through cooking time. Serve warm.

Skinny Fries

Servings: 2
Cooking Time: 15 Minutes
Ingredients:
- 2 to 3 russet potatoes, peeled and cut into ¼-inch sticks
- 2 to 3 teaspoons olive or vegetable oil
- salt

Directions:
1. Cut the potatoes into ¼-inch strips. Rinse the potatoes with cold water several times and let them soak in cold water for at least 10 minutes or as long as overnight.
2. Preheat the air fryer to 380°F.
3. Drain and dry the potato sticks really well, using a clean kitchen towel. Toss the fries with the oil in a bowl and then air-

fry the fries in two batches at 380°F for 15 minutes, shaking the basket a couple of times while they cook.

4. Add the first batch of French fries back into the air fryer basket with the finishing batch and let everything warm through for a few minutes. As soon as the fries are done, season them with salt and transfer to a plate or basket. Serve them warm with ketchup or your favorite dip.

Potato Chips

Servings: 2
Cooking Time: 15 Minutes
Ingredients:
- 2 medium potatoes
- 2 teaspoons extra-light olive oil
- oil for misting or cooking spray
- salt and pepper

Directions:
1. Peel the potatoes.
2. Using a mandoline or paring knife, shave potatoes into thin slices, dropping them into a bowl of water as you cut them.
3. Dry potatoes as thoroughly as possible with paper towels or a clean dish towel. Toss potato slices with the oil to coat completely.
4. Spray air fryer basket with cooking spray and add potato slices.
5. Stir and separate with a fork.
6. Cook 390°F for 5minutes. Stir and separate potato slices. Cook 5 more minutes. Stir and separate potatoes again. Cook another 5 minutes.
7. Season to taste.

Italian Bruschetta With Mushrooms & Cheese

Servings: 4
Cooking Time: 25 Minutes
Ingredients:
- ½ cup button mushrooms, chopped
- ½ baguette, sliced
- 1 garlic clove, minced
- 3 oz sliced Parmesan cheese
- 1 tbsp extra virgin olive oil
- Salt and pepper to taste

Directions:
1. Preheat air fryer to 350°F. Add the mushrooms, olive oil, salt, pepper, and garlic to a mixing bowl and stir thoroughly to combine. Divide the mushroom mixture between the bread slices, drizzling all over the surface with olive oil, then cover with Parmesan slices. Place the covered bread slices in the greased frying basket and Bake for 15 minutes. Serve and enjoy!

Herbed Cheese Brittle

Servings: 4
Cooking Time: 5 Minutes
Ingredients:
- ½ cup shredded Parmesan cheese
- ½ cup shredded white cheddar cheese
- 1 tablespoon fresh chopped rosemary
- 1 teaspoon garlic powder
- 1 large egg white

Directions:
1. Preheat the air fryer to 400°F.

2. In a large bowl, mix the cheeses, rosemary, and garlic powder. Mix in the egg white. Then pour the batter into a 7-inch pan. Place the pan in the air fryer basket and cook for 4 to 5 minutes, or until the cheese is melted and slightly browned.
3. Remove the pan from the air fryer, and let it cool for 2 minutes. Invert the pan before the cheese brittle completely cools but is semi-hardened to allow it to easily slide out of the pan.
4. Let the pan cool another 5 minutes. Break into pieces and serve.

Bacon-wrapped Onion Rings

Servings:8
Cooking Time: 10 Minutes
Ingredients:
- 1 large white onion, peeled and cut into 16 (¼"-thick) slices
- 8 slices sugar-free bacon

Directions:
1. Stack 2 slices onion and wrap with 1 slice bacon. Secure with a toothpick. Repeat with remaining onion slices and bacon.
2. Place onion rings into ungreased air fryer basket. Adjust the temperature to 350°F and set the timer for 10 minutes, turning rings halfway through cooking. Bacon will be crispy when done. Serve warm.

Cheesy Pigs In A Blanket

Servings: 4
Cooking Time: 7 Minutes
Ingredients:
- 24 cocktail size smoked sausages
- 6 slices deli-sliced Cheddar cheese, each cut into 8 rectangular pieces
- 1 tube refrigerated crescent roll dough
- ketchup or mustard for dipping

Directions:
1. Unroll the crescent roll dough into one large sheet. If your crescent roll dough has perforated seams, pinch or roll all the perforated seams together. Cut the large sheet of dough into 4 rectangles. Then cut each rectangle into 6 pieces by making one slice lengthwise in the middle and 2 slices horizontally. You should have 24 pieces of dough.
2. Make a deep slit lengthwise down the center of the cocktail sausage. Stuff two pieces of cheese into the slit in the sausage. Roll one piece of crescent dough around the stuffed cocktail sausage leaving the ends of the sausage exposed. Pinch the seam together. Repeat with the remaining sausages.
3. Preheat the air fryer to 350°F.
4. Air-fry in 2 batches, placing the sausages seam side down in the basket. Air-fry for 7 minutes. Serve hot with ketchup or your favorite mustard for dipping.

Za'atar Garbanzo Beans

Servings: 6
Cooking Time: 12 Minutes
Ingredients:
- One 14.5-ounce can garbanzo beans, drained and rinsed
- 1 tablespoon extra-virgin olive oil
- 6 teaspoons za'atar seasoning mix
- 2 tablespoons chopped parsley
- Salt and pepper, to taste

Directions:
1. Preheat the air fryer to 390°F.

2. In a medium bowl, toss the garbanzo beans with olive oil and za'atar seasoning.

3. Pour the beans into the air fryer basket and cook for 12 minutes, or until toasted as you like. Stir every 3 minutes while roasting.

4. Remove the beans from the air fryer basket into a serving bowl, top with fresh chopped parsley, and season with salt and pepper.

Onion Ring Nachos

Servings: 3
Cooking Time: 8 Minutes
Ingredients:
- ¾ pound Frozen breaded (not battered) onion rings (do not thaw)
- 1½ cups Shredded Cheddar, Monterey Jack, or Swiss cheese, or a purchased Tex-Mex blend
- Up to 12 Pickled jalapeño rings

Directions:
1. Preheat the air fryer to 400°F.
2. When the machine is at temperature, spread the onion rings in the basket in a fairly even layer. Air-fry undisturbed for 6 minutes, or until crisp. Remove the basket from the machine.
3. Cut a circle of parchment paper to line a 6-inch round cake pan for a small air fryer, a 7-inch round cake pan for a medium air fryer, or an 8-inch round cake pan for a large machine.
4. Pour the onion rings into a fairly even layer in the cake pan, then sprinkle the cheese evenly over them. Dot with the jalapeño rings.
5. Set the pan in the basket and air-fry undisturbed for 2 minutes, until the cheese has melted and is bubbling.
6. Remove the pan from the basket. Cool for 5 minutes before serving.

Tomato & Garlic Roasted Potatoes

Servings: 4
Cooking Time: 25 Minutes
Ingredients:
- 16 cherry tomatoes, halved
- 6 red potatoes, cubed
- 3 garlic cloves, minced
- Salt and pepper to taste
- 1 tsp chopped chives
- 1 tbsp extra-virgin olive oil

Directions:
1. Preheat air fryer to 370°F. Combine cherry potatoes, garlic, salt, pepper, chives and olive oil in a resealable plastic bag. Seal and shake the bag. Put the potatoes in the greased frying basket and Roast for 10 minutes. Shake the basket, place the cherry tomatoes in, and cook for 10 more minutes. Allow to cool slightly and serve.

Pickled Chips

Servings:4
Cooking Time: 10 Minutes
Ingredients:
- 1 cup pickles, sliced
- 2 eggs, beaten
- ½ cup coconut flakes
- 1 teaspoon dried cilantro
- ¼ cup Provolone cheese, grated

Directions:

1. Mix up coconut flakes, dried cilantro, and Provolone cheese. Then dip the sliced pickles in the egg and coat in coconut flakes mixture. Preheat the air fryer to 400°F. Arrange the pickles in the air fryer in one layer and cook them for 5 minutes. Then flip the pickles on another side and cook for another 5 minutes.

Fried Mozzarella Sticks

Servings: 7
Cooking Time: 5 Minutes
Ingredients:
- 7 1-ounce string cheese sticks, unwrapped
- ½ cup All-purpose flour or tapioca flour
- 2 Large egg(s), well beaten
- 2¼ cups Seasoned Italian-style dried bread crumbs (gluten-free, if a concern)
- Olive oil spray

Directions:
1. Unwrap the string cheese and place the pieces in the freezer for 20 minutes.
2. Preheat the air fryer to 400°F.
3. Set up and fill three shallow soup plates or small pie plates on your counter: one for the flour, one for the egg(s), and one for the bread crumbs.
4. Dip a piece of cold string cheese in the flour until well coated. Gently tap off any excess flour, then set the stick in the egg(s). Roll it around to coat, let any excess egg mixture slip back into the rest, and set the stick in the bread crumbs. Gently roll it around to coat it evenly, even the ends. Now dip it back in the egg(s), then again in the bread crumbs, rolling it to coat well and evenly. Set the stick aside on a cutting board and coat the remaining pieces of string cheese in the same way.
5. Lightly coat the sticks all over with olive oil spray. Place them in the basket in one layer and air-fry undisturbed for 5 minutes, or until golden brown and crisp.
6. Remove the basket from the machine and cool for 5 minutes. Use a nonstick-safe spatula to transfer the mozzarella sticks to a serving platter. Serve hot.

Bacon-y Cauliflower Skewers

Servings:4
Cooking Time: 12 Minutes
Ingredients:
- 4 slices sugar-free bacon, cut into thirds
- ¼ medium yellow onion, peeled and cut into 1" pieces
- 4 ounces cauliflower florets
- 1½ tablespoons olive oil
- ¼ teaspoon salt
- ¼ teaspoon garlic powder

Directions:
1. Place 1 piece bacon and 2 pieces onion on a 6" skewer. Add a second piece bacon, and 2 cauliflower florets, followed by another piece of bacon onto skewer. Repeat with remaining ingredients and three additional skewers to make four total skewers.
2. Drizzle skewers with olive oil, then sprinkle with salt and garlic powder. Place skewers into ungreased air fryer basket. Adjust the temperature to 375°F and set the timer for 12 minutes, turning the skewers halfway through cooking. When done, vegetables will be tender and bacon will be crispy. Serve warm.

Crispy Salami Roll-ups

Servings:16
Cooking Time: 4 Minutes
Ingredients:
- 4 ounces cream cheese, broken into 16 equal pieces
- 16 deli slices Genoa salami

Directions:
1. Place a piece of cream cheese at the edge of a slice of salami and roll to close. Secure with a toothpick. Repeat with remaining cream cheese pieces and salami.
2. Place roll-ups in an ungreased 6" round nonstick baking dish and place into air fryer basket. Adjust the temperature to 350°F and set the timer for 4 minutes. Salami will be crispy and cream cheese will be warm when done. Let cool 5 minutes before serving.

Easy Crispy Prawns

Servings:4
Cooking Time:10 Minutes
Ingredients:
- 1 egg
- ½ pound nacho chips, crushed
- 18 prawns, peeled and deveined
- Salt and black pepper, to taste

Directions:
1. Preheat the Air fryer to 355°F and grease an Air fryer basket.
2. Crack egg in a shallow dish and beat well.
3. Place the crushed nacho chips in another shallow dish.
4. Coat prawns into egg and then roll into nacho chips.
5. Place the coated prawns into the Air fryer basket and cook for about 10 minutes.
6. Dish out and serve warm.

Pepperoni Chips

Servings:2
Cooking Time: 8 Minutes
Ingredients:
- 14 slices pepperoni

Directions:
1. Place pepperoni slices into ungreased air fryer basket. Adjust the temperature to 350°F and set the timer for 8 minutes. Pepperoni will be browned and crispy when done. Let cool 5 minutes before serving. Store in airtight container at room temperature up to 3 days.

Zucchini Chips

Servings: 3
Cooking Time: 17 Minutes
Ingredients:
- 1½ small Zucchini, washed but not peeled, and cut into ¼-inch-thick rounds
- Olive oil spray
- ¼ teaspoon Table salt

Directions:
1. Preheat the air fryer to 375°F.
2. Lay some paper towels on your work surface. Set the zucchini rounds on top, then set more paper towels over the rounds. Press gently to remove some of the moisture. Remove the top layer of paper towels and lightly coat the rounds with olive oil spray on both sides.

3. When the machine is at temperature, set the rounds in the basket, overlapping them a bit as needed. Air-fry for 15 minutes, tossing and rearranging the rounds at the 5- and 10-minute marks, until browned, soft, yet crisp at the edges.
4. Gently pour the contents of the basket onto a wire rack. Cool for at least 10 minutes or up to 2 hours before serving.

Buffalo Cauliflower Wings

Servings:4
Cooking Time: 14 Minutes
Ingredients:
- 1 cauliflower head, cut into florets
- 1 tbsp butter, melted
- 1/2 cup buffalo sauce
- Pepper
- Salt

Directions:
1. Spray air fryer basket with cooking spray.
2. In a bowl, mix together buffalo sauce, butter, pepper, and salt.
3. Add cauliflower florets into the air fryer basket and cook at 400 °F for 7 minutes.
4. Transfer cauliflower florets into the buffalo sauce mixture and toss well.
5. Again, add cauliflower florets into the air fryer basket and cook for 7 minutes more at 400 °F.
6. Serve and enjoy.

Eggplant Fries

Servings: 18
Cooking Time: 10 Minutes
Ingredients:
- ¾ cup All-purpose flour or tapioca flour
- 1 Large egg(s), well beaten
- 1 cup Seasoned Italian-style dried bread crumbs (gluten-free, if a concern)
- 3 tablespoons (about ½ ounce) Finely grated Asiago or Parmesan cheese
- 3 Peeled ½-inch-thick eggplant slices
- Olive oil spray

Directions:
1. Preheat the air fryer to 375°F.
2. Set up and fill three shallow soup plates or small pie plates on your counter: one for the flour, one for the egg(s), and one for the bread crumbs mixed with the cheese until well combined.
3. Cut each eggplant slice into six ½-inch-wide strips or sticks. Dip one strip in the flour, coating it well on all sides. Gently shake off the excess flour, then dip the strip in the beaten egg(s) to coat it without losing the flour. Let any excess egg slip back into the rest, then roll the strip in the bread-crumb mixture to coat evenly on all sides, even the ends. Set the strips aside on a cutting board and continue dipping and coating the remaining strips as you did the first one.
4. Generously coat the strips with olive oil spray on all sides. Set them in the basket in one layer and air-fry undisturbed for 10 minutes, or until golden brown and crisp. If the machine is at 390°F, the strips may be done in 8 minutes.
5. Remove the basket from the machine and cool for a couple of minutes. Then use kitchen tongs to transfer the eggplant fries to a wire rack to cool for only a minute or two more before serving.

Honey Tater Tots With Bacon

Servings: 4
Cooking Time: 25 Minutes
Ingredients:
- 24 frozen tater tots
- 6 bacon slices
- 1 tbsp honey
- 1 cup grated cheddar

Directions:
1. Preheat air fryer to 400°F. Air Fry the tater tots for 10 minutes, shaking the basket once halfway through cooking. Cut the bacon into pieces. When the tater tots are done, remove them from the fryer to a baking pan. Top them with bacon and drizzle with honey. Air Fry for 5 minutes to crisp up the bacon. Top the tater tots with cheese and cook for 2 minutes to melt the cheese. Serve.

Chapter 4. Beef , pork & Lamb Recipes

Honey-sriracha Pork Ribs

Servings:4
Cooking Time: 25 Minutes
Ingredients:
- 3 pounds pork back ribs, white membrane removed
- 2 teaspoons salt
- 1 teaspoon ground black pepper
- ½ cup sriracha
- ⅓ cup honey
- 1 tablespoon lemon juice

Directions:
1. Preheat the air fryer to 400°F.
2. Place ribs on a work surface and cut the rack into two pieces to fit in the air fryer basket.
3. Sprinkle ribs with salt and pepper and place in the air fryer basket meat side down. Cook 15 minutes.
4. In a small bowl, combine the sriracha, honey, and lemon juice to make a sauce.
5. Remove ribs from the air fryer basket and pour sauce over both sides. Return them to the air fryer basket meat side up and cook an additional 10 minutes until brown and the internal temperature reaches at least 190°F. Serve warm.

Pork Belly Marinated In Onion-coconut Cream

Servings:3
Cooking Time: 25 Minutes
Ingredients:
- ½ pork belly, sliced to thin strips
- 1 onion, diced
- 1 tablespoon butter
- 4 tablespoons coconut cream
- Salt and pepper to taste

Directions:
1. Place all ingredients in a mixing bowl and allow to marinate in the fridge for 2 hours.
2. Preheat the air fryer for 5 minutes.
3. Place the pork strips in the air fryer and bake for 25 minutes at 350°F.

Marinated Steak Kebabs

Servings:4
Cooking Time: 5 Minutes

Ingredients:
- 1 pound strip steak, fat trimmed, cut into 1" cubes
- ½ cup soy sauce
- ¼ cup olive oil
- 1 tablespoon granular brown erythritol
- ½ teaspoon salt
- ¼ teaspoon ground black pepper
- 1 medium green bell pepper, seeded and chopped into 1" cubes

Directions:
1. Place steak into a large sealable bowl or bag and pour in soy sauce and olive oil. Add erythritol, then stir to coat steak. Marinate at room temperature 30 minutes.
2. Remove streak from marinade and sprinkle with salt and black pepper.
3. Place meat and vegetables onto 6" skewer sticks, alternating between steak and bell pepper.
4. Place kebabs into ungreased air fryer basket. Adjust the temperature to 400°F and set the timer for 5 minutes. Steak will be done when crispy at the edges and peppers are tender. Serve warm.

Rosemary Lamb Chops

Servings: 4
Cooking Time: 6 Minutes
Ingredients:
- 8 lamb chops
- 1 tablespoon extra-virgin olive oil
- 1 teaspoon dried rosemary, crushed
- 2 cloves garlic, minced
- 1 teaspoon sea salt
- ¼ teaspoon black pepper

Directions:
1. In a large bowl, mix together the lamb chops, olive oil, rosemary, garlic, salt, and pepper. Let sit at room temperature for 10 minutes.
2. Meanwhile, preheat the air fryer to 380°F.
3. Cook the lamb chops for 3 minutes, flip them over, and cook for another 3 minutes.

Mustard Pork

Servings: 4
Cooking Time: 30 Minutes
Ingredients:
- 1 pound pork tenderloin, trimmed
- A pinch of salt and black pepper
- 2 tablespoons olive oil
- 3 tablespoons mustard
- 2 tablespoons balsamic vinegar

Directions:
1. In a bowl, mix the pork tenderloin with the rest of the ingredients and rub well. Put the roast in your air fryer's basket and cook at 380°F for 30 minutes. Slice the roast, divide between plates and serve.

Chicken-fried Steak

Servings: 2
Cooking Time: 12 Minutes
Ingredients:
- 1½ cups All-purpose flour
- 2 Large egg(s)
- 2 tablespoons Regular or low-fat sour cream
- 2 tablespoons Worcestershire sauce
- 2 ¼-pound thin beef cube steak(s)
- Vegetable oil spray

Directions:
1. Preheat the air fryer to 400°F.
2. Set up and fill two shallow soup plates or small pie plates on your counter: one for the flour; and one for the egg(s), whisked with the sour cream and Worcestershire sauce until uniform.
3. Dredge a piece of beef in the flour, coating it well on both sides and even along the edge. Shake off any excess; then dip the meat in the egg mixture, coating both sides while retaining the flour on the meat. Let any excess egg mixture slip back into the rest. Dredge the meat in the flour once again, coating all surfaces well. Gently shake off the excess coating and set the steak aside if you're coating another steak or two. Once done, coat the steak(s) on both sides with the vegetable oil spray.
4. Set the steak(s) in the basket. If there's more than one steak, make sure they do not overlap or even touch, although the smallest gap between them is enough to get them crunchy. Air-fry undisturbed for 6 minutes.
5. Use kitchen tongs to pick up one of the steaks. Coat it again on both sides with vegetable oil spray. Turn it upside down and set it back in the basket with that same regard for the space between them in larger batches. Repeat with any other steaks. Continue air-frying undisturbed for 6 minutes, or until golden brown and crunchy.
6. Use kitchen tongs to transfer the steak(s) to a wire rack. Cool for 5 minutes before serving.

Barbecue-style Beef Cube Steak

Servings: 2
Cooking Time: 14 Minutes
Ingredients:
- 2 4-ounce beef cube steak(s)
- 2 cups Fritos (original flavor) or a generic corn chip equivalent, crushed to crumbs
- 6 tablespoons Purchased smooth barbecue sauce, any flavor (gluten-free, if a concern)

Directions:

1. Preheat the air fryer to 375°F.
2. Spread the Fritos crumbs in a shallow soup plate or a small pie plate. Rub the barbecue sauce onto both sides of the steak(s). Dredge the steak(s) in the Fritos crumbs to coat well and thoroughly, turning several times and pressing down to get the little bits to adhere to the meat.
3. When the machine is at temperature, set the steak(s) in the basket. Leave as much air space between them as possible if you're working with more than one piece of beef. Air-fry undisturbed for 12 minutes, or until lightly brown and crunchy. If the machine is at 360°F, you may need to add 2 minutes to the cooking time.
4. Use kitchen tongs to transfer the steak(s) to a wire rack. Cool for 5 minutes before serving.

London Broil

Servings:4
Cooking Time: 12 Minutes
Ingredients:
- 1 pound top round steak
- 1 tablespoon Worcestershire sauce
- ¼ cup soy sauce
- 2 cloves garlic, peeled and finely minced
- ½ teaspoon ground black pepper
- ½ teaspoon salt
- 2 tablespoons salted butter, melted

Directions:
1. Place steak in a large sealable bowl or bag. Pour in Worcestershire sauce and soy sauce, then add garlic, pepper, and salt. Toss to coat. Seal and place into refrigerator to let marinate 2 hours.
2. Remove steak from marinade and pat dry. Drizzle top side with butter, then place into ungreased air fryer basket. Adjust the temperature to 375°F and set the timer for 12 minutes, turning steak halfway through cooking. Steak will be done when browned at the edges and it has an internal temperature of 150°F for medium or 180°F for well-done.
3. Let steak rest on a large plate 10 minutes before slicing into thin pieces. Serve warm.

Crispy Pork Pork Escalopes

Servings: 4
Cooking Time: 20 Minutes
Ingredients:
- 4 pork loin steaks
- Salt and pepper to taste
- ¼ cup flour
- 2 tbsp bread crumbs
- Cooking spray

Directions:
1. Preheat air fryer to 380°F. Season pork with salt and pepper. In one shallow bowl, add flour. In another, add bread crumbs. Dip the steaks first in the flour, then in the crumbs. Place them in the fryer and spray with oil. Bake for 12-14 minutes, flipping once until crisp. Serve.

Delicious Cheeseburgers

Servings: 4
Cooking Time: 12 Minutes
Ingredients:
- 1 lb ground beef
- 4 cheddar cheese slices

- 1/2 tsp Italian seasoning
- Pepper
- Salt
- Cooking spray

Directions:
1. Spray air fryer basket with cooking spray.
2. In a bowl, mix together ground beef, Italian seasoning, pepper, and salt.
3. Make four equal shapes of patties from meat mixture and place into the air fryer basket.
4. Cook at 375°F for 5 minutes. Turn patties to another side and cook for 5 minutes more.
5. Place cheese slices on top of each patty and cook for 2 minutes more.
6. Serve and enjoy.

Mustard And Rosemary Pork Tenderloin With Fried Apples

Servings: 2
Cooking Time: 26 Minutes

Ingredients:
- 1 pork tenderloin
- 2 tablespoons coarse brown mustard
- salt and freshly ground black pepper
- 1½ teaspoons finely chopped fresh rosemary, plus sprigs for garnish
- 2 apples, cored and cut into 8 wedges
- 1 tablespoon butter, melted
- 1 teaspoon brown sugar

Directions:
1. Preheat the air fryer to 370°F.
2. Cut the pork tenderloin in half so that you have two pieces that fit into the air fryer basket. Brush the mustard onto both halves of the pork tenderloin and then season with salt, pepper and the fresh rosemary. Place the pork tenderloin halves into the air fryer basket and air-fry for 10 minutes. Turn the pork over and air-fry for an additional 8 minutes or until the internal temperature of the pork registers 155°F on an instant read thermometer. If your pork tenderloin is especially thick, you may need to add a minute or two, but it's better to check the pork and add time, than to overcook it.
3. Let the pork rest for 5 minutes. In the meantime, toss the apple wedges with the butter and brown sugar and air-fry at 400°F for 8 minutes, shaking the basket once or twice during the cooking process so the apples cook and brown evenly.
4. Slice the pork on the bias. Serve with the fried apples scattered over the top and a few sprigs of rosemary as garnish.

Baby Back Ribs

Servings: 4
Cooking Time: 36 Minutes

Ingredients:
- 2¼ pounds Pork baby back rib rack(s)
- 1 tablespoon Dried barbecue seasoning blend or rub (gluten-free, if a concern)
- 1 cup Water
- 3 tablespoons Purchased smooth barbecue sauce (gluten-free, if a concern)

Directions:
1. Preheat the air fryer to 350°F.

2. Cut the racks into 4- to 5-bone sections, about two sections for the small batch, three for the medium, and four for the large. Sprinkle both sides of these sections with the seasoning blend.
3. Pour the water into the bottom of the air-fryer drawer or into a tray placed under the rack. Set the rib sections in the basket so that they're not touching. Air-fry for 30 minutes, turning once.
4. If using a tray with water, check it a couple of times to make sure it still has water in it or hasn't overflowed from the rendered fat.
5. Brush half the barbecue sauce on the exposed side of the ribs. Air-fry undisturbed for 3 minutes. Turn the racks over, brush with the remaining sauce, and air-fry undisturbed for 3 minutes more, or until sizzling and brown.
6. Use kitchen tongs to transfer the racks to a cutting board. Let stand for 5 minutes, then slice between the bones to serve.

Stuffed Peppers

Servings:4
Cooking Time: 15 Minutes

Ingredients:
- ½ pound cooked Italian sausage, drained
- 1 can diced tomatoes and green chilies, drained
- 2 teaspoons Italian seasoning
- 1 teaspoon salt
- 4 large green bell peppers, trimmed and seeded
- 1 cup shredded Italian-blend cheese
- Cooking spray

Directions:
1. Preheat the air fryer to 320°F.
2. In a large bowl, mix sausage, tomatoes and chilies, Italian seasoning, and salt.
3. Spoon one-fourth of meat mixture into each pepper. Sprinkle ¼ cup cheese on top of each pepper. Spritz peppers with cooking spray and place in the air fryer basket.
4. Cook 15 minutes until peppers are tender and cheese is melted and bubbling. Serve warm.

Bourbon-bbq Sauce Marinated Beef Bbq

Servings:4
Cooking Time: 60 Minutes

Ingredients:
- ¼ cup bourbon
- ¼ cup barbecue sauce
- 1 tablespoon Worcestershire sauce
- 2 pounds beef steak, pounded
- Salt and pepper to taste

Directions:
1. Place all ingredients in a Ziploc bag and allow to marinate in the fridge for at least 2 hours.
2. Preheat the air fryer to 390°F.
3. Place the grill pan accessory in the air fryer.
4. Place on the grill pan and cook for 20 minutes per batch.
5. Halfway through the cooking time, give a stir to cook evenly.
6. Meanwhile, pour the marinade on a saucepan and allow to simmer until the sauce thickens.
7. Serve beef with the bourbon sauce.

City "chicken"

Servings: 3
Cooking Time: 10 Minutes
Ingredients:
- 1 pound Pork tenderloin, cut into 2-inch cubes
- ½ cup All-purpose flour or tapioca flour
- 1 Large egg(s)
- 1 teaspoon Dried poultry seasoning blend
- 1¼ cups Plain panko bread crumbs (gluten-free, if a concern)
- Vegetable oil spray

Directions:
1. Preheat the air fryer to 350°F .
2. Thread 3 or 4 pieces of pork on a 4-inch bamboo skewer. You'll need 2 or 3 skewers for a small batch, 3 or 4 for a medium, and up to 6 for a large batch.
3. Set up and fill three shallow soup plates or small pie plates on your counter: one for the flour; one for the egg(s), beaten with the poultry seasoning until foamy; and one for the bread crumbs.
4. Dip and roll one skewer into the flour, coating all sides of the meat. Gently shake off any excess flour, then dip and roll the skewer in the egg mixture. Let any excess egg mixture slip back into the rest, then set the skewer in the bread crumbs and roll it around, pressing gently, until the exterior surfaces of the meat are evenly coated. Generously coat the meat on the skewer with vegetable oil spray. Set aside and continue dredging, dipping, coating, and spraying the remaining skewers.
5. Set the skewers in the basket in one layer and air-fry undisturbed for 10 minutes, or until brown and crunchy.
6. Use kitchen tongs to transfer the skewers to a wire rack. Cool for a minute or two before serving.

Garlic And Oregano Lamb Chops

Servings: 4
Cooking Time: 17 Minutes
Ingredients:
- 1½ tablespoons Olive oil
- 1 tablespoon Minced garlic
- 1 teaspoon Dried oregano
- 1 teaspoon Finely minced orange zest
- ¾ teaspoon Fennel seeds
- ¾ teaspoon Table salt
- ¾ teaspoon Ground black pepper
- 6 4-ounce, 1-inch-thick lamb loin chops

Directions:
1. Mix the olive oil, garlic, oregano, orange zest, fennel seeds, salt, and pepper in a large bowl. Add the chops and toss well to coat. Set aside as the air fryer heats, tossing one more time.
2. Preheat the air fryer to 400°F.
3. Set the chops bone side down in the basket with as much air space between them as possible. Air-fry undisturbed for 14 minutes for medium-rare, or until an instant-read meat thermometer inserted into the thickest part of a chop registers 132°F. Or air-fry undisturbed for 17 minutes for well done, or until an instant-read meat thermometer registers 145°F.
4. Use kitchen tongs to transfer the chops to a wire rack. Cool for 5 minutes before serving.

Cheeseburgers

Servings:4
Cooking Time: 10 Hours

Ingredients:
- 1 pound 70/30 ground beef
- ½ teaspoon salt
- ¼ teaspoon ground black pepper
- 4 slices American cheese
- 4 hamburger buns

Directions:
1. Preheat the air fryer to 360°F.
2. Separate beef into four equal portions and form into patties.
3. Sprinkle both sides of patties with salt and pepper. Place in the air fryer basket and cook 10 minutes, turning halfway through cooking time, until internal temperature reaches at least 160°F.
4. For each burger, place a slice of cheese on a patty and place on a hamburger bun. Serve warm.

Peppered Steak Bites

Servings: 4
Cooking Time: 14 Minutes
Ingredients:
- 1 pound sirloin steak, cut into 1-inch cubes
- ½ teaspoon coarse sea salt
- 1 teaspoon coarse black pepper
- 2 teaspoons Worcestershire sauce
- ½ teaspoon garlic powder
- ¼ teaspoon red pepper flakes
- ¼ cup chopped parsley

Directions:
1. Preheat the air fryer to 390°F.
2. In a large bowl, place the steak cubes and toss with the salt, pepper, Worcestershire sauce, garlic powder, and red pepper flakes.
3. Pour the steak into the air fryer basket and cook for 10 to 14 minutes, depending on how well done you prefer your bites. Starting at the 8-minute mark, toss the steak bites every 2 minutes to check for doneness.
4. When the steak is cooked, remove it from the basket to a serving bowl and top with the chopped parsley. Allow the steak to rest for 5 minutes before serving.

Simple Pork Chops

Servings: 4
Cooking Time: 20 Minutes
Ingredients:
- 4 pork chops, boneless
- 1 1/2 tbsp Mr. Dash seasoning
- Pepper
- Salt

Directions:
1. Coat pork chops with Mr. dash seasoning, pepper, and salt.
2. Place pork chops in the air fryer and cook at 360°F for 10 minutes.
3. Turn pork chops to another side and cook for 10 minutes more.
4. Serve and enjoy.

Champagne-vinegar Marinated Skirt Steak

Servings:2
Cooking Time: 40 Minutes
Ingredients:
- ¼ cup Dijon mustard
- 1 tablespoon rosemary leaves
- 1-pound skirt steak, trimmed
- 2 tablespoons champagne vinegar
- Salt and pepper to taste

Directions:
1. Place all ingredients in a Ziploc bag and marinate in the fridge for 2 hours.
2. Preheat the air fryer to 390°F.
3. Place the grill pan accessory in the air fryer.
4. Grill the skirt steak for 20 minutes per batch.
5. Flip the beef halfway through the cooking time.

Beef & Mushrooms

Servings: 1
Cooking Time: 3 Hours 15 Minutes
Ingredients:
- 6 oz. beef
- ¼ onion, diced
- ½ cup mushroom slices
- 2 tbsp. favorite marinade [preferably bulgogi]

Directions:
1. Slice or cube the beef and put it in a bowl.
2. Cover the meat with the marinade, place a layer of aluminum foil or saran wrap over the bowl, and place the bowl in the refrigerator for 3 hours.
3. Put the meat in a baking dish along with the onion and mushrooms
4. Air Fry at 350°F for 10 minutes. Serve hot.

Canadian-style Rib Eye Steak

Servings: 2
Cooking Time: 15 Minutes
Ingredients:
- 2 tsp Montreal steak seasoning
- 1 ribeye steak
- 1 tbsp butter, halved
- 1 tsp chopped parsley
- ½ tsp fresh rosemary

Directions:
1. Preheat air fryer at 400ºF. Sprinkle ribeye with steak seasoning and rosemary on both sides. Place it in the basket and Bake for 10 minutes, turning once. Remove it to a cutting board and top with butter halves. Let rest for 5 minutes and scatter with parsley. Serve immediately.

Teriyaki Country-style Pork Ribs

Servings: 3
Cooking Time: 30 Minutes
Ingredients:
- 3 tablespoons Regular or low-sodium soy sauce or gluten-free tamari sauce
- 3 tablespoons Honey
- ¾ teaspoon Ground dried ginger
- ¾ teaspoon Garlic powder
- 3 8-ounce boneless country-style pork ribs
- Vegetable oil spray

Directions:
1. Preheat the air fryer to 350°F .
2. Mix the soy or tamari sauce, honey, ground ginger, and garlic powder in another bowl until uniform.
3. Smear about half of this teriyaki sauce over all sides of the country-style ribs. Reserve the remainder of the teriyaki sauce. Generously coat the meat with vegetable oil spray.
4. When the machine is at temperature, place the country-style ribs in the basket with as much air space between them as possible. Air-fry undisturbed for 15 minutes. Turn the country-style ribs and brush them all over with the remaining teriyaki sauce. Continue air-frying undisturbed for 15 minutes, or until an instant-read meat thermometer inserted into the center of one rib registers at least 145°F.
5. Use kitchen tongs to transfer the country-style ribs to a wire rack. Cool for 5 minutes before serving.

Salty Lamb Chops

Servings: 4
Cooking Time: 8 Minutes
Ingredients:
- 1-pound lamb chops
- 1 egg, beaten
- ½ teaspoon salt
- ½ cup coconut flour
- Cooking spray

Directions:
1. Chop the lamb chops into small pieces (popcorn) and sprinkle with salt. Then add a beaten egg and stir the meat well. After this, add coconut flour and shake the lamb popcorn until all meat pieces are coated. Preheat the air fryer to 380°F. Put the lamb popcorn in the air fryer and spray it with cooking spray. Cook the lamb popcorn for 4 minutes. Then shake the meat well and cook it for 4 minutes more.

Tasty Filet Mignon

Servings:2
Cooking Time: 30 Minutes
Ingredients:
- 2 filet mignon steaks
- ¼ tsp garlic powder
- Salt and pepper to taste
- 1 tbsp butter, melted

Directions:
1. Preheat air fryer to 370ºF. Sprinkle the steaks with salt, garlic and pepper on both sides. Place them in the greased frying basket and Air Fry for 12 minutes to yield a medium-rare steak, turning twice. Transfer steaks to a cutting board, brush them with butter and let rest 5 minutes before serving.

Orange And Brown Sugar–glazed Ham

Servings:8
Cooking Time: 15 Minutes
Ingredients:
- ½ cup brown sugar
- ¼ cup orange juice
- 2 tablespoons yellow mustard
- 1 fully cooked boneless ham
- 1 teaspoon salt
- ½ teaspoon ground black pepper

Directions:

1. Preheat the air fryer to 375°F.
2. In a medium bowl, whisk together brown sugar, orange juice, and mustard until combined. Brush over ham until well coated. Sprinkle with salt and pepper.
3. Place in the air fryer basket and cook 15 minutes until heated through and edges are caramelized. Serve warm.

Cheese-stuffed Steak Burgers

Servings:4
Cooking Time: 10 Minutes
Ingredients:
- 1 pound 80/20 ground sirloin
- 4 ounces mild Cheddar cheese, cubed
- ½ teaspoon salt
- ¼ teaspoon ground black pepper

Directions:
1. Form ground sirloin into four equal balls, then separate each ball in half and flatten into two thin patties, for eight total patties. Place 1 ounce Cheddar into center of one patty, then top with a second patty and press edges to seal burger closed. Repeat with remaining patties and Cheddar to create four burgers.
2. Sprinkle salt and pepper over both sides of burgers and carefully place burgers into ungreased air fryer basket. Adjust the temperature to 350°F and set the timer for 10 minutes. Burgers will be done when browned on the edges and top. Serve warm.

Barbecue-style London Broil

Servings: 5
Cooking Time: 17 Minutes
Ingredients:
- ¾ teaspoon Mild smoked paprika
- ¾ teaspoon Dried oregano
- ¾ teaspoon Table salt
- ¾ teaspoon Ground black pepper
- ¼ teaspoon Garlic powder
- ¼ teaspoon Onion powder
- 1½ pounds Beef London broil (in one piece)
- Olive oil spray

Directions:
1. Preheat the air fryer to 400°F.
2. Mix the smoked paprika, oregano, salt, pepper, garlic powder, and onion powder in a small bowl until uniform.
3. Pat and rub this mixture across all surfaces of the beef. Lightly coat the beef on all sides with olive oil spray.
4. When the machine is at temperature, lay the London broil flat in the basket and air-fry undisturbed for 8 minutes for the small batch, 10 minutes for the medium batch, or 12 minutes for the large batch for medium-rare, until an instant-read meat thermometer inserted into the center of the meat registers 130°F. Add 1, 2, or 3 minutes, respectively for medium, until an instant-read meat thermometer registers 135°F. Or add 3, 4, or 5 minutes respectively for medium, until an instant-read meat thermometer registers 145°F.
5. Use kitchen tongs to transfer the London broil to a cutting board. Let the meat rest for 10 minutes. It needs a long time for the juices to be reincorporated into the meat's fibers. Carve it against the grain into very thin slices to serve.

Rib Eye Steak

Servings:4
Cooking Time: 15 Minutes
Ingredients:
- 4 rib eye steaks
- 1 teaspoon salt
- ½ teaspoon ground black pepper
- 2 tablespoons salted butter

Directions:
1. Preheat the air fryer to 400°F.
2. Sprinkle steaks with salt and pepper and place in the air fryer basket.
3. Cook 15 minutes, turning halfway through cooking time, until edges are firm, and the internal temperature reaches at least 160°F for well-done.
4. Top each steak with ½ tablespoon butter immediately after removing from the air fryer. Let rest 5 minutes before cutting. Serve warm.

Sweet And Spicy Spare Ribs

Servings:6
Cooking Time: 30 Minutes
Ingredients:
- ¼ cup granular brown erythritol
- 2 teaspoons paprika
- 2 teaspoons chili powder
- 1 teaspoon garlic powder
- ½ teaspoon cayenne pepper
- 2 teaspoons salt
- 1 teaspoon ground black pepper
- 1 rack pork spare ribs

Directions:
1. In a small bowl, mix erythritol, paprika, chili powder, garlic powder, cayenne pepper, salt, and black pepper. Rub spice mix over ribs on both sides. Place ribs on ungreased aluminum foil sheet and wrap to cover.
2. Place ribs into ungreased air fryer basket. Adjust the temperature to 400°F and set the timer for 25 minutes.
3. When timer beeps, remove ribs from foil, then place back into air fryer basket to cook an additional 5 minutes, turning halfway through cooking. Ribs will be browned and have an internal temperature of at least 180°F when done. Serve warm.

Wasabi-coated Pork Loin Chops

Servings: 3
Cooking Time: 14 Minutes
Ingredients:
- 1½ cups Wasabi peas
- ¼ cup Plain panko bread crumbs
- 1 Large egg white(s)
- 2 tablespoons Water
- 3 5- to 6-ounce boneless center-cut pork loin chops (about ½ inch thick)

Directions:
1. Preheat the air fryer to 375°F.
2. Put the wasabi peas in a food processor. Cover and process until finely ground, about like panko bread crumbs. Add the bread crumbs and pulse a few times to blend.
3. Set up and fill two shallow soup plates or small pie plates on your counter: one for the egg white(s), whisked with the water until uniform; and one for the wasabi pea mixture.
4. Dip a pork chop in the egg white mixture, coating the chop on both sides as well as around the edge. Allow any excess egg white mixture to slip back into the rest, then set the chop in the wasabi pea mixture. Press gently and turn it several times to

coat evenly on both sides and around the edge. Set aside, then dip and coat the remaining chop(s).

5. Set the chops in the basket with as much air space between them as possible. Air-fry, turning once at the 6-minute mark, for 12 minutes, or until the chops are crisp and browned and an instant-read meat thermometer inserted into the center of a chop registers 145°F. If the machine is at 360°F, you may need to add 2 minutes to the cooking time.

6. Use kitchen tongs to transfer the chops to a wire rack. Cool for a couple of minutes before serving.

Mexican-style Shredded Beef

Servings:6
Cooking Time: 35 Minutes
Ingredients:
- 1 beef chuck roast, cut into 2" cubes
- 1 teaspoon salt
- ½ teaspoon ground black pepper
- ½ cup no-sugar-added chipotle sauce

Directions:
1. In a large bowl, sprinkle beef cubes with salt and pepper and toss to coat. Place beef into ungreased air fryer basket. Adjust the temperature to 400°F and set the timer for 30 minutes, shaking the basket halfway through cooking. Beef will be done when internal temperature is at least 160°F.

2. Place cooked beef into a large bowl and shred with two forks. Pour in chipotle sauce and toss to coat.

3. Return beef to air fryer basket for an additional 5 minutes at 400°F to crisp with sauce. Serve warm.

Bacon With Shallot And Greens

Servings: 2
Cooking Time: 10 Minutes
Ingredients:
- 7 ounces mixed greens
- 8 thick slices pork bacon
- 2 shallots, peeled and diced
- Nonstick cooking spray

Directions:
1. Begin by preheating the air fryer to 345°F.

2. Now, add the shallot and bacon to the Air Fryer cooking basket; set the timer for 2 minutes. Spritz with a nonstick cooking spray.

3. After that, pause the Air Fryer; throw in the mixed greens; give it a good stir and cook an additional 5 minutes. Serve warm.

Air Fried Steak

Servings: 2
Cooking Time: 10 Minutes
Ingredients:
- 2 sirloin steaks
- 2 tsp olive oil
- 2 tbsp steak seasoning
- Pepper
- Salt

Directions:
1. Preheat the air fryer to 350°F.

2. Coat steak with olive oil and season with steak seasoning, pepper, and salt.

3. Spray air fryer basket with cooking spray and place steak in the air fryer basket.

4. Cook for 10 minutes. Turn halfway through.

5. Slice and serve.

Spinach And Provolone Steak Rolls

Servings:8
Cooking Time: 12 Minutes
Ingredients:
- 1 flank steak, butterflied
- 8 deli slices provolone cheese
- 1 cup fresh spinach leaves
- ½ teaspoon salt
- ¼ teaspoon ground black pepper

Directions:
1. Place steak on a large plate. Place provolone slices to cover steak, leaving 1" at the edges. Lay spinach leaves over cheese. Gently roll steak and tie with kitchen twine or secure with toothpicks. Carefully slice into eight pieces. Sprinkle each with salt and pepper.

2. Place rolls into ungreased air fryer basket, cut side up. Adjust the temperature to 400°F and set the timer for 12 minutes. Steak rolls will be browned and cheese will be melted when done and have an internal temperature of at least 150°F for medium steak and 180°F for well-done steak. Serve warm.

Venison Backstrap

Servings: 4
Cooking Time: 10 Minutes
Ingredients:
- 2 eggs
- ¼ cup milk
- 1 cup whole wheat flour
- ½ teaspoon salt
- ¼ teaspoon pepper
- 1 pound venison backstrap, sliced
- salt and pepper
- oil for misting or cooking spray

Directions:
1. Beat together eggs and milk in a shallow dish.

2. In another shallow dish, combine the flour, salt, and pepper. Stir to mix well.

3. Sprinkle venison steaks with additional salt and pepper to taste. Dip in flour, egg wash, then in flour again, pressing in coating.

4. Spray steaks with oil or cooking spray on both sides.

5. Cooking in 2 batches, place steaks in the air fryer basket in a single layer. Cook at 360°F for 8minutes. Spray with oil, turn over, and spray other side. Cook for 2 minutes longer, until coating is crispy brown and meat is done to your liking.

6. Repeat to cook remaining venison.

7. Spray both sides with oil and cook for 5minutes. If needed, mist with oil and continue cooking for 3 minutes longer. This second batch will cook a little faster than the first because your air fryer is already hot.

8. Serve with marinara sauce on the side for dipping.

Pork Chops

Servings: 2
Cooking Time: 16 Minutes
Ingredients:
- 2 bone-in, centercut pork chops, 1-inch thick
- 2 teaspoons Worcestershire sauce
- salt and pepper

- cooking spray

Directions:
1. Rub the Worcestershire sauce into both sides of pork chops.
2. Season with salt and pepper to taste.
3. Spray air fryer basket with cooking spray and place the chops in basket side by side.
4. Cook at 360°F for 16 minutes or until well done. Let rest for 5minutes before serving.

Parmesan-crusted Pork Chops

Servings:4
Cooking Time: 12 Minutes
Ingredients:
- 1 large egg
- ½ cup grated Parmesan cheese
- 4 boneless pork chops
- ½ teaspoon salt
- ¼ teaspoon ground black pepper

Directions:
1. Whisk egg in a medium bowl and place Parmesan in a separate medium bowl.
2. Sprinkle pork chops on both sides with salt and pepper. Dip each pork chop into egg, then press both sides into Parmesan.
3. Place pork chops into ungreased air fryer basket. Adjust the temperature to 400°F and set the timer for 12 minutes, turning chops halfway through cooking. Pork chops will be golden and have an internal temperature of at least 145°F when done. Serve warm.

Easy Garlic Butter Steak

Servings: 2
Cooking Time: 6 Minutes
Ingredients:
- 2 steaks
- 2 tsp garlic butter
- 1/4 tsp Italian seasoning
- Pepper
- Salt

Directions:
1. Season steaks with Italian seasoning, pepper, and salt.
2. Rub steaks with garlic butter and place into the air fryer basket and cook at 350°F for 6 minutes.
3. Serve and enjoy.

Bacon Wrapped Filets Mignons

Servings: 4
Cooking Time: 18 Minutes
Ingredients:
- 4 slices bacon (not thick cut)
- 4 filets mignons
- 1 tablespoon fresh thyme leaves
- salt and freshly ground black pepper

Directions:
1. Preheat the air fryer to 400°F.
2. Lay the bacon slices down on a cutting board and sprinkle the thyme leaves on the bacon slices. Remove any string tying the filets and place the steaks down on their sides on top of the bacon slices. Roll the bacon around the side of the filets and secure the bacon to the fillets with a toothpick or two.
3. Season the steaks generously with salt and freshly ground black pepper and transfer the steaks to the air fryer.

4. Air-fry for 18 minutes, turning the steaks over halfway through the cooking process. This should cook your steaks to about medium, depending on how thick they are. If you'd prefer your steaks medium-rare or medium-well, simply add or subtract two minutes from the cooking time. Remove the steaks from the air fryer and let them rest for 5 minutes before removing the toothpicks and serving.

Cheddar Bacon Ranch Pinwheels

Servings:5
Cooking Time: 12 Minutes Per Batch
Ingredients:
- 4 ounces full-fat cream cheese, softened
- 1 tablespoon dry ranch seasoning
- ½ cup shredded Cheddar cheese
- 1 sheet frozen puff pastry dough, thawed
- 6 slices bacon, cooked and crumbled

Directions:
1. Preheat the air fryer to 320°F. Cut parchment paper to fit the air fryer basket.
2. In a medium bowl, mix cream cheese, ranch seasoning, and Cheddar. Unfold puff pastry and gently spread cheese mixture over pastry.
3. Sprinkle crumbled bacon on top. Starting from a long side, roll dough into a log, pressing in the edges to seal.
4. Cut log into ten pieces, then place on parchment in the air fryer basket, working in batches as necessary.
5. Cook 12 minutes, turning each piece after 7 minutes. Let cool 5 minutes before serving.

Lamb Chops

Servings: 2
Cooking Time: 20 Minutes
Ingredients:
- 2 teaspoons oil
- ½ teaspoon ground rosemary
- ½ teaspoon lemon juice
- 1 pound lamb chops, approximately 1-inch thick
- salt and pepper
- cooking spray

Directions:
1. Mix the oil, rosemary, and lemon juice together and rub into all sides of the lamb chops. Season to taste with salt and pepper.
2. For best flavor, cover lamb chops and allow them to rest in the fridge for 20 minutes.
3. Spray air fryer basket with nonstick spray and place lamb chops in it.
4. Cook at 360°F for approximately 20minutes. This will cook chops to medium. The meat will be juicy but have no remaining pink. Cook for a minute or two longer for well done chops. For rare chops, stop cooking after about 12minutes and check for doneness.

Air Fried Grilled Steak

Servings:2
Cooking Time: 45 Minutes
Ingredients:
- 2 top sirloin steaks
- 3 tablespoons butter, melted
- 3 tablespoons olive oil
- Salt and pepper to taste

Directions:
1. Preheat the air fryer for 5 minutes.
2. Season the sirloin steaks with olive oil, salt and pepper.
3. Place the beef in the air fryer basket.
4. Cook for 45 minutes at 350°F.
5. Once cooked, serve with butter.

Empanadas

Servings:4
Cooking Time: 28 Minutes
Ingredients:
- 1 pound 80/20 ground beef
- ¼ cup taco seasoning
- ⅓ cup salsa
- 2 refrigerated piecrusts
- 1 cup shredded Colby-jack cheese

Directions:
1. In a medium skillet over medium heat, brown beef about 10 minutes until cooked through. Drain fat, then add taco seasoning and salsa to the pan. Bring to a boil, then cook 30 seconds. Reduce heat and simmer 5 minutes. Remove from heat.
2. Preheat the air fryer to 370°F.
3. Cut three 5" circles from each piecrust, forming six total. Reroll scraps out to ½" thickness. Cut out two more 5" circles to make eight circles total.
4. For each empanada, place ¼ cup meat mixture onto the lower half of a pastry circle and top with 2 tablespoons cheese. Dab a little water along the edge of pastry and fold circle in half to fully cover meat and cheese, pressing the edges together. Use a fork to gently seal the edges. Repeat with remaining pastry, meat, and cheese.
5. Spritz empanadas with cooking spray. Place in the air fryer basket and cook 12 minutes, turning halfway through cooking time, until crust is golden. Serve warm.

Roast Beef

Servings:6
Cooking Time: 60 Minutes
Ingredients:
- 1 top round beef roast
- 1 teaspoon salt
- ½ teaspoon ground black pepper
- 1 teaspoon dried rosemary
- ½ teaspoon garlic powder
- 1 tablespoon coconut oil, melted

Directions:
1. Sprinkle all sides of roast with salt, pepper, rosemary, and garlic powder. Drizzle with coconut oil. Place roast into ungreased air fryer basket, fatty side down. Adjust the temperature to 375°F and set the timer for 60 minutes, turning the roast halfway through cooking. Roast will be done when no pink remains and internal temperature is at least 180°F. Serve warm.

Air Fried Thyme Garlic Lamb Chops

Servings: 4
Cooking Time: 12 Minutes
Ingredients:
- 4 lamb chops
- 4 garlic cloves, minced
- 3 tbsp olive oil
- 1 tbsp dried thyme

- Pepper
- Salt

Directions:
1. Preheat the air fryer to 390°F.
2. Season lamb chops with pepper and salt.
3. In a small bowl, mix together thyme, oil, and garlic and rub over lamb chops.
4. Place lamb chops into the air fryer and cook for 12 minutes. Turn halfway through.
5. Serve and enjoy.

Boneless Ribeyes

Servings: 2
Cooking Time: 10-15 Minutes
Ingredients:
- 2 8-ounce boneless ribeye steaks
- 4 teaspoons Worcestershire sauce
- ½ teaspoon garlic powder
- pepper
- 4 teaspoons extra virgin olive oil
- salt

Directions:
1. Season steaks on both sides with Worcestershire sauce. Use the back of a spoon to spread evenly.
2. Sprinkle both sides of steaks with garlic powder and coarsely ground black pepper to taste.
3. Drizzle both sides of steaks with olive oil, again using the back of a spoon to spread evenly over surfaces.
4. Allow steaks to marinate for 30minutes.
5. Place both steaks in air fryer basket and cook at 390°F for 5minutes.
6. Turn steaks over and cook until done: medium rare: additional 5 minutes, medium: additional 7 minutes, well done: additional 10 minutes.
7. Remove steaks from air fryer basket and let sit 5minutes. Salt to taste and serve.

Crouton-breaded Pork Chops

Servings:4
Cooking Time: 14 Minutes
Ingredients:
- 4 boneless pork chops
- 1 teaspoon salt
- ½ teaspoon ground black pepper
- 2 cups croutons
- ½ teaspoon dried thyme
- ¼ teaspoon dried sage
- 1 large egg, whisked
- Cooking spray

Directions:
1. Preheat the air fryer to 400°F.
2. Sprinkle pork chops with salt and pepper on both sides.
3. In a food processor, add croutons, thyme, and sage. Pulse five times until croutons are mostly broken down with a few medium-sized pieces remaining. Transfer to a medium bowl.
4. In a separate medium bowl, place egg. Dip each pork chop into egg, then press into crouton mixture to coat both sides. Spritz with cooking spray.
5. Place pork in the air fryer basket and cook 14 minutes, turning halfway through cooking time, until chops are golden brown and internal temperature reaches at least 145°F. Serve warm.

Friday Night Cheeseburgers

Servings: 4
Cooking Time: 20 Minutes
Ingredients:
- 1 lb ground beef
- 1 tsp Worcestershire sauce
- 1 tbsp allspice
- Salt and pepper to taste
- 4 cheddar cheese slices
- 4 buns

Directions:
1. Preheat air fryer to 360°F. Combine beef, Worcestershire sauce, allspice, salt and pepper in a large bowl. Divide into 4 equal portions and shape into patties. Place the burgers in the greased frying basket and Air Fry for 8 minutes. Flip and cook for another 3-4 minutes. Top each burger with cheddar cheese and cook for another minute so the cheese melts. Transfer to a bun and serve.

Extra Crispy Country-style Pork Riblets

Servings: 3
Cooking Time: 30 Minutes
Ingredients:
- ⅓ cup Tapioca flour
- 2½ tablespoons Chile powder
- ¾ teaspoon Table salt (optional)
- 1¼ pounds Boneless country-style pork ribs, cut into 1½-inch chunks
- Vegetable oil spray

Directions:
1. Preheat the air fryer to 375°F.
2. Mix the tapioca flour, chile powder, and salt in a large bowl until well combined. Add the country-style rib chunks and toss well to coat thoroughly.
3. When the machine is at temperature, gently shake off any excess tapioca coating from the chunks. Generously coat them on all sides with vegetable oil spray. Arrange the chunks in the basket in one layer. The pieces may touch. Air-fry for 30 minutes, rearranging the pieces at the 10- and 20-minute marks to expose any touching bits, until very crisp and well browned.
4. Gently pour the contents of the basket onto a wire rack. Cool for 5 minutes before serving.

Ground Beef

Servings: 4
Cooking Time: 9 Minutes
Ingredients:
- 1 pound 70/30 ground beef
- ¼ cup water
- 1 teaspoon salt
- ½ teaspoon ground black pepper
- 1 teaspoon garlic powder

Directions:
1. Preheat the air fryer to 400°F.
2. In a medium bowl, mix beef with remaining ingredients. Place beef in a 6" round cake pan and press into an even layer.
3. Place in the air fryer basket and set the timer to 10 minutes. After 5 minutes, open the air fryer and stir ground beef with a spatula. Return to the air fryer.
4. After 2 more minutes, open the air fryer, remove the pan and drain any excess fat from the ground beef. Return to the air

fryer for and cook 2 more minutes until beef is brown and no pink remains.

Herbed Beef Roast

Servings: 5
Cooking Time: 45 Minutes
Ingredients:
- 2 pounds beef roast
- 1 tablespoon olive oil
- 1 teaspoon dried rosemary, crushed
- 1 teaspoon dried thyme, crushed
- Salt, to taste

Directions:
1. Preheat the Air fryer to 360°F and grease an Air fryer basket.
2. Rub the roast generously with herb mixture and coat with olive oil.
3. Arrange the roast in the Air fryer basket and cook for about 45 minutes.
4. Dish out the roast and cover with foil for about 10 minutes.
5. Cut into desired size slices and serve.

Lamb Burgers

Servings: 2
Cooking Time: 16 Minutes
Ingredients:
- 8 oz lamb, minced
- ½ teaspoon salt
- ½ teaspoon ground black pepper
- ½ teaspoon dried cilantro
- 1 tablespoon water
- Cooking spray

Directions:
1. In the mixing bowl mix up minced lamb, salt, ground black pepper, dried cilantro, and water.
2. Stir the meat mixture carefully with the help of the spoon and make 2 burgers.
3. Preheat the air fryer to 375°F.
4. Spray the air fryer basket with cooking spray and put the burgers inside.
5. Cook them for 8 minutes from each side.

Buttery Pork Chops

Servings: 4
Cooking Time: 12 Minutes
Ingredients:
- 4 boneless pork chops
- 1 teaspoon salt
- ½ teaspoon ground black pepper
- 4 tablespoons salted butter, sliced into 8 (½-tablespoon) pats, divided

Directions:
1. Preheat the air fryer to 400°F.
2. Sprinkle pork chops with salt and pepper. Top each pork chop with a ½-tablespoon butter pat.
3. Place chops in the air fryer basket and cook 12 minutes, turning halfway through cooking time, until tops and edges are golden brown and internal temperature reaches at least 145°F.
4. Use remaining butter pats to top each pork chop while hot, then let cool 5 minutes before serving warm.

Pepperoni Pockets

Servings: 4
Cooking Time: 8 Minutes
Ingredients:

- 4 bread slices, 1-inch thick
- olive oil for misting
- 24 slices pepperoni
- 1 ounce roasted red peppers, drained and patted dry
- 1 ounce Pepper Jack cheese cut into 4 slices
- pizza sauce (optional)

Directions:
1. Spray both sides of bread slices with olive oil.
2. Stand slices upright and cut a deep slit in the top to create a pocket—almost to the bottom crust but not all the way through.
3. Stuff each bread pocket with 6 slices of pepperoni, a large strip of roasted red pepper, and a slice of cheese.
4. Place bread pockets in air fryer basket, standing up. Cook at 360°F for 8 minutes, until filling is heated through and bread is lightly browned. Serve while hot as is or with pizza sauce for dipping.

Mozzarella-stuffed Meatloaf

Servings:6
Cooking Time: 30 Minutes
Ingredients:

- 1 pound 80/20 ground beef
- ½ medium green bell pepper, seeded and chopped
- ¼ medium yellow onion, peeled and chopped
- ½ teaspoon salt
- ¼ teaspoon ground black pepper
- 2 ounces mozzarella cheese, sliced into ¼"-thick slices
- ¼ cup low-carb ketchup

Directions:
1. In a large bowl, combine ground beef, bell pepper, onion, salt, and black pepper. Cut a piece of parchment to fit air fryer basket. Place half beef mixture on ungreased parchment and form a 9" × 4" loaf, about ½" thick.
2. Center mozzarella slices on beef loaf, leaving at least ¼" around each edge.
3. Press remaining beef into a second 9" × 4" loaf and place on top of mozzarella, pressing edges of loaves together to seal.
4. Place parchment with meatloaf into air fryer basket. Adjust the temperature to 350°F and set the timer for 30 minutes, carefully turning loaf and brushing top with ketchup halfway through cooking. Loaf will be browned and have an internal temperature of at least 180°F when done. Slice and serve warm.

Meatloaf

Servings:4
Cooking Time: 40 Minutes
Ingredients:

- 1 pound 80/20 lean ground beef
- 1 large egg
- 3 tablespoons Italian bread crumbs
- 1 teaspoon salt
- 2 tablespoons ketchup
- 2 tablespoons brown sugar

Directions:
1. Preheat the air fryer to 350°F.
2. In a large bowl, combine beef, egg, bread crumbs, and salt.
3. In a small bowl, mix ketchup and brown sugar.

4. Form meat mixture into a 6" × 3" loaf and brush with ketchup mixture.
5. Place in the air fryer basket and cook 40 minutes until internal temperature reaches at least 160°F. Serve warm.

Lemon-butter Veal Cutlets

Servings: 2
Cooking Time: 4 Minutes
Ingredients:

- 3 strips Butter
- 3 Thinly pounded 2-ounce veal leg cutlets (less than ¼ inch thick)
- ¼ teaspoon Lemon-pepper seasoning

Directions:
1. Preheat the air fryer to 400°F.
2. Run a vegetable peeler lengthwise along a hard, cold stick of butter, making 2, 3, or 4 long strips as the recipe requires for the number of cutlets you're making.
3. Lay the veal cutlets on a clean, dry cutting board or work surface. Sprinkle about ⅛ teaspoon lemon-pepper seasoning over each. Set a strip of butter on top of each cutlet.
4. When the machine is at temperature, set the topped cutlets in the basket so that they don't overlap or even touch. Air-fry undisturbed for 4 minutes without turning.
5. Use a nonstick-safe spatula to transfer the cutlets to a serving plate or plates, taking care to keep as much of the butter on top as possible. Remove the basket from the drawer or from over the baking tray. Carefully pour the browned butter over the cutlets.

Easy & The Traditional Beef Roast Recipe

Servings:12
Cooking Time: 2 Hours
Ingredients:

- 1 cup organic beef broth
- 3 pounds beef round roast
- 4 tablespoons olive oil
- Salt and pepper to taste

Directions:
1. Place in a Ziploc bag all the ingredients and allow to marinate in the fridge for 2 hours.
2. Preheat the air fryer for 5 minutes.
3. Transfer all ingredients in a baking dish that will fit in the air fryer.
4. Place in the air fryer and cook for 2 hours for 400°F.

Mustard Beef Mix

Servings: 7
Cooking Time: 30 Minutes
Ingredients:

- 2-pound beef ribs, boneless
- 1 tablespoon Dijon mustard
- 1 tablespoon sunflower oil
- 1 teaspoon ground paprika
- 1 teaspoon cayenne pepper

Directions:
1. In the shallow bowl mix up Dijon mustard and sunflower oil. Then sprinkle the beef ribs with ground paprika and cayenne pepper. After this, brush the meat with Dijon mustard mixture and leave for 10 minutes to marinate. Meanwhile, preheat the air fryer to 400°F. Put the beef ribs in the air fryer to and cook them for 10 minutes. Then flip the ribs on another

side and reduce the air fryer heat to 325°F. Cook the ribs for 20 minutes more.

Egg Stuffed Pork Meatballs

Servings: 2
Cooking Time: 40 Minutes
Ingredients:
- 3 soft boiled eggs, peeled
- 8 oz ground pork
- 2 tsp dried tarragon
- ½ tsp hot paprika
- 2 tsp garlic powder
- Salt and pepper to taste

Directions:
1. Preheat air fryer to 350°F. Combine the pork, tarragon, hot paprika, garlic powder, salt, and pepper in a bowl and stir until all spices are evenly spread throughout the meat. Divide the meat mixture into three equal portions in the mixing bowl, and shape each into balls.
2. Flatten one of the meatballs on top to make a wide, flat meat circle. Place an egg in the middle. Use your hands to mold the mixture up and around to enclose the egg. Repeat with the remaining eggs. Place the stuffed balls in the air fryer. Air Fry for 18-20 minutes, shaking the basket once until the meat is crispy and golden brown. Serve.

Beef Al Carbon (street Taco Meat)

Servings: 6
Cooking Time: 8 Minutes
Ingredients:
- 1½ pounds sirloin steak, cut into ½-inch cubes
- ¾ cup lime juice
- ½ cup extra-virgin olive oil
- 1 teaspoon ground cumin
- 2 teaspoons garlic powder
- 1 teaspoon salt

Directions:
1. In a large bowl, toss together the steak, lime juice, olive oil, cumin, garlic powder, and salt. Allow the meat to marinate for 30 minutes. Drain off all the marinade and pat the meat dry with paper towels.
2. Preheat the air fryer to 400°F.
3. Place the meat in the air fryer basket and spray with cooking spray. Cook the meat for 5 minutes, toss the meat, and continue cooking another 3 minutes, until slightly crispy.

Bacon And Blue Cheese Burgers

Servings:4
Cooking Time: 15 Minutes
Ingredients:
- 1 pound 70/30 ground beef
- 6 slices cooked sugar-free bacon, finely chopped
- ½ cup crumbled blue cheese
- ¼ cup peeled and chopped yellow onion
- ½ teaspoon salt
- ¼ teaspoon ground black pepper

Directions:
1. In a large bowl, mix ground beef, bacon, blue cheese, and onion. Separate into four sections and shape each section into a patty. Sprinkle with salt and pepper.
2. Place patties into ungreased air fryer basket. Adjust the temperature to 350°F and set the timer for 15 minutes, turning

patties halfway through cooking. Burgers will be done when internal temperature is at least 150°F for medium and 180°F for well. Serve warm.

Stress-free Beef Patties

Servings: 2
Cooking Time: 30 Minutes
Ingredients:
- ½ lb ground beef
- 1 ½ tbsp ketchup
- 1 ½ tbsp tamari
- ½ tsp jalapeño powder
- ½ tsp mustard powder
- Salt and pepper to taste

Directions:
1. Preheat air fryer to 350°F.Add the beef, ketchup, tamari, jalapeño, mustard salt, and pepper in a bowl and mix until evenly combined. Shape into 2 patties, then place them on the greased frying basket. Air Fry for 18-20 minutes, turning once. Serve and enjoy!

Honey Mesquite Pork Chops

Servings: 2
Cooking Time: 10 Minutes
Ingredients:
- 2 tablespoons mesquite seasoning
- ¼ cup honey
- 1 tablespoon olive oil
- 1 tablespoon water
- freshly ground black pepper
- 2 bone-in center cut pork chops

Directions:
1. Whisk the mesquite seasoning, honey, olive oil, water and freshly ground black pepper together in a shallow glass dish. Pierce the chops all over and on both sides with a fork or meat tenderizer. Add the pork chops to the marinade and massage the marinade into the chops. Cover and marinate for 30 minutes.
2. Preheat the air fryer to 330°F.
3. Transfer the pork chops to the air fryer basket and pour half of the marinade over the chops, reserving the remaining marinade. Air-fry the pork chops for 6 minutes. Flip the pork chops over and pour the remaining marinade on top. Air-fry for an additional 3 minutes at 330°F. Then, increase the air fryer temperature to 400°F and air-fry the pork chops for an additional minute.
4. Transfer the pork chops to a serving plate, and let them rest for 5 minutes before serving. If you'd like a sauce for these chops, pour the cooked marinade from the bottom of the air fryer over the top.

Bacon-wrapped Pork Tenderloin

Servings:6
Cooking Time: 20 Minutes
Ingredients:
- 1 pork tenderloin
- ½ teaspoon salt
- ½ teaspoon garlic powder
- ¼ teaspoon ground black pepper
- 8 slices sugar-free bacon

Directions:

1. Sprinkle tenderloin with salt, garlic powder, and pepper. Wrap each piece of bacon around tenderloin and secure with toothpicks.
2. Place tenderloin into ungreased air fryer basket. Adjust the temperature to 400°F and set the timer for 20 minutes, turning tenderloin after 15 minutes. When done, bacon will be crispy and tenderloin will have an internal temperature of at least 145°F.
3. Cut the tenderloin into six even portions and transfer each to a medium plate and serve warm.

Steak Bites And Spicy Dipping Sauce

Servings:4
Cooking Time: 8 Minutes
Ingredients:
- 2 pounds sirloin steak, cut into 2" cubes
- 2 teaspoons salt
- 1 teaspoon ground black pepper
- 1 teaspoon garlic powder
- ½ cup mayonnaise
- 2 tablespoons sriracha

Directions:
1. Preheat the air fryer to 400°F.
2. Sprinkle steak with salt, pepper, and garlic powder.
3. Place steak in the air fryer basket and cook 8 minutes, shaking the basket twice during cooking, until internal temperature reaches at least 160°F.
4. In a small bowl, combine mayonnaise and sriracha. Serve with steak bites for dipping.

Mustard-crusted Rib-eye

Servings: 2
Cooking Time: 9 Minutes
Ingredients:
- Two 6-ounce rib-eye steaks, about 1-inch thick
- 1 teaspoon coarse salt
- ½ teaspoon coarse black pepper
- 2 tablespoons Dijon mustard

Directions:
1. Rub the steaks with the salt and pepper. Then spread the mustard on both sides of the steaks. Cover with foil and let the steaks sit at room temperature for 30 minutes.
2. Preheat the air fryer to 390°F.
3. Cook the steaks for 9 minutes. Check for an internal temperature of 140°F and immediately remove the steaks and let them rest for 5 minutes before slicing.

Salted Porterhouse With Sage 'n Thyme Medley

Servings:2
Cooking Time: 40 Minutes
Ingredients:
- ¼ cup fish sauce
- 2 porterhouse steaks
- 2 tablespoons marjoram
- 2 tablespoons sage
- 2 tablespoons thyme
- Salt and pepper to taste

Directions:
1. Place all ingredients in a Ziploc bag and allow to marinate in the fridge for at least 2 hours.
2. Preheat the air fryer to 390°F.

3. Place the grill pan accessory in the air fryer.
4. Grill for 20 minutes per batch.
5. Flip every 10 minutes for even grilling.

Simple Beef

Servings: 1
Cooking Time: 25 Minutes
Ingredients:
- 1 thin beef schnitzel
- 1 egg, beaten
- ½ cup friendly bread crumbs
- 2 tbsp. olive oil
- Pepper and salt to taste

Directions:
1. Pre-heat the Air Fryer to 350°F.
2. In a shallow dish, combine the bread crumbs, oil, pepper, and salt.
3. In a second shallow dish, place the beaten egg.
4. Dredge the schnitzel in the egg before rolling it in the bread crumbs.
5. Put the coated schnitzel in the fryer basket and air fry for 12 minutes.

Mustard Herb Pork Tenderloin

Servings:6
Cooking Time: 20 Minutes
Ingredients:
- ¼ cup mayonnaise
- 2 tablespoons Dijon mustard
- ½ teaspoon dried thyme
- ¼ teaspoon dried rosemary
- 1 pork tenderloin
- ½ teaspoon salt
- ¼ teaspoon ground black pepper

Directions:
1. In a small bowl, mix mayonnaise, mustard, thyme, and rosemary. Brush tenderloin with mixture on all sides, then sprinkle with salt and pepper on all sides.
2. Place tenderloin into ungreased air fryer basket. Adjust the temperature to 400°F and set the timer for 20 minutes, turning tenderloin halfway through cooking. Tenderloin will be golden and have an internal temperature of at least 145°F when done. Serve warm.

Sweet Potato–crusted Pork Rib Chops

Servings: 2
Cooking Time: 14 Minutes
Ingredients:
- 2 Large egg white(s), well beaten
- 1½ cups Crushed sweet potato chips (certified gluten-free, if a concern)
- 1 teaspoon Ground cinnamon
- 1 teaspoon Ground dried ginger
- 1 teaspoon Table salt (optional)
- 2 10-ounce, 1-inch-thick bone-in pork rib chop(s)

Directions:
1. Preheat the air fryer to 375°F .
2. Set up and fill two shallow soup plates or small pie plates on your counter: one for the beaten egg white(s); and one for the crushed chips, mixed with the cinnamon, ginger, and salt.
3. Dip a chop in the egg white(s), coating it on both sides as well as the edges. Let the excess egg white slip back into the

rest, then set it in the crushed chip mixture. Turn it several times, pressing gently, until evenly coated on both sides and the edges. If necessary, set the chop aside and coat the remaining chop(s).

4. Set the chop(s) in the basket with as much air space between them as possible. Air-fry undisturbed for 12 minutes, or until crunchy and browned and an instant-read meat thermometer inserted into the center of a chop registers 145°F. If the machine is at 360°F, you may need to add 2 minutes to the cooking time.

5. Use kitchen tongs to transfer the chop(s) to a wire rack. Cool for 2 or 3 minutes before serving.

Marinated Rib Eye

Servings:4
Cooking Time: 10 Minutes
Ingredients:
- 1 pound rib eye steak
- ¼ cup soy sauce
- 1 tablespoon Worcestershire sauce
- 1 tablespoon granular brown erythritol
- 2 tablespoons olive oil
- ½ teaspoon salt
- ¼ teaspoon ground black pepper

Directions:
1. Place rib eye in a large sealable bowl or bag and pour in soy sauce, Worcestershire sauce, erythritol, and olive oil. Seal and let marinate 30 minutes in the refrigerator.

2. Remove rib eye from marinade, pat dry, and sprinkle on all sides with salt and pepper. Place rib eye into ungreased air fryer basket. Adjust the temperature to 400°F and set the timer for 10 minutes. Steak will be done when browned at the edges and has an internal temperature of 150°F for medium or 180°F for well-done. Serve warm.

Maple'n Soy Marinated Beef

Servings:4
Cooking Time: 45 Minutes
Ingredients:
- 2 pounds sirloin flap steaks, pounded
- 3 tablespoons balsamic vinegar
- 3 tablespoons maple syrup
- 3 tablespoons soy sauce
- 4 cloves of garlic, minced

Directions:
1. Preheat the air fryer to 390°F.
2. Place the grill pan accessory in the air fryer.
3. On a deep dish, place the flap steaks and season with soy sauce, balsamic vinegar, and maple syrup, and garlic.
4. Place on the grill pan and cook for 15 minutes in batches.

Simple Air Fryer Steak

Servings: 2
Cooking Time: 18 Minutes
Ingredients:
- 12 oz steaks, 3/4-inch thick
- 1 tsp garlic powder
- 1 tsp olive oil
- Pepper
- Salt

Directions:

1. Coat steaks with oil and season with garlic powder, pepper, and salt.
2. Preheat the air fryer to 400°F.
3. Place steaks in air fryer basket and cook for 15-18 minutes. Turn halfway through.
4. Serve and enjoy.

Almond And Sun-dried Tomato Crusted Pork Chops

Servings: 4
Cooking Time: 10 Minutes
Ingredients:
- ½ cup oil-packed sun-dried tomatoes
- ½ cup toasted almonds
- ¼ cup grated Parmesan cheese
- ½ cup olive oil
- 2 tablespoons water
- ½ teaspoon salt
- freshly ground black pepper
- 4 center-cut boneless pork chops

Directions:
1. Place the sun-dried tomatoes into a food processor and pulse them until they are coarsely chopped. Add the almonds, Parmesan cheese, olive oil, water, salt and pepper. Process all the ingredients into a smooth paste. Spread most of the paste onto both sides of the pork chops and then pierce the meat several times with a needle-style meat tenderizer or a fork. Let the pork chops sit and marinate for at least 1 hour.

2. Preheat the air fryer to 370°F.
3. Brush a little olive oil on the bottom of the air fryer basket. Transfer the pork chops into the air fryer basket, spooning a little more of the sun-dried tomato paste onto the pork chops if there are any gaps where the paste may have been rubbed off. Air-fry the pork chops at 370°F for 10 minutes, turning the chops over halfway through the cooking process.

4. When the pork chops have finished cooking, transfer them to a serving plate and serve with mashed potatoes and vegetables for a hearty meal.

Fajita Flank Steak Rolls

Servings:4
Cooking Time: 12 Minutes
Ingredients:
- 1 pound flank steak
- 4 slices pepper jack cheese
- 1 medium green bell pepper, seeded and chopped
- ½ medium red bell pepper, seeded and chopped
- ¼ cup finely chopped yellow onion
- 1 teaspoon salt
- ½ teaspoon ground black pepper
- Cooking spray

Directions:
1. Preheat the air fryer to 400°F.
2. Carefully butterfly steak, leaving the two halves connected. Place slices of cheese on top of steak. Scatter bell peppers and onion over cheese in an even layer.

3. Place steak so that the grain runs horizontally. Tightly roll up steak and secure it with eight evenly spaced toothpicks or eight sections of butcher's twine.

4. Slice steak into four even rolls. Spritz with cooking spray, then sprinkle with salt and black pepper. Place in the air fryer basket and cook 12 minutes until steak is brown on the edges and internal temperature reaches at least 160°F for well-done. Serve.

Bjorn's Beef Steak

Servings: 1
Cooking Time: 15 Minutes
Ingredients:
- 1 steak, 1-inch thick
- 1 tbsp. olive oil
- Black pepper to taste
- Sea salt to taste

Directions:
1. Place the baking tray inside the Air Fryer and pre-heat for about 5 minutes at 390°F.
2. Brush or spray both sides of the steak with the oil.
3. Season both sides with salt and pepper.
4. Take care when placing the steak in the baking tray and allow to cook for 3 minutes. Flip the meat over, and cook for an additional 3 minutes.
5. Take it out of the fryer and allow to sit for roughly 3 minutes before serving.

Perfect Strip Steaks

Servings: 2
Cooking Time: 17 Minutes
Ingredients:
- 1½ tablespoons Olive oil
- 1½ tablespoons Minced garlic
- 2 teaspoons Ground black pepper
- 1 teaspoon Table salt
- 2 ¾-pound boneless beef strip steak(s)

Directions:
1. Preheat the air fryer to 375°F.
2. Mix the oil, garlic, pepper, and salt in a small bowl, then smear this mixture over both sides of the steak(s).
3. When the machine is at temperature, put the steak(s) in the basket with as much air space as possible between them for the larger batch. They should not overlap or even touch. That said, even just a ¼-inch between them will work. Air-fry for 12 minutes, turning once, until an instant-read meat thermometer inserted into the thickest part of a steak registers 127°F for rare. Or air-fry for 15 minutes, turning once, until an instant-read meat thermometer registers 145°F for medium. If the machine is at 390°F, the steaks may cook 2 minutes more quickly than the stated timing.
4. Use kitchen tongs to transfer the steak(s) to a wire rack. Cool for 5 minutes before serving.

Mccornick Pork Chops

Servings: 2
Cooking Time: 15 Minutes
Ingredients:
- 2 pork chops
- 1/2 tsp McCormick Montreal chicken seasoning
- 2 tbsp arrowroot flour
- 1 1/2 tbsp coconut milk
- Salt

Directions:
1. Season pork chops with pepper and salt.
2. Drizzle milk over the pork chops.
3. Place pork chops in a zip-lock bag with flour and shake well to coat. Marinate pork chops for 30 minutes.

4. Place marinated pork chops into the air fryer basket and cook at 380°F for 15 minutes. Turn halfway through.
5. Serve and enjoy.

Smokehouse-style Beef Ribs

Servings: 3
Cooking Time: 25 Minutes
Ingredients:
- ¼ teaspoon Mild smoked paprika
- ¼ teaspoon Garlic powder
- ¼ teaspoon Onion powder
- ¼ teaspoon Table salt
- ¼ teaspoon Ground black pepper
- 3 10- to 12-ounce beef back ribs (not beef short ribs)

Directions:
1. Preheat the air fryer to 350°F .
2. Mix the smoked paprika, garlic powder, onion powder, salt, and pepper in a small bowl until uniform. Massage and pat this mixture onto the ribs.
3. When the machine is at temperature, set the ribs in the basket in one layer, turning them on their sides if necessary, sort of like they're spooning but with at least ¼ inch air space between them. Air-fry for 25 minutes, turning once, until deep brown and sizzling.
4. Use kitchen tongs to transfer the ribs to a wire rack. Cool for 5 minutes before serving.

German-style Pork Patties

Servings: 6
Cooking Time: 35 Minutes
Ingredients:
- 1 lb ground pork
- ¼ cup diced fresh pear
- 1 tbsp minced sage leaves
- 1 garlic clove, minced
- 2 tbsp chopped chives
- Salt and pepper to taste

Directions:
1. Preheat the air fryer to 375°F. Combine the pork, pear, sage, chives, garlic, salt, and pepper in a bowl and mix gently but thoroughly with your hands, then make 8 patties about ½ inch thick. Lay the patties in the frying basket in a single layer and Air Fry for 15-20 minutes, flipping once halfway through. Remove and drain on paper towels, then serve. Serve and enjoy!

Crispy Five-spice Pork Belly

Servings: 6
Cooking Time: 60-75 Minutes
Ingredients:
- 1½ pounds Pork belly with skin
- 3 tablespoons Shaoxing (Chinese cooking rice wine), dry sherry, or white grape juice
- 1½ teaspoons Granulated white sugar
- ¾ teaspoon Five-spice powder
- 1¼ cups Coarse sea salt or kosher salt

Directions:
1. Preheat the air fryer to 350°F .
2. Set the pork belly skin side up on a cutting board. Use a meat fork to make dozens and dozens of tiny holes all across the surface of the skin. You can hardly make too many holes. These will allow the skin to bubble up and keep it from becoming hard as it roasts.

3. Turn the pork belly over so that one of its longer sides faces you. Make four evenly spaced vertical slits in the meat. The slits should go about halfway into the meat toward the fat.

4. Mix the Shaoxing or its substitute, sugar, and five-spice powder in a small bowl until the sugar dissolves. Massage this mixture across the meat and into the cuts.

5. Turn the pork belly over again. Blot dry any moisture on the skin. Make a double-thickness aluminum foil tray by setting two 10-inch-long pieces of foil on top of another. Set the pork belly skin side up in the center of this tray. Fold the sides of the tray up toward the pork, crimping the foil as you work to make a high-sided case all around the pork belly. Seal the foil to the meat on all sides so that only the skin is exposed.

6. Pour the salt onto the skin and pat it down and in place to create a crust. Pick up the foil tray with the pork in it and set it in the basket.

7. Air-fry undisturbed for 35 minutes for a small batch, 45 minutes for a medium batch, or 50 minutes for a large batch.

8. Remove the foil tray with the pork belly still in it. Warning: The foil tray is full of scalding-hot fat. Discard the fat in the tray, as well as the tray itself. Transfer the pork belly to a cutting board.

9. Raise the air fryer temperature to 375°F. Brush the salt crust off the pork, removing any visible salt from the sides of the meat, too.

10. When the machine is at temperature, return the pork belly skin side up to the basket. Air-fry undisturbed for 25 minutes, or until crisp and very well browned. If the machine is at 390°F, you may be able to shave 5 minutes off the cooking time so that the skin doesn't blacken.

11. Use a nonstick-safe spatula, and perhaps a silicone baking mitt, to transfer the pork belly to a wire rack. Cool for 10 minutes before serving.

Tonkatsu

Servings: 3
Cooking Time: 10 Minutes
Ingredients:
- ½ cup All-purpose flour or tapioca flour
- 1 Large egg white(s), well beaten
- ¾ cup Plain panko bread crumbs (gluten-free, if a concern)
- 3 4-ounce center-cut boneless pork loin chops (about ½ inch thick)
- Vegetable oil spray

Directions:
1. Preheat the air fryer to 375°F .
2. Set up and fill three shallow soup plates or small pie plates on your counter: one for the flour, one for the beaten egg white(s), and one for the bread crumbs.
3. Set a chop in the flour and roll it to coat all sides, even the ends. Gently shake off any excess flour and set it in the egg white(s). Gently roll and turn it to coat all sides. Let any excess egg white slip back into the rest, then set the chop in the bread crumbs. Turn it several times, pressing gently to get an even coating on all sides and the ends. Generously coat the breaded chop with vegetable oil spray, then set it aside so you can dredge, coat, and spray the remaining chop(s).
4. Set the chops in the basket with as much air space between them as possible. Air-fry undisturbed for 10 minutes, or until golden brown and crisp.
5. Use kitchen tongs to transfer the chops to a wire rack and cool for a couple of minutes before serving.

Provençal Grilled Rib-eye

Servings: 4
Cooking Time: 25 Minutes
Ingredients:
- 4 ribeye steaks
- 1 tbsp herbs de Provence
- Salt and pepper to taste

Directions:
1. Preheat air fryer to 360°F. Season the steaks with herbs, salt and pepper. Place them in the greased frying basket and cook for 8-12 minutes, flipping once. Use a thermometer to check for doneness and adjust time as needed. Let the steak rest for a few minutes and serve.

Corn Dogs

Servings:4
Cooking Time: 8 Minutes
Ingredients:
- 1½ cups shredded mozzarella cheese
- 1 ounce cream cheese
- ½ cup blanched finely ground almond flour
- 4 beef hot dogs

Directions:
1. Place mozzarella, cream cheese, and flour in a large microwave-safe bowl. Microwave on high 45 seconds, then stir with a fork until a soft ball of dough forms.
2. Press dough out into a 12" × 6" rectangle, then use a knife to separate into four smaller rectangles.
3. Wrap each hot dog in one rectangle of dough and place into ungreased air fryer basket. Adjust the temperature to 400°F and set the timer for 8 minutes, turning corn dogs halfway through cooking. Corn dogs will be golden brown when done. Serve warm.

Beef Short Ribs

Servings:4
Cooking Time: 25 Minutes
Ingredients:
- 3 pounds beef short ribs
- 2 tablespoons olive oil
- 3 teaspoons salt
- 3 teaspoons ground black pepper
- ½ cup barbecue sauce

Directions:
1. Preheat the air fryer to 375°F.
2. Place short ribs in a large bowl. Drizzle with oil and sprinkle both sides with salt and pepper.
3. Place in the air fryer basket and cook 20 minutes. Remove from basket and brush with barbecue sauce. Return to the air fryer basket and cook 5 additional minutes until sauce is dark brown and internal temperature reaches at least 160°F. Serve warm.

Steakhouse Filets Mignons

Servings: 3
Cooking Time: 12-15 Minutes
Ingredients:
- ¾ ounce Dried porcini mushrooms
- ¼ teaspoon Granulated white sugar
- ¼ teaspoon Ground white pepper
- ¼ teaspoon Table salt
- 6 ¼-pound filets mignons or beef tenderloin steaks

- 6 Thin-cut bacon strips (gluten-free, if a concern)

Directions:

1. Preheat the air fryer to 400°F.
2. Grind the dried mushrooms in a clean spice grinder until powdery. Add the sugar, white pepper, and salt. Grind to blend.
3. Rub this mushroom mixture into both cut sides of each filet. Wrap the circumference of each filet with a strip of bacon.
4. Set the filets mignons in the basket on their sides with the bacon seam side down. Do not let the filets touch; keep at least ¼ inch open between them. Air-fry undisturbed for 12 minutes for rare, or until an instant-read meat thermometer inserted into the center of a filet registers 125°F; 13 minutes for medium-rare, or until an instant-read meat thermometer inserted into the center of a filet registers 132°F; or 15 minutes for medium, or until an instant-read meat thermometer inserted into the center of a filet registers 145°F.
5. Use kitchen tongs to transfer the filets to a wire rack, setting them cut side down. Cool for 5 minutes before serving.

Crispy Ham And Eggs

Servings: 3
Cooking Time: 9 Minutes

Ingredients:

- 2 cups Rice-puff cereal, such as Rice Krispies
- ¼ cup Maple syrup
- ½ pound ¼- to ½-inch-thick ham steak (gluten-free, if a concern)
- 1 tablespoon Unsalted butter
- 3 Large eggs
- ⅛ teaspoon Table salt
- ⅛ teaspoon Ground black pepper

Directions:

1. Preheat the air fryer to 400°F.
2. Pour the cereal into a food processor, cover, and process until finely ground. Pour the ground cereal into a shallow soup plate or a small pie plate.
3. Smear the maple syrup on both sides of the ham, then set the ham into the ground cereal. Turn a few times, pressing gently, until evenly coated.
4. Set the ham steak in the basket and air-fry undisturbed for 5 minutes, or until browned.
5. Meanwhile, melt the butter in a medium or large nonstick skillet set over medium heat. Crack the eggs into the skillet and cook until the whites are set and the yolks are hot, about 3 minutes. Season with the salt and pepper.
6. When the ham is ready, transfer it to a serving platter, then slip the eggs from the skillet on top of it. Divide into portions to serve.

Crunchy Veal Cutlets

Servings: 2
Cooking Time: 5 Minutes

Ingredients:

- ½ cup All-purpose flour or tapioca flour
- 1 Large egg(s), well beaten
- ¾ cup Seasoned Italian-style dried bread crumbs (gluten-free, if a concern)
- 2 tablespoons Yellow cornmeal
- 4 Thinly pounded 2-ounce veal leg cutlets (less than ¼ inch thick)
- Olive oil spray

Directions:

1. Preheat the air fryer to 400°F.
2. Set up and fill three shallow soup plates or small pie plates on your counter: one for the flour; one for the egg(s); and one for the bread crumbs, whisked with the cornmeal until well combined.
3. Dredge a veal cutlet in the flour, coating it on both sides. Gently shake off any excess flour, then gently dip it in the beaten egg(s), coating both sides. Let the excess egg slip back into the rest. Dip the cutlet in the bread-crumb mixture, turning it several times and pressing gently to make an even coating on both sides. Coat it on both sides with olive oil spray, then set it aside and continue dredging and coating more cutlets.
4. When the machine is at temperature, set the cutlets in the basket so that they don't touch each other. Air-fry undisturbed for 5 minutes, or until crisp and brown. (If only some of the veal cutlets will fit in one layer for any selected batch—the sizes of air fryer baskets vary dramatically—work in batches as necessary.)
5. Use kitchen tongs to transfer the cutlets to a wire rack. Cool for only 1 to 2 minutes before serving.

Pesto Coated Rack Of Lamb

Servings:4
Cooking Time:15 Minutes

Ingredients:

- ½ bunch fresh mint
- 1 rack of lamb
- 1 garlic clove
- ¼ cup extra-virgin olive oil
- ½ tablespoon honey
- Salt and black pepper, to taste

Directions:

1. Preheat the Air fryer to 200°F and grease an Air fryer basket.
2. Put the mint, garlic, oil, honey, salt, and black pepper in a blender and pulse until smooth to make pesto.
3. Coat the rack of lamb with this pesto on both sides and arrange in the Air fryer basket.
4. Cook for about 15 minutes and cut the rack into individual chops to serve.

Steak Kebabs

Servings:4
Cooking Time: 10 Minutes Per Batch

Ingredients:

- 1 ½ pounds sirloin steak, cut into 1" cubes
- 1 medium yellow onion, peeled and cut into 1" pieces
- 1 medium green bell pepper, seeded and cut into 1" pieces
- 1 medium red bell pepper, seeded and cut into 1" pieces
- 1 teaspoon salt
- ½ teaspoon ground black pepper
- 2 tablespoons olive oil

Directions:

1. Soak twelve 6" skewers in water 10 minutes to prevent burning. Preheat the air fryer to 400°F.
2. To assemble kebabs, place one piece of steak on skewer, then a piece of onion, green bell pepper, and red bell pepper. Repeat three times per skewer.
3. Sprinkle assembled kebabs with salt and black pepper, then drizzle with oil.
4. Place kebabs in the air fryer basket in a single layer, working in batches as necessary. Cook 10 minutes, turning

halfway through cooking time, until vegetables are tender, meat is brown, and internal temperature reaches at least 160°F. Serve warm.

Crispy Pierogi With Kielbasa And Onions

Servings: 3
Cooking Time: 20 Minutes
Ingredients:
- 6 Frozen potato and cheese pierogi, thawed
- ½ pound Smoked kielbasa, sliced into ½-inch-thick rounds
- ¾ cup Very roughly chopped sweet onion, preferably Vidalia
- Vegetable oil spray

Directions:
1. Preheat the air fryer to 375°F .
2. Put the pierogi, kielbasa rounds, and onion in a large bowl. Coat them with vegetable oil spray, toss well, spray again, and toss until everything is glistening.
3. When the machine is at temperature, dump the contents of the bowl it into the basket. Air-fry, tossing and rearranging everything twice so that all covered surfaces get exposed, for 20 minutes, or until the sausages have begun to brown and the pierogi are crisp.
4. Pour the contents of the basket onto a serving platter. Wait a minute or two just to take make sure nothing's searing hot before serving.

Salted 'n Peppered Scored Beef Chuck

Servings:6
Cooking Time: 1 Hour And 30 Minutes
Ingredients:
- 2 ounces black peppercorns
- 2 tablespoons olive oil
- 3 pounds beef chuck roll, scored with knife
- 3 tablespoons salt

Directions:
1. Preheat the air fryer to 390°F.
2. Place the grill pan accessory in the air fryer.
3. Season the beef chuck roll with black peppercorns and salt.
4. Brush with olive oil and cover top with foil.
5. Grill for 1 hour and 30 minutes.
6. Flip the beef every 30 minutes for even grilling on all sides.

Garlic Fillets

Servings: 4
Cooking Time: 15 Minutes
Ingredients:
- 1-pound beef filet mignon
- 1 teaspoon minced garlic
- 1 tablespoon peanut oil
- ½ teaspoon salt
- 1 teaspoon dried oregano

Directions:
1. Chop the beef into the medium size pieces and sprinkle with salt and dried oregano. Then add minced garlic and peanut oil and mix up the meat well. Place the bowl with meat in the fridge for 10 minutes to marinate. Meanwhile, preheat the air fryer to 400°F. Put the marinated beef pieces in the air fryer and cook them for 10 minutes Then flip the beef on another side and cook for 5 minutes more.

Jumbo Italian Meatballs

Servings:6

Cooking Time: 15 Minutes
Ingredients:
- 1 pound 80/20 ground beef
- ⅓ cup Italian bread crumbs
- 1 large egg
- 2 teaspoons Italian seasoning
- ¼ cup grated Parmesan cheese
- 1 teaspoon salt
- ½ teaspoon ground black pepper

Directions:
1. Preheat the air fryer to 400°F.
2. In a large bowl, mix all the ingredients. Roll mixture into balls, about 3" each, making twelve total.
3. Place meatballs in the air fryer basket and cook 15 minutes, shaking the basket twice during cooking, until meatballs are brown on the outside and internal temperature reaches at least 160°F. Serve warm.

Brown Sugar Mustard Pork Loin

Servings:4
Cooking Time: 35 Minutes
Ingredients:
- 1 pound boneless pork loin
- 1 tablespoon olive oil
- ¼ cup Dijon mustard
- ¼ cup brown sugar
- 1 teaspoon salt
- ½ teaspoon ground black pepper

Directions:
1. Preheat the air fryer to 400°F. Brush pork loin with oil.
2. In a small bowl, mix mustard, brown sugar, salt, and pepper. Brush mixture over both sides of pork loin and let sit 15 minutes.
3. Place in the air fryer basket and cook 20 minutes until internal temperature reaches 145°F. Let rest 10 minutes before slicing. Serve warm.

Sweet And Spicy Pork Ribs

Servings:4
Cooking Time: 20 Minutes Per Batch
Ingredients:
- 1 rack pork spareribs, white membrane removed
- ¼ cup brown sugar
- 2 teaspoons salt
- 2 teaspoons ground black pepper
- 1 tablespoon chili powder
- 1 teaspoon garlic powder
- ½ teaspoon cayenne pepper

Directions:
1. Preheat the air fryer to 400°F.
2. Place ribs on a work surface and cut the rack into two pieces to fit in the air fryer basket.
3. In a medium bowl, whisk together brown sugar, salt, black pepper, chili powder, garlic powder, and cayenne to make a dry rub.
4. Massage dry rub onto both sides of ribs until well coated. Place a portion of ribs in the air fryer basket, working in batches as necessary.
5. Cook 20 minutes until internal temperature reaches at least 190°F and no pink remains. Let rest 5 minutes before cutting and serving.

Spinach And Mushroom Steak Rolls

Servings:4
Cooking Time: 19 Minutes
Ingredients:
- ½ medium yellow onion, peeled and chopped
- ½ cup chopped baby bella mushrooms
- 1 cup chopped fresh spinach
- 1 pound flank steak
- 8 slices provolone cheese
- 1 teaspoon salt
- ½ teaspoon ground black pepper
- Cooking spray

Directions:
1. In a medium skillet over medium heat, sauté onion 2 minutes until fragrant and beginning to soften. Add mushrooms and spinach and continue cooking 5 more minutes until spinach is wilted and mushrooms are soft.
2. Preheat the air fryer to 400°F.
3. Carefully butterfly steak, leaving the two halves connected. Place slices of cheese on top of steak, then top with cooked vegetables.
4. Place steak so that the grain runs horizontally. Tightly roll up steak and secure it closed with eight evenly placed toothpicks or eight sections of butcher's twine.
5. Slice steak into four rolls. Spritz with cooking spray, then sprinkle with salt and pepper. Place in the air fryer basket and cook 12 minutes until steak is brown on the edges and internal temperature reaches at least 160°F for well-done. Serve.

Grilled Prosciutto Wrapped Fig

Servings:2
Cooking Time: 8 Minutes
Ingredients:
- 2 whole figs, sliced in quarters
- 8 prosciutto slices
- Pepper and salt to taste

Directions:
1. Wrap a prosciutto slice around one slice of figs and then thread into skewer. Repeat process for remaining Ingredients. Place on skewer rack in air fryer.
2. For 8 minutes, cook on 390°F. Halfway through cooking time, turnover skewers.
3. Serve and enjoy.

Chapter 5. Poultry Recipes

Crispy Cajun Fried Chicken

Servings: 4
Cooking Time: 50 Minutes
Ingredients:
- 4 boneless, skinless chicken thighs
- ¾ cup buttermilk
- ⅓ cup hot sauce
- 1 ½ tablespoons Cajun seasoning, divided
- 1 cup all-purpose flour
- 1 large egg

Directions:
1. Preheat the air fryer to 375°F.
2. In a large bowl, combine chicken thighs, buttermilk, hot sauce, and ½ tablespoon Cajun seasoning, and toss to coat. Cover and let marinate in refrigerator at least 30 minutes.
3. In a large bowl, whisk flour with ½ tablespoon Cajun seasoning. In a medium bowl, whisk egg.
4. Remove chicken from marinade and sprinkle with remaining ½ tablespoon Cajun seasoning.
5. Dredge chicken by dipping into egg, then pressing into flour to fully coat. Spritz with cooking spray and place into the air fryer basket.
6. Cook 20 minutes, turning halfway through cooking time, until chicken is golden brown and internal temperature reaches at least 165°F. Serve warm.

Chicken Nuggets

Servings:4
Cooking Time: 10 Minutes
Ingredients:
- 1 pound ground chicken breast
- 1 ½ teaspoons salt, divided
- ¾ teaspoon ground black pepper, divided
- 1 ½ cups plain bread crumbs, divided
- 2 large eggs

Directions:
1. Preheat the air fryer to 400°F.
2. In a large bowl, mix chicken, 1 teaspoon salt, ½ teaspoon pepper, and ½ cup bread crumbs.
3. In a small bowl, whisk eggs. In a separate medium bowl, mix remaining 1 cup bread crumbs with remaining ½ teaspoon salt and ¼ teaspoon pepper.
4. Scoop 1 tablespoon chicken mixture and flatten it into a nugget shape.
5. Dip into eggs, shaking off excess before rolling in bread crumb mixture. Repeat with remaining chicken mixture to make twenty nuggets.
6. Place nuggets in the air fryer basket and spritz with cooking spray. Cook 10 minutes, turning halfway through cooking time, until internal temperature reaches 165°F. Serve warm.

Cajun-breaded Chicken Bites

Servings:4
Cooking Time: 12 Minutes
Ingredients:
- 1 pound boneless, skinless chicken breasts, cut into 1" cubes
- ½ cup heavy whipping cream
- ½ teaspoon salt
- ¼ teaspoon ground black pepper

- 1 ounce plain pork rinds, finely crushed
- ¼ cup unflavored whey protein powder
- ½ teaspoon Cajun seasoning

Directions:

1. Place chicken in a medium bowl and pour in cream. Stir to coat. Sprinkle with salt and pepper.

2. In a separate large bowl, combine pork rinds, protein powder, and Cajun seasoning. Remove chicken from cream, shaking off any excess, and toss in dry mix until fully coated.

3. Place bites into ungreased air fryer basket. Adjust the temperature to 400°F and set the timer for 12 minutes, shaking the basket twice during cooking. Bites will be done when golden brown and have an internal temperature of at least 165°F. Serve warm.

Bacon-wrapped Chicken

Servings: 6
Cooking Time: 20 Minutes
Ingredients:

- 1 chicken breast, cut into 6 pieces
- 6 rashers back bacon
- 1 tbsp. soft cheese

Directions:

1. Put the bacon rashers on a flat surface and cover one side with the soft cheese.

2. Lay the chicken pieces on each bacon rasher. Wrap the bacon around the chicken and use a toothpick stick to hold each one in place. Put them in Air Fryer basket.

3. Air fry at 350°F for 15 minutes.

Tuscan Stuffed Chicken

Servings: 4
Cooking Time: 30 Minutes
Ingredients:

- 1/3 cup ricotta cheese
- 1 cup Tuscan kale, chopped
- 4 chicken breasts
- 1 tbsp chicken seasoning
- Salt and pepper to taste
- 1 tsp paprika

Directions:

1. Preheat air fryer to 370°F. Soften the ricotta cheese in a microwave-safe bowl for 15 seconds. Combine in a bowl along with Tuscan kale. Set aside. Cut 4-5 slits in the top of each chicken breast about ¾ of the way down. Season with chicken seasoning, salt, and pepper.

2. Place the chicken with the slits facing up in the greased frying basket. Lightly spray the chicken with oil. Bake for 6-8 minutes. Slide-out and stuff the cream cheese mixture into the chicken slits. Sprinkle ½ tsp of paprika and cook for another 3 minutes. Serve and enjoy!

Fried Chicken Halves

Servings: 4
Cooking Time: 75 Minutes
Ingredients:

- 16 oz whole chicken
- 1 tablespoon dried thyme
- 1 teaspoon ground cumin
- 1 teaspoon salt
- 1 tablespoon avocado oil

Directions:

1. Cut the chicken into halves and sprinkle it with dried thyme, cumin, and salt. Then brush the chicken halves with avocado oil. Preheat the air fryer to 365°F. Put the chicken halves in the air fryer and cook them for 60 minutes. Then flip the chicken halves on another side and cook them for 15 minutes more.

Hot Chicken Skin

Servings: 4
Cooking Time: 30 Minutes
Ingredients:

- ½ teaspoon chili paste
- 8 oz chicken skin
- 1 teaspoon sesame oil
- ½ teaspoon chili powder
- ½ teaspoon salt

Directions:

1. In the shallow bowl mix up chili paste, sesame oil, chili powder, and salt. Then brush the chicken skin with chili mixture well and leave for 10 minutes to marinate. Meanwhile, preheat the air fryer to 365°F. Put the marinated chicken skin in the air fryer and cook it for 20 minutes. When the time is finished, flip the chicken skin on another side and cook it for 10 minutes more or until the chicken skin is crunchy.

Roasted Chicken

Servings: 6
Cooking Time: 90 Minutes
Ingredients:

- 6 lb. whole chicken
- 1 tsp. olive oil
- 1 tbsp. minced garlic
- 1 white onion, peeled and halved
- 3 tbsp. butter

Directions:

1. Pre-heat the fryer at 360°F.

2. Massage the chicken with the olive oil and the minced garlic.

3. Place the peeled and halved onion, as well as the butter, inside of the chicken.

4. Cook the chicken in the fryer for seventy-five minutes.

5. Take care when removing the chicken from the fryer, then carve and serve.

Herb-marinated Chicken

Servings: 4
Cooking Time: 25 Minutes
Ingredients:

- 4 chicken breasts
- 2 tsp rosemary, minced
- 2 tsp thyme, minced
- Salt and pepper to taste
- ½ cup chopped cilantro
- 1 lime, juiced
- Cooking spray

Directions:

1. Place chicken in a resealable bag. Add rosemary, thyme, salt, pepper, cilantro, and lime juice. Seal the bag and toss to coat, then place in the refrigerator for 2 hours.

2. Preheat air fryer to 400°F. Arrange the chicken in a single layer in the greased frying basket. Spray the chicken with cooking oil. Air Fry for 6-7 minutes, then flip the chicken. Cook for another 3 minutes. Serve and enjoy!

Gingered Chicken Drumsticks

Servings:3
Cooking Time:25 Minutes
Ingredients:
- ¼ cup full-fat coconut milk
- 3 chicken drumsticks
- 2 teaspoons fresh ginger, minced
- 2 teaspoons galangal, minced
- 2 teaspoons ground turmeric
- Salt, to taste

Directions:
1. Preheat the Air fryer to 375°F and grease an Air fryer basket.
2. Mix the coconut milk, galangal, ginger, and spices in a bowl.
3. Add the chicken drumsticks and coat generously with the marinade.
4. Refrigerate to marinate for at least 8 hours and transfer into the Air fryer basket.
5. Cook for about 25 minutes and dish out the chicken drumsticks onto a serving platter.

Mustardy Chicken Bites

Servings: 4
Cooking Time: 20 Minutes + Chilling Time
Ingredients:
- 2 tbsp horseradish mustard
- 1 tbsp mayonnaise
- 1 tbsp olive oil
- 2 chicken breasts, cubes
- 1 tbsp parsley

Directions:
1. Combine all ingredients, excluding parsley, in a bowl. Let marinate covered in the fridge for 30 minutes. Preheat air fryer at 350°F. Place chicken cubes in the greased frying basket and Air Fry for 9 minutes, tossing once. Serve immediately sprinkled with parsley.

Jerk Chicken Kebabs

Servings:4
Cooking Time: 14 Minutes
Ingredients:
- 8 ounces boneless, skinless chicken thighs, cut into 1" cubes
- 2 tablespoons jerk seasoning
- 2 tablespoons coconut oil
- ½ medium red bell pepper, seeded and cut into 1" pieces
- ¼ medium red onion, peeled and cut into 1" pieces
- ½ teaspoon salt

Directions:
1. Place chicken in a medium bowl and sprinkle with jerk seasoning and coconut oil. Toss to coat on all sides.
2. Using eight 6" skewers, build skewers by alternating chicken, pepper, and onion pieces, about three repetitions per skewer.
3. Sprinkle salt over skewers and place into ungreased air fryer basket. Adjust the temperature to 370°F and set the timer for 14 minutes, turning skewers halfway through cooking.

Chicken will be golden and have an internal temperature of at least 165°F when done. Serve warm.

Pickle-brined Fried Chicken

Servings:4
Cooking Time: 20 Minutes
Ingredients:
- 4 boneless, skinless chicken thighs
- ⅓ cup dill pickle juice
- 1 large egg
- 2 ounces plain pork rinds, crushed
- ½ teaspoon salt
- ¼ teaspoon ground black pepper

Directions:
1. Place chicken thighs in a large sealable bowl or bag and pour pickle juice over them. Place sealed bowl or bag into refrigerator and allow to marinate at least 1 hour up to overnight.
2. In a small bowl, whisk egg. Place pork rinds in a separate medium bowl.
3. Remove chicken thighs from marinade. Shake off excess pickle juice and pat thighs dry with a paper towel. Sprinkle with salt and pepper.
4. Dip each thigh into egg and gently shake off excess. Press into pork rinds to coat each side. Place thighs into ungreased air fryer basket. Adjust the temperature to 400°F and set the timer for 20 minutes. When chicken thighs are done, they will be golden and crispy on the outside with an internal temperature of at least 165°F. Serve warm.

Chicken Wings

Servings: 4
Cooking Time: 55 Minutes
Ingredients:
- 3 lb. bone-in chicken wings
- ¾ cup flour
- 1 tbsp. old bay seasoning
- 4 tbsp. butter
- Couple fresh lemons

Directions:
1. In a bowl, combine the all-purpose flour and Old Bay seasoning.
2. Toss the chicken wings with the mixture to coat each one well.
3. Pre-heat the Air Fryer to 375°F.
4. Give the wings a shake to shed any excess flour and place each one in the Air Fryer. You may have to do this in multiple batches, so as to not overlap any.
5. Cook for 30 – 40 minutes, shaking the basket frequently, until the wings are cooked through and crispy.
6. In the meantime, melt the butter in a frying pan over a low heat. Squeeze one or two lemons and add the juice to the pan. Mix well.
7. Serve the wings topped with the sauce.

Crispy Tender Parmesan Chicken

Servings:2
Cooking Time: 20 Minutes
Ingredients:
- 1 tablespoon butter, melted
- 2 chicken breasts
- 2 tablespoons parmesan cheese

- 6 tablespoons almond flour

Directions:
1. Preheat the air fryer for 5 minutes.
2. Combine the almond flour and parmesan cheese in a plate.
3. Drizzle the chicken breasts with butter.
4. Dredge in the almond flour mixture.
5. Place in the fryer basket.
6. Cook for 20 minutes at 350°F.

Spinach And Feta Stuffed Chicken Breasts

Servings: 4
Cooking Time: 27 Minutes
Ingredients:
- 1 package frozen spinach, thawed and drained well
- 1 cup feta cheese, crumbled
- ½ teaspoon freshly ground black pepper
- 4 boneless chicken breasts
- salt and freshly ground black pepper
- 1 tablespoon olive oil

Directions:
1. Prepare the filling. Squeeze out as much liquid as possible from the thawed spinach. Rough chop the spinach and transfer it to a mixing bowl with the feta cheese and the freshly ground black pepper.
2. Prepare the chicken breast. Place the chicken breast on a cutting board and press down on the chicken breast with one hand to keep it stabilized. Make an incision about 1-inch long in the fattest side of the breast. Move the knife up and down inside the chicken breast, without poking through either the top or the bottom, or the other side of the breast. The inside pocket should be about 3-inches long, but the opening should only be about 1-inch wide. If this is too difficult, you can make the incision longer, but you will have to be more careful when cooking the chicken breast since this will expose more of the stuffing.
3. Once you have prepared the chicken breasts, use your fingers to stuff the filling into each pocket, spreading the mixture down as far as you can.
4. Preheat the air fryer to 380°F.
5. Lightly brush or spray the air fryer basket and the chicken breasts with olive oil. Transfer two of the stuffed chicken breasts to the air fryer. Air-fry for 12 minutes, turning the chicken breasts over halfway through the cooking time. Remove the chicken to a resting plate and air-fry the second two breasts for 12 minutes. Return the first batch of chicken to the air fryer with the second batch and air-fry for 3 more minutes. When the chicken is cooked, an instant read thermometer should register 165°F in the thickest part of the chicken, as well as in the stuffing.
6. Remove the chicken breasts and let them rest on a cutting board for 2 to 3 minutes. Slice the chicken on the bias and serve with the slices fanned out.

Buffalo Chicken Meatballs

Servings:5
Cooking Time: 12 Minutes
Ingredients:
- 1 pound ground chicken breast
- 1 packet dry ranch seasoning
- ⅓ cup plain bread crumbs
- 3 tablespoons mayonnaise
- 5 tablespoons buffalo sauce, divided

Directions:

1. Preheat the air fryer to 370°F.
2. In a large bowl, mix chicken, ranch seasoning, bread crumbs, and mayonnaise. Pour in 2 tablespoons buffalo sauce and stir to combine.
3. Roll meat mixture into balls, about 2 tablespoons for each, to make twenty meatballs.
4. Place meatballs in the air fryer basket and cook 12 minutes, shaking the basket twice during cooking, until brown and internal temperature reaches at least 165°F.
5. Toss meatballs in remaining buffalo sauce and serve.

Thyme Turkey Nuggets

Servings:2
Cooking Time: 20 Minutes
Ingredients:
- 1 egg, beaten
- 1 cup breadcrumbs
- 1 tbsp dried thyme
- ½ tbsp dried parsley
- Salt and pepper, to taste

Directions:
1. Preheat air fryer to 350°F. In a bowl, mix ground chicken, thyme, parsley, salt and pepper. Shape the mixture into balls. Dip in the breadcrumbs, then egg, then in the breadcrumbs again. Place the nuggets in the air fryer basket, spray with cooking spray cook for 10 minutes, shaking once.

Parmesan Chicken Tenders

Servings:4
Cooking Time: 12 Minutes
Ingredients:
- 1 pound boneless, skinless chicken breast tenderloins
- ½ cup mayonnaise
- 1 cup grated Parmesan cheese
- 1 cup panko bread crumbs
- ½ teaspoon garlic powder
- 1 teaspoon salt
- ½ teaspoon ground black pepper
- Cooking spray

Directions:
1. Preheat the air fryer to 400°F.
2. In a large bowl, add chicken and mayonnaise and toss to coat.
3. In a medium bowl, mix Parmesan, bread crumbs, garlic powder, salt, and pepper. Press chicken into bread crumb mixture to fully coat. Spritz with cooking spray and place in the air fryer basket.
4. Cook 12 minutes, turning halfway through cooking time, until tenders are golden and crisp on the edges and internal temperature reaches at least 165°F. Serve warm.

Grilled Chicken Pesto

Servings:8
Cooking Time: 30 Minutes
Ingredients:
- 1 ¾ cup commercial pesto
- 8 chicken thighs
- Salt and pepper to taste

Directions:
1. Place all Ingredients in the Ziploc bag and allow to marinate in the fridge for at least 2 hours.
2. Preheat the air fryer to 390°F.

3. Place the grill pan accessory in the air fryer.
4. Grill the chicken for at least 30 minutes.
5. Make sure to flip the chicken every 10 minutes for even grilling.

Popcorn Chicken

Servings:4
Cooking Time: 12 Minutes
Ingredients:
- 1 ½ teaspoons salt, divided
- 1 teaspoon ground black pepper, divided
- 1 ½ teaspoons garlic powder, divided
- 1 tablespoon mayonnaise
- 1 pound boneless, skinless chicken breast, cut into 1" cubes
- 1 cup panko bread crumbs

Directions:
1. Preheat the air fryer to 350°F.
2. In a large bowl, combine 1 teaspoon salt, ½ teaspoon pepper, 1 teaspoon garlic powder, and mayonnaise. Add chicken cubes and toss to coat.
3. Place bread crumbs in a large resealable bag and add remaining ½ teaspoon salt, ½ teaspoon pepper, and ½ teaspoon garlic powder. Place chicken into the bag and toss to evenly coat.
4. Spritz chicken with cooking spray and place in the air fryer basket. Cook 12 minutes, turning halfway through cooking time, until chicken is golden brown and internal temperature reaches at least 165°F. Serve warm.

Crunchy Chicken Strips

Servings: 4
Cooking Time: 40 Minutes
Ingredients:
- 1 chicken breast, sliced into strips
- 1 tbsp grated Parmesan cheese
- 1 cup breadcrumbs
- 1 tbsp chicken seasoning
- 2 eggs, beaten
- Salt and pepper to taste

Directions:
1. Preheat air fryer to 350°F. Mix the breadcrumbs, Parmesan cheese, chicken seasoning, salt, and pepper in a mixing bowl. Coat the chicken with the crumb mixture, then dip in the beaten eggs. Finally, coat again with the dry ingredients. Arrange the coated chicken pieces on the greased frying basket and Air Fry for 15 minutes. Turn over halfway through cooking and cook for another 15 minutes. Serve immediately.

Party Buffalo Chicken Drumettes

Servings: 6
Cooking Time: 30 Minutes
Ingredients:
- 16 chicken drumettes
- 1 tsp garlic powder
- 1 tbsp chicken seasoning
- Black pepper to taste
- ¼ cup Buffalo wings sauce
- 2 spring onions, sliced
- Cooking spray

Directions:
1. Preheat air fryer to 400°F. Sprinkle garlic, chicken seasoning, and black pepper on the drumettes. Place them in the fryer and spray with cooking oil. Air Fry for 10 minutes, shaking the basket once. Transfer the drumettes to a large bowl. Drizzle with Buffalo wing sauce and toss to coat. Place in the fryer and Fry for 7-8 minutes, until crispy. Allow to cool slightly. Top with spring onions and serve warm.

Dill Pickle–ranch Wings

Servings:4
Cooking Time: 2 Hours 20 Minutes
Ingredients:
- 1 cup pickle juice
- 2 pounds chicken wings, flats and drums separated
- ½ teaspoon salt
- ½ teaspoon ground black pepper
- 2 teaspoons dry ranch seasoning

Directions:
1. In a large bowl or resealable plastic bag, combine pickle juice and wings. Cover and let marinate in refrigerator 2 hours.
2. Preheat the air fryer to 400°F.
3. In a separate bowl, mix salt, pepper, and ranch seasoning. Remove wings from marinade and toss in dry seasoning.
4. Place wings in the air fryer basket in a single layer, working in batches as necessary. Cook 20 minutes, turning halfway through cooking time, until wings reach an internal temperature of at least 165°F. Cool 5 minutes before serving.

Fantasy Sweet Chili Chicken Strips

Servings: 2
Cooking Time: 20 Minutes
Ingredients:
- 1 lb chicken strips
- 1 cup sweet chili sauce
- ½ cup bread crumbs
- ½ cup cornmeal

Directions:
1. Preheat air fryer at 350°F. Combine chicken strips and sweet chili sauce in a bowl until fully coated. In another bowl, mix the remaining ingredients. Dredge strips in the mixture. Shake off any excess. Place chicken strips in the greased frying basket and Air Fry for 10 minutes, tossing once. Serve right away.

Italian Chicken Thighs

Servings: 4
Cooking Time: 30 Minutes
Ingredients:
- 4 skin-on bone-in chicken thighs
- 2 tbsp. unsalted butter, melted
- 3 tsp. Italian herbs
- ½ tsp. garlic powder
- ¼ tsp. onion powder

Directions:
1. Using a brush, coat the chicken thighs with the melted butter. Combine the herbs with the garlic powder and onion powder, then massage into the chicken thighs. Place the thighs in the fryer.
2. Cook at 380°F for 20 minutes, turning the chicken halfway through to cook on the other side.
3. When the thighs have achieved a golden color, test the temperature with a meat thermometer. Once they have reached 165°F, remove from the fryer and serve.

Butter And Bacon Chicken

Servings:6
Cooking Time: 65 Minutes
Ingredients:
- 1 whole chicken
- 2 tablespoons salted butter, softened
- 1 teaspoon dried thyme
- ½ teaspoon garlic powder
- 1 teaspoon salt
- ½ teaspoon ground black pepper
- 6 slices sugar-free bacon

Directions:
1. Pat chicken dry with a paper towel, then rub with butter on all sides. Sprinkle thyme, garlic powder, salt, and pepper over chicken.
2. Place chicken into ungreased air fryer basket, breast side up. Lay strips of bacon over chicken and secure with toothpicks.
3. Adjust the temperature to 350°F and set the timer for 65 minutes. Halfway through cooking, remove and set aside bacon and flip chicken over. Chicken will be done when the skin is golden and crispy and the internal temperature is at least 165°F. Serve warm with bacon.

Creamy Chicken Tenders

Servings:8
Cooking Time:20 Minutes
Ingredients:
- 2 pounds chicken tenders
- 1 cup feta cheese
- 4 tablespoons olive oil
- 1 cup cream
- Salt and black pepper, to taste

Directions:
1. Preheat the Air fryer to 340°F and grease an Air fryer basket.
2. Season the chicken tenders with salt and black pepper.
3. Arrange the chicken tenderloins in the Air fryer basket and drizzle with olive oil.
4. Cook for about 15 minutes and set the Air fryer to 390°F.
5. Cook for about 5 more minutes and dish out to serve warm.
6. Repeat with the remaining mixture and dish out to serve hot.

Cinnamon Chicken Thighs

Servings: 4
Cooking Time: 30 Minutes
Ingredients:
- 2 pounds chicken thighs
- A pinch of salt and black pepper
- 2 tablespoons olive oil
- ½ teaspoon cinnamon, ground

Directions:
1. Season the chicken thighs with salt and pepper, and rub with the rest of the ingredients. Put the chicken thighs in air fryer's basket, cook at 360°F for 15 minutes on each side, divide between plates and serve.

Chipotle Drumsticks

Servings:4
Cooking Time: 25 Minutes
Ingredients:
- 1 tablespoon tomato paste

- ½ teaspoon chipotle powder
- ¼ teaspoon apple cider vinegar
- ¼ teaspoon garlic powder
- 8 chicken drumsticks
- ½ teaspoon salt
- ⅛ teaspoon ground black pepper

Directions:
1. In a small bowl, combine tomato paste, chipotle powder, vinegar, and garlic powder.
2. Sprinkle drumsticks with salt and pepper, then place into a large bowl and pour in tomato paste mixture. Toss or stir to evenly coat all drumsticks in mixture.
3. Place drumsticks into ungreased air fryer basket. Adjust the temperature to 400°F and set the timer for 25 minutes, turning drumsticks halfway through cooking. Drumsticks will be dark red with an internal temperature of at least 165°F when done. Serve warm.

Blackened Chicken Tenders

Servings:4
Cooking Time: 12 Minutes
Ingredients:
- 1 pound boneless, skinless chicken tenders
- 2 teaspoons paprika
- 1 teaspoon garlic powder
- 1 teaspoon salt
- ½ teaspoon cayenne pepper
- ½ teaspoon dried thyme
- ½ teaspoon ground black pepper
- Cooking spray

Directions:
1. Preheat the air fryer to 400°F.
2. Place chicken tenders into a large bowl.
3. In a small bowl, mix paprika, garlic powder, salt, cayenne, thyme, and black pepper. Add spice mixture to chicken and toss to coat. Spritz chicken with cooking spray.
4. Place chicken in the air fryer basket and cook 12 minutes, turning halfway through cooking time, until chicken is brown at the edges and internal temperature reaches at least 165°F. Serve warm.

Spinach 'n Bacon Egg Cups

Servings:4
Cooking Time: 10 Minutes
Ingredients:
- ¼ cup spinach, chopped finely
- 1 bacon strip, fried and crumbled
- 3 tablespoons butter
- 4 eggs, beaten
- Salt and pepper to taste

Directions:
1. Preheat the air fryer for 5 minutes.
2. In a mixing bowl, combine the eggs, butter, and spinach. Season with salt and pepper to taste.
3. Grease a ramekin with cooking spray and pour the egg mixture inside.
4. Sprinkle with bacon bits.
5. Place the ramekin in the air fryer.
6. Cook for 10 minutes at 350°F.

15-minute Chicken

Servings:4
Cooking Time: 15 Minutes
Ingredients:
- 4 boneless, skinless chicken breasts
- 2 tablespoons olive oil
- 1 teaspoon salt
- 1 teaspoon garlic powder
- 1 teaspoon paprika
- ½ teaspoon ground black pepper

Directions:
1. Preheat the air fryer to 375°F.
2. Carefully butterfly chicken breasts lengthwise, leaving the two halves connected. Drizzle chicken with oil, then sprinkle with salt, garlic powder, paprika, and pepper.
3. Place in the air fryer basket and cook 15 minutes, turning halfway through cooking time, until chicken is golden brown and the internal temperature reaches at least 165°F. Serve warm.

Barbecue Chicken Enchiladas

Servings:4
Cooking Time: 15 Minutes Per Batch
Ingredients:
- 1 ½ cups barbecue sauce, divided
- 3 cups shredded cooked chicken
- 8 flour tortillas
- 1 ½ cups shredded Mexican-blend cheese, divided
- ⅓ cup diced red onion

Directions:
1. Preheat the air fryer to 350°F.
2. In a large bowl, mix 1 cup barbecue sauce and shredded chicken.
3. Place ¼ cup chicken onto each tortilla and top with 2 tablespoons cheese.
4. Roll each tortilla and place seam side down into two 6" round baking dishes. Brush tortillas with remaining sauce, top with remaining cheese, and sprinkle with onion.
5. Working in batches, place in the air fryer basket and cook 15 minutes until the sauce is bubbling and cheese is melted. Serve warm.

Family Chicken Fingers

Servings: 4
Cooking Time: 30 Minutes
Ingredients:
- 1 lb chicken breast fingers
- 1 tbsp chicken seasoning
- ½ tsp mustard powder
- Salt and pepper to taste
- 2 eggs
- 1 cup bread crumbs

Directions:
1. Preheat air fryer to 400°F. Add the chicken fingers to a large bowl along with chicken seasoning, mustard, salt, and pepper; mix well. Set up two small bowls. In one bowl, beat the eggs. In the second bowl, add the bread crumbs. Dip the chicken in the egg, then dredge in breadcrumbs. Place the nuggets in the air fryer. Lightly spray with cooking oil, then Air Fry for 8 minutes, shaking the basket once until crispy and cooked through. Serve warm.

Pretzel-crusted Chicken

Servings:4
Cooking Time: 12 Minutes
Ingredients:
- 2 cups mini twist pretzels
- ½ cup mayonnaise
- 2 tablespoons honey
- 2 tablespoons yellow mustard
- 4 boneless, skinless chicken breasts, sliced in half lengthwise
- 1 teaspoon salt
- ½ teaspoon ground black pepper
- Cooking spray

Directions:
1. Preheat the air fryer to 375°F.
2. In a food processor, place pretzels and pulse ten times.
3. In a medium bowl, mix mayonnaise, honey, and mustard.
4. Sprinkle chicken with salt and pepper, then brush with sauce mixture until well coated.
5. Pour pretzel crumbs onto a shallow plate and press each piece of chicken into them until well coated.
6. Spritz chicken with cooking spray and place in the air fryer basket. Cook 12 minutes, turning halfway through cooking time, until edges are golden brown and the internal temperature reaches at least 165°F. Serve warm.

Chipotle Aioli Wings

Servings:6
Cooking Time: 25 Minutes
Ingredients:
- 2 pounds bone-in chicken wings
- ½ teaspoon salt
- ¼ teaspoon ground black pepper
- 2 tablespoons mayonnaise
- 2 teaspoons chipotle powder
- 2 tablespoons lemon juice

Directions:
1. In a large bowl, toss wings in salt and pepper, then place into ungreased air fryer basket. Adjust the temperature to 400°F and set the timer for 25 minutes, shaking the basket twice while cooking. Wings will be done when golden and have an internal temperature of at least 165°F.
2. In a small bowl, whisk together mayonnaise, chipotle powder, and lemon juice. Place cooked wings into a large serving bowl and drizzle with aioli. Toss to coat. Serve warm.

Chicken Chunks

Servings: 4
Cooking Time: 10 Minutes
Ingredients:
- 1 pound chicken tenders cut in large chunks, about 1½ inches
- salt and pepper
- ½ cup cornstarch
- 2 eggs, beaten
- 1 cup panko breadcrumbs
- oil for misting or cooking spray

Directions:
1. Season chicken chunks to your liking with salt and pepper.
2. Dip chicken chunks in cornstarch. Then dip in egg and shake off excess. Then roll in panko crumbs to coat well.

3. Spray all sides of chicken chunks with oil or cooking spray.
4. Place chicken in air fryer basket in single layer and cook at 390°F for 5minutes. Spray with oil, turn chunks over, and spray other side.
5. Cook for an additional 5minutes or until chicken juices run clear and outside is golden brown.
6. Repeat steps 4 and 5 to cook remaining chicken.

Sticky Drumsticks

Servings: 4
Cooking Time: 45 Minutes
Ingredients:
- 1 lb chicken drumsticks
- 1 tbsp chicken seasoning
- 1 tsp dried chili flakes
- Salt and pepper to taste
- ¼ cup honey
- 1 cup barbecue sauce

Directions:
1. Preheat air fryer to 390°F. Season drumsticks with chicken seasoning, chili flakes, salt, and pepper. Place one batch of drumsticks in the greased frying basket and Air Fry for 18-20 minutes, flipping once until golden.
2. While the chicken is cooking, combine honey and barbecue sauce in a small bowl. Remove the drumsticks to a serving dish. Drizzle honey-barbecue sauce over and serve.

Pecan-crusted Chicken Tenders

Servings:4
Cooking Time: 12 Minutes
Ingredients:
- 2 tablespoons mayonnaise
- 1 teaspoon Dijon mustard
- 1 pound boneless, skinless chicken tenders
- ½ teaspoon salt
- ¼ teaspoon ground black pepper
- ½ cup chopped roasted pecans, finely ground

Directions:
1. In a small bowl, whisk mayonnaise and mustard until combined. Brush mixture onto chicken tenders on both sides, then sprinkle tenders with salt and pepper.
2. Place pecans in a medium bowl and press each tender into pecans to coat each side.
3. Place tenders into ungreased air fryer basket in a single layer, working in batches if needed. Adjust the temperature to 375°F and set the timer for 12 minutes, turning tenders halfway through cooking. Tenders will be golden brown and have an internal temperature of at least 165°F when done. Serve warm.

Chicken Parmesan Casserole

Servings:4
Cooking Time: 20 Minutes
Ingredients:
- 2 cups cubed cooked chicken breast
- ½ teaspoon salt
- ¼ teaspoon ground black pepper
- ¾ cup marinara sauce
- 2 teaspoons Italian seasoning, divided
- 1 cup shredded mozzarella cheese
- ½ cup grated Parmesan cheese

Directions:
1. Preheat the air fryer to 320°F.

2. In a large bowl, toss chicken with salt, pepper, marinara, and 1 teaspoon Italian seasoning.
3. Scrape mixture into a 6" round baking dish. Top with mozzarella, Parmesan, and remaining 1 teaspoon Italian seasoning.
4. Place in the air fryer basket and cook 20 minutes until the sauce is bubbling and cheese is brown and melted. Serve warm.

Chicken Fajita Poppers

Servings:18
Cooking Time: 20 Minutes
Ingredients:
- 1 pound ground chicken thighs
- ½ medium green bell pepper, seeded and finely chopped
- ¼ medium yellow onion, peeled and finely chopped
- ½ cup shredded pepper jack cheese
- 1 packet gluten-free fajita seasoning

Directions:
1. In a large bowl, combine all ingredients. Form mixture into eighteen 2" balls and place in a single layer into ungreased air fryer basket, working in batches if needed.
2. Adjust the temperature to 350°F and set the timer for 20 minutes. Carefully use tongs to turn poppers halfway through cooking. When 5 minutes remain on timer, increase temperature to 400°F to give the poppers a dark golden-brown color. Shake air fryer basket once more when 2 minutes remain on timer. Serve warm.

Sweet Lime 'n Chili Chicken Barbecue

Servings:2
Cooking Time: 40 Minutes
Ingredients:
- ¼ cup soy sauce
- 1 cup sweet chili sauce
- 1-pound chicken breasts
- Juice from 2 limes, freshly squeezed

Directions:
1. In a Ziploc bag, combine all Ingredients and give a good shake. Allow to marinate for at least 2 hours in the fridge.
2. Preheat the air fryer to 390°F.
3. Place the grill pan accessory in the air fryer.
4. Place chicken on the grill and cook for 30 to 40 minutes. Make sure to flip the chicken every 10 minutes to cook evenly.
5. Meanwhile, use the remaining marinade and put it in a saucepan. Simmer until the sauce thickens.
6. Once the chicken is cooked, brush with the thickened marinade.

Garlic Dill Wings

Servings:4
Cooking Time: 25 Minutes
Ingredients:
- 2 pounds bone-in chicken wings, separated at joints
- ½ teaspoon salt
- ½ teaspoon ground black pepper
- ½ teaspoon onion powder
- ½ teaspoon garlic powder
- 1 teaspoon dried dill

Directions:
1. In a large bowl, toss wings with salt, pepper, onion powder, garlic powder, and dill until evenly coated. Place wings into

ungreased air fryer basket in a single layer, working in batches if needed.

2. Adjust the temperature to 400°F and set the timer for 25 minutes, shaking the basket every 7 minutes during cooking. Wings should have an internal temperature of at least 165°F and be golden brown when done. Serve warm.

Salt And Pepper Wings

Servings:4
Cooking Time: 25 Minutes
Ingredients:
- 2 pounds bone-in chicken wings, separated at joints
- 1 teaspoon salt
- ½ teaspoon ground black pepper

Directions:
1. Sprinkle wings with salt and pepper, then place into ungreased air fryer basket in a single layer, working in batches if needed.
2. Adjust the temperature to 400°F and set the timer for 25 minutes, shaking the basket every 7 minutes during cooking. Wings should have an internal temperature of at least 165°F and be golden brown when done. Serve warm.

Lemon Sage Roast Chicken

Servings: 4
Cooking Time: 60 Minutes
Ingredients:
- 1 chicken
- 1 bunch sage, divided
- 1 lemon, zest and juice
- salt and freshly ground black pepper

Directions:
1. Preheat the air fryer to 350°F and pour a little water into the bottom of the air fryer drawer.
2. Run your fingers between the skin and flesh of the chicken breasts and thighs. Push a couple of sage leaves up underneath the skin of the chicken on each breast and each thigh.
3. Push some of the lemon zest up under the skin of the chicken next to the sage. Sprinkle some of the zest inside the chicken cavity, and reserve any leftover zest. Squeeze the lemon juice all over the chicken and in the cavity as well.
4. Season the chicken, inside and out, with the salt and freshly ground black pepper. Set a few sage leaves aside for the final garnish. Crumple up the remaining sage leaves and push them into the cavity of the chicken, along with one of the squeezed lemon halves.
5. Place the chicken breast side up into the air fryer basket and air-fry for 20 minutes at 350°F. Flip the chicken over so that it is breast side down and continue to air-fry for another 20 minutes. Return the chicken to breast side up and finish air-frying for 20 more minutes. The internal temperature of the chicken should register 165°F in the thickest part of the thigh when fully cooked. Remove the chicken from the air fryer and let it rest on a cutting board for at least 5 minutes.
6. Cut the rested chicken into pieces, sprinkle with the reserved lemon zest and garnish with the reserved sage leaves.

Shishito Pepper Rubbed Wings

Servings:6
Cooking Time: 30 Minutes
Ingredients:
- 1 ½ cups shishito peppers, pureed
- 2 tablespoons sesame oil

- 3 pounds chicken wings
- Salt and pepper to taste

Directions:
1. Place all Ingredients in a Ziploc bowl and allow to marinate for at least 2 hours in the fridge.
2. Preheat the air fryer to 390°F.
3. Place the grill pan accessory in the air fryer.
4. Grill for at least 30 minutes flipping the chicken every 5 minutes and basting with the remaining sauce.

Creamy Onion Chicken

Servings:4
Cooking Time: 20 Minutes
Ingredients:
- 1 ½ cup onion soup mix
- 1 cup mushroom soup
- ½ cup cream

Directions:
1. Preheat Fryer to 400°F. Add mushrooms, onion mix and cream in a frying pan. Heat on low heat for 1 minute. Pour the warm mixture over chicken slices and allow to sit for 25 minutes. Place the marinated chicken in the air fryer cooking basket and cook for 15 minutes. Serve with the remaining cream.

Basic Chicken Breasts.

Servings:4
Cooking Time: 15 Minutes
Ingredients:
- 2 tsp olive oil
- 2 chicken breasts
- Salt and pepper to taste
- ½ tsp garlic powder
- ½ tsp rosemary

Directions:
1. Preheat air fryer to 350°F. Rub the chicken breasts with olive oil over tops and bottom and sprinkle with garlic powder, rosemary, salt, and pepper. Place the chicken in the frying basket and Air Fry for 9 minutes, flipping once. Let rest onto a serving plate for 5 minutes before cutting into cubes. Serve and enjoy!

Pulled Turkey Quesadillas

Servings: 4
Cooking Time: 15 Minutes
Ingredients:
- ¾ cup pulled cooked turkey breast
- 6 tortilla wraps
- 1/3 cup grated Swiss cheese
- 1 small red onion, sliced
- 2 tbsp Mexican chili sauce

Directions:
1. Preheat air fryer to 400°F. Lay 3 tortilla wraps on a clean workspace, then spoon equal amounts of Swiss cheese, turkey, Mexican chili sauce, and red onion on the tortillas. Spritz the exterior of the tortillas with cooking spray. Air Fry the quesadillas, one at a time, for 5-8 minutes. The cheese should be melted and the outsides crispy. Serve.

Bacon Chicken Mix

Servings: 2
Cooking Time: 25 Minutes
Ingredients:
- 2 chicken legs
- 4 oz bacon, sliced
- ½ teaspoon salt
- ½ teaspoon ground black pepper
- 1 teaspoon sesame oil

Directions:
1. Sprinkle the chicken legs with salt and ground black pepper and wrap in the sliced bacon. After this, preheat the air fryer to 385°F. Put the chicken legs in the air fryer and sprinkle with sesame oil. Cook the bacon chicken legs for 25 minutes.

Barbecue Chicken Drumsticks

Servings:4
Cooking Time: 25 Minutes
Ingredients:
- 1 teaspoon salt
- 1 teaspoon chili powder
- 1 teaspoon garlic powder
- ½ teaspoon ground black pepper
- ½ teaspoon onion powder
- 8 chicken drumsticks
- 1 cup barbecue sauce, divided

Directions:
1. Preheat the air fryer to 375°F.
2. In a large bowl, combine salt, chili powder, garlic powder, pepper, and onion powder. Add drumsticks and toss to fully coat.
3. Brush drumsticks with ¾ cup barbecue sauce to coat.
4. Place in the air fryer basket and cook 25 minutes, turning three times during cooking, until drumsticks are brown and internal temperature reaches at least 165°F.
5. Before serving, brush remaining ¼ cup barbecue sauce over drumsticks. Serve warm.

Air Fried Chicken Tenderloin

Servings:8
Cooking Time: 15 Minutes
Ingredients:
- ½ cup almond flour
- 1 egg, beaten
- 2 tablespoons coconut oil
- 8 chicken tenderloins
- Salt and pepper to taste

Directions:
1. Preheat the air fryer for 5 minutes.
2. Season the chicken tenderloin with salt and pepper to taste.
3. Soak in beaten eggs then dredge in almond flour.
4. Place in the air fryer and brush with coconut oil.
5. Cook for 15 minutes at 375°F.
6. Halfway through the cooking time, give the fryer basket a shake to cook evenly.

Garlic Parmesan Drumsticks

Servings:4
Cooking Time: 25 Minutes
Ingredients:
- 8 chicken drumsticks
- ½ teaspoon salt
- ⅛ teaspoon ground black pepper
- ½ teaspoon garlic powder
- 2 tablespoons salted butter, melted
- ½ cup grated Parmesan cheese
- 1 tablespoon dried parsley

Directions:
1. Sprinkle drumsticks with salt, pepper, and garlic powder. Place drumsticks into ungreased air fryer basket.
2. Adjust the temperature to 400°F and set the timer for 25 minutes, turning drumsticks halfway through cooking. Drumsticks will be golden and have an internal temperature of at least 165°F when done.
3. Transfer drumsticks to a large serving dish. Pour butter over drumsticks, and sprinkle with Parmesan and parsley. Serve warm.

Easy & Crispy Chicken Wings

Servings: 8
Cooking Time: 20 Minutes
Ingredients:
- 1 1/2 lbs chicken wings
- 2 tbsp olive oil
- Pepper
- Salt

Directions:
1. Toss chicken wings with oil and place in the air fryer basket.
2. Cook chicken wings at 370°F for 15 minutes.
3. Shake basket and cook at 400 F for 5 minutes more.
4. Season chicken wings with pepper and salt.
5. Serve and enjoy.

Chicken Tenders With Basil-strawberry Glaze

Servings:4
Cooking Time: 20 Minutes
Ingredients:
- 1 lb chicken tenderloins
- ¼ cup strawberry preserves
- 3 tbsp chopped basil
- 1 tsp orange juice
- ½ tsp orange zest
- Salt and pepper to taste

Directions:
1. Combine all ingredients, except for 1 tbsp of basil, in a bowl. Marinade in the fridge covered for 30 minutes.
2. Preheat air fryer to 350ºF. Place the chicken tenders in the frying basket and Air Fry for 4-6 minutes. Shake gently the basket and turn over the chicken. Cook for 5 more minutes. Top with the remaining basil to serve.

Balsamic Duck And Cranberry Sauce

Servings: 4
Cooking Time: 25 Minutes
Ingredients:
- 4 duck breasts, boneless, skin-on and scored
- A pinch of salt and black pepper
- 1 tablespoon olive oil
- ¼ cup balsamic vinegar
- ½ cup dried cranberries

Directions:

1. Heat up a pan that fits your air fryer with the oil over medium-high heat, add the duck breasts skin side down and cook for 5 minutes. Add the rest of the ingredients, toss, put the pan in the fryer and cook at 380°F for 20 minutes. Divide between plates and serve.

Turkey-hummus Wraps

Servings: 4
Cooking Time: 7 Minutes Per Batch
Ingredients:
- 4 large whole wheat wraps
- ½ cup hummus
- 16 thin slices deli turkey
- 8 slices provolone cheese
- 1 cup fresh baby spinach (or more to taste)

Directions:

1. To assemble, place 2 tablespoons of hummus on each wrap and spread to within about a half inch from edges. Top with 4 slices of turkey and 2 slices of provolone. Finish with ¼ cup of baby spinach—or pile on as much as you like.
2. Roll up each wrap. You don't need to fold or seal the ends.
3. Place 2 wraps in air fryer basket, seam side down.
4. Cook at 360°F for 4minutes to warm filling and melt cheese. If you like, you can continue cooking for 3 more minutes, until the wrap is slightly crispy.
5. Repeat step 4 to cook remaining wraps.

Hasselback Alfredo Chicken

Servings:4
Cooking Time: 20 Minutes
Ingredients:
- 4 boneless, skinless chicken breasts
- 4 teaspoons coconut oil
- ½ teaspoon salt
- ¼ teaspoon ground black pepper
- 4 strips cooked sugar-free bacon, broken into 24 pieces
- ½ cup Alfredo sauce
- 1 cup shredded mozzarella cheese
- ¼ teaspoon crushed red pepper flakes

Directions:

1. Cut six horizontal slits in the top of each chicken breast. Drizzle with coconut oil and sprinkle with salt and black pepper. Place into an ungreased 6" round nonstick baking dish.
2. Place 1 bacon piece in each slit in chicken breasts. Pour Alfredo sauce over chicken and sprinkle with mozzarella and red pepper flakes.
3. Place dish into air fryer basket. Adjust the temperature to 370°F and set the timer for 20 minutes. Chicken will be done when internal temperature is at least 165°F and cheese is browned. Serve warm.

Teriyaki Chicken Legs

Servings: 2
Cooking Time: 20 Minutes
Ingredients:
- 4 tablespoons teriyaki sauce
- 1 tablespoon orange juice
- 1 teaspoon smoked paprika
- 4 chicken legs
- cooking spray

Directions:

1. Mix together the teriyaki sauce, orange juice, and smoked paprika. Brush on all sides of chicken legs.
2. Spray air fryer basket with nonstick cooking spray and place chicken in basket.
3. Cook at 360°F for 6minutes. Turn and baste with sauce. Cook for 6 moreminutes, turn and baste. Cook for 8 minutes more, until juices run clear when chicken is pierced with a fork.

Yummy Stuffed Chicken Breast

Servings:4
Cooking Time:15 Minutes
Ingredients:
- 2 chicken fillets, skinless and boneless, each cut into 2 pieces
- 4 brie cheese slices
- 1 tablespoon chive, minced
- 4 cured ham slices
- Salt and black pepper, to taste

Directions:

1. Preheat the Air fryer to 355°F and grease an Air fryer basket.
2. Make a slit in each chicken piece horizontally and season with the salt and black pepper.
3. Insert cheese slice in the slits and sprinkle with chives.
4. Wrap each chicken piece with one ham slice and transfer into the Air fryer basket.
5. Cook for about 15 minutes and dish out to serve warm.

Fried Herbed Chicken Wings

Servings: 4
Cooking Time: 11 Minutes
Ingredients:
- 1 tablespoon Emperor herbs chicken spices
- 8 chicken wings
- Cooking spray

Directions:

1. Generously sprinkle the chicken wings with Emperor herbs chicken spices and place in the preheated to 400°F air fryer. Cook the chicken wings for 6 minutes from each side.

Buffalo Chicken Wings

Servings: 3
Cooking Time: 37 Minutes
Ingredients:
- 2 lb. chicken wings
- 1 tsp. salt
- ¼ tsp. black pepper
- 1 cup buffalo sauce

Directions:

1. Wash the chicken wings and pat them dry with clean kitchen towels.
2. Place the chicken wings in a large bowl and sprinkle on salt and pepper.
3. Pre-heat the Air Fryer to 380°F.
4. Place the wings in the fryer and cook for 15 minutes, giving them an occasional stir throughout.
5. Place the wings in a bowl. Pour over the buffalo sauce and toss well to coat.
6. Put the chicken back in the Air Fryer and cook for a final 5 – 6 minutes.

Crispy Italian Chicken Thighs

Servings:4
Cooking Time: 25 Minutes
Ingredients:
- ½ cup mayonnaise
- 4 bone-in, skin-on chicken thighs
- 1 teaspoon salt
- ½ teaspoon ground black pepper
- 2 teaspoons Italian seasoning
- 1 cup Italian bread crumbs

Directions:
1. Preheat the air fryer to 370°F.
2. Brush mayonnaise over chicken thighs on both sides.
3. Sprinkle thighs with salt, pepper, and Italian seasoning.
4. Place bread crumbs into a resealable plastic bag and add thighs. Shake to coat.
5. Remove thighs from bag and spritz with cooking spray. Place in the air fryer basket and cook 25 minutes, turning thighs after 15 minutes, until skin is golden and crispy and internal temperature reaches at least 165°F.
6. Serve warm.

Chicken & Pepperoni Pizza

Servings: 6
Cooking Time: 20 Minutes
Ingredients:
- 2 cups cooked chicken, cubed
- 20 slices pepperoni
- 1 cup sugar-free pizza sauce
- 1 cup mozzarella cheese, shredded
- ¼ cup parmesan cheese, grated

Directions:
1. Place the chicken into the base of a four-cup baking dish and add the pepperoni and pizza sauce on top. Mix well so as to completely coat the meat with the sauce.
2. Add the parmesan and mozzarella on top of the chicken, then place the baking dish into your fryer.
3. Cook for 15 minutes at 375°F.
4. When everything is bubbling and melted, remove from the fryer. Serve hot.

Perfect Grill Chicken Breast

Servings: 2
Cooking Time: 12 Minutes
Ingredients:
- 2 chicken breast, skinless and boneless
- 2 tsp olive oil
- Pepper
- Salt

Directions:
1. Remove air fryer basket and replace it with air fryer grill pan.
2. Place chicken breast to the grill pan. Season chicken with pepper and salt. Drizzle with oil.
3. Cook chicken for 375°F for 12 minutes.
4. Serve and enjoy.

Spice-rubbed Chicken Thighs

Servings:4
Cooking Time: 25 Minutes
Ingredients:
- 4 bone-in, skin-on chicken thighs
- ½ teaspoon salt
- ½ teaspoon garlic powder
- 2 teaspoons chili powder
- 1 teaspoon paprika
- 1 teaspoon ground cumin
- 1 small lime, halved

Directions:
1. Pat chicken thighs dry and sprinkle with salt, garlic powder, chili powder, paprika, and cumin.
2. Squeeze juice from ½ lime over thighs. Place thighs into ungreased air fryer basket. Adjust the temperature to 380°F and set the timer for 25 minutes, turning thighs halfway through cooking. Thighs will be crispy and browned with an internal temperature of at least 165°F when done.
3. Transfer thighs to a large serving plate and drizzle with remaining lime juice. Serve warm.

Broccoli And Cheese–stuffed Chicken

Servings:4
Cooking Time: 20 Minutes
Ingredients:
- 2 ounces cream cheese, softened
- 1 cup chopped fresh broccoli, steamed
- ½ cup shredded sharp Cheddar cheese
- 4 boneless, skinless chicken breasts
- 2 tablespoons mayonnaise
- ¼ teaspoon salt
- ¼ teaspoon garlic powder
- ⅛ teaspoon ground black pepper

Directions:
1. In a medium bowl, combine cream cheese, broccoli, and Cheddar. Cut a 4" pocket into each chicken breast. Evenly divide mixture between chicken breasts; stuff the pocket of each chicken breast with the mixture.
2. Spread ¼ tablespoon mayonnaise per side of each chicken breast, then sprinkle both sides of breasts with salt, garlic powder, and pepper.
3. Place stuffed chicken breasts into ungreased air fryer basket so that the open seams face up. Adjust the temperature to 350°F and set the timer for 20 minutes, turning chicken halfway through cooking. When done, chicken will be golden and have an internal temperature of at least 165°F. Serve warm.

Quick Chicken For Filling

Servings: 2
Cooking Time: 8 Minutes
Ingredients:
- 1 pound chicken tenders, skinless and boneless
- ½ teaspoon ground cumin
- ½ teaspoon garlic powder
- cooking spray

Directions:
1. Sprinkle raw chicken tenders with seasonings.
2. Spray air fryer basket lightly with cooking spray to prevent sticking.
3. Place chicken in air fryer basket in single layer.
4. Cook at 390°F for 4minutes, turn chicken strips over, and cook for an additional 4minutes.
5. Test for doneness. Thick tenders may require an additional minute or two.

Crispy "fried" Chicken

Servings: 4
Cooking Time: 14 Minutes
Ingredients:
- ¾ cup all-purpose flour
- ½ teaspoon paprika
- ¼ teaspoon black pepper
- ¼ teaspoon salt
- 2 large eggs
- 1½ cups panko breadcrumbs
- 1 pound boneless, skinless chicken tenders

Directions:
1. Preheat the air fryer to 400°F.
2. In a shallow bowl, mix the flour with the paprika, pepper, and salt.
3. In a separate bowl, whisk the eggs; set aside.
4. In a third bowl, place the breadcrumbs.
5. Liberally spray the air fryer basket with olive oil spray.
6. Pat the chicken tenders dry with a paper towel. Dredge the tenders one at a time in the flour, then dip them in the egg, and toss them in the breadcrumb coating. Repeat until all tenders are coated.
7. Set each tender in the air fryer, leaving room on each side of the tender to allow for flipping.
8. When the basket is full, cook 4 to 7 minutes, flip, and cook another 4 to 7 minutes.
9. Remove the tenders and let cool 5 minutes before serving. Repeat until all tenders are cooked.

Zesty Ranch Chicken Drumsticks

Servings: 4
Cooking Time: 20 Minutes
Ingredients:
- 8 chicken drumsticks
- 1 teaspoon salt
- ½ teaspoon ground black pepper
- ¼ cup dry ranch seasoning
- ½ cup panko bread crumbs
- ½ cup grated Parmesan cheese

Directions:
1. Preheat the air fryer to 375°F.
2. Sprinkle drumsticks with salt, pepper, and ranch seasoning.
3. In a paper lunch bag, combine bread crumbs and Parmesan. Add drumsticks to the bag and shake to coat. Spritz with cooking spray.
4. Place drumsticks in the air fryer basket and cook 20 minutes, turning halfway through cooking time, until the internal temperature reaches at least 165°F. Serve warm.

Ginger Turmeric Chicken Thighs

Servings: 4
Cooking Time: 25 Minutes
Ingredients:
- 4 boneless, skin-on chicken thighs
- 2 tablespoons coconut oil, melted
- ½ teaspoon ground turmeric
- ½ teaspoon salt
- ½ teaspoon garlic powder
- ½ teaspoon ground ginger
- ¼ teaspoon ground black pepper

Directions:

1. Place chicken thighs in a large bowl and drizzle with coconut oil. Sprinkle with remaining ingredients and toss to coat both sides of thighs.
2. Place thighs skin side up into ungreased air fryer basket. Adjust the temperature to 400°F and set the timer for 25 minutes. After 10 minutes, turn thighs. When 5 minutes remain, flip thighs once more. Chicken will be done when skin is golden brown and the internal temperature is at least 165°F. Serve warm.

Lemon Pepper Chicken Wings

Servings: 4
Cooking Time: 16 Minutes
Ingredients:
- 1 lb chicken wings
- 1 tsp lemon pepper
- 1 tbsp olive oil
- 1 tsp salt

Directions:
1. Add chicken wings into the large mixing bowl.
2. Add remaining ingredients over chicken and toss well to coat.
3. Place chicken wings in the air fryer basket.
4. Cook chicken wings for 8 minutes at 400°F.
5. Turn chicken wings to another side and cook for 8 minutes more.
6. Serve and enjoy.

Chicken Pesto Pizzas

Servings:4
Cooking Time: 12 Minutes
Ingredients:
- 1 pound ground chicken thighs
- ¼ teaspoon salt
- ⅛ teaspoon ground black pepper
- ¼ cup basil pesto
- 1 cup shredded mozzarella cheese
- 4 grape tomatoes, sliced

Directions:
1. Cut four squares of parchment paper to fit into your air fryer basket.
2. Place ground chicken in a large bowl and mix with salt and pepper. Divide mixture into four equal sections.
3. Wet your hands with water to prevent sticking, then press each section into a 6" circle onto a piece of ungreased parchment. Place each chicken crust into air fryer basket, working in batches if needed.
4. Adjust the temperature to 350°F and set the timer for 10 minutes, turning crusts halfway through cooking.
5. When the timer beeps, spread 1 tablespoon pesto across the top of each crust, then sprinkle with ¼ cup mozzarella and top with 1 sliced tomato. Continue cooking at 350°F for 2 minutes. Cheese will be melted and brown when done. Serve warm.

Cornish Hens With Honey-lime Glaze

Servings: 2
Cooking Time: 30 Minutes
Ingredients:
- 1 Cornish game hen
- 1 tablespoon honey
- 1 tablespoon lime juice
- 1 teaspoon poultry seasoning

- salt and pepper
- cooking spray

Directions:
1. To split the hen into halves, cut through breast bone and down one side of the backbone.
2. Mix the honey, lime juice, and poultry seasoning together and brush or rub onto all sides of the hen. Season to taste with salt and pepper.
3. Spray air fryer basket with cooking spray and place hen halves in the basket, skin-side down.
4. Cook at 330°F for 30 minutes. Hen will be done when juices run clear when pierced at leg joint with a fork. Let hen rest for 5 to 10 minutes before cutting.

Chicken Gruyere

Servings:4
Cooking Time: 20 Minutes
Ingredients:
- ¼ cup Gruyere cheese, grated
- 1 pound chicken breasts, boneless, skinless
- ½ cup flour
- 2 eggs, beaten
- Sea salt and black pepper to taste
- 4 lemon slices
- Cooking spray

Directions:
1. Preheat your Air Fryer to 370°F. Spray the air fryer basket with cooking spray.
2. Mix the breadcrumbs with Gruyere cheese in a bowl, pour the eggs in another bowl, and the flour in a third bowl. Toss the chicken in the flour, then in the eggs, and then in the breadcrumb mixture. Place in the fryer basket, close and cook for 12 minutes. At the 6-minute mark, turn the chicken over. Once golden brown, remove onto a serving plate and serve topped with lemon slices.

Sweet Nutty Chicken Breasts

Servings:4
Cooking Time: 30 Minutes
Ingredients:
- 2 chicken breasts, halved lengthwise
- ¼ cup honey mustard
- ¼ cup chopped pecans
- 1 tbsp olive oil
- 1 tbsp parsley, chopped

Directions:
1. Preheat air fryer to 350°F. Brush chicken breasts with honey mustard and olive oil on all sides. Place the pecans in a bowl. Add and coat the chicken breasts. Place the breasts in the greased frying basket and Air Fry for 25 minutes, turning once. Let chill onto a serving plate for 5 minutes. Sprinkle with parsley and serve.

Simple Salsa Chicken Thighs

Servings:2
Cooking Time: 35 Minutes
Ingredients:
- 1 lb boneless, skinless chicken thighs
- 1 cup mild chunky salsa
- ½ tsp taco seasoning
- 2 lime wedges for serving

Directions:

1. Preheat air fryer to 350°F. Add chicken thighs into a baking pan and pour salsa and taco seasoning over. Place the pan in the frying basket and Air Fry for 30 minutes until golden brown. Serve with lime wedges.

Peppery Lemon-chicken Breast

Servings:1
Cooking Time:
Ingredients:
- 1 chicken breast
- 1 teaspoon minced garlic
- 2 lemons, rinds and juice reserved
- Salt and pepper to taste

Directions:
1. Preheat the air fryer.
2. Place all ingredients in a baking dish that will fit in the air fryer.
3. Place in the air fryer basket.
4. Close and cook for 20 minutes at 400°F.

Basic Chicken Breasts

Servings: 4
Cooking Time: 15 Minutes
Ingredients:
- 2 tsp olive oil
- 4 chicken breasts
- Salt and pepper to taste
- 1 tbsp Italian seasoning

Directions:
1. Preheat air fryer at 350°F. Rub olive oil over chicken breasts and sprinkle with salt, Italian seasoning and black pepper. Place them in the frying basket and Air Fry for 8-10 minutes. Let rest for 5 minutes before cutting. Store it covered in the fridge for up to 1 week.

Herb Seasoned Turkey Breast

Servings: 4
Cooking Time: 35 Minutes
Ingredients:
- 2 lbs turkey breast
- 1 tsp fresh sage, chopped
- 1 tsp fresh rosemary, chopped
- 1 tsp fresh thyme, chopped
- Pepper
- Salt

Directions:
1. Spray air fryer basket with cooking spray.
2. In a small bowl, mix together sage, rosemary, and thyme.
3. Season turkey breast with pepper and salt and rub with herb mixture.
4. Place turkey breast in air fryer basket and cook at 390°F for 30-35 minutes.
5. Slice and serve.

Buttermilk Brined Turkey Breast

Servings:8
Cooking Time:20 Minutes
Ingredients:
- ¾ cup brine from a can of olives
- 3½ pounds boneless, skinless turkey breast
- 2 fresh thyme sprigs
- 1 fresh rosemary sprig

- ½ cup buttermilk

Directions:

1. Preheat the Air fryer to 350°F and grease an Air fryer basket.
2. Mix olive brine and buttermilk in a bowl until well combined.
3. Place the turkey breast, buttermilk mixture and herb sprigs in a resealable plastic bag.
4. Seal the bag and refrigerate for about 12 hours.
5. Remove the turkey breast from bag and arrange the turkey breast into the Air fryer basket.
6. Cook for about 20 minutes, flipping once in between.
7. Dish out the turkey breast onto a cutting board and cut into desired size slices to serve.

Air Fried Cheese Chicken

Servings:6
Cooking Time: 15 Minutes
Ingredients:

- 6 tbsp seasoned breadcrumbs
- 2 tbsp Parmesan cheese, grated
- 1 tbsp melted butter
- ½ cup mozzarella cheese, shredded
- 1 tbsp marinara sauce
- Cooking spray as needed

Directions:

1. Preheat your air fryer to 390°F. Grease the cooking basket with cooking spray. In a small bowl, mix breadcrumbs and Parmesan cheese. Brush the chicken pieces with butter and dredge into the breadcrumbs. Add chicken to the cooking basket and cook for 6 minutes. Turn over and top with marinara sauce and shredded mozzarella; cook for 3 more minutes.

Chicken Thighs In Salsa Verde

Servings: 4
Cooking Time: 35 Minutes
Ingredients:

- 4 boneless, skinless chicken thighs
- 1 cup salsa verde
- 1 tsp mashed garlic

Directions:

1. Preheat air fryer at 350ºF. Add chicken thighs to a cake pan and cover with salsa verde and mashed garlic. Place cake pan in the frying basket and Bake for 30 minutes. Let rest for 5 minutes before serving.

Quick 'n Easy Garlic Herb Wings

Servings:4
Cooking Time: 35 Minutes
Ingredients:

- ¼ cup chopped rosemary
- 2 pounds chicken wings
- 6 medium garlic cloves , grated
- Salt and pepper to taste

Directions:

1. Season the chicken with garlic, rosemary, salt and pepper.
2. Preheat the air fryer to 390°F.
3. Place the grill pan accessory in the air fryer.
4. Grill for 35 minutes and make sure to flip the chicken every 10 minutes.

Spicy Pork Rind Fried Chicken

Servings:4
Cooking Time: 20 Minutes
Ingredients:

- ¼ cup buffalo sauce
- 4 boneless, skinless chicken breasts
- ½ teaspoon paprika
- ½ teaspoon garlic powder
- ¼ teaspoon ground black pepper
- 2 ounces plain pork rinds, finely crushed

Directions:

1. Pour buffalo sauce into a large sealable bowl or bag. Add chicken and toss to coat. Place sealed bowl or bag into refrigerator and let marinate at least 30 minutes up to overnight.
2. Remove chicken from marinade but do not shake excess sauce off chicken. Sprinkle both sides of thighs with paprika, garlic powder, and pepper.
3. Place pork rinds into a large bowl and press each chicken breast into pork rinds to coat evenly on both sides.
4. Place chicken into ungreased air fryer basket. Adjust the temperature to 400°F and set the timer for 20 minutes, turning chicken halfway through cooking. Chicken will be golden and have an internal temperature of at least 165°F when done. Serve warm.

Baked Chicken Nachos

Servings:4
Cooking Time: 7 Minutes
Ingredients:

- 50 tortilla chips
- 2 cups shredded cooked chicken breast, divided
- 2 cups shredded Mexican-blend cheese, divided
- ½ cup sliced pickled jalapeño peppers, divided
- ½ cup diced red onion, divided

Directions:

1. Preheat the air fryer to 300°F.
2. Use foil to make a bowl shape that fits the shape of the air fryer basket. Place half tortilla chips in the bottom of foil bowl, then top with 1 cup chicken, 1 cup cheese, ¼ cup jalapeños, and ¼ cup onion. Repeat with remaining chips and toppings.
3. Place foil bowl in the air fryer basket and cook 7 minutes until cheese is melted and toppings heated through. Serve warm.

Buttermilk-fried Drumsticks

Servings: 2
Cooking Time: 25 Minutes
Ingredients:

- 1 egg
- ½ cup buttermilk
- ¾ cup self-rising flour
- ¾ cup seasoned panko breadcrumbs
- 1 teaspoon salt
- ¼ teaspoon ground black pepper (to mix into coating)
- 4 chicken drumsticks, skin on
- oil for misting or cooking spray

Directions:

1. Beat together egg and buttermilk in shallow dish.
2. In a second shallow dish, combine the flour, panko crumbs, salt, and pepper.
3. Sprinkle chicken legs with additional salt and pepper to taste.

4. Dip legs in buttermilk mixture, then roll in panko mixture, pressing in crumbs to make coating stick. Mist with oil or cooking spray.

5. Spray air fryer basket with cooking spray.

6. Cook drumsticks at 360°F for 10 minutes. Turn pieces over and cook an additional 10minutes.

7. Turn pieces to check for browning. If you have any white spots that haven't begun to brown, spritz them with oil or cooking spray. Continue cooking for 5 more minutes or until crust is golden brown and juices run clear. Larger, meatier drumsticks will take longer to cook than small ones.

Chicken Cordon Bleu

Servings:4
Cooking Time: 15 Minutes
Ingredients:
- 4 boneless, skinless chicken breasts
- ¾ teaspoon salt
- ½ teaspoon ground black pepper
- 8 slices deli Black Forest ham
- 8 slices Gruyère cheese
- 1 large egg, beaten
- 2 cups panko bread crumbs

Directions:
1. Preheat the air fryer to 375°F.

2. Cut each chicken breast in half lengthwise. Use a mallet to pound to ¼" thickness. Sprinkle salt and pepper on each side of chicken.

3. Place a slice of ham and a slice of cheese on each piece of chicken. Roll up chicken and secure with toothpicks.

4. In a medium bowl, add egg. In a separate medium bowl, add bread crumbs. Dip each chicken roll into egg, then into bread crumbs, pressing gently to adhere.

5. Spritz rolls with cooking spray and place in the air fryer basket. Cook 15 minutes, turning halfway through cooking time, until rolls are golden brown and internal temperature reaches at least 165°F. Serve warm.

Italian Roasted Chicken Thighs

Servings: 6
Cooking Time: 14 Minutes
Ingredients:
- 6 boneless chicken thighs
- ½ teaspoon dried oregano
- ½ teaspoon garlic powder
- ½ teaspoon sea salt
- ½ teaspoon black pepper
- ¼ teaspoon crushed red pepper flakes

Directions:
1. Pat the chicken thighs with paper towel.

2. In a small bowl, mix the oregano, garlic powder, salt, pepper, and crushed red pepper flakes. Rub the spice mixture onto the chicken thighs.

3. Preheat the air fryer to 400°F.

4. Place the chicken thighs in the air fryer basket and spray with cooking spray. Cook for 10 minutes, turn over, and cook another 4 minutes. When cooking completes, the internal temperature should read 165°F.

Surprisingly Tasty Chicken

Servings:4
Cooking Time:1 Hour

Ingredients:
- 1 whole chicken
- 1 pound small potatoes
- Salt and black pepper, to taste
- 1 tablespoon olive oil, scrubbed

Directions:
1. Preheat the Air fryer to 390°F and grease an Air fryer basket.

2. Season the chicken with salt and black pepper and transfer into the Air fryer.

3. Cook for about 40 minutes and dish out in a plate, covering with a foil paper.

4. Mix potato, oil, salt and black pepper in a bowl and toss to coat well

5. Arrange the potatoes into the Air fryer basket and cook for 20 minutes.

6. Dish out and serve warm.

Celery Chicken Mix

Servings: 4
Cooking Time: 9 Minutes
Ingredients:
- 1 teaspoon fennel seeds
- ½ teaspoon ground celery
- ½ teaspoon salt
- 1 tablespoon olive oil
- 12 oz chicken fillet

Directions:
1. Cut the chicken fillets on 4 chicken chops. In the shallow bowl mix up fennel seeds and olive oil. Rub the chicken chops with salt and ground celery. Preheat the air fryer to 365°F. Brush the chicken chops with the fennel oil and place it in the air fryer basket. Cook them for 9 minutes.

Breaded Chicken Patties

Servings:4
Cooking Time: 15 Minutes
Ingredients:
- 1 pound ground chicken breast
- 1 cup shredded sharp Cheddar cheese
- ½ cup plain bread crumbs
- 1 teaspoon salt
- ½ teaspoon ground black pepper
- 2 tablespoons mayonnaise
- 1 cup panko bread crumbs
- Cooking spray

Directions:
1. Preheat the air fryer to 400°F.

2. In a large bowl, mix chicken, Cheddar, plain bread crumbs, salt, and pepper until well combined. Separate into four portions and form into patties ½" thick.

3. Brush each patty with mayonnaise, then press into panko bread crumbs to fully coat. Spritz with cooking spray.

4. Place in the air fryer basket and cook 15 minutes, turning halfway through cooking time, until patties are golden brown and internal temperature reaches at least 165°F. Serve warm.

Harissa Chicken Wings

Servings: 4
Cooking Time: 25 Minutes
Ingredients:
- 8 whole chicken wings

- 1 tsp garlic powder
- ¼ tsp dried oregano
- 1 tbsp harissa seasoning

Directions:

1. Preheat air fryer to 400°F. Season the wings with garlic, harissa seasoning, and oregano. Place them in the greased frying basket and spray with cooking oil spray. Air Fry for 10 minutes, shake the basket, and cook for another 5-7 minutes until golden and crispy. Serve warm.

Chicken Adobo

Servings: 6
Cooking Time: 12 Minutes
Ingredients:

- 6 boneless chicken thighs
- ¼ cup soy sauce or tamari
- ½ cup rice wine vinegar
- 4 cloves garlic, minced
- ⅛ teaspoon crushed red pepper flakes
- ½ teaspoon black pepper

Directions:

1. Place the chicken thighs into a resealable plastic bag with the soy sauce or tamari, the rice wine vinegar, the garlic, and the crushed red pepper flakes. Seal the bag and let the chicken marinate at least 1 hour in the refrigerator.
2. Preheat the air fryer to 400°F.
3. Drain the chicken and pat dry with a paper towel. Season the chicken with black pepper and liberally spray with cooking spray.
4. Place the chicken in the air fryer basket and cook for 9 minutes, turn over at 9 minutes and check for an internal temperature of 165°F, and cook another 3 minutes.

Yummy Shredded Chicken

Servings: 2
Cooking Time: 15 Minutes
Ingredients:

- 2 large chicken breasts
- ¼ tsp Pepper
- 1 tsp garlic puree
- 1 tsp mustard
- Salt

Directions:

1. Add all ingredients to the bowl and toss well.
2. Transfer chicken into the air fryer basket and cook at 360°F for 15 minutes.
3. Remove chicken from air fryer and shred using a fork.
4. Serve and enjoy.

Jerk Chicken Wings

Servings:4
Cooking Time: 1 Hour 20 Minutes
Ingredients:

- ¼ cup Jamaican jerk marinade
- 1 teaspoon onion powder
- 1 teaspoon garlic powder
- 1 teaspoon salt
- 2 pounds chicken wings, flats and drums separated

Directions:

1. In a large bowl, combine jerk seasoning, onion powder, garlic powder, and salt. Add chicken wings and toss to coat well. Cover and let marinate in refrigerator at least 1 hour.

2. Preheat the air fryer to 400°F.
3. Place wings in the air fryer basket in a single layer, working in batches as necessary. Cook wings 20 minutes, turning halfway through cooking time, until internal temperature reaches at least 165°F. Cool 5 minutes before serving.

Za'atar Chicken Drumsticks

Servings: 4
Cooking Time: 45 Minutes
Ingredients:

- 2 tbsp butter, melted
- 8 chicken drumsticks
- 1 ½ tbsp Za'atar seasoning
- Salt and pepper to taste
- 1 lemon, zested
- 2 tbsp parsley, chopped

Directions:

1. Preheat air fryer to 390°F. Mix the Za'atar seasoning, lemon zest, parsley, salt, and pepper in a bowl. Add the chicken drumsticks and toss to coat. Place them in the air fryer and brush them with butter. Air Fry for 18-20 minutes, flipping once until crispy. Serve and enjoy!

Garlic Ginger Chicken

Servings:4
Cooking Time: 12 Minutes
Ingredients:

- 1 pound boneless, skinless chicken thighs, cut into 1" pieces
- ¼ cup soy sauce
- 2 cloves garlic, peeled and finely minced
- 1 tablespoon minced ginger
- ¼ teaspoon salt

Directions:

1. Place all ingredients in a large sealable bowl or bag. Place sealed bowl or bag into refrigerator and let marinate at least 30 minutes up to overnight.
2. Remove chicken from marinade and place into ungreased air fryer basket. Adjust the temperature to 375°F and set the timer for 12 minutes, shaking the basket twice during cooking. Chicken will be golden and have an internal temperature of at least 165°F when done. Serve warm.

Tangy Mustard Wings

Servings:4
Cooking Time: 25 Minutes
Ingredients:

- 1 pound bone-in chicken wings, separated at joints
- ¼ cup yellow mustard
- ½ teaspoon salt
- ¼ teaspoon ground black pepper

Directions:

1. Place wings in a large bowl and toss with mustard to fully coat. Sprinkle with salt and pepper.
2. Place wings into ungreased air fryer basket. Adjust the temperature to 400°F and set the timer for 25 minutes, shaking the basket three times during cooking. Wings will be done when browned and cooked to an internal temperature of at least 165°F. Serve warm.

Chapter 6. Fish And Seafood Recipes

Garlic Lemon Scallops

Servings:4
Cooking Time: 10 Minutes
Ingredients:
- 4 tablespoons salted butter, melted
- 4 teaspoons peeled and finely minced garlic
- ½ small lemon, zested and juiced
- 8 sea scallops, cleaned and patted dry
- ¼ teaspoon salt
- ¼ teaspoon ground black pepper

Directions:
1. In a small bowl, mix butter, garlic, lemon zest, and lemon juice. Place scallops in an ungreased 6" round nonstick baking dish. Pour butter mixture over scallops, then sprinkle with salt and pepper.
2. Place dish into air fryer basket. Adjust the temperature to 360°F and set the timer for 10 minutes. Scallops will be opaque and firm, and have an internal temperature of 130°F when done. Serve warm.

Garlic-lemon Scallops

Servings:4
Cooking Time: 12 Minutes
Ingredients:
- ¼ teaspoon salt
- ¼ teaspoon ground black pepper
- 8 sea scallops, rinsed and patted dry
- 4 tablespoons salted butter, melted
- 4 teaspoons finely minced garlic
- Zest and juice of ½ small lemon

Directions:
1. Preheat the air fryer to 375°F.
2. Sprinkle salt and pepper evenly over scallops. Spritz scallops lightly with cooking spray. Place in the air fryer basket in a single layer and cook 12 minutes, turning halfway through cooking time, until scallops are opaque and firm and internal temperature reaches at least 130°F.
3. While scallops are cooking, in a small bowl, mix butter, garlic, lemon zest, and juice. Set aside.
4. When scallops are done, drizzle with garlic–lemon butter. Serve warm.

Crispy Smelts

Servings:3
Cooking Time: 20 Minutes
Ingredients:
- 1 pound Cleaned smelts
- 3 tablespoons Tapioca flour
- Vegetable oil spray
- To taste Coarse sea salt or kosher salt

Directions:
1. Preheat the air fryer to 400°F.
2. Toss the smelts and tapioca flour in a large bowl until the little fish are evenly coated.
3. Lay the smelts out on a large cutting board. Lightly coat both sides of each fish with vegetable oil spray.
4. When the machine is at temperature, set the smelts close together in the basket, with a few even overlapping on top. Air-fry undisturbed for 20 minutes, until lightly browned and crisp.
5. Remove the basket from the machine and turn out the fish onto a wire rack. The smelts will most likely come out as one large block, or maybe in a couple of large pieces. Cool for a minute or two, then sprinkle the smelts with salt and break the block(s) into much smaller sections or individual fish to serve.

French Clams

Servings: 5
Cooking Time: 3 Minutes
Ingredients:
- 2-pounds clams, raw, shells removed
- 1 tablespoon Herbs de Provence
- 1 tablespoon sesame oil
- 1 garlic clove, diced

Directions:
1. Put the clams in the bowl and sprinkle with Herbs de Provence, sesame oil, and diced garlic. Shake the seafood well. Preheat the air fryer to 390°F. Put the clams in the air fryer and cook them for 3 minutes. When the clams are cooked, shake them well and transfer in the serving plates.

Teriyaki Salmon

Servings:4
Cooking Time: 27 Minutes
Ingredients:
- ½ cup teriyaki sauce
- ¼ teaspoon salt
- 1 teaspoon ground ginger
- ½ teaspoon garlic powder
- 4 boneless, skinless salmon fillets
- 2 tablespoons toasted sesame seeds

Directions:
1. In a large bowl, whisk teriyaki sauce, salt, ginger, and garlic powder. Add salmon to the bowl, being sure to coat each side with marinade. Cover and let marinate in refrigerator 15 minutes.
2. Preheat the air fryer to 375°F.
3. Spritz fillets with cooking spray and place in the air fryer basket. Cook 12 minutes, turning halfway through cooking time, until glaze has caramelized to a dark brown color, salmon flakes easily, and internal temperature reaches at least 145°F. Sprinkle sesame seeds on salmon and serve warm.

Great Cat Fish

Servings:4
Cooking Time: 25 Minutes
Ingredients:
- ¼ cup seasoned fish fry
- 1 tbsp olive oil
- 1 tbsp parsley, chopped

Directions:
1. Preheat your air fryer to 400°F, and add seasoned fish fry, and fillets in a large Ziploc bag; massage well to coat. Place the fillets in your air fryer's cooking basket and cook for 10 minutes. Flip the fish and cook for 2-3 more minutes. Top with parsley and serve.

Cajun Lobster Tails

Servings:4
Cooking Time: 10 Minutes
Ingredients:
- 4 lobster tails
- 2 tablespoons salted butter, melted
- 2 teaspoons lemon juice
- 1 tablespoon Cajun seasoning

Directions:
1. Preheat the air fryer to 400°F.
2. Carefully cut open lobster tails with kitchen scissors and pull back the shell a little to expose the meat. Drizzle butter and lemon juice over each tail, then sprinkle with Cajun seasoning.
3. Place tails in the air fryer basket and cook 10 minutes until lobster shells are bright red and internal temperature reaches at least 145°F. Serve warm.

Crunchy Coconut Shrimp

Servings:2
Cooking Time: 8 Minutes
Ingredients:
- 8 ounces jumbo shrimp, peeled and deveined
- 2 tablespoons salted butter, melted
- ½ teaspoon Old Bay Seasoning
- ¼ cup unsweetened shredded coconut
- ¼ cup coconut flour

Directions:
1. In a large bowl, toss shrimp in butter and Old Bay Seasoning.
2. In a medium bowl, combine shredded coconut with coconut flour. Coat each piece of shrimp in coconut mixture.
3. Place shrimp into ungreased air fryer basket. Adjust the temperature to 400°F and set the timer for 8 minutes, gently turning shrimp halfway through cooking. Shrimp will be pink and C-shaped when done. Serve warm.

Easy Lobster Tail With Salted Butetr

Servings:4
Cooking Time: 6 Minutes
Ingredients:
- 2 tablespoons melted butter
- 4 lobster tails
- Salt and pepper to taste

Directions:
1. Preheat the air fryer to 390°F.
2. Place the grill pan accessory.
3. Cut the lobster through the tail section using a pair of kitchen scissors.
4. Brush the lobster tails with melted butter and season with salt and pepper to taste.
5. Place on the grill pan and cook for 6 minutes.

Ahi Tuna Steaks

Servings:2
Cooking Time: 14 Minutes
Ingredients:
- 2 ahi tuna steaks
- 2 tablespoons olive oil
- 3 tablespoons everything bagel seasoning

Directions:
1. Preheat the air fryer to 400°F.

2. Drizzle both sides of steaks with oil. Place seasoning on a medium plate and press each side of tuna steaks into seasoning to form a thick layer.
3. Place steaks in the air fryer basket and cook 14 minutes, turning halfway through cooking time, until internal temperature reaches at least 145°F for well-done. Serve warm.

Shrimp Burgers

Servings:4
Cooking Time: 10 Minutes
Ingredients:
- 10 ounces medium shrimp, peeled and deveined
- ¼ cup mayonnaise
- ½ cup panko bread crumbs
- ½ teaspoon Old Bay Seasoning
- ¼ teaspoon salt
- ⅛ teaspoon ground black pepper
- 4 hamburger buns

Directions:
1. Preheat the air fryer to 400°F.
2. In a food processor, add shrimp and pulse four times until broken down.
3. Scoop shrimp into a large bowl and mix with mayonnaise, bread crumbs, Old Bay, salt, and pepper until well combined.
4. Separate mixture into four portions and form into patties. They will feel wet but should be able to hold their shape.
5. Place in the air fryer basket and cook 10 minutes, turning halfway through cooking time, until burgers are brown and internal temperature reaches at least 145°F. Serve warm on buns.

Ham Tilapia

Servings: 4
Cooking Time: 10 Minutes
Ingredients:
- 16 oz tilapia fillet
- 4 ham slices
- 1 teaspoon sunflower oil
- ½ teaspoon salt
- 1 teaspoon dried rosemary

Directions:
1. Cut the tilapia on 4 servings. Sprinkle every fish serving with salt, dried rosemary, and sunflower oil. Then carefully wrap the fish fillets in the ham slices and secure with toothpicks Preheat the air fryer to 400°F. Put the wrapped tilapia in the air fryer basket in one layer and cook them for 10 minutes. Gently flip the fish on another side after 5 minutes of cooking.

Sesame Tuna Steak

Servings: 2
Cooking Time: 12 Minutes
Ingredients:
- 1 tbsp. coconut oil, melted
- 2 x 6-oz. tuna steaks
- ½ tsp. garlic powder
- 2 tsp. black sesame seeds
- 2 tsp. white sesame seeds

Directions:
1. Apply the coconut oil to the tuna steaks with a brunch, then season with garlic powder.

2. Combine the black and white sesame seeds. Embed them in the tuna steaks, covering the fish all over. Place the tuna into your air fryer.

3. Cook for eight minutes at 400°F, turning the fish halfway through.

4. The tuna steaks are ready when they have reached a temperature of 145°F. Serve straightaway.

Fish-in-chips

Servings:4
Cooking Time: 11 Minutes
Ingredients:
- 1 cup All-purpose flour or potato starch
- 2 Large egg(s), well beaten
- 1½ cups Crushed plain potato chips, preferably thick-cut or ruffled (gluten-free, if a concern)
- 4 4-ounce skinless cod fillets

Directions:
1. Preheat the air fryer to 400°F.

2. Set up and fill three shallow soup plates or small pie plates on your counter: one for the flour, one for the beaten egg(s), and one for the crushed potato chips.

3. Dip a piece of cod in the flour, turning it to coat on all sides, even the ends and sides. Gently shake off any excess flour, then dip it in the beaten egg(s). Gently turn to coat it on all sides, then let any excess egg slip back into the rest. Set the fillet in the crushed potato chips and turn several times and onto all sides, pressing gently to coat the fish. Dip it back in the egg(s), coating all sides but taking care that the coating doesn't slip off; then dip it back in the potato chips for a thick, even coating. Set it aside and coat more fillets in the same way.

4. When the machine is at temperature, set the fillets in the basket with as much air space between them as possible. Air-fry undisturbed for 11 minutes, until golden brown and firm but not hard.

5. Use kitchen tongs to transfer the fillets to a wire rack. Cool for just a minute or two before serving.

Timeless Garlic-lemon Scallops

Servings:2
Cooking Time: 15 Minutes
Ingredients:
- 2 tbsp butter, melted
- 1 garlic clove, minced
- 1 tbsp lemon juice
- 1 lb jumbo sea scallops

Directions:
1. Preheat air fryer to 400ºF. Whisk butter, garlic, and lemon juice in a bowl. Roll scallops in the mixture to coat all sides. Place scallops in the frying basket and Air Fry for 4 minutes, flipping once. Brush the tops of each scallop with butter mixture and cook for 4 more minutes, flipping once. Serve and enjoy!

Crispy Sweet-and-sour Cod Fillets

Servings:3
Cooking Time: 12 Minutes
Ingredients:
- 1½ cups Plain panko bread crumbs (gluten-free, if a concern)
- 2 tablespoons Regular or low-fat mayonnaise (not fat-free; gluten-free, if a concern)
- ¼ cup Sweet pickle relish

- 3 4- to 5-ounce skinless cod fillets

Directions:
1. Preheat the air fryer to 400°F.

2. Pour the bread crumbs into a shallow soup plate or a small pie plate. Mix the mayonnaise and relish in a small bowl until well combined. Smear this mixture all over the cod fillets. Set them in the crumbs and turn until evenly coated on all sides, even on the ends.

3. Set the coated cod fillets in the basket with as much air space between them as possible. They should not touch. Air-fry undisturbed for 12 minutes, or until browned and crisp.

4. Use a nonstick-safe spatula to transfer the cod pieces to a wire rack. Cool for only a minute or two before serving hot.

Crab-stuffed Avocado Boats

Servings:4
Cooking Time: 7 Minutes
Ingredients:
- 2 medium avocados, halved and pitted
- 8 ounces cooked crabmeat
- ¼ teaspoon Old Bay Seasoning
- 2 tablespoons peeled and diced yellow onion
- 2 tablespoons mayonnaise

Directions:
1. Scoop out avocado flesh in each avocado half, leaving ½" around edges to form a shell. Chop scooped-out avocado.

2. In a medium bowl, combine crabmeat, Old Bay Seasoning, onion, mayonnaise, and chopped avocado. Place ¼ mixture into each avocado shell.

3. Place avocado boats into ungreased air fryer basket. Adjust the temperature to 350°F and set the timer for 7 minutes. Avocado will be browned on the top and mixture will be bubbling when done. Serve warm.

Crunchy And Buttery Cod With Ritz Cracker Crust

Servings: 2
Cooking Time: 10 Minutes
Ingredients:
- 4 tablespoons butter, melted
- 8 to 10 RITZ crackers, crushed into crumbs
- 2 cod fillets
- salt and freshly ground black pepper
- 1 lemon

Directions:
1. Preheat the air fryer to 380°F.

2. Melt the butter in a small saucepan on the stovetop or in a microwavable dish in the microwave, and then transfer the butter to a shallow dish. Place the crushed RITZ crackers into a second shallow dish.

3. Season the fish fillets with salt and freshly ground black pepper. Dip them into the butter and then coat both sides with the RITZ crackers.

4. Place the fish into the air fryer basket and air-fry at 380°F for 10 minutes, flipping the fish over halfway through the cooking time.

5. Serve with a wedge of lemon to squeeze over the top.

Potato-wrapped Salmon Fillets

Servings:3
Cooking Time: 8 Minutes
Ingredients:
- 1 Large 1-pound elongated yellow potato(es), peeled
- 3 6-ounce, 1½-inch-wide, quite thick skinless salmon fillets
- Olive oil spray
- ¼ teaspoon Table salt
- ¼ teaspoon Ground black pepper

Directions:
1. Preheat the air fryer to 400°F.
2. Use a vegetable peeler or mandoline to make long strips from the potato(es). You'll need anywhere from 8 to 12 strips per fillet, depending on the shape of the potato and of the salmon fillet.
3. Drape potato strips over a salmon fillet, overlapping the strips to create an even "crust." Tuck the potato strips under the fillet, overlapping the strips underneath to create as smooth a bottom as you can. Wrap the remaining fillet(s) in the same way.
4. Gently turn the fillets over. Generously coat the bottoms with olive oil spray. Turn them back seam side down and generously coat the tops with the oil spray. Sprinkle the salt and pepper over the wrapped fillets.
5. Use a nonstick-safe spatula to gently transfer the fillets seam side down to the basket. It helps to remove the basket from the machine and set it on your work surface (keeping in mind that the basket's hot). Leave as much air space as possible between the fillets. Air-fry undisturbed for 8 minutes, or until golden brown and crisp.
6. Use a nonstick-safe spatula to gently transfer the fillets to serving plates. Cool for a couple of minutes before serving.

Herbed Haddock

Servings:2
Cooking Time:8 Minutes
Ingredients:
- 2 haddock fillets
- 2 tablespoons pine nuts
- 3 tablespoons fresh basil, chopped
- 1 tablespoon Parmesan cheese, grated
- ½ cup extra-virgin olive oil
- Salt and black pepper, to taste

Directions:
1. Preheat the Air fryer to 355°F and grease an Air fryer basket.
2. Coat the haddock fillets evenly with olive oil and season with salt and black pepper.
3. Place the haddock fillets in the Air fryer basket and cook for about 8 minutes.
4. Dish out the haddock fillets in serving plates.
5. Meanwhile, put remaining ingredients in a food processor and pulse until smooth.
6. Top this cheese sauce over the haddock fillets and serve hot.

Honey-glazed Salmon

Servings:4
Cooking Time: 30 Minutes
Ingredients:
- 2 tablespoons soy sauce

- 1 teaspoon sriracha
- ½ teaspoon minced garlic
- 4 skin-on salmon fillets
- 2 teaspoons honey

Directions:
1. In a large bowl, whisk together soy sauce, sriracha, and garlic. Place salmon in bowl. Cover and let marinate in refrigerator at least 20 minutes.
2. Preheat the air fryer to 375°F.
3. Place salmon in the air fryer basket and cook 8 minutes. Open air fryer and brush honey on salmon. Continue cooking 2 more minutes until salmon flakes easily and internal temperature reaches at least 145°F. Serve warm.

Super-simple Scallops

Servings:2
Cooking Time:4 Minutes
Ingredients:
- ¾ pound sea scallops
- 1 tablespoon butter, melted
- ½ tablespoon fresh thyme, minced
- Salt and black pepper, to taste

Directions:
1. Preheat the Air fryer to 390°F and grease an Air fryer basket.
2. Mix all the ingredients in a bowl and toss to coat well.
3. Arrange the scallops in the Air fryer basket and cook for about 4 minutes.
4. Dish out and serve warm.

Cod Nuggets

Servings:4
Cooking Time: 12 Minutes
Ingredients:
- 2 boneless, skinless cod fillets
- 1 ½ teaspoons salt, divided
- ¾ teaspoon ground black pepper, divided
- 2 large eggs
- 1 cup plain bread crumbs

Directions:
1. Preheat the air fryer to 350°F.
2. Cut cod fillets into sixteen even-sized pieces. In a large bowl, add cod nuggets and sprinkle with 1 teaspoon salt and ½ teaspoon pepper.
3. In a small bowl, whisk eggs. In another small bowl, mix bread crumbs with remaining ½ teaspoon salt and ¼ teaspoon pepper.
4. One by one, dip nuggets in the eggs, shaking off excess before rolling in the bread crumb mixture. Repeat to make sixteen nuggets.
5. Place nuggets in the air fryer basket and spritz with cooking spray. Cook 12 minutes, turning halfway through cooking time. Nuggets will be done when golden brown and have an internal temperature of at least 145°F. Serve warm.

Fish Taco Bowl

Servings:4
Cooking Time: 12 Minutes
Ingredients:
- 2 cups finely shredded cabbage
- ½ cup mayonnaise
- Juice of 1 medium lime, divided
- 4 boneless, skinless tilapia fillets
- 2 teaspoons chili powder
- 1 teaspoon salt
- ½ teaspoon ground black pepper

Directions:
1. In a large bowl, mix cabbage, mayonnaise, and half of lime juice to make a slaw. Cover and refrigerate while the fish cooks.
2. Preheat the air fryer to 400°F.
3. Sprinkle tilapia with chili powder, salt, and pepper. Spritz each side with cooking spray.
4. Place fillets in the air fryer basket and cook 12 minutes, turning halfway through cooking time, until fish is opaque, flakes easily, and reaches an internal temperature of 145°F.
5. Allow fish to cool 5 minutes before chopping into bite-sized pieces. To serve, place ½ cup slaw into each bowl and top with one-fourth of fish. Squeeze remaining lime juice over fish. Serve warm.

Garlic And Dill Salmon

Servings: 2
Cooking Time: 8 Minutes
Ingredients:
- 12 ounces salmon filets with skin
- 2 tablespoons melted butter
- 1 tablespoon extra-virgin olive oil
- 2 garlic cloves, minced
- 1 tablespoon fresh dill
- ½ teaspoon sea salt
- ½ lemon

Directions:
1. Pat the salmon dry with paper towels.
2. In a small bowl, mix together the melted butter, olive oil, garlic, and dill.
3. Sprinkle the top of the salmon with sea salt. Brush all sides of the salmon with the garlic and dill butter.
4. Preheat the air fryer to 350°F.
5. Place the salmon, skin side down, in the air fryer basket. Cook for 6 to 8 minutes, or until the fish flakes in the center.
6. Remove the salmon and plate on a serving platter. Squeeze fresh lemon over the top of the salmon. Serve immediately.

Tuna Cakes

Servings:4
Cooking Time: 10 Minutes
Ingredients:
- 4 pouches tuna, drained
- 1 large egg, whisked
- 2 tablespoons peeled and chopped white onion
- ½ teaspoon Old Bay Seasoning

Directions:
1. In a large bowl, mix all ingredients together and form into four patties.
2. Place patties into ungreased air fryer basket. Adjust the temperature to 400°F and set the timer for 10 minutes. Patties

will be browned and crispy when done. Let cool 5 minutes before serving.

Simple Sesame Squid On The Grill

Servings:3
Cooking Time: 10 Minutes
Ingredients:
- 1 ½ pounds squid, cleaned
- 2 tablespoon toasted sesame oil
- Salt and pepper to taste

Directions:
1. Preheat the air fryer at 390°F.
2. Place the grill pan accessory in the air fryer.
3. Season the squid with sesame oil, salt and pepper.
4. Grill the squid for 10 minutes.

Lemon And Thyme Sea Bass

Servings: 3
Cooking Time: 15 Minutes
Ingredients:
- 8 oz sea bass, trimmed, peeled
- 4 lemon slices
- 1 tablespoon thyme
- 2 teaspoons sesame oil
- 1 teaspoon salt

Directions:
1. Fill the sea bass with lemon slices and rub with thyme, salt, and sesame oil. Then preheat the air fryer to 385°F and put the fish in the air fryer basket. Cook it for 12 minutes. Then flip the fish on another side and cook it for 3 minutes more.

Miso Fish

Servings: 2
Cooking Time: 10 Minutes
Ingredients:
- 2 cod fish fillets
- 1 tbsp garlic, chopped
- 2 tsp swerve
- 2 tbsp miso

Directions:
1. Add all ingredients to the zip-lock bag. Shake well place in the refrigerator for overnight.
2. Place marinated fish fillets into the air fryer basket and cook at 350°F for 10 minutes.
3. Serve and enjoy.

Lime Flaming Halibut

Servings:2
Cooking Time: 20 Minutes
Ingredients:
- 2 tbsp butter, melted
- ½ tsp chili powder
- ½ cup bread crumbs
- 2 halibut fillets

Directions:
1. Preheat air fryer to 350°F. In a bowl, mix the butter, chili powder and bread crumbs. Press mixture onto tops of halibut fillets. Place halibut in the greased frying basket and Air Fry for 10 minutes or until the fish is opaque and flake easily with a fork. Serve right away.

Sardinas Fritas

Servings: 2
Cooking Time: 15 Minutes
Ingredients:
- 2 cans boneless, skinless sardines in mustard sauce
- Salt and pepper to taste
- ½ cup bread crumbs
- 2 lemon wedges
- 1 tsp chopped parsley

Directions:
1. Preheat air fryer at 350ºF. Add breadcrumbs, salt and black pepper to a bowl. Roll sardines in the breadcrumbs to coat. Place them in the greased frying basket and Air Fry for 6 minutes, flipping once. Transfer them to a serving dish. Serve topped with parsley and lemon wedges.

Fried Catfish Fillets

Servings:2
Cooking Time: 40 Minutes
Ingredients:
- 3 tbsp breadcrumbs
- 1 tsp cayenne pepper
- 1 tsp dry fish seasoning, of choice
- 2 sprigs parsley, chopped
- Salt to taste, optional
- Cooking spray

Directions:
1. Preheat air fryer to 400°F. Pour all the dry ingredients, except the parsley, in a zipper bag. Pat dry and add the fish pieces. Close the bag and shake to coat the fish well. Do this with one fish piece at a time.
2. Lightly spray the fish with olive oil. Arrange them in the fryer basket, one at a time depending on the size of the fish. Close the air fryer and cook for 10 minutes. Flip the fish and cook further for 10 minutes. For extra crispiness, cook for 3 more minutes. Garnish with parsley and serve.

Mediterranean-style Cod

Servings:4
Cooking Time: 12 Minutes
Ingredients:
- 4 cod fillets
- 3 tablespoons fresh lemon juice
- 1 tablespoon olive oil
- ¼ teaspoon salt
- 6 cherry tomatoes, halved
- ¼ cup pitted and sliced kalamata olives

Directions:
1. Place cod into an ungreased 6" round nonstick baking dish. Pour lemon juice into dish and drizzle cod with olive oil. Sprinkle with salt. Place tomatoes and olives around baking dish in between fillets.
2. Place dish into air fryer basket. Adjust the temperature to 350°F and set the timer for 12 minutes, carefully turning cod halfway through cooking. Fillets will be lightly browned, easily flake, and have an internal temperature of at least 145°F when done. Serve warm.

Simple Salmon Fillets

Servings: 2
Cooking Time: 7 Minutes
Ingredients:
- 2 salmon fillets
- 2 tsp olive oil
- 2 tsp paprika
- Pepper
- Salt

Directions:
1. Rub salmon fillet with oil, paprika, pepper, and salt.
2. Place salmon fillets in the air fryer basket and cook a 390°F for 7 minutes.
3. Serve and enjoy.

Shrimp Al Pesto

Servings: 4
Cooking Time: 10 Minutes
Ingredients:
- 1 lb peeled shrimp, deveined
- ¼ cup pesto sauce
- 1 lime, sliced
- 2 cups cooked farro

Directions:
1. Preheat air fryer to 360°F. Coat the shrimp with the pesto sauce in a bowl. Put the shrimp in a single layer in the frying basket. Put the lime slices over the shrimp and Roast for 5 minutes. Remove lime and discard. Serve the shrimp over a bed of farro pilaf. Enjoy!

Catalan Sardines With Romesco Sauce

Servings:2
Cooking Time: 15 Minutes
Ingredients:
- 2 cans skinless, boneless sardines in oil, drained
- ½ cup warmed romesco sauce
- ½ cup bread crumbs

Directions:
1. Preheat air fryer to 350ºF. In a shallow dish, add bread crumbs. Roll in sardines to coat. Place sardines in the greased frying basket and Air Fry for 6 minutes, turning once. Serve with romesco sauce.

Lemon Butter Cod

Servings:4
Cooking Time: 12 Minutes
Ingredients:
- 4 cod fillets
- 2 tablespoons salted butter, melted
- 1 teaspoon Old Bay Seasoning
- ½ medium lemon, cut into 4 slices

Directions:
1. Place cod fillets into an ungreased 6" round nonstick baking dish. Brush tops of fillets with butter and sprinkle with Old Bay Seasoning. Lay 1 lemon slice on each fillet.
2. Cover dish with aluminum foil and place into air fryer basket. Adjust the temperature to 350°F and set the timer for 12 minutes, turning fillets halfway through cooking. Fish will be opaque and have an internal temperature of at least 145°F when done. Serve warm.

Chili-lime Shrimp

Servings:4
Cooking Time: 10 Minutes
Ingredients:
- 1 pound medium shrimp, peeled and deveined
- ½ cup lime juice
- 2 tablespoons olive oil
- 2 tablespoons sriracha
- 1 teaspoon salt
- ¼ teaspoon ground black pepper

Directions:
1. Preheat the air fryer to 375°F.
2. In an 6" round cake pan, combine all ingredients.
3. Place pan in the air fryer and cook 10 minutes, stirring halfway through cooking time, until the inside of shrimp are pearly white and opaque and internal temperature reaches at least 145°F. Serve warm.

Air Fried Cod With Basil Vinaigrette

Servings:4
Cooking Time: 15 Minutes
Ingredients:
- ¼ cup olive oil
- 4 cod fillets
- A bunch of basil, torn
- Juice from 1 lemon, freshly squeezed
- Salt and pepper to taste

Directions:
1. Preheat the air fryer for 5 minutes.
2. Season the cod fillets with salt and pepper to taste.
3. Place in the air fryer and cook for 15 minutes at 350°F.
4. Meanwhile, mix the rest of the ingredients in a bowl and toss to combine.
5. Serve the air fried cod with the basil vinaigrette.

Lemon-roasted Salmon Fillets

Servings:3
Cooking Time: 7 Minutes
Ingredients:
- 3 6-ounce skin-on salmon fillets
- Olive oil spray
- 9 Very thin lemon slices
- ¾ teaspoon Ground black pepper
- ¼ teaspoon Table salt

Directions:
1. Preheat the air fryer to 400°F.
2. Generously coat the skin of each of the fillets with olive oil spray. Set the fillets skin side down on your work surface. Place three overlapping lemon slices down the length of each salmon fillet. Sprinkle them with the pepper and salt. Coat lightly with olive oil spray.
3. Use a nonstick-safe spatula to transfer the fillets one by one to the basket, leaving as much air space between them as possible. Air-fry undisturbed for 7 minutes, or until cooked through.
4. Use a nonstick-safe spatula to transfer the fillets to serving plates. Cool for only a minute or two before serving.

Better Fish Sticks

Servings:3
Cooking Time: 8 Minutes
Ingredients:

- ¾ cup Seasoned Italian-style dried bread crumbs (gluten-free, if a concern)
- 3 tablespoons (about ½ ounce) Finely grated Parmesan cheese
- 10 ounces Skinless cod fillets, cut lengthwise into 1-inch-wide pieces
- 3 tablespoons Regular or low-fat mayonnaise (not fat-free; gluten-free, if a concern)
- Vegetable oil spray

Directions:
1. Preheat the air fryer to 400°F.
2. Mix the bread crumbs and grated Parmesan in a shallow soup bowl or a small pie plate.
3. Smear the fish fillet sticks completely with the mayonnaise, then dip them one by one in the bread-crumb mixture, turning and pressing gently to make an even and thorough coating. Coat each stick on all sides with vegetable oil spray.
4. Set the fish sticks in the basket with at least ¼ inch between them. Air-fry undisturbed for 8 minutes, or until golden brown and crisp.
5. Use a nonstick-safe spatula to gently transfer them from the basket to a wire rack. Cool for only a minute or two before serving.

Very Easy Lime-garlic Shrimps

Servings:1
Cooking Time: 6 Minutes
Ingredients:
- 1 clove of garlic, minced
- 1 cup raw shrimps
- 1 lime, juiced and zested
- Salt and pepper to taste

Directions:
1. In a mixing bowl, combine all Ingredients and give a good stir.
2. Preheat the air fryer to 390°F.
3. Skewer the shrimps onto the metal skewers that come with the double layer rack accessory.
4. Place on the rack and cook for 6 minutes.

Seared Scallops In Beurre Blanc

Servings: 4
Cooking Time: 15 Minutes
Ingredients:
- 1 lb sea scallops
- Salt and pepper to taste
- 2 tbsp butter, melted
- 1 lemon, zested and juiced
- 2 tbsp dry white wine

Directions:
1. Preheat the air fryer to 400°F. Sprinkle the scallops with salt and pepper, then set in a bowl. Combine the butter, lemon zest, lemon juice, and white wine in another bowl; mix well. Put the scallops in a baking pan and drizzle over them the mixture. Air Fry for 8-11 minutes, flipping over at about 5 minutes until opaque. Serve and enjoy!

Sea Scallops

Servings: 4
Cooking Time: 8 Minutes
Ingredients:
- 1½ pounds sea scallops
- salt and pepper
- 2 eggs
- ½ cup flour
- ½ cup plain breadcrumbs
- oil for misting or cooking spray

Directions:
1. Rinse scallops and remove the tough side muscle. Sprinkle to taste with salt and pepper.
2. Beat eggs together in a shallow dish. Place flour in a second shallow dish and breadcrumbs in a third.
3. Preheat air fryer to 390°F.
4. Dip scallops in flour, then eggs, and then roll in breadcrumbs. Mist with oil or cooking spray.
5. Place scallops in air fryer basket in a single layer, leaving some space between. You should be able to cook about a dozen at a time.
6. Cook at 390°F for 8 minutes, watching carefully so as not to overcook. Scallops are done when they turn opaque all the way through. They will feel slightly firm when pressed with tines of a fork.
7. Repeat step 6 to cook remaining scallops.

Italian Tuna Roast

Servings: 8
Cooking Time: 21 Minutes
Ingredients:
- cooking spray
- 1 tablespoon Italian seasoning
- ⅛ teaspoon ground black pepper
- 1 tablespoon extra-light olive oil
- 1 teaspoon lemon juice
- 1 tuna loin

Directions:
1. Spray baking dish with cooking spray and place in air fryer basket. Preheat air fryer to 390°F.
2. Mix together the Italian seasoning, pepper, oil, and lemon juice.
3. Using a dull table knife or butter knife, pierce top of tuna about every half inch: Insert knife into top of tuna roast and pierce almost all the way to the bottom.
4. Spoon oil mixture into each of the holes and use the knife to push seasonings into the tuna as deeply as possible.
5. Spread any remaining oil mixture on all outer surfaces of tuna.
6. Place tuna roast in baking dish and cook at 390°F for 20 minutes. Check temperature with a meat thermometer. Cook for an additional 1 minutes or until temperature reaches 145°F.
7. Remove basket from fryer and let tuna sit in basket for 10minutes.

Potato-crusted Cod

Servings:4
Cooking Time: 15 Minutes
Ingredients:
- 4 boneless, skinless cod fillets
- 2 tablespoons olive oil
- ½ teaspoon salt, divided
- 1 teaspoon dried dill
- 2 cups mashed potato flakes

Directions:
1. Preheat the air fryer to 350°F.
2. Place cod fillets on a work surface and brush with oil. Sprinkle with ¼ teaspoon salt and dill.
3. In a large bowl, combine mashed potato flakes with remaining salt.
4. Roll each fillet in the potato mixture and spritz with cooking spray.
5. Place in the air fryer basket and cook 15 minutes, turning halfway through cooking time. Cod will be golden brown and have an internal temperature of at least 145°F when done. Serve warm.

Snapper Fillets With Thai Sauce

Servings: 2
Cooking Time: 30 Minutes + Marinating Time
Ingredients:
- 1/2 cup full-fat coconut milk
- 2 tablespoons lemon juice
- 1 teaspoon fresh ginger, grated
- 2 snapper fillets
- 1 tablespoon olive oil
- Salt and white pepper, to taste

Directions:
1. Place the milk, lemon juice, and ginger in a glass bowl; add fish and let it marinate for 1 hour.
2. Removed the fish from the milk mixture and place in the Air Fryer basket. Drizzle olive oil all over the fish fillets.
3. Cook in the preheated Air Fryer at 390°F for 15 minutes.
4. Meanwhile, heat the milk mixture over medium-high heat; bring to a rapid boil, stirring continuously. Reduce to simmer and add the salt, and pepper; continue to cook 12 minutes more.
5. Spoon the sauce over the warm snapper fillets and serve immediately. Bon appétit!

Crab Cakes

Servings:4
Cooking Time: 12 Minutes
Ingredients:
- 2 cans lump crabmeat, drained
- ½ cup plain bread crumbs
- ½ cup mayonnaise
- 1 ½ teaspoons Old Bay Seasoning
- Zest and juice of ½ medium lemon
- ½ teaspoon salt
- ½ teaspoon ground black pepper
- Cooking spray

Directions:
1. Preheat the air fryer to 375°F.
2. In a large bowl, mix all ingredients.
3. Scoop ¼ cup mixture and form into a 4" patty. Repeat to make eight crab cakes. Spritz cakes with cooking spray.
4. Place in the air fryer basket and cook 12 minutes, turning halfway through cooking time, until edges are brown and center is firm. Serve warm.

Lemon Pepper–breaded Tilapia

Servings:4
Cooking Time: 10 Minutes
Ingredients:
- 1 large egg
- ⅓ cup all-purpose flour
- ¼ cup grated Parmesan cheese
- ½ tablespoon lemon pepper seasoning
- 4 boneless, skinless tilapia fillets

Directions:
1. Preheat the air fryer to 375°F.
2. In a medium bowl, whisk egg. On a large plate, mix flour, Parmesan, and lemon pepper seasoning.
3. Pat tilapia dry. Dip each fillet into egg, gently shaking off excess. Press into flour mixture, then spritz both sides with cooking spray.
4. Place in the air fryer basket and cook 10 minutes, turning halfway through cooking, until fillets are golden and crispy and internal temperature reaches at least 145°F. Serve warm.

Italian Baked Cod

Servings:4
Cooking Time: 12 Minutes
Ingredients:
- 4 cod fillets
- 2 tablespoons salted butter, melted
- 1 teaspoon Italian seasoning
- ¼ teaspoon salt
- ½ cup low-carb marinara sauce

Directions:
1. Place cod into an ungreased 6" round nonstick baking dish. Pour butter over cod and sprinkle with Italian seasoning and salt. Top with marinara.
2. Place dish into air fryer basket. Adjust the temperature to 350°F and set the timer for 12 minutes. Fillets will be lightly browned, easily flake, and have an internal temperature of at least 145°F when done. Serve warm.

Nacho Chips Crusted Prawns

Servings:2
Cooking Time: 8 Minutes
Ingredients:
- ¾ pound prawns, peeled and deveined
- 1 large egg
- 5 ounces Nacho flavored chips, finely crushed

Directions:
1. In a shallow bowl, beat the egg.
2. In another bowl, place the nacho chips.
3. Dip each prawn into the beaten egg and then, coat with the crushed nacho chips.
4. Set the temperature of air fryer to 350°F. Grease an air fryer basket.
5. Arrange prawns into the prepared air fryer basket.
6. Air fry for about 8 minutes.
7. Remove from air fryer and transfer the prawns onto serving plates.
8. Serve hot.

Super Crunchy Flounder Fillets

Servings:2
Cooking Time: 6 Minutes
Ingredients:

- ½ cup All-purpose flour or tapioca flour
- 1 Large egg white(s)
- 1 tablespoon Water
- ¾ teaspoon Table salt
- 1 cup Plain panko bread crumbs (gluten-free, if a concern)
- 2 4-ounce skinless flounder fillet(s)
- Vegetable oil spray

Directions:
1. Preheat the air fryer to 400°F.
2. Set up and fill three shallow soup plates or small pie plates on your counter: one for the flour; one for the egg white(s), beaten with the water and salt until foamy; and one for the bread crumbs.
3. Dip one fillet in the flour, turning it to coat both sides. Gently shake off any excess flour, then dip the fillet in the egg white mixture, turning it to coat. Let any excess egg white mixture slip back into the rest, then set the fish in the bread crumbs. Turn it several times, gently pressing it into the crumbs to create an even crust. Generously coat both sides of the fillet with vegetable oil spray. If necessary, set it aside and continue coating the remaining fillet(s) in the same way.
4. Set the fillet(s) in the basket. If working with more than one fillet, they should not touch, although they may be quite close together, depending on the basket's size. Air-fry undisturbed for 6 minutes, or until lightly browned and crunchy.
5. Use a nonstick-safe spatula to transfer the fillet(s) to a wire rack. Cool for only a minute or two before serving.

Horseradish-crusted Salmon Fillets

Servings:3
Cooking Time: 8 Minutes
Ingredients:
- ½ cup Fresh bread crumbs
- 4 tablespoons (¼ cup/½ stick) Butter, melted and cooled
- ¼ cup Jarred prepared white horseradish
- Vegetable oil spray
- 4 6-ounce skin-on salmon fillets

Directions:
1. Preheat the air fryer to 400°F.
2. Mix the bread crumbs, butter, and horseradish in a bowl until well combined.
3. Take the basket out of the machine. Generously spray the skin side of each fillet. Pick them up one by one with a nonstick-safe spatula and set them in the basket skin side down with as much air space between them as possible. Divide the bread-crumb mixture between the fillets, coating the top of each fillet with an even layer. Generously coat the bread-crumb mixture with vegetable oil spray.
4. Return the basket to the machine and air-fry undisturbed for 8 minutes, or until the topping has lightly browned and the fish is firm but not hard.
5. Use a nonstick-safe spatula to transfer the salmon fillets to serving plates. Cool for 5 minutes before serving. Because of the butter in the topping, it will stay very hot for quite a while. Take care, especially if you're serving these fillets to children.

Maple Butter Salmon

Servings:4
Cooking Time: 12 Minutes
Ingredients:
- 2 tablespoons salted butter, melted
- 1 teaspoon low-carb maple syrup
- 1 teaspoon yellow mustard
- 4 boneless, skinless salmon fillets
- ½ teaspoon salt

Directions:
1. In a small bowl, whisk together butter, syrup, and mustard. Brush ½ mixture over each fillet on both sides. Sprinkle fillets with salt on both sides.
2. Place salmon into ungreased air fryer basket. Adjust the temperature to 400°F and set the timer for 12 minutes. Halfway through cooking, brush fillets on both sides with remaining syrup mixture. Salmon will easily flake and have an internal temperature of at least 145°F when done. Serve warm.

Tortilla-crusted With Lemon Filets

Servings:4
Cooking Time: 15 Minutes
Ingredients:
- 1 cup tortilla chips, pulverized
- 1 egg, beaten
- 1 tablespoon lemon juice
- 4 fillets of white fish fillet
- Salt and pepper to taste

Directions:
1. Preheat the air fryer to 390°F.
2. Place a grill pan in the air fryer.
3. Season the fish fillet with salt, pepper, and lemon juice.
4. Soak in beaten eggs and dredge in tortilla chips.
5. Place on the grill pan.
6. Cook for 15 minutes.
7. Make sure to flip the fish halfway through the cooking time.

Lemon-basil On Cod Filet

Servings:4
Cooking Time: 15 Minutes
Ingredients:
- ¼ cup olive oil
- 4 cod fillets
- A bunch of basil, torn
- Juice from 1 lemon, freshly squeezed
- Salt and pepper to taste

Directions:
1. Preheat the air fryer for 5 minutes.
2. Season the cod fillets with salt and pepper to taste. Place on lightly greased air fryer baking pan.
3. Mix the rest of the ingredients in a bowl and toss to combine. Pour over fish.
4. Cook for 15 minutes at 330°F.
5. Serve and enjoy.

Lemon Shrimp And Zucchinis

Servings: 4
Cooking Time: 15 Minutes
Ingredients:
- 1 pound shrimp, peeled and deveined
- A pinch of salt and black pepper
- 2 zucchinis, cut into medium cubes
- 1 tablespoon lemon juice
- 1 tablespoon olive oil
- 1 tablespoon garlic, minced

Directions:
1. In a pan that fits the air fryer, combine all the ingredients, toss, put the pan in the machine and cook at 370°F for 15 minutes. Divide between plates and serve right away.

Salmon Patties

Servings:4
Cooking Time: 12 Minutes
Ingredients:
- 1 pouch cooked salmon
- 6 tablespoons panko bread crumbs
- ½ cup mayonnaise
- 2 teaspoons Old Bay Seasoning

Directions:
1. Preheat the air fryer to 350°F.
2. In a large bowl, combine all ingredients.
3. Divide mixture into four equal portions. Using your hands, form into patties and spritz with cooking spray.
4. Place in the air fryer basket and cook 12 minutes, turning halfway through cooking time, until brown and firm. Serve warm.

Chili Blackened Shrimp

Servings: 4
Cooking Time: 15 Minutes
Ingredients:
- 1 lb peeled shrimp, deveined
- 1 tsp paprika
- ½ tsp dried dill
- ½ tsp red chili flakes
- ½ lemon, juiced
- Salt and pepper to taste

Directions:
1. Preheat air fryer to 400°F. In a resealable bag, add shrimp, paprika, dill, red chili flakes, lemon juice, salt and pepper. Seal and shake well. Place the shrimp in the greased frying basket and Air Fry for 7-8 minutes, shaking the basket once until blackened. Let cool slightly and serve.

Coriander Cod And Green Beans

Servings: 4
Cooking Time: 15 Minutes
Ingredients:
- 12 oz cod fillet
- ½ cup green beans, trimmed and halved
- 1 tablespoon avocado oil
- 1 teaspoon salt
- 1 teaspoon ground coriander

Directions:
1. Cut the cod fillet on 4 servings and sprinkle every serving with salt and ground coriander. After this, place the fish on 4 foil squares. Top them with green beans and avocado oil and wrap them into parcels. Preheat the air fryer to 400°F. Place the cod parcels in the air fryer and cook them for 15 minutes.

Lemon Butter–dill Salmon

Servings: 4
Cooking Time: 10 Minutes
Ingredients:
- 4 skin-on salmon fillets
- ¾ teaspoon salt
- ½ teaspoon ground black pepper
- 1 medium lemon, halved
- 2 tablespoons salted butter, melted
- 1 teaspoon dried dill

Directions:
1. Preheat the air fryer to 375°F.
2. Sprinkle salmon with salt and pepper.
3. Juice half the lemon and slice the other half into ¼"-thick pieces. In a small bowl, combine juice with butter. Brush mixture over salmon.
4. Sprinkle dill evenly over salmon. Place lemon slices on top of salmon.
5. Place salmon in the air fryer basket and cook 10 minutes until salmon flakes easily and internal temperature reaches at least 145°F. Remove lemon slices before serving.

Beer-battered Cod

Servings:3
Cooking Time: 12 Minutes
Ingredients:
- 1½ cups All-purpose flour
- 3 tablespoons Old Bay seasoning
- 1 Large egg(s)
- ¼ cup Amber beer, pale ale, or IPA
- 3 4-ounce skinless cod fillets
- Vegetable oil spray

Directions:
1. Preheat the air fryer to 400°F.
2. Set up and fill two shallow soup plates or small pie plates on your counter: one with the flour, whisked with the Old Bay until well combined; and one with the egg(s), whisked with the beer until foamy and uniform.
3. Dip a piece of cod in the flour mixture, turning it to coat on all sides. Gently shake off any excess flour and dip the fish in the egg mixture, turning it to coat. Let any excess egg mixture slip back into the rest, then set the fish back in the flour mixture and coat it again, then back in the egg mixture for a second wash, then back in the flour mixture for a third time. Coat the fish on all sides with vegetable oil spray and set it aside. "Batter" the remaining piece(s) of cod in the same way.
4. Set the coated cod fillets in the basket with as much space between them as possible. They should not touch. Air-fry undisturbed for 12 minutes, or until brown and crisp.
5. Use kitchen tongs to gently transfer the fish to a wire rack. Cool for only a couple of minutes before serving.

Flounder Fillets

Servings: 4
Cooking Time: 8 Minutes
Ingredients:
- 1 egg white
- 1 tablespoon water
- 1 cup panko breadcrumbs
- 2 tablespoons extra-light virgin olive oil
- 4 4-ounce flounder fillets
- salt and pepper

- oil for misting or cooking spray

Directions:
1. Preheat air fryer to 390°F.
2. Beat together egg white and water in shallow dish.
3. In another shallow dish, mix panko crumbs and oil until well combined and crumbly.
4. Season flounder fillets with salt and pepper to taste. Dip each fillet into egg mixture and then roll in panko crumbs, pressing in crumbs so that fish is nicely coated.
5. Spray air fryer basket with nonstick cooking spray and add fillets. Cook at 390°F for 3minutes.
6. Spray fish fillets but do not turn. Cook 5 minutes longer or until golden brown and crispy. Using a spatula, carefully remove fish from basket and serve.

Tuna-stuffed Tomatoes

Servings:2
Cooking Time: 5 Minutes
Ingredients:
- 2 medium beefsteak tomatoes, tops removed, seeded, membranes removed
- 2 pouches tuna packed in water, drained
- 1 medium stalk celery, trimmed and chopped
- 2 tablespoons mayonnaise
- ¼ teaspoon salt
- ¼ teaspoon ground black pepper
- 2 teaspoons coconut oil
- ¼ cup shredded mild Cheddar cheese

Directions:
1. Scoop pulp out of each tomato, leaving ½" shell.
2. In a medium bowl, mix tuna, celery, mayonnaise, salt, and pepper. Drizzle with coconut oil. Spoon ½ mixture into each tomato and top each with 2 tablespoons Cheddar.
3. Place tomatoes into ungreased air fryer basket. Adjust the temperature to 320°F and set the timer for 5 minutes. Cheese will be melted when done. Serve warm.

Crab Rangoon

Servings:4
Cooking Time: 5 Minutes
Ingredients:
- ½ cup imitation crabmeat
- 4 ounces full-fat cream cheese, softened
- ¼ teaspoon Worcestershire sauce
- 8 wonton wrappers

Directions:
1. Preheat the air fryer to 400°F.
2. In a medium bowl, mix crabmeat, cream cheese, and Worcestershire until combined.
3. Place wonton wrappers on work surface. For each rangoon, scoop ½ tablespoon crab mixture onto center of a wonton wrapper. Press opposing edges toward the center and pinch to close. Spray with cooking spray to coat well. Repeat with remaining crab mixture and wontons.
4. Place in the air fryer basket and cook 5 minutes until brown at the edges. Serve warm.

Quick And Easy Shrimp

Servings:2
Cooking Time:5 Minutes
Ingredients:
- ½ pound tiger shrimp
- 1 tablespoon olive oil
- ½ teaspoon old bay seasoning
- ¼ teaspoon smoked paprika
- ¼ teaspoon cayenne pepper
- Salt, to taste

Directions:
1. Preheat the Air fryer to 390°F and grease an Air fryer basket.
2. Mix all the ingredients in a large bowl until well combined.
3. Place the shrimps in the Air fryer basket and cook for about 5 minutes.
4. Dish out and serve warm.

Fish Sticks For Kids

Servings: 8
Cooking Time: 6 Minutes
Ingredients:
- 8 ounces fish fillets (pollock or cod)
- salt (optional)
- ½ cup plain breadcrumbs
- oil for misting or cooking spray

Directions:
1. Cut fish fillets into "fingers" about ½ x 3 inches. Sprinkle with salt to taste, if desired.
2. Roll fish in breadcrumbs. Spray all sides with oil or cooking spray.
3. Place in air fryer basket in single layer and cook at 390°F for 6 minutes, until golden brown and crispy.

Thyme Scallops

Servings: 1
Cooking Time: 12 Minutes
Ingredients:
- 1 lb. scallops
- Salt and pepper
- ½ tbsp. butter
- ½ cup thyme, chopped

Directions:
1. Wash the scallops and dry them completely. Season with pepper and salt, then set aside while you prepare the pan.
2. Grease a foil pan in several spots with the butter and cover the bottom with the thyme. Place the scallops on top.
3. Pre-heat the fryer at 400°F and set the rack inside.
4. Place the foil pan on the rack and allow to cook for seven minutes.
5. Take care when removing the pan from the fryer and transfer the scallops to a serving dish. Spoon any remaining butter in the pan over the fish and enjoy.

Easy-peasy Shrimp

Servings:2
Cooking Time: 15 Minutes
Ingredients:
- 1 lb tail-on shrimp, deveined
- 2 tbsp butter, melted
- 1 tbsp lemon juice

- 1 tbsp dill, chopped

Directions:
1. Preheat air fryer to 350°F. Combine shrimp and butter in a bowl. Place shrimp in the greased frying basket and Air Fry for 6 minutes, flipping once. Squeeze lemon juice over and top with dill. Serve hot.

Italian Shrimp

Servings: 4
Cooking Time: 12 Minutes
Ingredients:
- 1 pound shrimp, peeled and deveined
- A pinch of salt and black pepper
- 1 tablespoon sesame seeds, toasted
- ½ teaspoon Italian seasoning
- 1 tablespoon olive oil

Directions:
1. In a bowl, mix the shrimp with the rest of the ingredients and toss well. Put the shrimp in the air fryer's basket, cook at 370°F for 12 minutes, divide into bowls and serve,

Mahi-mahi "burrito" Fillets

Servings:3
Cooking Time: 10 Minutes
Ingredients:
- 1 Large egg white
- 1½ cups Crushed corn tortilla chips (gluten-free, if a concern)
- 1 tablespoon Chile powder
- 3 5-ounce skinless mahi-mahi fillets
- 6 tablespoons Canned refried beans
- Vegetable oil spray

Directions:
1. Preheat the air fryer to 400°F.
2. Set up and fill two shallow soup plates or small pie plates on your counter: one with the egg white, beaten until foamy; and one with the crushed tortilla chips.
3. Gently rub ½ teaspoon chile powder on each side of each fillet.
4. Spread 1 tablespoon refried beans over both sides and the edges of a fillet. Dip the fillet in the egg white, turning to coat it on both sides. Let any excess egg white slip back into the rest, then set the fillet in the crushed tortilla chips. Turn several times, pressing gently to coat it evenly. Coat the fillet on all sides with the vegetable oil spray, then set it aside. Prepare the remaining fillet(s) in the same way.
5. When the machine is at temperature, set the fillets in the basket with as much air space between them as possible. Air-fry undisturbed for 10 minutes, or until crisp and browned.
6. Use a nonstick-safe spatula to transfer the fillets to a serving platter or plates. Cool for only a minute or so, then serve hot.

Simple Salmon

Servings:2
Cooking Time:10 Minutes
Ingredients:
- 2 salmon fillets
- Salt and black pepper, as required
- 1 tablespoon olive oil

Directions:

1. Preheat the Air fryer to 390°F and grease an Air fryer basket.
2. Season each salmon fillet with salt and black pepper and drizzle with olive oil.
3. Arrange salmon fillets into the Air fryer basket and cook for about 10 minutes.
4. Remove from the Air fryer and dish out the salmon fillets onto the serving plates.

Zesty Mahi Mahi

Servings:3
Cooking Time:8 Minutes
Ingredients:
- 1½ pounds Mahi Mahi fillets
- 1 lemon, cut into slices
- 1 tablespoon fresh dill, chopped
- ½ teaspoon red chili powder
- Salt and ground black pepper, as required

Directions:
1. Preheat the Air fryer to 375°F and grease an Air fryer basket.
2. Season the Mahi Mahi fillets evenly with chili powder, salt, and black pepper.
3. Arrange the Mahi Mahi fillets into the Air fryer basket and top with the lemon slices.
4. Cook for about 8 minutes and dish out
5. Place the lemon slices over the salmon the salmon fillets in the serving plates.
6. Garnish with fresh dill and serve warm.

Bacon-wrapped Scallops

Servings: 4
Cooking Time: 8 Minutes
Ingredients:
- 16 large scallops
- 8 bacon strips
- ½ teaspoon black pepper
- ¼ teaspoon smoked paprika

Directions:
1. Pat the scallops dry with a paper towel. Slice each of the bacon strips in half. Wrap 1 bacon strip around 1 scallop and secure with a toothpick. Repeat with the remaining scallops. Season the scallops with pepper and paprika.
2. Preheat the air fryer to 350°F.
3. Place the bacon-wrapped scallops in the air fryer basket and cook for 4 minutes, shake the basket, cook another 3 minutes, shake the basket, and cook another 1 to 3 to minutes. When the bacon is crispy, the scallops should be cooked through and slightly firm, but not rubbery. Serve immediately.

Coconut Shrimp

Servings:4
Cooking Time: 10 Minutes
Ingredients:
- 1 cup all-purpose flour
- 1 teaspoon salt
- 2 large eggs
- ½ cup panko bread crumbs
- 1 cup shredded unsweetened coconut flakes
- 1 pound large shrimp, peeled and deveined
- Cooking spray

Directions:

1. Preheat the air fryer to 375°F.
2. In a medium bowl, mix flour and salt. In a separate medium bowl, whisk eggs. In a third medium bowl, mix bread crumbs and coconut flakes.
3. Dredge shrimp first in flour mixture, shaking off excess, then in eggs, letting any additional egg drip off, and finally in bread crumb mixture. Spritz with cooking spray.
4. Place shrimp in the air fryer basket. Cook 10 minutes, turning and spritzing opposite side with cooking spray halfway through cooking, until insides are pearly white and opaque and internal temperature reaches at least 145°F. Serve warm.

Tilapia Fish Fillets

Servings: 2
Cooking Time: 7 Minutes
Ingredients:
- 2 tilapia fillets
- 1 tsp old bay seasoning
- 1/2 tsp butter
- 1/4 tsp lemon pepper
- Pepper
- Salt

Directions:
1. Spray air fryer basket with cooking spray.
2. Place fish fillets into the air fryer basket and season with lemon pepper, old bay seasoning, pepper, and salt.
3. Spray fish fillets with cooking spray and cook at 400°F for 7 minutes.
4. Serve and enjoy.

Tilapia Teriyaki

Servings: 3
Cooking Time: 10 Minutes
Ingredients:
- 4 tablespoons teriyaki sauce
- 1 tablespoon pineapple juice
- 1 pound tilapia fillets
- cooking spray
- 6 ounces frozen mixed peppers with onions, thawed and drained
- 2 cups cooked rice

Directions:
1. Mix the teriyaki sauce and pineapple juice together in a small bowl.
2. Split tilapia fillets down the center lengthwise.
3. Brush all sides of fish with the sauce, spray air fryer basket with nonstick cooking spray, and place fish in the basket.
4. Stir the peppers and onions into the remaining sauce and spoon over the fish. Save any leftover sauce for drizzling over the fish when serving.
5. Cook at 360°F for 10 minutes, until fish flakes easily with a fork and is done in center.
6. Divide into 3 or 4 servings and serve each with approximately ½ cup cooked rice.

Catfish Nuggets

Servings: 4
Cooking Time: 7 Minutes Per Batch
Ingredients:
- 2 medium catfish fillets, cut in chunks
- salt and pepper
- 2 eggs
- 2 tablespoons skim milk
- ½ cup cornstarch
- 1 cup panko breadcrumbs, crushed
- oil for misting or cooking spray

Directions:
1. Season catfish chunks with salt and pepper to your liking.
2. Beat together eggs and milk in a small bowl.
3. Place cornstarch in a second small bowl.
4. Place breadcrumbs in a third small bowl.
5. Dip catfish chunks in cornstarch, dip in egg wash, shake off excess, then roll in breadcrumbs.
6. Spray all sides of catfish chunks with oil or cooking spray.
7. Place chunks in air fryer basket in a single layer, leaving space between for air circulation.
8. Cook at 390°F for 4minutes, turn, and cook an additional 3 minutes, until fish flakes easily and outside is crispy brown.
9. Repeat steps 7 and 8 to cook remaining catfish nuggets.

Coconut Jerk Shrimp

Servings:3
Cooking Time: 8 Minutes
Ingredients:
- 1 Large egg white(s)
- 1 teaspoon Purchased or homemade jerk dried seasoning blend
- ¾ cup Plain panko bread crumbs (gluten-free, if a concern)
- ¾ cup Unsweetened shredded coconut
- 12 Large shrimp, peeled and deveined
- Coconut oil spray

Directions:
1. Preheat the air fryer to 375°F .
2. Whisk the egg white(s) and seasoning blend in a bowl until foamy. Add the shrimp and toss well to coat evenly.
3. Mix the bread crumbs and coconut on a dinner plate until well combined. Use kitchen tongs to pick up a shrimp, letting the excess egg white mixture slip back into the rest. Set the shrimp in the bread-crumb mixture. Turn several times to coat evenly and thoroughly. Set on a cutting board and continue coating the remainder of the shrimp.
4. Lightly coat all the shrimp on both sides with the coconut oil spray. Set them in the basket in one layer with as much space between them as possible. Air-fry undisturbed for 6 minutes, or until the coating is lightly browned. If the air fryer is at 360°F, you may need to add 2 minutes to the cooking time.
5. Use clean kitchen tongs to transfer the shrimp to a wire rack. Cool for only a minute or two before serving.

Lemon Butter Scallops

Servings: 1
Cooking Time: 30 Minutes
Ingredients:
- 1 lemon
- 1 lb. scallops
- ½ cup butter

- ¼ cup parsley, chopped

Directions:
1. Juice the lemon into a Ziploc bag.
2. Wash your scallops, dry them, and season to taste. Put them in the bag with the lemon juice. Refrigerate for an hour.
3. Remove the bag from the refrigerator and leave for about twenty minutes until it returns to room temperature. Transfer the scallops into a foil pan that is small enough to be placed inside the fryer.
4. Pre-heat the fryer at 400°F and put the rack inside.
5. Place the foil pan on the rack and cook for five minutes.
6. In the meantime, melt the butter in a saucepan over a medium heat. Zest the lemon over the saucepan, then add in the chopped parsley. Mix well.
7. Take care when removing the pan from the fryer. Transfer the contents to a plate and drizzle with the lemon-butter mixture. Serve hot.

Air Fried Catfish

Servings: 4
Cooking Time: 20 Minutes
Ingredients:
- 4 catfish fillets
- 1 tbsp olive oil
- 1/4 cup fish seasoning
- 1 tbsp fresh parsley, chopped

Directions:
1. Preheat the air fryer to 400°F.
2. Spray air fryer basket with cooking spray.
3. Seasoned fish with seasoning and place into the air fryer basket.
4. Drizzle fish fillets with oil and cook for 10 minutes.
5. Turn fish to another side and cook for 10 minutes more.
6. Garnish with parsley and serve.

Smoked Halibut And Eggs In Brioche

Servings: 4
Cooking Time: 25 Minutes
Ingredients:
- 4 brioche rolls
- 1 pound smoked halibut, chopped
- 4 eggs
- 1 teaspoon dried thyme
- 1 teaspoon dried basil
- Salt and black pepper, to taste
- Cooking spray

Directions:
1. Cut off the top of each brioche; then, scoop out the insides to make the shells.
2. Lay the prepared brioche shells in the lightly greased cooking basket.
3. Spritz with cooking oil; add the halibut. Crack an egg into each brioche shell; sprinkle with thyme, basil, salt, and black pepper.
4. Bake in the preheated Air Fryer at 325°F for 20 minutes. Bon appétit!

Fried Oysters

Servings:12
Cooking Time: 8 Minutes
Ingredients:
- 1½ cups All-purpose flour
- 1½ cups Yellow cornmeal
- 1½ tablespoons Cajun dried seasoning blend
- 1¼ cups, plus more if needed Amber beer, pale ale, or IPA
- 12 Large shucked oysters, any liquid drained off
- Vegetable oil spray

Directions:
1. Preheat the air fryer to 400°F.
2. Whisk ⅔ cup of the flour, ½ cup of the cornmeal, and the seasoning blend in a bowl until uniform. Set aside.
3. Whisk the remaining ⅓ cup flour and the remaining ½ cup cornmeal with the beer in a second bowl, adding more beer in dribs and drabs until the mixture is the consistency of pancake batter.
4. Using a fork, dip a shucked oyster in the beer batter, coating it thoroughly. Gently shake off any excess batter, then set the oyster in the dry mixture and turn gently to coat well and evenly. Set the coated oyster on a cutting board and continue dipping and coating the remainder of the oysters.
5. Coat the oysters with vegetable oil spray, then set them in the basket with as much air space between them as possible. Air-fry undisturbed for 8 minutes, or until lightly browned and crisp.
6. Use a nonstick-safe spatula to transfer the oysters to a wire rack. Cool for a couple of minutes before serving.

Panko-breaded Cod Fillets

Servings:2
Cooking Time: 20 Minutes
Ingredients:
- 1 lemon wedge, juiced and zested
- ½ cup panko bread crumbs
- Salt to taste
- 1 tbsp Dijon mustard
- 1 tbsp butter, melted
- 2 cod fillets

Directions:
1. Preheat air fryer to 350ºF. Combine all ingredients, except for the fish, in a bowl. Press mixture evenly across tops of cod fillets. Place fillets in the greased frying basket and Air Fry for 10 minutes until the cod is opaque and flakes easily with a fork. Serve immediately.

Perfect Soft-shelled Crabs

Servings:2
Cooking Time: 12 Minutes
Ingredients:
- ½ cup All-purpose flour
- 1 tablespoon Old Bay seasoning
- 1 Large egg(s), well beaten
- 1 cup Ground oyster crackers
- 2 2½-ounce cleaned soft-shelled crab(s), about 4 inches across
- Vegetable oil spray

Directions:
1. Preheat the air fryer to 375°F.
2. Set up and fill three shallow soup plates or small pie plates on your counter: one for the flour, whisked with the Old Bay until well combined; one for the beaten egg(s); and one for the cracker crumbs.
3. Set a soft-shelled crab in the flour mixture and turn to coat evenly and well on all sides, even inside the legs. Dip the crab into the egg(s) and coat well, turning at least once, again getting some of the egg between the legs. Let any excess egg slip back into the rest, then set the crab in the cracker crumbs. Turn several times, pressing very gently to get the crab evenly coated with crumbs, even between the legs. Generously coat the crab on all sides with vegetable oil spray. Set it aside if you're making more than one and coat these in the same way.
4. Set the crab(s) in the basket with as much air space between them as possible. They may overlap slightly, particularly at the ends of their legs, depending on the basket's size. Air-fry undisturbed for 12 minutes, or until very crisp and golden brown. If the machine is at 390°F, the crabs may be done in only 10 minutes.
5. Use kitchen tongs to gently transfer the crab(s) to a wire rack. Cool for a couple of minutes before serving.

Southern-style Catfish

Servings:4
Cooking Time: 12 Minutes
Ingredients:
- 4 catfish fillets
- ⅓ cup heavy whipping cream
- 1 tablespoon lemon juice
- 1 cup blanched finely ground almond flour
- 2 teaspoons Old Bay Seasoning
- ½ teaspoon salt
- ¼ teaspoon ground black pepper

Directions:
1. Place catfish fillets into a large bowl with cream and pour in lemon juice. Stir to coat.
2. In a separate large bowl, mix flour and Old Bay Seasoning.
3. Remove each fillet and gently shake off excess cream. Sprinkle with salt and pepper. Press each fillet gently into flour mixture on both sides to coat.
4. Place fillets into ungreased air fryer basket. Adjust the temperature to 400°F and set the timer for 12 minutes, turning fillets halfway through cooking. Catfish will be golden brown and have an internal temperature of at least 145°F when done. Serve warm.

Spicy Mackerel

Servings: 2
Cooking Time: 20 Minutes
Ingredients:
- 2 mackerel fillets
- 2 tbsp. red chili flakes
- 2 tsp. garlic, minced
- 1 tsp. lemon juice

Directions:
1. Season the mackerel fillets with the red pepper flakes, minced garlic, and a drizzle of lemon juice. Allow to sit for five minutes.
2. Preheat your fryer at 350°F.
3. Cook the mackerel for five minutes, before opening the drawer, flipping the fillets, and allowing to cook on the other side for another five minutes.
4. Plate the fillets, making sure to spoon any remaining juice over them before serving.

Crispy Parmesan Lobster Tails

Servings:4
Cooking Time: 7 Minutes
Ingredients:
- 4 lobster tails
- 2 tablespoons salted butter, melted
- 1½ teaspoons Cajun seasoning, divided
- ¼ teaspoon salt
- ¼ teaspoon ground black pepper
- ¼ cup grated Parmesan cheese
- ½ ounce plain pork rinds, finely crushed

Directions:
1. Cut lobster tails open carefully with a pair of scissors and gently pull meat away from shells, resting meat on top of shells.
2. Brush lobster meat with butter and sprinkle with 1 teaspoon Cajun seasoning, ¼ teaspoon per tail.
3. In a small bowl, mix remaining Cajun seasoning, salt, pepper, Parmesan, and pork rinds. Gently press ¼ mixture onto meat on each lobster tail.
4. Carefully place tails into ungreased air fryer basket. Adjust the temperature to 400°F and set the timer for 7 minutes. Lobster tails will be crispy and golden on top and have an internal temperature of at least 145°F when done. Serve warm.

Outrageous Crispy Fried Salmon Skin

Servings:4
Cooking Time: 10 Minutes
Ingredients:
- ½ pound salmon skin, patted dry
- 4 tablespoons coconut oil
- Salt and pepper to taste

Directions:
1. Preheat the air fryer for 5 minutes.
2. In a large bowl, combine everything and mix well.
3. Place in the fryer basket and close.
4. Cook for 10 minutes at 400°F.
5. Halfway through the cooking time, give a good shake to evenly cook the skin.

Maple Balsamic Glazed Salmon

Servings: 4
Cooking Time: 10 Minutes
Ingredients:
- 4 fillets of salmon
- salt and freshly ground black pepper
- vegetable oil
- ¼ cup pure maple syrup
- 3 tablespoons balsamic vinegar
- 1 teaspoon Dijon mustard

Directions:
1. Preheat the air fryer to 400°F.
2. Season the salmon well with salt and freshly ground black pepper. Spray or brush the bottom of the air fryer basket with vegetable oil and place the salmon fillets inside. Air-fry the salmon for 5 minutes.
3. While the salmon is air-frying, combine the maple syrup, balsamic vinegar and Dijon mustard in a small saucepan over medium heat and stir to blend well. Let the mixture simmer while the fish is cooking. It should start to thicken slightly, but keep your eye on it so it doesn't burn.
4. Brush the glaze on the salmon fillets and air-fry for an additional 5 minutes. The salmon should feel firm to the touch when finished and the glaze should be nicely browned on top. Brush a little more glaze on top before removing and serving with rice and vegetables, or a nice green salad.

Spicy Prawns

Servings: 2
Cooking Time: 8 Minutes
Ingredients:
- 6 prawns
- 1/4 tsp pepper
- 1/2 tsp chili powder
- 1 tsp chili flakes
- 1/4 tsp salt

Directions:
1. Preheat the air fryer to 350°F.
2. In a bowl, mix together spices add prawns.
3. Spray air fryer basket with cooking spray.
4. Transfer prawns into the air fryer basket and cook for 8 minutes.
5. Serve and enjoy.

Cajun Flounder Fillets

Servings:2
Cooking Time: 5 Minutes
Ingredients:
- 2 4-ounce skinless flounder fillet(s)
- 2 teaspoons Peanut oil
- 1 teaspoon Purchased or homemade Cajun dried seasoning blend

Directions:
1. Preheat the air fryer to 400°F.
2. Oil the fillet(s) by drizzling on the peanut oil, then gently rubbing in the oil with your clean, dry fingers. Sprinkle the seasoning blend evenly over both sides of the fillet(s).
3. When the machine is at temperature, set the fillet(s) in the basket. If working with more than one fillet, they should not touch, although they may be quite close together, depending on the basket's size. Air-fry undisturbed for 5 minutes, or until lightly browned and cooked through.
4. Use a nonstick-safe spatula to transfer the fillets to a serving platter or plate(s). Serve at once.

Restaurant-style Flounder Cutlets

Servings: 2
Cooking Time: 15 Minutes
Ingredients:
- 1 egg
- 1 cup Pecorino Romano cheese, grated
- Sea salt and white pepper, to taste
- 1/2 teaspoon cayenne pepper
- 1 teaspoon dried parsley flakes
- 2 flounder fillets

Directions:
1. To make a breading station, whisk the egg until frothy.
2. In another bowl, mix Pecorino Romano cheese, and spices.
3. Dip the fish in the egg mixture and turn to coat evenly; then, dredge in the cracker crumb mixture, turning a couple of times to coat evenly.
4. Cook in the preheated Air Fryer at 390°F for 5 minutes turn them over and cook another 5 minutes. Enjoy!

Miso-rubbed Salmon Fillets

Servings:3
Cooking Time: 5 Minutes
Ingredients:

- ¼ cup White (shiro) miso paste (usually made from rice and soy beans)
- 1½ tablespoons Mirin or a substitute
- 2½ teaspoons Unseasoned rice vinegar
- Vegetable oil spray
- 3 6-ounce skin-on salmon fillets

Directions:

1. Preheat the air fryer to 400°F.
2. Mix the miso, mirin, and vinegar in a small bowl until uniform.
3. Remove the basket from the machine. Generously spray the skin side of each fillet. Pick them up one by one with a nonstick-safe spatula and set them in the basket skin side down with as much air space between them as possible. Coat the top of each fillet with the miso mixture, dividing it evenly between them.
4. Return the basket to the machine. Air-fry undisturbed for 5 minutes, or until lightly browned and firm.
5. Use a nonstick-safe spatula to transfer the fillets to serving plates. Cool for only a minute or so before serving.

Buttery Lobster Tails

Servings:4
Cooking Time: 6 Minutes
Ingredients:

- 4 6- to 8-ounce shell-on raw lobster tails
- 2 tablespoons Butter, melted and cooled
- 1 teaspoon Lemon juice
- ½ teaspoon Finely grated lemon zest
- ½ teaspoon Garlic powder
- ½ teaspoon Table salt
- ½ teaspoon Ground black pepper

Directions:

1. Preheat the air fryer to 375°F .
2. To give the tails that restaurant look, you need to butterfly the meat. To do so, place a tail on a cutting board so that the shell is convex. Use kitchen shears to cut a line down the middle of the shell from the larger end to the smaller, cutting only the shell and not the meat below, and stopping before the back fins. Pry open the shell, leaving it intact. Use your clean fingers to separate the meat from the shell's sides and bottom, keeping it attached to the shell at the back near the fins. Pull the meat up and out of the shell through the cut line, laying the meat on top of the shell and closing the shell under the meat. Make two equidistant cuts down the meat from the larger end to near the smaller end, each about ¼ inch deep, for the classic restaurant look on the plate. Repeat this procedure with the remaining tail(s).
3. Stir the butter, lemon juice, zest, garlic powder, salt, and pepper in a small bowl until well combined. Brush this mixture over the lobster meat set atop the shells.
4. When the machine is at temperature, place the tails shell side down in the basket with as much air space between them as possible. Air-fry undisturbed for 6 minutes, or until the lobster meat has pink streaks over it and is firm.
5. Use kitchen tongs to transfer the tails to a wire rack. Cool for only a minute or two before serving.

Stevia Cod

Servings: 4
Cooking Time: 14 Minutes
Ingredients:

- 1/3 cup stevia
- 2 tablespoons coconut aminos
- 4 cod fillets, boneless
- A pinch of salt and black pepper

Directions:

1. In a pan that fits the air fryer, combine all the ingredients and toss gently. Introduce the pan in the fryer and cook at 350°F for 14 minutes, flipping the fish halfway. Divide everything between plates and serve.

Fish Fillet Sandwich

Servings:4
Cooking Time: 18 Minutes
Ingredients:

- 4 cod fillets
- ½ teaspoon salt
- ¼ teaspoon ground black pepper
- 2 cups unsweetened cornflakes, crushed
- 1 cup Italian bread crumbs
- 2 large eggs
- 4 sandwich buns

Directions:

1. Preheat the air fryer to 375°F.
2. Sprinkle cod with salt and pepper on both sides.
3. In a large bowl, combine cornflakes and bread crumbs.
4. In a medium bowl, whisk eggs. Press each piece of cod into eggs to coat, shaking off excess, then into cornflake mixture to coat evenly on both sides. Spritz with cooking spray.
5. Place in the air fryer basket and cook 18 minutes, turning halfway through cooking time, until fillets are brown and internal temperature reaches at least 145°F. Place on buns to serve.

Lime Bay Scallops

Servings:4
Cooking Time: 10 Minutes
Ingredients:

- 2 tbsp butter, melted
- 1 lime, juiced
- ¼ tsp salt
- 1 lb bay scallops
- 2 tbsp chopped cilantro

Directions:

1. Preheat air fryer to 350ºF. Combine all ingredients in a bowl, except for the cilantro. Place scallops in the frying basket and Air Fry for 5 minutes, tossing once. Serve immediately topped with cilantro.

Air Fried Calamari

Servings:3
Cooking Time: 30 Minutes
Ingredients:
- ½ cup cornmeal or cornstarch
- 2 large eggs, beaten
- 2 mashed garlic cloves
- 1 cup breadcrumbs
- lemon juice

Directions:
1. Coat calamari with the cornmeal. The first mixture is prepared by mixing the eggs and garlic. Dip the calamari in the eggs' mixture. Then dip them in the breadcrumbs. Put the rings in the fridge for 2 hours.
2. Then, line them in the air fryer and add oil generously. Fry for 10 to 13 minutes at 390°F, shaking once halfway through. Serve with garlic mayonnaise and top with lemon juice.

Sweet Potato–wrapped Shrimp

Servings:3
Cooking Time: 6 Minutes
Ingredients:
- 24 Long spiralized sweet potato strands
- Olive oil spray
- ¼ teaspoon Garlic powder
- ¼ teaspoon Table salt
- Up to a ⅛ teaspoon Cayenne
- 12 Large shrimp, peeled and deveined

Directions:
1. Preheat the air fryer to 400°F.
2. Lay the spiralized sweet potato strands on a large swath of paper towels and straighten out the strands to long ropes. Coat them with olive oil spray, then sprinkle them with the garlic powder, salt, and cayenne.
3. Pick up 2 strands and wrap them around the center of a shrimp, with the ends tucked under what now becomes the bottom side of the shrimp. Continue wrapping the remainder of the shrimp.
4. Set the shrimp bottom side down in the basket with as much air space between them as possible. Air-fry undisturbed for 6 minutes, or until the sweet potato strands are crisp and the shrimp are pink and firm.
5. Use kitchen tongs to transfer the shrimp to a wire rack. Cool for only a minute or two before serving.

Chapter 7. Vegetable Side Dishes Recipes

Bacon-balsamic Brussels Sprouts

Servings:4
Cooking Time: 12 Minutes
Ingredients:
- 2 cups trimmed and halved fresh Brussels sprouts
- 2 tablespoons olive oil
- ¼ teaspoon salt
- ¼ teaspoon ground black pepper
- 2 tablespoons balsamic vinegar
- 2 slices cooked sugar-free bacon, crumbled

Directions:
1. In a large bowl, toss Brussels sprouts in olive oil, then sprinkle with salt and pepper. Place into ungreased air fryer basket. Adjust the temperature to 375°F and set the timer for 12 minutes, shaking the basket halfway through cooking. Brussels sprouts will be tender and browned when done.
2. Place sprouts in a large serving dish and drizzle with balsamic vinegar. Sprinkle bacon over top. Serve warm.

Honey-mustard Asparagus Puffs

Servings: 4
Cooking Time: 35 Minutes
Ingredients:
- 8 asparagus spears
- ½ sheet puff pastry
- 2 tbsp honey mustard
- 1 egg, lightly beaten

Directions:
1. Preheat the air fryer to 375°F. Spread the pastry with honey mustard and cut it into 8 strips. Wrap the pastry, honey mustard–side in, around the asparagus. Put a rack in the frying basket and lay the asparagus spears on the rack. Brush all over pastries with beaten egg and Air Fry for 12-17 minutes or until the pastry is golden. Serve.

Savory Roasted Carrots

Servings:4
Cooking Time: 12 Minutes
Ingredients:
- 1 pound baby carrots
- 2 tablespoons dry ranch seasoning
- 3 tablespoons salted butter, melted

Directions:
1. Preheat the air fryer to 360°F.
2. Place carrots into a 6" round baking dish. Sprinkle carrots with ranch seasoning and drizzle with butter. Gently toss to coat.
3. Place in the air fryer basket and cook 12 minutes, stirring twice during cooking, until carrots are tender. Serve warm.

Fingerling Potatoes

Servings: 4
Cooking Time: 15 Minutes
Ingredients:
- 1 pound fingerling potatoes
- 1 tablespoon light olive oil
- ½ teaspoon dried parsley
- ½ teaspoon lemon juice

- coarsely ground sea salt

Directions:

1. Cut potatoes in half lengthwise.
2. In a large bowl, combine potatoes, oil, parsley, and lemon juice. Stir well to coat potatoes.
3. Place potatoes in air fryer basket and cook at 360°F for 15 minutes or until lightly browned and tender inside.
4. Sprinkle with sea salt before serving.

Zucchini Bites

Servings: 4
Cooking Time: 15 Minutes

Ingredients:

- 4 zucchinis
- 1 egg
- ½ cup parmesan cheese, grated
- 1 tbsp. Italian herbs
- 1 cup coconut, grated

Directions:

1. Thinly grate the zucchini and dry with a cheesecloth, ensuring to remove all of the moisture.
2. In a bowl, combine the zucchini with the egg, parmesan, Italian herbs, and grated coconut, mixing well to incorporate everything. Using your hands, mold the mixture into balls.
3. Pre-heat the fryer at 400°F and place a rack inside. Lay the zucchini balls on the rack and cook for ten minutes. Serve hot.

Crispy Herbed Potatoes

Servings: 6
Cooking Time: 20 Minutes

Ingredients:

- 3 medium baking potatoes, washed and cubed
- ½ teaspoon dried thyme
- 1 teaspoon minced dried rosemary
- ½ teaspoon garlic powder
- 1 teaspoon sea salt
- ½ teaspoon black pepper
- 2 tablespoons extra-virgin olive oil
- ¼ cup chopped parsley

Directions:

1. Preheat the air fryer to 390°F.
2. Pat the potatoes dry. In a large bowl, mix together the cubed potatoes, thyme, rosemary, garlic powder, sea salt, and pepper. Drizzle and toss with olive oil.
3. Pour the herbed potatoes into the air fryer basket. Cook for 20 minutes, stirring every 5 minutes.
4. Toss the cooked potatoes with chopped parsley and serve immediately.
5. VARY IT! Potatoes are versatile — add any spice or seasoning mixture you prefer and create your own favorite side dish.

Perfect Broccoli

Servings: 4
Cooking Time: 12 Minutes

Ingredients:

- 5 cups 1- to 1½-inch fresh broccoli florets (not frozen)
- Olive oil spray
- ¾ teaspoon Table salt

Directions:

1. Preheat the air fryer to 375°F .

2. Put the broccoli florets in a big bowl, coat them generously with olive oil spray, then toss to coat all surfaces, even down into the crannies, spraying them in a couple of times more. Sprinkle the salt on top and toss again.
3. When the machine is at temperature, pour the florets into the basket. Air-fry for 10 minutes, tossing and rearranging the pieces twice so that all the covered or touching bits are eventually exposed to the air currents, until lightly browned but still crunchy.
4. Pour the florets into a serving bowl. Cool for a minute or two, then serve hot.

Roasted Salsa

Servings: 2
Cooking Time: 30 Minutes

Ingredients:

- 2 large San Marzano tomatoes, cored and cut into large chunks
- ½ medium white onion, peeled and large-diced
- ½ medium jalapeño, seeded and large-diced
- 2 cloves garlic, peeled and diced
- ½ teaspoon salt
- 1 tablespoon coconut oil
- ¼ cup fresh lime juice

Directions:

1. Place tomatoes, onion, and jalapeño into an ungreased 6" round nonstick baking dish. Add garlic, then sprinkle with salt and drizzle with coconut oil.
2. Place dish into air fryer basket. Adjust the temperature to 300°F and set the timer for 30 minutes. Vegetables will be dark brown around the edges and tender when done.
3. Pour mixture into a food processor or blender. Add lime juice. Process on low speed 30 seconds until only a few chunks remain.
4. Transfer salsa to a sealable container and refrigerate at least 1 hour. Serve chilled.

Spicy Fries

Servings: 4
Cooking Time: 20 Minutes

Ingredients:

- 2 tsp olive oil
- 2 tsp cayenne pepper
- 1 tsp paprika
- Salt and black pepper

Directions:

1. Place the fries into a bowl and sprinkle with oil, cayenne, paprika, salt, and black pepper. Toss and place them in the fryer. Cook for 7 minutes at 360ºF, until golden and crispy. Give it a toss after 7-8 minutes and continue cooking for another 8 minutes. Serve.

Lemon Tempeh

Servings: 4
Cooking Time: 12 Minutes

Ingredients:

- 1 teaspoon lemon juice
- 1 tablespoon sunflower oil
- ¼ teaspoon ground coriander
- 6 oz tempeh, chopped

Directions:

1. Sprinkle the tempeh with lemon juice, sunflower oil, and ground coriander. Massage the tempeh gently with the help of the fingertips. After this, preheat the air fryer to 325ºF. Put the tempeh in the air fryer and cook it for 12 minutes. Flip the tempeh every 2 minutes during cooking.

Grilled Lime Scallions

Servings:6
Cooking Time: 15 Minutes
Ingredients:
- 2 bunches of scallions
- 1 tbsp olive oil
- 2 tsp lime juice
- Salt and pepper to taste
- ¼ tsp Italian seasoning
- 2 tsp lime zest

Directions:
1. Preheat air fryer to 370ºF. Trim the scallions and cut them in half lengthwise. Place them in a bowl and add olive oil and lime juice. Toss to coat. Place the mix in the frying basket and Air Fry for 7 minutes, tossing once. Transfer to a serving dish and stir in salt, pepper, Italian seasoning and lime zest. Serve immediately.

Lemon And Butter Artichokes

Servings: 4
Cooking Time: 15 Minutes
Ingredients:
- 12 ounces artichoke hearts
- Juice of ½ lemon
- 4 tablespoons butter, melted
- 2 tablespoons tarragon, chopped
- Salt and black pepper to the taste

Directions:
1. In a bowl, mix all the ingredients, toss, transfer the artichokes to your air fryer's basket and cook at 370ºF for 15 minutes. Divide between plates and serve as a side dish.

Steak Fries

Servings: 4
Cooking Time: 25 Minutes
Ingredients:
- 2 pounds Medium Yukon Gold or other yellow potatoes (peeled or not—your choice)
- 2 tablespoons Olive oil
- ½ teaspoon, or more to taste Table salt
- ½ teaspoon, or more to taste Ground black pepper

Directions:
1. Preheat the air fryer to 350°F .
2. Cut the potatoes lengthwise into wedges about 1 inch wide at the outer edge. Toss these wedges in a bowl with the oil, salt, and pepper until the wedges are evenly coated in the oil.
3. When the machine is at temperature, set the wedges in the basket in a crisscross stack, with about half of the wedges first lining in the basket's bottom, then others set on top of those at a 45-degree angle. Air-fry undisturbed for 15 minutes.
4. Increase the machine's temperature to 400°F. Toss the fries so they're no longer in a crisscross pattern but more like a mound. Air-fry for 10 minutes more, tossing and rearranging the fries once, until they're crisp and brown.
5. Pour them onto a wire rack and cool for a few minutes before serving hot.

Buttery Mushrooms

Servings:4
Cooking Time: 10 Minutes
Ingredients:
- 8 ounces cremini mushrooms, halved
- 2 tablespoons salted butter, melted
- ¼ teaspoon salt
- ¼ teaspoon ground black pepper

Directions:
1. In a medium bowl, toss mushrooms with butter, the sprinkle with salt and pepper. Place into ungreased air frye basket. Adjust the temperature to 400°F and set the timer for 1 minutes, shaking the basket halfway through cooking Mushrooms will be tender when done. Serve warm.

Fried Mashed Potato Balls

Servings:4
Cooking Time: 10 Minutes
Ingredients:
- 2 cups mashed potatoes
- ¾ cup sour cream, divided
- 1 teaspoon salt
- ½ teaspoon ground black pepper
- 1 cup shredded sharp Cheddar cheese
- 4 slices bacon, cooked and crumbled
- 1 cup panko bread crumbs
- Cooking spray

Directions:
1. Preheat the air fryer to 400°F. Cut parchment paper to f the air fryer basket.
2. In a large bowl, mix mashed potatoes, ½ cup sour crean salt, pepper, Cheddar, and bacon. Form twelve balls using tablespoons of the potato mixture per ball.
3. Divide remaining ¼ cup sour cream evenly among mashe potato balls, coating each before rolling in bread crumbs.
4. Place balls on parchment in the air fryer basket and sprit with cooking spray. Cook 10 minutes until brown. Serve warm

Brussels Sprout And Ham Salad

Servings: 3
Cooking Time: 12 Minutes
Ingredients:
- 1 pound 2-inch-in-length Brussels sprouts, quartere through the stem
- 6 ounces Smoked ham steak, any rind removed, dice (gluten-free, if a concern)
- ¼ teaspoon Caraway seeds
- Vegetable oil spray
- ¼ cup Brine from a jar of pickles (gluten-free, if a concern
- ¾ teaspoon Ground black pepper

Directions:
1. Preheat the air fryer to 375°F .
2. Toss the Brussels sprout quarters, ham, and caraway seed in a bowl until well combined. Generously coat the top of th mixture with vegetable oil spray, toss again, spray again, an repeat a couple of times until the vegetables and ham ar glistening.
3. When the machine is at temperature, scrape the contents o the bowl into the basket, spreading it into as close to one laye as you can. Air-fry for 12 minutes, tossing and rearranging th pieces at least twice so that any covered or touching parts ar

eventually exposed to the air currents, until the Brussels sprouts are tender and a little brown at the edges.

4. Dump the contents of the basket into a serving bowl. Scrape any caraway seeds from the bottom of the basket or the tray under the basket attachment into the bowl as well. Add the pickle brine and pepper. Toss well to coat. Serve warm.

Taco Okra

Servings: 3
Cooking Time: 10 Minutes
Ingredients:
- 9 oz okra, chopped
- 1 teaspoon taco seasoning
- 1 teaspoon sunflower oil

Directions:
1. In the mixing bowl mix up chopped okra, taco seasoning, and sunflower oil. Then preheat the air fryer to 385ºF. Put the okra mixture in the air fryer and cook it for 5 minutes. Then shake the vegetables well and cook them for 5 minutes more.

Mini Hasselback Potatoes

Servings: 4
Cooking Time: 25 Minutes
Ingredients:
- 1½ pounds baby Yukon Gold potatoes
- 5 tablespoons butter, cut into very thin slices
- salt and freshly ground black pepper
- 1 tablespoon vegetable oil
- ¼ cup grated Parmesan cheese (optional)
- chopped fresh parsley or chives

Directions:
1. Preheat the air fryer to 400°F.
2. Make six to eight deep vertical slits across the top of each potato about three quarters of the way down. Make sure the slits are deep enough to allow the slices to spread apart a little, but don't cut all the way through the potato. Place a thin slice of butter between each of the slices and season generously with salt and pepper.
3. Transfer the potatoes to the air fryer basket. Pack them in next to each other. It's alright if some of the potatoes sit on top or rest on another potato. Air-fry for 20 minutes.
4. Spray or brush the potatoes with a little vegetable oil and sprinkle the Parmesan cheese on top. Air-fry for an additional 5 minutes. Garnish with chopped parsley or chives and serve hot.

Beet Fries

Servings: 3
Cooking Time: 22 Minutes
Ingredients:
- 3 6-ounce red beets
- Vegetable oil spray
- To taste Coarse sea salt or kosher salt

Directions:
1. Preheat the air fryer to 375°F.
2. Remove the stems from the beets and peel them with a knife or vegetable peeler. Slice them into ½-inch-thick circles. Lay these flat on a cutting board and slice them into ½-inch-thick sticks. Generously coat the sticks on all sides with vegetable oil spray.
3. When the machine is at temperature, drop them into the basket, shake the basket to even the sticks out into as close to one layer as possible, and air-fry for 20 minutes, tossing and rearranging the beet matchsticks every 5 minutes, or until

brown and even crisp at the ends. If the machine is at 360°F, you may need to add 2 minutes to the cooking time.

4. Pour the fries into a big bowl, add the salt, toss well, and serve warm.

Mouth-watering Provençal Mushrooms

Servings: 4
Cooking Time: 35 Minutes
Ingredients:
- 2 lb mushrooms, quartered
- 2-3 tbsp olive oil
- ½ tsp garlic powder
- 2 tsp herbs de Provence
- 2 tbsp dry white wine

Directions:
1. Preheat air fryer to 320°F. Beat together the olive oil, garlic powder, herbs de Provence, and white wine in a bowl. Add the mushrooms and toss gently to coat. Spoon the mixture onto the frying basket and Bake for 16-18 minutes, stirring twice. Serve hot and enjoy!

Cauliflower

Servings: 4
Cooking Time: 6 Minutes
Ingredients:
- ½ cup water
- 1 10-ounce package frozen cauliflower (florets)
- 1 teaspoon lemon pepper seasoning

Directions:
1. Pour the water into air fryer drawer.
2. Pour the frozen cauliflower into the air fryer basket and sprinkle with lemon pepper seasoning.
3. Cook at 390°F for approximately 6 minutes.

Parmesan Herb Radishes

Servings:6
Cooking Time: 10 Minutes
Ingredients:
- 1 pound radishes, ends removed, quartered
- 2 tablespoons salted butter, melted
- ½ teaspoon garlic powder
- ½ teaspoon dried parsley
- ¼ teaspoon dried oregano
- ¼ teaspoon ground black pepper
- ¼ cup grated Parmesan cheese

Directions:
1. Place radishes into a medium bowl and drizzle with butter. Sprinkle with garlic powder, parsley, oregano, and pepper, then place into ungreased air fryer basket. Adjust the temperature to 350°F and set the timer for 10 minutes, shaking the basket three times during cooking. Radishes will be done when tender and golden.
2. Place radishes into a large serving dish and sprinkle with Parmesan. Serve warm.

Perfect Asparagus

Servings: 3
Cooking Time: 10 Minutes
Ingredients:
- 1 pound Very thin asparagus spears
- 2 tablespoons Olive oil
- 1 teaspoon Coarse sea salt or kosher salt

- ¾ teaspoon Finely grated lemon zest

Directions:

1. Preheat the air fryer to 400°F.
2. Trim just enough off the bottom of the asparagus spears so they'll fit in the basket. Put the spears on a large plate and drizzle them with some of the olive oil. Turn them over and drizzle more olive oil, working to get all the spears coated.
3. When the machine is at temperature, place the spears in one direction in the basket. They may be touching. Air-fry for 10 minutes, tossing and rearranging the spears twice, until tender.
4. Dump the contents of the basket on a serving platter. Spread out the spears. Sprinkle them with the salt and lemon zest while still warm. Serve at once.

Cheesy Vegetarian Lasagna

Servings: 4
Cooking Time: 40 Minutes

Ingredients:

- 1 ¼ cups shredded Italian-blend cheese, divided
- ½ cup grated vegetarian Parmesan cheese, divided
- ½ cup full-fat ricotta cheese
- ½ teaspoon salt
- ¼ teaspoon ground black pepper
- 2 cups tomato pasta sauce, divided
- 5 no-boil lasagna noodles

Directions:

1. Preheat the air fryer to 360°F. Spritz a 6" round baking pan with cooking spray.
2. In a medium bowl, mix 1 cup Italian-blend cheese, ¼ cup Parmesan, ricotta, salt, and pepper.
3. Pour ½ cup pasta sauce into the bottom of the prepared pan. Break the noodles into pieces to fit the pan. Place a layer of noodles into the pan.
4. Separate ricotta mixture into three portions. Spread one-third of the mixture over noodles in the pan. Pour ½ cup pasta sauce over ricotta mixture. Repeat layers of noodles, cheese mixture, and pasta sauce twice more until all ingredients are used, topping the final layer with remaining Italian-blend cheese.
5. Cover pan tightly with foil, being sure to tuck foil under the bottom of the pan to ensure the air fryer fan does not blow it off. Place in the air fryer basket. Cook 35 minutes, then remove foil and cook an additional 5 minutes until the top is golden brown and noodles are fork-tender.
6. Remove from the air fryer basket and top with remaining Parmesan and let cool 5 minutes before serving.

Dinner Rolls

Servings:6
Cooking Time: 12 Minutes

Ingredients:

- 1 cup shredded mozzarella cheese
- 1 ounce cream cheese, broken into small pieces
- 1 cup blanched finely ground almond flour
- ¼ cup ground flaxseed
- ½ teaspoon baking powder
- 1 large egg, whisked

Directions:

1. Place mozzarella, cream cheese, and flour in a large microwave-safe bowl. Microwave on high 1 minute. Mix until smooth.

2. Add flaxseed, baking powder, and egg to mixture until fully combined and smooth. Microwave an additional 15 seconds if dough becomes too firm.
3. Separate dough into six equal pieces and roll each into a ball. Place rolls into ungreased air fryer basket. Adjust the temperature to 320°F and set the timer for 12 minutes, turning rolls halfway through cooking. Allow rolls to cool completely before serving, about 5 minutes.

Polenta

Servings: 4
Cooking Time: 15 Minutes

Ingredients:

- 1 pound polenta
- ¼ cup flour
- oil for misting or cooking spray

Directions:

1. Cut polenta into ½-inch slices.
2. Dip slices in flour to coat well. Spray both sides with oil or cooking spray.
3. Cook at 390°F for 5minutes. Turn polenta and spray both sides again with oil.
4. Cook 10 more minutes or until brown and crispy.

Balsamic Green Beans With Bacon

Servings:4
Cooking Time: 15 Minutes

Ingredients:

- 2 cups green beans, trimmed
- 1 tbsp butter, melted
- Salt and pepper to taste
- 1 bacon slice, diced
- 1 clove garlic, minced
- 1 tbsp balsamic vinegar

Directions:

1. Preheat air fryer to 375ºF. Combine green beans, butter, salt, and pepper in a bowl. Put the bean mixture in the frying basket and Air Fry for 5 minutes. Stir in bacon and Air Fry for 4 more minutes. Mix in garlic and cook for 1 minute. Transfer it to a serving dish, drizzle with balsamic vinegar and combine. Serve right away.

Blistered Green Beans

Servings: 3
Cooking Time: 10 Minutes

Ingredients:

- ¾ pound Green beans, trimmed on both ends
- 1½ tablespoons Olive oil
- 3 tablespoons Pine nuts
- 1½ tablespoons Balsamic vinegar
- 1½ teaspoons Minced garlic
- ¾ teaspoon Table salt
- ¾ teaspoon Ground black pepper

Directions:

1. Preheat the air fryer to 400°F.
2. Toss the green beans and oil in a large bowl until all the green beans are glistening.
3. When the machine is at temperature, pile the green beans into the basket. Air-fry for 10 minutes, tossing often to rearrange the green beans in the basket, or until blistered and tender.

4. Dump the contents of the basket into a serving bowl. Add the pine nuts, vinegar, garlic, salt, and pepper. Toss well to coat and combine. Serve warm or at room temperature.

Home Fries

Servings: 4
Cooking Time: 20 Minutes
Ingredients:
- 3 pounds potatoes, cut into 1-inch cubes
- ½ teaspoon oil
- salt and pepper

Directions:
1. In a large bowl, mix the potatoes and oil thoroughly.
2. Cook at 390°F for 10minutes and shake the basket to redistribute potatoes.
3. Cook for an additional 10 minutes, until brown and crisp.
4. Season with salt and pepper to taste.

Sweet Roasted Pumpkin Rounds

Servings: 4
Cooking Time: 35 Minutes
Ingredients:
- 1 pumpkin
- 1 tbsp honey
- 1 tbsp melted butter
- ¼ tsp cardamom
- ¼ tsp sea salt

Directions:
1. Preheat the air fryer to 370°F. Cut the pumpkin in half lengthwise and remove the seeds. Slice each half crosswise into 1-inch-wide half-circles, then cut each half-circle in half again to make quarter rounds. Combine the honey, butter, cardamom, and salt in a bowl and mix well. Toss the pumpkin in the mixture until coated, then put into the frying basket. Bake for 15-20 minutes, shaking once during cooking until the edges start to brown and the squash is tender.

Grits Again

Servings: 2
Cooking Time: 10 Minutes
Ingredients:
- cooked grits
- plain breadcrumbs
- oil for misting or cooking spray
- honey or maple syrup for serving (optional)

Directions:
1. While grits are still warm, spread them into a square or rectangular baking pan, about ½-inch thick. If your grits are thicker than that, scoop some out into another pan.
2. Chill several hours or overnight, until grits are cold and firm.
3. When ready to cook, pour off any water that has collected in pan and cut grits into 2- to 3-inch squares.
4. Dip grits squares in breadcrumbs and place in air fryer basket in single layer, close but not touching.
5. Cook at 390°F for 10 minutes, until heated through and crispy brown on the outside.
6. Serve while hot either plain or with a drizzle of honey or maple syrup.

Sage Hasselback Potatoes

Servings: 4
Cooking Time: 45 Minutes

Ingredients:
- 1 lb fingerling potatoes
- 1 tbsp olive oil
- 1 tbsp butter
- 1tsp dried sage
- Salt and pepper to taste

Directions:
1. Preheat the air fryer to 400°F. Rinse the potatoes dry, then set them on a work surface and put two chopsticks lengthwise on either side of each so you won't cut all the way through. Make vertical, crosswise cuts in the potato, about ⅛ inch apart. Repeat with the remaining potatoes. Combine the olive oil and butter in a bowl and microwave for 30 seconds or until melted. Stir in the sage, salt, and pepper. Put the potatoes in a large bowl and drizzle with the olive oil mixture. Toss to coat, then put the potatoes in the fryer and Air Fry for 22-27 minutes, rearranging them after 10-12 minutes. Cook until the potatoes are tender. Serve hot and enjoy!

Hasselbacks

Servings: 4
Cooking Time: 41 Minutes
Ingredients:
- 2 large potatoes
- oil for misting or cooking spray
- salt, pepper, and garlic powder
- 1½ ounces sharp Cheddar cheese, sliced very thin
- ¼ cup chopped green onions
- 2 strips turkey bacon, cooked and crumbled
- light sour cream for serving (optional)

Directions:
1. Preheat air fryer to 390°F.
2. Scrub potatoes. Cut thin vertical slices ¼-inch thick crosswise about three-quarters of the way down so that bottom of potato remains intact.
3. Fan potatoes slightly to separate slices. Mist with oil and sprinkle with salt, pepper, and garlic powder to taste. Potatoes will be very stiff, but try to get some of the oil and seasoning between the slices.
4. Place potatoes in air fryer basket and cook for 40 minutes or until centers test done when pierced with a fork.
5. Top potatoes with cheese slices and cook for 30 seconds to 1 minute to melt cheese.
6. Cut each potato in half crosswise, and sprinkle with green onions and crumbled bacon. If you like, add a dollop of sour cream before serving.

Garlic-parmesan French Fries

Servings:4
Cooking Time: 45 Minutes
Ingredients:
- 3 large russet potatoes, peeled, trimmed, and sliced into ½" × 4" sticks
- 2 ½ tablespoons olive oil, divided
- 2 teaspoons minced garlic
- ½ teaspoon salt
- ¼ teaspoon ground black pepper
- 1 teaspoon dried parsley
- ¼ cup grated Parmesan cheese

Directions:
1. Place potato sticks in a large bowl of cold water and let soak 30 minutes.

2. Preheat the air fryer to 350°F.

3. Drain potatoes and gently pat dry. Place in a large, dry bowl.

4. Pour 2 tablespoons oil over potatoes. Add garlic, salt, and pepper, then toss to fully coat.

5. Place fries in the air fryer basket and cook 15 minutes, shaking the basket twice during cooking, until fries are golden and crispy on the edges.

6. Place fries into a clean medium bowl and drizzle with remaining ½ tablespoon oil. Sprinkle parsley and Parmesan over fries and toss to coat. Serve warm.

Roasted Peppers With Balsamic Vinegar And Basil

Servings: 6
Cooking Time: 12 Minutes
Ingredients:
- 4 Small or medium red or yellow bell peppers
- 3 tablespoons Olive oil
- 1 tablespoon Balsamic vinegar
- Up to 6 Fresh basil leaves, torn up

Directions:
1. Preheat the air fryer to 400°F.

2. When the machine is at temperature, put the peppers in the basket with at least ¼ inch between them. Air-fry undisturbed for 12 minutes, until blistered, even blackened in places.

3. Use kitchen tongs to transfer the peppers to a medium bowl. Cover the bowl with plastic wrap. Set aside at room temperature for 30 minutes.

4. Uncover the bowl and use kitchen tongs to transfer the peppers to a cutting board or work surface. Peel off the filmy exterior skin. If there are blackened bits under it, these can stay on the peppers. Cut off and remove the stem ends. Split open the peppers and discard any seeds and their spongy membranes. Slice the peppers into ½-inch- to 1-inch-wide strips.

5. Put these in a clean bowl and gently toss them with the oil, vinegar, and basil. Serve at once. Or cover and store at room temperature for up to 4 hours or in the refrigerator for up to 5 days.

Mashed Potato Pancakes

Servings: 6
Cooking Time: 10 Minutes
Ingredients:
- 2 cups leftover mashed potatoes
- ½ cup grated cheddar cheese
- ¼ cup thinly sliced green onions
- ½ teaspoon salt
- ¼ teaspoon black pepper
- 1 cup breadcrumbs

Directions:
1. Preheat the air fryer to 380°F.

2. In a large bowl, mix together the potatoes, cheese, and onions. Using a ¼ cup measuring cup, measure out 6 patties. Form the potatoes into ½-inch thick patties. Season the patties with salt and pepper on both sides.

3. In a small bowl, place the breadcrumbs. Gently press the potato pancakes into the breadcrumbs.

4. Place the potato pancakes into the air fryer basket and spray with cooking spray. Cook for 5 minutes, turn the pancakes over, and cook another 3 to 5 minutes or until golden brown on the outside and cooked through on the inside.

Garlic Knots

Servings: 5
Cooking Time: 15 Minutes
Ingredients:
- 1 cup self-rising flour
- 1 cup plain full-fat Greek yogurt
- ⅓ cup salted butter, melted
- 1 teaspoon garlic powder
- ¼ cup grated Parmesan cheese

Directions:
1. Preheat the air fryer to 320°F.

2. In a large bowl, mix flour and yogurt and let sit 5 minutes.

3. Turn dough onto a lightly floured surface and gently knead about 3 minutes until it's no longer sticky.

4. Form dough into a rectangle and roll out until it measures 10" × 6". Cut dough into ten 1"× 6" strips.

5. Tie each dough strip into a knot. Brush each knot with butter and sprinkle with garlic powder.

6. Place in the air fryer basket and cook 8 minutes, turning after 6 minutes. Let cool 2 minutes, sprinkle with Parmesan, and serve.

Macaroni And Cheese

Servings: 4
Cooking Time: 25 Minutes
Ingredients:
- 1 ½ cups dry elbow macaroni
- 1 cup chicken broth
- ½ cup whole milk
- 2 tablespoons salted butter, melted
- 8 ounces sharp Cheddar cheese, shredded, divided
- ½ teaspoon ground black pepper

Directions:
1. Preheat the air fryer to 350°F.

2. In a 6" baking dish, combine macaroni, broth, milk, butter, half the Cheddar, and pepper. Stir to combine.

3. Place in the air fryer basket and cook 12 minutes.

4. Stir in remaining Cheddar, then return the basket to the air fryer and cook 13 additional minutes.

5. Stir macaroni and cheese until creamy. Let cool 10 minutes before serving.

Cheesy Baked Asparagus

Servings:4
Cooking Time: 18 Minutes
Ingredients:
- ½ cup heavy whipping cream
- ½ cup grated Parmesan cheese
- 2 ounces cream cheese, softened
- 1 pound asparagus, ends trimmed, chopped into 1" pieces
- ¼ teaspoon salt
- ¼ teaspoon ground black pepper

Directions:
1. In a medium bowl, whisk together heavy cream, Parmesan, and cream cheese until combined.

2. Place asparagus into an ungreased 6" round nonstick baking dish. Pour cheese mixture over top and sprinkle with salt and pepper.

3. Place dish into air fryer basket. Adjust the temperature to 350°F and set the timer for 18 minutes. Asparagus will be tender when done. Serve warm.

Roasted Yellow Squash And Onions

Servings: 3
Cooking Time: 20 Minutes
Ingredients:
- 1 medium squash Yellow or summer crookneck squash, cut into ½-inch-thick rounds
- 1½ cups Yellow or white onion, roughly chopped
- ¾ teaspoon Table salt
- ¼ teaspoon Ground cumin (optional)
- Olive oil spray
- 1½ tablespoons Lemon or lime juice

Directions:
1. Preheat the air fryer to 375°F.
2. Toss the squash rounds, onion, salt, and cumin in a large bowl. Lightly coat the vegetables with olive oil spray, toss again, spray again, and keep at it until the vegetables are evenly coated.
3. When the machine is at temperature, scrape the contents of the bowl into the basket, spreading the vegetables out into as close to one layer as you can. Air-fry for 20 minutes, tossing once very gently, until the squash and onions are soft, even a little browned at the edges.
4. Pour the contents of the basket into a serving bowl, add the lemon or lime juice, and toss gently but well to coat. Serve warm or at room temperature.

Onions

Servings: 4
Cooking Time: 18 Minutes
Ingredients:
- 2 yellow onions
- salt and pepper
- ¼ teaspoon ground thyme
- ¼ teaspoon smoked paprika
- 2 teaspoons olive oil
- 1 ounce Gruyère cheese, grated

Directions:
1. Peel onions and halve lengthwise.
2. Sprinkle cut sides of onions with salt, pepper, thyme, and paprika.
3. Place each onion half, cut-surface up, on a large square of aluminum foil. Pull sides of foil up to cup around onion. Drizzle cut surface of onions with oil.
4. Crimp foil at top to seal closed.
5. Place wrapped onions in air fryer basket and cook at 390°F for 18 minutes. When done, onions should be soft enough to pierce with fork but still slightly firm.
6. Open foil just enough to sprinkle each onion with grated cheese.
7. Cook for 30 seconds to 1 minute to melt cheese.

Simple Roasted Sweet Potatoes

Servings: 2
Cooking Time: 45 Minutes
Ingredients:
- 2 10- to 12-ounce sweet potato(es)

Directions:
1. Preheat the air fryer to 350°F.
2. Prick the sweet potato(es) in four or five different places with the tines of a flatware fork.
3. When the machine is at temperature, set the sweet potato(es) in the basket with as much air space between them as possible. Air-fry undisturbed for 45 minutes, or until soft when pricked with a fork.
4. Use kitchen tongs to transfer the sweet potato(es) to a wire rack. Cool for 5 minutes before serving.

Smashed Fried Baby Potatoes

Servings: 3
Cooking Time: 18 Minutes
Ingredients:
- 1½ pounds baby red or baby Yukon gold potatoes
- ¼ cup butter, melted
- 1 teaspoon olive oil
- ½ teaspoon paprika
- 1 teaspoon dried parsley
- salt and freshly ground black pepper
- 2 scallions, finely chopped

Directions:
1. Bring a large pot of salted water to a boil. Add the potatoes and boil for 18 minutes or until the potatoes are fork-tender.
2. Drain the potatoes and transfer them to a cutting board to cool slightly. Spray or brush the bottom of a drinking glass with a little oil. Smash or flatten the potatoes by pressing the glass down on each potato slowly. Try not to completely flatten the potato or smash it so hard that it breaks apart.
3. Combine the melted butter, olive oil, paprika, and parsley together.
4. Preheat the air fryer to 400°F.
5. Spray the bottom of the air fryer basket with oil and transfer one layer of the smashed potatoes into the basket. Brush with some of the butter mixture and season generously with salt and freshly ground black pepper.
6. Air-fry at 400°F for 10 minutes. Carefully flip the potatoes over and air-fry for an additional 8 minutes until crispy and lightly browned.
7. Keep the potatoes warm in a 170°F oven or tent with aluminum foil while you cook the second batch. Sprinkle minced scallions over the potatoes and serve warm.

Asparagus Wrapped In Pancetta

Servings: 4
Cooking Time: 30 Minutes
Ingredients:
- 20 asparagus trimmed
- Salt and pepper pepper
- 4 pancetta slices
- 1 tbsp fresh sage, chopped

Directions:
1. Sprinkle the asparagus with fresh sage, salt and pepper. Toss to coat. Make 4 bundles of 5 spears by wrapping the center of the bunch with one slice of pancetta.
2. Preheat air fryer to 400°F. Put the bundles in the greased frying basket and Air Fry for 8-10 minutes or until the pancetta is brown and the asparagus are starting to char on the edges. Serve immediately.

Honey-roasted Parsnips

Servings: 3
Cooking Time: 23 Minutes
Ingredients:
- 1½ pounds Medium parsnips, peeled
- Olive oil spray
- 1 tablespoon Honey
- 1½ teaspoons Water
- ¼ teaspoon Table salt

Directions:
1. Preheat the air fryer to 350°F .
2. If the thick end of a parsnip is more than ½ inch in diameter, cut the parsnip just below where it swells to its large end, then slice the large section in half lengthwise. If the parsnips are larger than the basket, trim off the thin end so the parsnips will fit. Generously coat the parsnips on all sides with olive oil spray.
3. When the machine is at temperature, set the parsnips in the basket with as much air space between them as possible. Air-fry undisturbed for 20 minutes.
4. Whisk the honey, water, and salt in a small bowl until smooth. Brush this mixture over the parsnips. Air-fry undisturbed for 3 minutes more, or until the glaze is lightly browned.
5. Use kitchen tongs to transfer the parsnips to a wire rack or a serving platter. Cool for a couple of minutes before serving.

Potato Wedges

Servings: 4
Cooking Time: 20 Minutes
Ingredients:
- 6 cups water
- 4 large russet potatoes, sliced into wedges
- 2 teaspoons seasoned salt
- ½ cup whole milk
- ½ cup all-purpose flour

Directions:
1. In a large saucepan over medium-high heat, bring water to a boil.
2. Carefully place potato wedges into boiling water and cook 5 minutes.
3. Preheat the air fryer to 400°F.
4. Drain potatoes into a colander, then rinse under cold running water 1 minute until they feel cool to the touch.
5. Place potatoes in a large bowl and sprinkle with seasoned salt. Pour milk into bowl, then toss wedges to coat.
6. Place flour on a large plate. Gently dredge each potato wedge in flour on both sides to lightly coat.
7. Place wedges in the air fryer basket and spritz both sides with cooking spray. Cook 15 minutes, turning after 10 minutes, until wedges are golden brown. Serve warm.

Mediterranean Zucchini Boats

Servings:4
Cooking Time: 10 Minutes
Ingredients:
- 1 large zucchini, ends removed, halved lengthwise
- 6 grape tomatoes, quartered
- ¼ teaspoon salt
- ¼ cup feta cheese
- 1 tablespoon balsamic vinegar
- 1 tablespoon olive oil

Directions:
1. Use a spoon to scoop out 2 tablespoons from center of each zucchini half, making just enough space to fill with tomatoes and feta.
2. Place tomatoes evenly in centers of zucchini halves and sprinkle with salt. Place into ungreased air fryer basket. Adjust the temperature to 350°F and set the timer for 10 minutes. When done, zucchini will be tender.
3. Transfer boats to a serving tray and sprinkle with feta, then drizzle with vinegar and olive oil. Serve warm.

Twice-baked Potatoes With Pancetta

Servings: 5
Cooking Time: 30 Minutes
Ingredients:
- 2 teaspoons canola oil
- 5 large russet potatoes, peeled
- Sea salt and ground black pepper, to taste
- 5 slices pancetta, chopped
- 5 tablespoons Swiss cheese, shredded

Directions:
1. Start by preheating your Air Fryer to 360 °F.
2. Drizzle the canola oil all over the potatoes. Place the potatoes in the Air Fryer basket and cook approximately 20 minutes, shaking the basket periodically.
3. Lightly crush the potatoes to split and season them with salt and ground black pepper. Add the pancetta and cheese.
4. Place in the preheated Air Fryer and bake an additional 5 minutes or until cheese has melted. Bon appétit!

Roasted Fennel Salad

Servings: 3
Cooking Time: 20 Minutes
Ingredients:
- 3 cups (about ¾ pound) Trimmed fennel, roughly chopped
- 1½ tablespoons Olive oil
- ¼ teaspoon Table salt
- ¼ teaspoon Ground black pepper
- 1½ tablespoons White balsamic vinegar

Directions:
1. Preheat the air fryer to 400°F.
2. Toss the fennel, olive oil, salt, and pepper in a large bowl until the fennel is well coated in the oil.
3. When the machine is at temperature, pour the fennel into the basket, spreading it out into as close to one layer as possible. Air-fry for 20 minutes, tossing and rearranging the fennel pieces twice so that any covered or touching parts get exposed to the air currents, until golden at the edges and softened.
4. Pour the fennel into a serving bowl. Add the vinegar while hot. Toss well, then cool a couple of minutes before serving. Or serve at room temperature.

Roasted Broccoli Salad

Servings:4
Cooking Time: 7 Minutes
Ingredients:
- 2 cups fresh broccoli florets, chopped
- 1 tablespoon olive oil
- ¼ teaspoon salt
- ⅛ teaspoon ground black pepper
- ¼ cup lemon juice, divided
- ¼ cup shredded Parmesan cheese

- ¼ cup sliced roasted almonds

Directions:

1. In a large bowl, toss broccoli and olive oil together. Sprinkle with salt and pepper, then drizzle with 2 tablespoons lemon juice.
2. Place broccoli into ungreased air fryer basket. Adjust the temperature to 350°F and set the timer for 7 minutes, shaking the basket halfway through cooking. Broccoli will be golden on the edges when done.
3. Place broccoli into a large serving bowl and drizzle with remaining lemon juice. Sprinkle with Parmesan and almonds. Serve warm.

Foil Packet Lemon Butter Asparagus

Servings: 4
Cooking Time: 15 Minutes

Ingredients:

- 1 pound asparagus, ends trimmed
- ¼ cup salted butter, cubed
- Zest and juice of ½ medium lemon
- ½ teaspoon salt
- ¼ teaspoon ground black pepper

Directions:

1. Preheat the air fryer to 375°F. Cut a 6" × 6" square of foil.
2. Place asparagus on foil square.
3. Dot asparagus with butter. Sprinkle lemon zest, salt, and pepper on top of asparagus. Drizzle lemon juice over asparagus.
4. Fold foil over asparagus and seal the edges closed to form a packet.
5. Place in the air fryer basket and cook 15 minutes until tender. Serve warm.

Corn Muffins

Servings: 12
Cooking Time: 10 Minutes

Ingredients:

- ½ cup all-purpose flour
- ½ cup cornmeal
- ¼ cup granulated sugar
- ½ teaspoon baking powder
- ¼ cup salted butter, melted
- ½ cup buttermilk
- 1 large egg

Directions:

1. Preheat the air fryer to 350°F.
2. In a large bowl, whisk together flour, cornmeal, sugar, and baking powder.
3. Add butter, buttermilk, and egg to dry mixture. Stir until well combined.
4. Divide batter evenly among twelve silicone or aluminum muffin cups, filling cups about halfway. Working in batches as needed, place in the air fryer and cook 10 minutes until golden brown. Let cool 5 minutes before serving.

Mushrooms, Sautéed

Servings: 4
Cooking Time: 4 Minutes

Ingredients:

- 8 ounces sliced white mushrooms, rinsed and well drained
- ¼ teaspoon garlic powder
- 1 tablespoon Worcestershire sauce

Directions:

1. Place mushrooms in a large bowl and sprinkle with garlic powder and Worcestershire. Stir well to distribute seasonings evenly.
2. Place in air fryer basket and cook at 390°F for 4 minutes, until tender.

Okra

Servings: 4
Cooking Time: 12 Minutes

Ingredients:

- 7–8 ounces fresh okra
- 1 egg
- 1 cup milk
- 1 cup breadcrumbs
- ½ teaspoon salt
- oil for misting or cooking spray

Directions:

1. Remove stem ends from okra and cut in ½-inch slices.
2. In a medium bowl, beat together egg and milk. Add okra slices and stir to coat.
3. In a sealable plastic bag or container with lid, mix together the breadcrumbs and salt.
4. Remove okra from egg mixture, letting excess drip off, and transfer into bag with breadcrumbs.
5. Shake okra in crumbs to coat well.
6. Place all of the coated okra into the air fryer basket and mist with oil or cooking spray. Okra doesn't need to cook in a single layer, nor is it necessary to spray all sides at this point. A good spritz on top will do.
7. Cook at 390°F for 5minutes. Shake basket to redistribute and give it another spritz as you shake.
8. Cook 5 more minutes. Shake and spray again. Cook for 2 minutes longer or until golden brown and crispy.

Tomato Salad

Servings: 4
Cooking Time: 15 Minutes

Ingredients:

- 10 cherry tomatoes, halved
- ½ pound kale leaves, torn
- Salt and black pepper to the taste
- ¼ cup veggie stock
- 2 tablespoons keto tomato sauce

Directions:

1. In a pan that fits your air fryer, mix tomatoes with the remaining ingredients, toss, put the pan in the fryer and cook at 360ºF for 15 minutes. Divide between plates and serve right away.

Yellow Squash And Zucchinis Dish

Servings: 4
Cooking Time:45 Minutes

Ingredients:

- 1 yellow squash; halved, deseeded and cut into chunks
- 6 tsp. olive oil
- 1 lb. zucchinis; sliced
- 1/2 lb. carrots; cubed
- 1 tbsp. tarragon; chopped
- Salt and white pepper to the taste

Directions:

1. In your air fryer's basket; mix zucchinis with carrots, squash, salt, pepper and oil; toss well and cook at 400 °F, for 25

minutes. Divide them on plates and serve as a side dish with tarragon sprinkled on top.

Sweet Butternut Squash

Servings:8
Cooking Time: 15 Minutes
Ingredients:
- 1 medium butternut squash, peeled and cubed
- 2 tablespoons salted butter, melted
- ½ teaspoon salt
- 1 ½ tablespoons brown sugar
- ½ teaspoon ground cinnamon

Directions:
1. Preheat the air fryer to 400°F.
2. In a large bowl, place squash and add butter. Toss to coat. Sprinkle salt, brown sugar, and cinnamon over squash and toss to fully coat.
3. Place squash in the air fryer basket and cook 15 minutes, shaking the basket three times during cooking, until the edges are golden and the center is fork-tender. Serve warm.

Roasted Brussels Sprouts

Servings:6
Cooking Time: 10 Minutes
Ingredients:
- 1 pound fresh Brussels sprouts, trimmed and halved
- 2 tablespoons coconut oil
- ½ teaspoon salt
- ¼ teaspoon ground black pepper
- ½ teaspoon garlic powder
- 1 tablespoon salted butter, melted

Directions:
1. Place Brussels sprouts into a large bowl. Drizzle with coconut oil and sprinkle with salt, pepper, and garlic powder.
2. Place Brussels sprouts into ungreased air fryer basket. Adjust the temperature to 350°F and set the timer for 10 minutes, shaking the basket three times during cooking. Brussels sprouts will be dark golden and tender when done.
3. Place cooked sprouts in a large serving dish and drizzle with butter. Serve warm.

Turmeric Cauliflower Rice

Servings: 4
Cooking Time: 20 Minutes
Ingredients:
- 1 big cauliflower, florets separated and riced
- 1 and ½ cups chicken stock
- 1 tablespoon olive oil
- Salt and black pepper to the taste
- ½ teaspoon turmeric powder

Directions:
1. In a pan that fits the air fryer, combine the cauliflower with the oil and the rest of the ingredients, toss, introduce in the air fryer and cook at 360°F for 20 minutes. Divide between plates and serve as a side dish.

French Fries

Servings: 4
Cooking Time: 25 Minutes
Ingredients:
- 2 cups fresh potatoes
- 2 teaspoons oil

- ½ teaspoon salt

Directions:
1. Cut potatoes into ½-inch-wide slices, then lay slices flat and cut into ½-inch sticks.
2. Rinse potato sticks and blot dry with a clean towel.
3. In a bowl or sealable plastic bag, mix the potatoes, oil, and salt together.
4. Pour into air fryer basket.
5. Cook at 390°F for 10minutes. Shake basket to redistribute fries and continue cooking for approximately 15minutes, until fries are golden brown.

Crunchy Green Beans

Servings: 4
Cooking Time: 15 Minutes
Ingredients:
- 1 tbsp tahini
- 1 tbsp lemon juice
- 1 tsp allspice
- 1 lb green beans, trimmed

Directions:
1. Preheat air fryer to 400°F. Whisk tahini, lemon juice, tbsp of water, and allspice in a bowl. Put in the green beans and toss to coat. Roast for 5 minutes until golden brown and cooked. Serve immediately.

Asparagus Fries

Servings: 4
Cooking Time: 5 Minutes Per Batch
Ingredients:
- 12 ounces fresh asparagus spears with tough ends trimmed off
- 2 egg whites
- ¼ cup water
- ¾ cup panko breadcrumbs
- ¼ cup grated Parmesan cheese, plus 2 tablespoons
- ¼ teaspoon salt
- oil for misting or cooking spray

Directions:
1. Preheat air fryer to 390°F.
2. In a shallow dish, beat egg whites and water until slightly foamy.
3. In another shallow dish, combine panko, Parmesan, and salt.
4. Dip asparagus spears in egg, then roll in crumbs. Spray with oil or cooking spray.
5. Place a layer of asparagus in air fryer basket, leaving just a little space in between each spear. Stack another layer on top crosswise. Cook at 390°F for 5 minutes, until crispy and golden brown.
6. Repeat to cook remaining asparagus.

Roman Artichokes

Servings: 4
Cooking Time: 12 Minutes
Ingredients:
- 2 9-ounce box(es) frozen artichoke heart quarters, thawed
- 1½ tablespoons Olive oil
- 2 teaspoons Minced garlic
- 1 teaspoon Table salt
- Up to ½ teaspoon Red pepper flakes

Directions:

1. Preheat the air fryer to 400°F.
2. Gently toss the artichoke heart quarters, oil, garlic, salt, and red pepper flakes in a bowl until the quarters are well coated.
3. When the machine is at temperature, scrape the contents of the bowl into the basket. Spread the artichoke heart quarters out into as close to one layer as possible. Air-fry undisturbed for 8 minutes. Gently toss and rearrange the quarters so that any covered or touching parts are now exposed to the air currents, then air-fry undisturbed for 4 minutes more, until very crisp.
4. Gently pour the contents of the basket onto a wire rack. Cool for a few minutes before serving.

Grilled Cheese

Servings: 2
Cooking Time: 25 Minutes
Ingredients:
- 4 slices bread
- ½ cup sharp cheddar cheese
- ¼ cup butter, melted

Directions:
1. Pre-heat the Air Fryer at 360°F.
2. Put cheese and butter in separate bowls.
3. Apply the butter to each side of the bread slices with a brush.
4. Spread the cheese across two of the slices of bread and make two sandwiches. Transfer both to the fryer.
5. Cook for 5 – 7 minutes or until a golden brown color is achieved and the cheese is melted.

Buttermilk Biscuits

Servings: 5
Cooking Time: 14 Minutes
Ingredients:
- 1⅔ cups, plus more for dusting All-purpose flour
- 1½ teaspoons Baking powder
- ¼ teaspoon Table salt
- 3 tablespoons plus 1 teaspoon Butter, cold and cut into small pieces
- ½ cup plus ½ tablespoon Cold buttermilk, regular or low-fat
- 2½ tablespoons Butter, melted and cooled

Directions:
1. Preheat the air fryer to 400°F.
2. Mix the flour, baking powder, and salt in a large bowl. Use a pastry cutter or a sturdy flatware fork to cut the cold butter pieces into the flour mixture, working the fat through the tines again and again until the mixture resembles coarse dry sand. Stir in the buttermilk to make a dough.
3. Very lightly dust a clean, dry work surface with flour. Turn the dough out onto it, dip your clean hands into flour, and press the dough into a ¾-inch-thick circle. Use a 3-inch round cookie cutter or sturdy drinking glass to cut the dough into rounds. Gather the dough scraps together, lightly shape again into a ¾-inch-thick circle, and cut out a few more rounds. You'll end up with 4 raw biscuits for a small air fryer, 5 for a medium, or 6 for a large.
4. For a small air fryer, brush the inside of a 6-inch round cake pan with a little more than half of the melted butter, then set the 4 raw biscuits in it, letting them touch but without squishing them.
5. For a medium air fryer, do the same with half of the melted butter in a 7-inch round cake pan and 5 raw biscuits.

6. And for a large air fryer, use a little more than half the melted butter to brush the inside of an 8-inch round cake pan, and set the 6 raw biscuits in it in the same way.
7. Brush the tops of the raw biscuits with the remaining melted butter.
8. Air-fry undisturbed for 14 minutes, or until the biscuits are golden brown and dry to the touch.
9. Using kitchen tongs and a nonstick-safe spatula, two hot pads, or silicone baking mitts, remove the cake pan from the basket and set it on a wire rack. Cool undisturbed for a couple of minutes. Turn the biscuits out onto the wire rack to cool for a couple of minutes more before serving.

Savory Brussels Sprouts

Servings: 4
Cooking Time: 15 Minutes
Ingredients:
- 1 lb Brussels sprouts, quartered
- 2 tbsp balsamic vinegar
- 1 tbsp olive oil
- 1 tbsp honey
- Salt and pepper to taste
- 1 ½ tbsp lime juice
- Parsley for sprinkling

Directions:
1. Preheat air fryer at 350ºF. Combine all ingredients in a bowl. Transfer them to the frying basket. Air Fry for 10 minutes, tossing once. Top with lime juice and parsley.

Rich Baked Sweet Potatoes

Servings: 2
Cooking Time: 55 Minutes
Ingredients:
- 1 lb sweet potatoes, scrubbed and perforated with a fork
- 2 tsp olive oil
- Salt and pepper to taste
- 2 tbsp butter
- 3 tbsp honey

Directions:
1. Preheat air fryer at 400ºF. Mix olive oil, salt, black pepper, and honey. Brush with the prepared mix over both sweet potatoes. Place them in the frying basket and Bake for 45 minutes, turning at 30 minutes mark. Let cool on a cutting board for 10 minutes until cool enough to handle. Slice each potato lengthwise. Press ends of one potato together to open up the slices. Top with butter to serve.

Fried Corn On The Cob

Servings: 2
Cooking Time: 10 Minutes
Ingredients:
- 1½ tablespoons Regular or low-fat mayonnaise (not fat-free; gluten-free, if a concern)
- 1½ teaspoons Minced garlic
- ¼ teaspoon Table salt
- ¾ cup Plain panko bread crumbs (gluten-free, if a concern)
- 3 4-inch lengths husked and de-silked corn on the cob
- Vegetable oil spray

Directions:
1. Preheat the air fryer to 400°F.
2. Stir the mayonnaise, garlic, and salt in a small bowl until well combined. Spread the panko on a dinner plate.

3. Brush the mayonnaise mixture over the kernels of a piece of corn on the cob. Set the corn in the bread crumbs, then roll, pressing gently, to coat it. Lightly coat with vegetable oil spray. Set it aside, then coat the remaining piece(s) of corn in the same way.

4. Set the coated corn on the cob in the basket with as much air space between the pieces as possible. Air-fry undisturbed for 10 minutes, or until brown and crisp along the coating.

5. Use kitchen tongs to gently transfer the pieces of corn to a wire rack. Cool for 5 minutes before serving.

Easy Parmesan Asparagus

Servings: 4
Cooking Time: 15 Minutes
Ingredients:
- 3 tsp grated Parmesan cheese
- 1 lb asparagus, trimmed
- 2 tsp olive oil
- Salt to taste
- 1 clove garlic, minced
- ½ lemon

Directions:
1. Preheat air fryer at 375ºF. Toss the asparagus and olive oil in a bowl, place them in the frying basket, and Air Fry for 8-10 minutes, tossing once. Transfer them into a large serving dish. Sprinkle with salt, garlic, and Parmesan cheese and toss until coated. Serve immediately with a squeeze of lemon. Enjoy!

Green Beans And Tomatoes Recipe

Servings: 4
Cooking Time:25 Minutes
Ingredients:
- 1-pint cherry tomatoes
- 2 tbsp. olive oil
- 1 lb. green beans
- Salt and black pepper to the taste

Directions:
1. In a bowl; mix cherry tomatoes with green beans, olive oil, salt and pepper, toss, transfer to your air fryer and cook at 400 °F, for 15 minutes. Divide among plates and serve right away

Buttered Brussels Sprouts

Servings: 4
Cooking Time: 30 Minutes
Ingredients:
- ¼ cup grated Parmesan
- 2 tbsp butter, melted
- 1 lb Brussels sprouts
- Salt and pepper to taste

Directions:
1. Preheat air fryer to 330°F. Trim the bottoms of the sprouts and remove any discolored leaves. Place the sprouts in a medium bowl along with butter, salt and pepper. Toss to coat, then place them in the frying basket. Roast for 20 minutes, shaking the basket twice. When done, the sprouts should be crisp with golden-brown color. Plate the sprouts in a serving dish and toss with Parmesan cheese.

Turmeric Cabbage Mix

Servings: 4
Cooking Time: 12 Minutes
Ingredients:
- 1 tablespoon olive oil
- 1 big green cabbage head, shredded
- ½ cup yellow onion, chopped
- 2 teaspoons turmeric powder
- Salt and black pepper to taste
- 4 tablespoons tomato sauce

Directions:
1. Take the oil and grease a pan that fits your air fryer.
2. Add all of the other ingredients and toss.
3. Place the pan in the fryer and cook at 365ºF for 12 minutes.
4. Divide between plates and serve as a side dish.

Parmesan Asparagus

Servings: 2
Cooking Time: 5 Minutes
Ingredients:
- 1 bunch asparagus, stems trimmed
- 1 teaspoon olive oil
- salt and freshly ground black pepper
- ¼ cup coarsely grated Parmesan cheese
- ½ lemon

Directions:
1. Preheat the air fryer to 400°F.
2. Toss the asparagus with the oil and season with salt and freshly ground black pepper.
3. Transfer the asparagus to the air fryer basket and air-fry at 400°F for 5 minutes, shaking the basket to turn the asparagus once or twice during the cooking process.
4. When the asparagus is cooked to your liking, sprinkle the asparagus generously with the Parmesan cheese and close the air fryer drawer again. Let the asparagus sit for 1 minute in the turned-off air fryer. Then, remove the asparagus, transfer it to a serving dish and finish with a grind of black pepper and a squeeze of lemon juice.

Cheesy Garlic Bread

Servings: 6
Cooking Time: 12 Minutes
Ingredients:
- 1 cup self-rising flour
- 1 cup plain full-fat Greek yogurt
- ¼ cup salted butter, softened
- 1 tablespoon minced garlic
- 1 cup shredded mozzarella cheese

Directions:
1. Preheat the air fryer to 320°F. Cut parchment paper to fit the air fryer basket.
2. In a large bowl, mix flour and yogurt until a sticky, soft dough forms. Let sit 5 minutes.
3. Turn dough onto a lightly floured surface. Knead dough 1 minute, then transfer to prepared parchment. Press out into an 8" round.
4. In a small bowl, mix butter and garlic. Brush over dough. Sprinkle with mozzarella.
5. Place in the air fryer and cook 12 minutes until edges are golden and cheese is brown. Serve warm.

Cauliflower Rice Balls

Servings:4
Cooking Time: 8 Minutes
Ingredients:
- 1 steamer bag cauliflower rice, cooked according to package instructions
- ½ cup shredded mozzarella cheese
- 1 large egg
- 2 ounces plain pork rinds, finely crushed
- ¼ teaspoon salt
- ½ teaspoon Italian seasoning

Directions:
1. Place cauliflower into a large bowl and mix with mozzarella.
2. Whisk egg in a separate medium bowl. Place pork rinds into another large bowl with salt and Italian seasoning.
3. Separate cauliflower mixture into four equal sections and form each into a ball. Carefully dip a ball into whisked egg, then roll in pork rinds. Repeat with remaining balls.
4. Place cauliflower balls into ungreased air fryer basket. Adjust the temperature to 400°F and set the timer for 8 minutes. Rice balls will be golden when done.
5. Use a spatula to carefully move cauliflower balls to a large dish for serving. Serve warm.

Rosemary New Potatoes

Servings: 4
Cooking Time: 6 Minutes
Ingredients:
- 3 large red potatoes
- ¼ teaspoon ground rosemary
- ¼ teaspoon ground thyme
- ⅛ teaspoon salt
- ⅛ teaspoon ground black pepper
- 2 teaspoons extra-light olive oil

Directions:
1. Preheat air fryer to 330°F.
2. Place potatoes in large bowl and sprinkle with rosemary, thyme, salt, and pepper.
3. Stir with a spoon to distribute seasonings evenly.
4. Add oil to potatoes and stir again to coat well.
5. Cook at 330°F for 4minutes. Stir and break apart any that have stuck together.
6. Cook an additional 2 minutes or until fork-tender.

Dijon Roast Cabbage

Servings:4
Cooking Time: 10 Minutes
Ingredients:
- 1 small head cabbage, cored and sliced into 1"-thick slices
- 2 tablespoons olive oil, divided
- ½ teaspoon salt
- 1 tablespoon Dijon mustard
- 1 teaspoon apple cider vinegar
- 1 teaspoon granular erythritol

Directions:
1. Drizzle each cabbage slice with 1 tablespoon olive oil, then sprinkle with salt. Place slices into ungreased air fryer basket, working in batches if needed. Adjust the temperature to 350°F and set the timer for 10 minutes. Cabbage will be tender and edges will begin to brown when done.

2. In a small bowl, whisk remaining olive oil with mustard, vinegar, and erythritol. Drizzle over cabbage in a large serving dish. Serve warm.

Simple Taro Fries

Servings: 2
Cooking Time: 20 Minutes
Ingredients:
- 8 small taro, peel and cut into fries shape
- 1 tbsp olive oil
- 1/2 tsp salt

Directions:
1. Add taro slice in a bowl and toss well with olive oil and salt.
2. Transfer taro slices into the air fryer basket.
3. Cook at 360ºF for 20 minutes. Toss halfway through.
4. Serve and enjoy.

Sweet Potato Fries

Servings: 3
Cooking Time: 20 Minutes
Ingredients:
- 2 10-ounce sweet potato(es)
- Vegetable oil spray
- To taste Coarse sea salt or kosher salt

Directions:
1. Preheat the air fryer to 400°F.
2. Peel the sweet potato(es), then cut lengthwise into ¼-inch-thick slices. Cut these slices lengthwise into ¼-inch-thick matchsticks. Place these matchsticks in a bowl and coat them with vegetable oil spray. Toss well, spray them again, and toss several times to make sure they're all evenly coated.
3. When the machine is at temperature, pour the sweet potato matchsticks into the basket, spreading them out in as close to an even layer as possible. Air-fry for 20 minutes, tossing and rearranging the matchsticks every 5 minutes, until lightly browned and crisp.
4. Pour the contents of the basket into a bowl, add some salt to taste, and toss well to coat.

Yellow Squash

Servings: 4
Cooking Time: 10 Minutes
Ingredients:
- 1 large yellow squash
- 2 eggs
- ¼ cup buttermilk
- 1 cup panko breadcrumbs
- ¼ cup white cornmeal
- ½ teaspoon salt
- oil for misting or cooking spray

Directions:
1. Preheat air fryer to 390°F.
2. Cut the squash into ¼-inch slices.
3. In a shallow dish, beat together eggs and buttermilk.
4. In sealable plastic bag or container with lid, combine ¼ cup panko crumbs, white cornmeal, and salt. Shake to mix well.
5. Place the remaining ¾ cup panko crumbs in a separate shallow dish.
6. Dump all the squash slices into the egg/buttermilk mixture. Stir to coat.

7. Remove squash from buttermilk mixture with a slotted spoon, letting excess drip off, and transfer to the panko/cornmeal mixture. Close bag or container and shake well to coat.

8. Remove squash from crumb mixture, letting excess fall off. Return squash to egg/buttermilk mixture, stirring gently to coat. If you need more liquid to coat all the squash, add a little more buttermilk.

9. Remove each squash slice from egg wash and dip in a dish of ¾ cup panko crumbs.

10. Mist squash slices with oil or cooking spray and place in air fryer basket. Squash should be in a single layer, but it's okay if the slices crowd together and overlap a little.

11. Cook at 390°F for 5minutes. Shake basket to break up any that have stuck together. Mist again with oil or spray.

12. Cook 5minutes longer and check. If necessary, mist again with oil and cook an additional two minutes, until squash slices are golden brown and crisp.

Sea Salt Radishes

Servings: 4
Cooking Time: 25 Minutes
Ingredients:
- 1 lb radishes
- 2 tbsp olive oil
- ½ tsp sea salt
- ½ tsp garlic powder

Directions:
1. Preheat air fryer to 360°F. Toss the radishes with olive oil, garlic powder, and salt in a bowl. Pour them into the air fryer. Air Fry for 18 minutes, turning once. Serve.

Brussels Sprouts

Servings: 3
Cooking Time: 5 Minutes
Ingredients:
- 1 10-ounce package frozen brussels sprouts, thawed and halved
- 2 teaspoons olive oil
- salt and pepper

Directions:
1. Toss the brussels sprouts and olive oil together.
2. Place them in the air fryer basket and season to taste with salt and pepper.
3. Cook at 360°F for approximately 5minutes, until the edges begin to brown.

Simple Zucchini Ribbons

Servings:4
Cooking Time: 15 Minutes
Ingredients:
- 2 zucchini
- 2 tsp butter, melted
- ¼ tsp garlic powder
- ¼ tsp chili flakes
- 8 cherry tomatoes, halved
- Salt and pepper to taste

Directions:
1. Preheat air fryer to 275ºF. Cut the zucchini into ribbons with a vegetable peeler. Mix them with butter, garlic, chili flakes, salt, and pepper in a bowl. Transfer to the frying basket and Air Fry for 2 minutes. Toss and add the cherry tomatoes. Cook for another 2 minutes. Serve.

Mexican-style Frittata

Servings: 4
Cooking Time: 35 Minutes
Ingredients:
- ½ cup shredded Cotija cheese
- ½ cup cooked black beans
- 1 cooked potato, sliced
- 3 eggs, beaten
- Salt and pepper to taste

Directions:
1. Preheat air fryer to 350°F. Mix the eggs, beans, half o Cotija cheese, salt, and pepper in a bowl. Pour the mixture int a greased baking dish. Top with potato slices. Place the bakin dish in the frying basket and Air Fry for 10 minutes. Slide th basket out and sprinkle the remaining Cotija cheese over th dish. Cook for 10 more minutes or until golden and bubbling Slice into wedges to serve.

Chipotle Chickpea Tacos

Servings: 4
Cooking Time: 10 Minutes
Ingredients:
- 2 cans chickpeas, drained and rinsed
- ¼ cup adobo sauce
- ¾ teaspoon salt
- ¼ teaspoon ground black pepper
- 8 medium flour tortillas, warmed
- 1 ½ cups chopped avocado
- ½ cup chopped fresh cilantro

Directions:
1. Preheat the air fryer to 375°F.
2. In a large bowl, toss chickpeas, adobo, salt, and pepper t fully coat.
3. Using a slotted spoon, place chickpeas in the air frye basket and cook 10 minutes, shaking the basket twice durin cooking, until tender.
4. To assemble, scoop ¼ cup chickpeas into a tortilla, the top with avocado and cilantro. Repeat with remaining tortilla and filling. Serve warm.

Green Beans And Potatoes Recipe

Servings: 5
Cooking Time:25 Minutes
Ingredients:
- 2 lbs. green beans
- 6 new potatoes; halved
- Salt and black pepper to the taste
- 6 bacon slices; cooked and chopped.
- A drizzle of olive oil

Directions:
1. In a bowl; mix green beans with potatoes, salt, pepper an oil, toss, transfer to your air fryer and cook at 390 °F, for 1 minutes. Divide among plates and serve with bacon sprinkle on top.

Almond Green Beans

Servings: 4
Cooking Time: 20 Minutes
Ingredients:
- 2 cups green beans, trimmed
- ¼ cup slivered almonds
- 2 tbsp butter, melted
- Salt and pepper to taste
- 2 tsp lemon juice
- Lemon zest and slices

Directions:
1. Preheat air fryer at 375ºF. Add almonds to the frying basket and Air Fry for 2 minutes, tossing once. Set aside in a small bowl. Combine the remaining ingredients, except 1 tbsp of butter, in a bowl.
2. Place green beans in the frying basket and Air Fry for 10 minutes, tossing once. Then, transfer them to a large serving dish. Scatter with the melted butter, lemon juice and roasted almonds and toss. Serve immediately garnished with lemon zest and lemon slices.

Shoestring Butternut Squash Fries

Servings: 3
Cooking Time: 16 Minutes
Ingredients:
- 1 pound 2 ounces Spiralized butternut squash strands
- Vegetable oil spray
- To taste Coarse sea salt or kosher salt

Directions:
1. Preheat the air fryer to 375°F .
2. Place the spiralized squash in a big bowl. Coat the strands with vegetable oil spray, toss well, coat again, and toss several times to make sure all the strands have been oiled.
3. When the machine is at temperature, pour the strands into the basket and spread them out into as even a layer as possible. Air-fry for 16 minutes, tossing and rearranging the strands every 4 minutes, or until they're lightly browned and crisp.
4. Pour the contents of the basket into a serving bowl, add salt to taste, and toss well before serving hot.

Corn On The Cob

Servings: 4
Cooking Time: 12 Minutes
Ingredients:
- 2 large ears fresh corn
- olive oil for misting
- salt (optional)

Directions:
1. Shuck corn, remove silks, and wash.
2. Cut or break each ear in half crosswise.
3. Spray corn with olive oil.
4. Cook at 390°F for 12 minutes or until browned as much as you like.
5. Serve plain or with coarsely ground salt.

Spicy Fried Green Beans

Servings: 2
Cooking Time: 8 Minutes
Ingredients:
- 12 ounces green beans, trimmed
- 2 small dried hot red chili peppers (like árbol)
- ¼ cup panko breadcrumbs
- 1 tablespoon olive oil
- ½ teaspoon salt
- ⅛ teaspoon crushed red pepper flakes
- 2 scallions, thinly sliced

Directions:
1. Preheat the air fryer to 400°F.
2. Toss the green beans, chili peppers and panko breadcrumbs with the olive oil, salt and crushed red pepper flakes.
3. Air-fry for 8 minutes, shaking the basket once during the cooking process. The crumbs will fall into the bottom drawer – don't worry.
4. Transfer the green beans to a serving dish, sprinkle the scallions and the toasted crumbs from the air fryer drawer on top and serve. The dried peppers are not to be eaten, but they do look nice with the green beans. You can leave them in, or take them out as you please.

Cheesy Loaded Broccoli

Servings:2
Cooking Time: 10 Minutes
Ingredients:
- 3 cups fresh broccoli florets
- 1 tablespoon coconut oil
- ¼ teaspoon salt
- ½ cup shredded sharp Cheddar cheese
- ¼ cup sour cream
- 4 slices cooked sugar-free bacon, crumbled
- 1 medium scallion, trimmed and sliced on the bias

Directions:
1. Place broccoli into ungreased air fryer basket, drizzle with coconut oil, and sprinkle with salt. Adjust the temperature to 350°F and set the timer for 8 minutes. Shake basket three times during cooking to avoid burned spots.
2. When timer beeps, sprinkle broccoli with Cheddar and set the timer for 2 additional minutes. When done, cheese will be melted and broccoli will be tender.
3. Serve warm in a large serving dish, topped with sour cream, crumbled bacon, and scallion slices.

Crispy Brussels Sprouts

Servings: 3
Cooking Time: 12 Minutes
Ingredients:
- 1¼ pounds Medium, 2-inch-in-length Brussels sprouts
- 1½ tablespoons Olive oil
- ¾ teaspoon Table salt

Directions:
1. Preheat the air fryer to 400°F.
2. Halve each Brussels sprout through the stem end, pulling off and discarding any discolored outer leaves. Put the sprout halves in a large bowl, add the oil and salt, and stir well to coat evenly, until the Brussels sprouts are glistening.
3. When the machine is at temperature, scrape the contents of the bowl into the basket, gently spreading the Brussels sprout halves into as close to one layer as possible. Air-fry for 12 minutes, gently tossing and rearranging the vegetables twice to get all covered or touching parts exposed to the air currents, until crisp and browned at the edges.
4. Gently pour the contents of the basket onto a wire rack. Cool for a minute or two before serving.

Shallots Almonds Green Beans

Servings: 6
Cooking Time: 15 Minutes
Ingredients:
- 1/4 cup almonds, toasted
- 1 1/2 lbs green beans, trimmed and steamed
- 2 tbsp olive oil
- 1/2 lb shallots, chopped
- Pepper
- Salt

Directions:
1. Add all ingredients into the large bowl and toss well.
2. Transfer green bean mixture into the air fryer basket and cook at 400ºF for 15 minutes.
3. Serve and enjoy.

Crispy Green Beans

Servings:4
Cooking Time: 8 Minutes
Ingredients:
- 2 teaspoons olive oil
- ½ pound fresh green beans, ends trimmed
- ¼ teaspoon salt
- ¼ teaspoon ground black pepper

Directions:
1. In a large bowl, drizzle olive oil over green beans and sprinkle with salt and pepper.
2. Place green beans into ungreased air fryer basket. Adjust the temperature to 350°F and set the timer for 8 minutes, shaking the basket two times during cooking. Green beans will be dark golden and crispy at the edges when done. Serve warm.

Hot Okra Wedges

Servings: 2
Cooking Time: 35 Minutes
Ingredients:
- 1 cup okra, sliced
- 1 cup breadcrumbs
- 2 eggs, beaten
- A pinch of black pepper
- 1 tsp crushed red peppers
- 2 tsp hot Tabasco sauce

Directions:
1. Preheat air fryer to 350°F. Place the eggs and Tabasco sauce in a bowl and stir thoroughly; set aside. In a separate mixing bowl, combine the breadcrumbs, crushed red peppers, and pepper. Dip the okra into the beaten eggs, then coat in the crumb mixture. Lay the okra pieces on the greased frying basket. Air Fry for 14-16 minutes, shaking the basket several times during cooking. When ready, the okra will be crispy and golden brown. Serve.

Simple Peppared Carrot Chips

Servings: 4
Cooking Time: 15 Minutes
Ingredients:
- 3 carrots, cut into coins
- 1 tbsp sesame oil
- Salt and pepper to taste

Directions:

1. Preheat air fryer at 375ºF. Combine all ingredients in a bowl. Place carrots in the frying basket and Roast for 10 minutes, tossing once. Serve right away.

Glazed Carrots

Servings: 4
Cooking Time: 10 Minutes
Ingredients:
- 2 teaspoons honey
- 1 teaspoon orange juice
- ½ teaspoon grated orange rind
- ⅛ teaspoon ginger
- 1 pound baby carrots
- 2 teaspoons olive oil
- ¼ teaspoon salt

Directions:
1. Combine honey, orange juice, grated rind, and ginger in a small bowl and set aside.
2. Toss the carrots, oil, and salt together to coat well and pour them into the air fryer basket.
3. Cook at 390°F for 5minutes. Shake basket to stir a little and cook for 4 minutes more, until carrots are barely tender.
4. Pour carrots into air fryer baking pan.
5. Stir the honey mixture to combine well, pour glaze over carrots, and stir to coat.
6. Cook at 360°F for 1 minute or just until heated through.

Roasted Brussels Sprouts With Bacon

Servings: 4
Cooking Time: 20 Minutes
Ingredients:
- 4 slices thick-cut bacon, chopped (about ¼ pound)
- 1 pound Brussels sprouts, halved (or quartered if large)
- freshly ground black pepper

Directions:
1. Preheat the air fryer to 380°F.
2. Air-fry the bacon for 5 minutes, shaking the basket once or twice during the cooking time.
3. Add the Brussels sprouts to the basket and drizzle a little bacon fat from the bottom of the air fryer drawer into the basket Toss the sprouts to coat with the bacon fat. Air-fry for an additional 15 minutes, or until the Brussels sprouts are tender to a knifepoint.
4. Season with freshly ground black pepper.

Pancetta Mushroom & Onion Sautée

Servings:4
Cooking Time: 20 Minutes
Ingredients:
- 16 oz white button mushrooms, stems trimmed, halved
- 1 onion, cut into half-moons
- 4 pancetta slices, diced
- 1 clove garlic, minced

Directions:
1. Preheat air fryer to 350ºF. Add all ingredients, except for the garlic, to the frying basket and Air Fry for 8 minutes, tossing once. Stir in the garlic and cook for 1 more minute Serve right away.

Green Peas With Mint

Servings: 4
Cooking Time: 5 Minutes
Ingredients:
- 1 cup shredded lettuce
- 1 10-ounce package frozen green peas, thawed
- 1 tablespoon fresh mint, shredded
- 1 teaspoon melted butter

Directions:
1. Lay the shredded lettuce in the air fryer basket.
2. Toss together the peas, mint, and melted butter and spoon over the lettuce.
3. Cook at 360°F for 5minutes, until peas are warm and lettuce wilts.

Chapter 8. Vegetarians Recipes

Crispy Apple Fries With Caramel Sauce

Servings: 4
Cooking Time: 15 Minutes
Ingredients:
- 4 medium apples, cored
- ¼ tsp cinnamon
- ¼ tsp nutmeg
- 1 cup caramel sauce

Directions:
1. Preheat air fryer to 350°F. Slice the apples to a 1/3-inch thickness for a crunchy chip. Place in a large bowl and sprinkle with cinnamon and nutmeg. Place the slices in the air fryer basket. Bake for 6 minutes. Shake the basket, then cook for another 4 minutes or until crunchy. Serve drizzled with caramel sauce and enjoy!

Breadcrumbs Stuffed Mushrooms

Servings:4
Cooking Time:10 Minutes
Ingredients:
- 1½ spelt bread slices
- 1 tablespoon flat-leaf parsley, finely chopped
- 16 small button mushrooms, stemmed and gills removed
- 1½ tablespoons olive oil
- 1 garlic clove, crushed
- Salt and black pepper, to taste

Directions:
1. Preheat the Air fryer to 390°F and grease an Air fryer basket.
2. Put the bread slices in a food processor and pulse until fine crumbs form.
3. Transfer the crumbs into a bowl and stir in the olive oil, garlic, parsley, salt, and black pepper.
4. Stuff the breadcrumbs mixture in each mushroom cap and arrange the mushrooms in the Air fryer basket.
5. Cook for about 10 minutes and dish out in a bowl to serve warm.

Crispy Cabbage Steaks

Servings:4
Cooking Time: 10 Minutes
Ingredients:
- 1 small head green cabbage, cored and cut into ½"-thick slices
- ¼ teaspoon salt
- ¼ teaspoon ground black pepper
- 2 tablespoons olive oil
- 1 clove garlic, peeled and finely minced
- ½ teaspoon dried thyme
- ½ teaspoon dried parsley

Directions:
1. Sprinkle each side of cabbage with salt and pepper, then place into ungreased air fryer basket, working in batches if needed.
2. Drizzle each side of cabbage with olive oil, then sprinkle with remaining ingredients on both sides. Adjust the temperature to 350°F and set the timer for 10 minutes, turning "steaks" halfway through cooking. Cabbage will be browned at the edges and tender when done. Serve warm.

Roasted Vegetable Pita Pizza

Servings: 4
Cooking Time: 20 Minutes
Ingredients:
- 1 medium red bell pepper, seeded and cut into quarters
- 1 teaspoon extra-virgin olive oil
- ⅛ teaspoon black pepper
- ⅛ teaspoon salt
- Two 6-inch whole-grain pita breads
- 6 tablespoons pesto sauce
- ¼ small red onion, thinly sliced
- ½ cup shredded part-skim mozzarella cheese

Directions:
1. Preheat the air fryer to 400°F.
2. In a small bowl, toss the bell peppers with the olive oil, pepper, and salt.
3. Place the bell peppers in the air fryer and cook for 15 minutes, shaking every 5 minutes to prevent burning.
4. Remove the peppers and set aside. Turn the air fryer temperature down to 350°F.
5. Lay the pita bread on a flat surface. Cover each with half the pesto sauce; then top with even portions of the red bell peppers and onions. Sprinkle cheese over the top. Spray the air fryer basket with olive oil mist.
6. Carefully lift the pita bread into the air fryer basket with a spatula.
7. Cook for 5 to 8 minutes, or until the outer edges begin to brown and the cheese is melted.
8. Serve warm with desired sides.

Savory Herb Cloud Eggs

Servings:2
Cooking Time: 8 Minutes
Ingredients:

- 2 large eggs, whites and yolks separated
- ¼ teaspoon salt
- ¼ teaspoon dried oregano
- 2 tablespoons chopped fresh chives
- 2 teaspoons salted butter, melted

Directions:

1. In a large bowl, whip egg whites until stiff peaks form, about 3 minutes. Place egg whites evenly into two ungreased 4" ramekins. Sprinkle evenly with salt, oregano, and chives. Place 1 whole egg yolk in center of each ramekin and drizzle with butter.
2. Place ramekins into air fryer basket. Adjust the temperature to 350°F and set the timer for 8 minutes. Egg whites will be fluffy and browned when done. Serve warm.

Spaghetti Squash

Servings:4
Cooking Time: 45 Minutes
Ingredients:

- 1 large spaghetti squash, halved lengthwise and seeded
- 1 teaspoon salt
- ½ teaspoon ground black pepper
- 1 teaspoon garlic powder
- 1 teaspoon dried parsley
- 2 tablespoons salted butter, melted

Directions:

1. Preheat the air fryer to 350°F.
2. Sprinkle squash with salt, pepper, garlic powder, and parsley. Spritz with cooking spray.
3. Place skin side down in the air fryer basket and cook 30 minutes.
4. Turn squash skin side up and cook an additional 15 minutes until fork-tender. You should be able to easily use a fork to scrape across the surface to separate the strands.
5. Place strands in a medium bowl, top with butter, and toss. Serve warm.

Easy Baked Root Veggies

Servings:4
Cooking Time: 45 Minutes
Ingredients:

- ¼ cup olive oil
- 1 head broccoli, cut into florets
- 1 tablespoon dry onion powder
- 2 sweet potatoes, peeled and cubed
- 4 carrots, cut into chunks
- 4 zucchinis, sliced thickly
- salt and pepper to taste

Directions:

1. Preheat the air fryer to 400°F.
2. In a baking dish that can fit inside the air fryer, mix all the ingredients and bake for 45 minutes or until the vegetables are tender and the sides have browned.

Vegetable Nuggets

Servings:6
Cooking Time: 10 Minutes Per Batch
Ingredients:

- 1 cup shredded carrots
- 2 cups broccoli florets
- 2 large eggs
- 1 cup shredded Cheddar cheese
- 1 cup Italian bread crumbs
- 1 teaspoon salt
- ½ teaspoon ground black pepper

Directions:

1. Preheat the air fryer to 400°F.
2. In a food processor, combine carrots and broccoli and pulse five times. Add eggs, Cheddar, bread crumbs, salt, and pepper, and pulse ten times.
3. Carefully scoop twenty-four balls, about 1 heaping tablespoon each, out of the mixture. Spritz balls with cooking spray.
4. Place balls in the air fryer basket, working in batches as necessary, and cook 10 minutes, shaking the basket twice during cooking to ensure even browning. Serve warm.

Portobello Mini Pizzas

Servings:4
Cooking Time: 10 Minutes
Ingredients:

- 4 large portobello mushrooms, stems removed
- 2 cups shredded mozzarella cheese, divided
- ½ cup full-fat ricotta cheese
- 1 teaspoon salt, divided
- ½ teaspoon ground black pepper
- 1 teaspoon Italian seasoning
- 1 cup pizza sauce

Directions:

1. Preheat the air fryer to 350°F.
2. Use a spoon to hollow out mushroom caps. Spritz mushrooms with cooking spray. Place ¼ cup mozzarella into each mushroom cap.
3. In a small bowl, mix ricotta, ½ teaspoon salt, pepper, and Italian seasoning. Divide mixture evenly and spoon into mushroom caps.
4. Pour ¼ cup pizza sauce into each mushroom cap, then top each with ¼ cup mozzarella. Sprinkle tops of pizzas with remaining salt.
5. Place mushrooms in the air fryer basket and cook 10 minutes until cheese is brown and bubbling. Serve warm.

Cheese And Bean Enchiladas

Servings:4
Cooking Time: 9 Minutes
Ingredients:

- 1 can pinto beans, drained and rinsed
- 1 ½ tablespoons taco seasoning
- 1 cup red enchilada sauce, divided
- 1 ½ cups shredded Mexican-blend cheese, divided
- 4 fajita-size flour tortillas

Directions:

1. Preheat the air fryer to 320°F.
2. In a large microwave-safe bowl, microwave beans for minute. Mash half the beans and fold into whole beans. Mix in taco seasoning, ¼ cup enchilada sauce, and 1 cup cheese until well combined.
3. Place ¼ cup bean mixture onto each tortilla. Fold up one end about 1", then roll to close.

4. Place enchiladas into a 3-quart baking pan, pushing together as needed to make them fit. Pour remaining ¾ cup enchilada sauce over enchiladas and top with remaining ½ cup cheese.

5. Place pan in the air fryer basket and cook 8 minutes until cheese is brown and bubbling and the edges of tortillas are brown. Serve warm.

Broccoli With Olives

Servings:4
Cooking Time:19 Minutes
Ingredients:
- 2 pounds broccoli, stemmed and cut into 1-inch florets
- 1/3 cup Kalamata olives, halved and pitted
- ¼ cup Parmesan cheese, grated
- 2 tablespoons olive oil
- Salt and ground black pepper, as required
- 2 teaspoons fresh lemon zest, grated

Directions:
1. Preheat the Air fryer to 400°F and grease an Air fryer basket.
2. Boil the broccoli for about 4 minutes and drain well.
3. Mix broccoli, oil, salt, and black pepper in a bowl and toss to coat well.
4. Arrange broccoli into the Air fryer basket and cook for about 15 minutes.
5. Stir in the olives, lemon zest and cheese and dish out to serve.

Avocado Rolls

Servings:5
Cooking Time: 15 Minutes
Ingredients:
- 10 egg roll wrappers
- 1 tomato, diced
- ¼ tsp pepper
- ½ tsp salt

Directions:
1. Place all filling ingredients in a bowl; mash with a fork until somewhat smooth. There should be chunks left. Divide the feeling between the egg wrappers. Wet your finger and brush along the edges, so the wrappers can seal well. Roll and seal the wrappers.
2. Arrange them on a baking sheet lined dish, and place in the air fryer. Cook at 350°F for 5 minutes. Serve with sweet chili dipping and enjoy.

Garden Fresh Green Beans

Servings:4
Cooking Time:12 Minutes
Ingredients:
- 1 pound green beans, washed and trimmed
- 1 teaspoon butter, melted
- 1 tablespoon fresh lemon juice
- ¼ teaspoon garlic powder
- Salt and freshly ground pepper, to taste

Directions:
1. Preheat the Air fryer to 400°F and grease an Air fryer basket.
2. Put all the ingredients in a large bowl and transfer into the Air fryer basket.

3. Cook for about 8 minutes and dish out in a bowl to serve warm.

Crispy Wings With Lemony Old Bay Spice

Servings:4
Cooking Time: 25 Minutes
Ingredients:
- ½ cup butter
- ¾ cup almond flour
- 1 tablespoon old bay spices
- 1 teaspoon lemon juice, freshly squeezed
- 3 pounds chicken wings
- Salt and pepper to taste

Directions:
1. Preheat the air fryer for 5 minutes.
2. In a mixing bowl, combine all ingredients except for the butter.
3. Place in the air fryer basket.
4. Cook for 25 minutes at 350°F.
5. Halfway through the cooking time, shake the fryer basket for even cooking.
6. Once cooked, drizzle with melted butter.

Cheesy Broccoli Sticks

Servings:2
Cooking Time: 16 Minutes
Ingredients:
- 1 steamer bag broccoli florets, cooked according to package instructions
- 1 large egg
- 1 ounce Parmesan 100% cheese crisps, finely ground
- ½ cup shredded sharp Cheddar cheese
- ½ teaspoon salt
- ½ cup ranch dressing

Directions:
1. Let cooked broccoli cool 5 minutes, then place into a food processor with egg, cheese crisps, Cheddar, and salt. Process on low for 30 seconds until all ingredients are combined and begin to stick together.
2. Cut a sheet of parchment paper to fit air fryer basket. Take one scoop of mixture, about 3 tablespoons, and roll into a 4" stick shape, pressing down gently to flatten the top. Place stick on ungreased parchment into air fryer basket. Repeat with remaining mixture to form eight sticks.
3. Adjust the temperature to 350°F and set the timer for 16 minutes, turning sticks halfway through cooking. Sticks will be golden brown when done.
4. Serve warm with ranch dressing on the side for dipping.

Sweet Pepper Nachos

Servings:2
Cooking Time: 5 Minutes
Ingredients:
- 6 mini sweet peppers, seeded and sliced in half
- ¾ cup shredded Colby jack cheese
- ¼ cup sliced pickled jalapeños
- ½ medium avocado, peeled, pitted, and diced
- 2 tablespoons sour cream

Directions:
1. Place peppers into an ungreased 6" round nonstick baking dish. Sprinkle with Colby and top with jalapeños.

2. Place dish into air fryer basket. Adjust the temperature to 350°F and set the timer for 5 minutes. Cheese will be melted and bubbly when done.
3. Remove dish from air fryer and top with avocado. Drizzle with sour cream. Serve warm.

Chewy Glazed Parsnips

Servings:6
Cooking Time:44 Minutes
Ingredients:
- 2 pounds parsnips, peeled and cut into 1-inch chunks
- 1 tablespoon butter, melted
- 2 tablespoons maple syrup
- 1 tablespoon dried parsley flakes, crushed
- ¼ teaspoon red pepper flakes, crushed

Directions:
1. Preheat the Air fryer to 355°F and grease an Air fryer basket.
2. Mix parsnips and butter in a bowl and toss to coat well.
3. Arrange the parsnips in the Air fryer basket and cook for about 40 minutes.
4. Meanwhile, mix remaining ingredients in a large bowl.
5. Transfer this mixture into the Air fryer basket and cook for about 4 more minutes.
6. Dish out and serve warm.

Almond Flour Battered Wings

Servings:4
Cooking Time: 25 Minutes
Ingredients:
- ¼ cup butter, melted
- ¾ cup almond flour
- 16 pieces chicken wings
- 2 tablespoons stevia powder
- 4 tablespoons minced garlic
- Salt and pepper to taste

Directions:
1. Preheat the air fryer for 5 minutes.
2. In a mixing bowl, combine the chicken wings, almond flour, stevia powder, and garlic Season with salt and pepper to taste.
3. Place in the air fryer basket and cook for 25 minutes at 400°F.
4. Halfway through the cooking time, make sure that you give the fryer basket a shake.
5. Once cooked, place in a bowl and drizzle with melted butter. Toss to coat.

Green Bean Sautée

Servings: 4
Cooking Time: 25 Minutes
Ingredients:
- 1 ½ lb green beans, trimmed
- 1 tbsp olive oil
- ½ tsp garlic powder
- Salt and pepper to taste
- 4 garlic cloves, thinly sliced
- 1 tbsp fresh basil, chopped

Directions:
1. Preheat the air fryer to 375°F. Toss the beans with the olive oil, garlic powder, salt, and pepper in a bowl, then add to the frying basket. Air Fry for 6 minutes, shaking the basket halfway through the cooking time. Add garlic to the air fryer and cook for 3-6 minutes or until the green beans are tender and the garlic slices start to brown. Sprinkle with basil and serve warm.

Almond Asparagus

Servings:3
Cooking Time:6 Minutes
Ingredients:
- 1 pound asparagus
- 1/3 cup almonds, sliced
- 2 tablespoons olive oil
- 2 tablespoons balsamic vinegar
- Salt and black pepper, to taste

Directions:
1. Preheat the Air fryer to 400°F and grease an Air fryer basket.
2. Mix asparagus, oil, vinegar, salt, and black pepper in a bowl and toss to coat well.
3. Arrange asparagus into the Air fryer basket and sprinkle with the almond slices.
4. Cook for about 6 minutes and dish out to serve hot.

Twice-baked Broccoli-cheddar Potatoes

Servings:4
Cooking Time: 35 Minutes
Ingredients:
- 4 large russet potatoes
- 2 tablespoons plus 2 teaspoons ranch dressing
- 1 teaspoon salt
- ½ teaspoon ground black pepper
- ¼ cup chopped cooked broccoli florets
- 1 cup shredded sharp Cheddar cheese

Directions:
1. Preheat the air fryer to 400°F.
2. Using a fork, poke several holes in potatoes. Place in the air fryer basket and cook 30 minutes until fork-tender.
3. Once potatoes are cool enough to handle, slice lengthwise and scoop out the cooked potato into a large bowl, being careful to maintain the structural integrity of potato skins. Add ranch dressing, salt, pepper, broccoli, and Cheddar to potato flesh and stir until well combined.
4. Scoop potato mixture back into potato skins and return to the air fryer basket. Cook an additional 5 minutes until cheese is melted. Serve warm.

Buttered Broccoli

Servings:4
Cooking Time:7 Minutes
Ingredients:
- 4 cups fresh broccoli florets
- 2 tablespoons butter, melted
- ¼ cup water
- Salt and black pepper, to taste

Directions:
1. Preheat the Air fryer to 400°F and grease an Air fryer basket.
2. Mix broccoli, butter, salt, and black pepper in a bowl and toss to coat well.
3. Place water at the bottom of Air fryer pan and arrange the broccoli florets into the Air fryer basket.

4. Cook for about 7 minutes and dish out in a bowl to serve hot.

Roasted Vegetable Grilled Cheese

Servings:4
Cooking Time: 6 Minutes
Ingredients:
* 8 slices sourdough bread
* 4 slices provolone cheese
* ½ cup chopped roasted red peppers
* ¼ cup chopped yellow onion
* 4 slices white American cheese

Directions:
1. Preheat the air fryer to 300°F.
2. Place a slice of bread on a work surface. Top with a slice of provolone, then with 2 tablespoons roasted red peppers and 1 tablespoon onion. Repeat with three more bread slices and remaining provolone and vegetables.
3. Place loaded bread slices in the air fryer basket and cook 1 minute until cheese is melted and onion is softened.
4. Remove the air fryer basket and carefully place 1 slice of American cheese on top of each slice of bread, finishing each with a second slice of bread to complete each sandwich.
5. Spritz the top with cooking spray. Increase the air fryer temperature to 400°F and cook 5 minutes, turning carefully after 3 minutes, until bread is golden and cheese is melted. Serve warm.

Caprese Eggplant Stacks

Servings:4
Cooking Time: 8 Minutes
Ingredients:
* 1 medium eggplant, cut into 4 (½") slices
* ½ teaspoon salt
* ¼ teaspoon ground black pepper
* 4 (¼") slices tomato
* 2 ounces fresh mozzarella cheese, cut into 4 slices
* 1 tablespoon olive oil
* ¼ cup fresh basil, sliced

Directions:
1. Preheat the air fryer to 320°F.
2. In a 6" round pan, place eggplant slices. Sprinkle with salt and pepper. Top each with a tomato slice, then a mozzarella slice, and drizzle with oil.
3. Place in the air fryer basket and cook 8 minutes until eggplant is tender and cheese is melted. Garnish with fresh basil to serve.

Sweet And Sour Brussel Sprouts

Servings:2
Cooking Time:10 Minutes
Ingredients:
* 2 cups Brussels sprouts, trimmed and halved lengthwise
* 1 tablespoon balsamic vinegar
* 1 tablespoon maple syrup
* Salt, as required

Directions:
1. Preheat the Air fryer to 400°F and grease an Air fryer basket.
2. Mix all the ingredients in a bowl and toss to coat well.
3. Arrange the Brussel sprouts in the Air fryer basket and cook for about 10 minutes, shaking once halfway through.

4. Dish out in a bowl and serve hot.

Spicy Celery Sticks

Servings: 4
Cooking Time: 20 Minutes
Ingredients:
* 1 pound celery, cut into matchsticks
* 2 tablespoons peanut oil
* 1 jalapeño, seeded and minced
* 1/4 teaspoon dill
* 1/2 teaspoon basil
* Salt and white pepper to taste

Directions:
1. Start by preheating your Air Fryer to 380°F.
2. Toss all ingredients together and place them in the Air Fryer basket.
3. Cook for 15 minutes, shaking the basket halfway through the cooking time. Transfer to a serving platter and enjoy!

Pizza Dough

Servings:4
Cooking Time: 1 Hour 10 Minutes, Plus 10 Minutes For Additional Batches
Ingredients:
* 2 cups all-purpose flour
* 1 tablespoon granulated sugar
* 1 tablespoon quick-rise yeast
* 4 tablespoons olive oil, divided
* ¾ cup warm water

Directions:
1. In a large bowl, mix flour, sugar, and yeast until combined. Add 2 tablespoons oil and warm water and mix until dough becomes smooth.
2. On a lightly floured surface, knead dough 10 minutes, then form into a smooth ball. Drizzle with remaining 2 tablespoons oil, then cover with plastic. Let dough rise 1 hour until doubled in size.
3. Preheat the air fryer to 320°F.
4. Separate dough into four pieces and press each into a 6" pan or air fryer pizza tray that has been spritzed with cooking oil.
5. Add any desired toppings. Place in the air fryer basket, working in batches as necessary, and cook 10 minutes until crust is brown at the edges and toppings are heated through. Serve warm.

Cheese & Bean Burgers

Servings: 2
Cooking Time: 35 Minutes
Ingredients:
* 1 cup cooked black beans
* ½ cup shredded cheddar
* 1 egg, beaten
* Salt and pepper to taste
* 1 cup bread crumbs
* ½ cup grated carrots

Directions:
1. Preheat air fryer to 350°F. Mash the beans with a fork in a bowl. Mix in the cheese, salt, and pepper until evenly combined. Stir in half of the bread crumbs and egg. Shape the mixture into 2 patties. Coat each patty with the remaining bread crumbs and spray with cooking oil. Air Fry for 14-16 minutes, turning once.

When ready, remove to a plate. Top with grated carrots and serve.

Lemony Green Beans

Servings:3
Cooking Time:12 Minutes
Ingredients:
- 1 pound green beans, trimmed and halved
- 1 teaspoon butter, melted
- 1 tablespoon fresh lemon juice
- ¼ teaspoon garlic powder

Directions:
1. Preheat the Air fryer to 400°F and grease an Air fryer basket.
2. Mix all the ingredients in a bowl and toss to coat well.
3. Arrange the green beans into the Air fryer basket and cook for about 12 minutes.
4. Dish out in a serving plate and serve hot.

Caribbean-style Fried Plantains

Servings: 2
Cooking Time: 20 Minutes
Ingredients:
- 2 plantains, peeled and cut into slices
- 2 tablespoons avocado oil
- 2 teaspoons Caribbean Sorrel Rum Spice Mix

Directions:
1. Toss the plantains with the avocado oil and spice mix.
2. Cook in the preheated Air Fryer at 400°F for 10 minutes, shaking the cooking basket halfway through the cooking time.
3. Adjust the seasonings to taste and enjoy!

Two-cheese Grilled Sandwiches

Servings: 2
Cooking Time: 30 Minutes
Ingredients:
- 4 sourdough bread slices
- 2 cheddar cheese slices
- 2 Swiss cheese slices
- 1 tbsp butter
- 2 dill pickles, sliced

Directions:
1. Preheat air fryer to 360°F. Smear both sides of the sourdough bread with butter and place them in the frying basket. Toast the bread for 6 minutes, flipping once.
2. Divide the cheddar cheese between 2 of the bread slices. Cover the remaining 2 bread slices with Swiss cheese slices. Bake for 10 more minutes until the cheeses have melted and lightly bubbled and the bread has golden brown. Set the cheddar-covered bread slices on a serving plate, cover with pickles, and top each with the Swiss-covered slices. Serve and enjoy!

Parmesan Artichokes

Servings: 4
Cooking Time: 35 Minutes
Ingredients:
- 2 medium artichokes, trimmed and quartered, with the centers removed
- 2 tbsp. coconut oil, melted
- 1 egg, beaten
- ½ cup parmesan cheese, grated

- ¼ cup blanched, finely ground flour

Directions:
1. Place the artichokes in a bowl with the coconut oil and toss to coat, then dip the artichokes into a bowl of beaten egg.
2. In a separate bowl, mix together the parmesan cheese and the flour. Combine with the pieces of artichoke, making sure to coat each piece well. Transfer the artichoke to the fryer.
3. Cook at 400°F for ten minutes, shaking occasionally throughout the cooking time. Serve hot.

Broccoli With Cauliflower

Servings:4
Cooking Time:20 Minutes
Ingredients:
- 1½ cups broccoli, cut into 1-inch pieces
- 1½ cups cauliflower, cut into 1-inch pieces
- 1 tablespoon olive oil
- Salt, as required

Directions:
1. Preheat the Air fryer to 375°F and grease an Air fryer basket.
2. Mix the vegetables, olive oil, and salt in a bowl and toss to coat well.
3. Arrange the veggie mixture in the Air fryer basket and cook for about 20 minutes, tossing once in between.
4. Dish out in a bowl and serve hot.

Pesto Spinach Flatbread

Servings:4
Cooking Time: 8 Minutes
Ingredients:
- 1 cup blanched finely ground almond flour
- 2 ounces cream cheese
- 2 cups shredded mozzarella cheese
- 1 cup chopped fresh spinach leaves
- 2 tablespoons basil pesto

Directions:
1. Place flour, cream cheese, and mozzarella in a large microwave-safe bowl and microwave on high 45 seconds, then stir.
2. Fold in spinach and microwave an additional 15 seconds. Stir until a soft dough ball forms.
3. Cut two pieces of parchment paper to fit air fryer basket. Separate dough into two sections and press each out on ungreased parchment to create 6" rounds.
4. Spread 1 tablespoon pesto over each flatbread and place rounds on parchment into ungreased air fryer basket. Adjust the temperature to 350°F and set the timer for 8 minutes, turning crusts halfway through cooking. Flatbread will be golden when done.
5. Let cool 5 minutes before slicing and serving.

Cauliflower Steaks Gratin

Servings: 2
Cooking Time: 13 Minutes
Ingredients:
- 1 head cauliflower
- 1 tablespoon olive oil
- salt and freshly ground black pepper
- ½ teaspoon chopped fresh thyme leaves
- 3 tablespoons grated Parmigiano-Reggiano cheese
- 2 tablespoons panko breadcrumbs

Directions:
1. Preheat the air-fryer to 370°F.
2. Cut two steaks out of the center of the cauliflower. To do this, cut the cauliflower in half and then cut one slice about 1-inch thick off each half. The rest of the cauliflower will fall apart into florets, which you can roast on their own or save for another meal.
3. Brush both sides of the cauliflower steaks with olive oil and season with salt, freshly ground black pepper and fresh thyme. Place the cauliflower steaks into the air fryer basket and air-fry for 6 minutes. Turn the steaks over and air-fry for another 4 minutes. Combine the Parmesan cheese and panko breadcrumbs and sprinkle the mixture over the tops of both steaks and air-fry for another 3 minutes until the cheese has melted and the breadcrumbs have browned. Serve this with some sautéed bitter greens and air-fried blistered tomatoes.

Garlic Okra Chips

Servings: 4
Cooking Time: 20 Minutes
Ingredients:
- 2 cups okra, cut into rounds
- 1 ½ tbsp. melted butter
- 1 garlic clove, minced
- 1 tsp powdered paprika
- Salt and pepper to taste

Directions:
1. Preheat air fryer to 350°F. Toss okra, melted butter, paprika, garlic, salt and pepper in a medium bowl until okra is coated. Place okra in the frying basket and Air Fry for 5 minutes. Shake the basket and Air Fry for another 5 minutes. Shake one more time and Air Fry for 2 minutes until crispy. Serve warm and enjoy.

Wine Infused Mushrooms

Servings:6
Cooking Time: 32 Minutes
Ingredients:
- 1 tablespoon butter
- 2 teaspoons Herbs de Provence
- ½ teaspoon garlic powder
- 2 pounds fresh mushrooms, quartered
- 2 tablespoons white vermouth

Directions:
1. Set the temperature of air fryer to 320°F.
2. In an air fryer pan, mix together the butter, Herbs de Provence, and garlic powder and air fry for about 2 minutes.
3. Stir in the mushrooms and air fry for about 25 minutes.
4. Stir in the vermouth and air fry for 5 more minutes.
5. Remove from air fryer and transfer the mushrooms onto serving plates.
6. Serve hot.

Brussels Sprouts With Balsamic Oil

Servings:4
Cooking Time: 15 Minutes
Ingredients:
- ¼ teaspoon salt
- 1 tablespoon balsamic vinegar
- 2 cups Brussels sprouts, halved
- 2 tablespoons olive oil

Directions:

1. Preheat the air fryer for 5 minutes.
2. Mix all ingredients in a bowl until the zucchini fries are well coated.
3. Place in the air fryer basket.
4. Close and cook for 15 minutes for 350°F.

Lemon Caper Cauliflower Steaks

Servings:4
Cooking Time: 15 Minutes
Ingredients:
- 1 small head cauliflower, leaves and core removed, cut into 4 (½"-thick) "steaks"
- 4 tablespoons olive oil, divided
- 1 medium lemon, zested and juiced, divided
- ¼ teaspoon salt
- ⅛ teaspoon ground black pepper
- 1 tablespoon salted butter, melted
- 1 tablespoon capers, rinsed

Directions:
1. Brush each cauliflower "steak" with ½ tablespoon olive oil on both sides and sprinkle with lemon zest, salt, and pepper on both sides.
2. Place cauliflower into ungreased air fryer basket. Adjust the temperature to 400°F and set the timer for 15 minutes, turning cauliflower halfway through cooking. Steaks will be golden at the edges and browned when done.
3. Transfer steaks to four medium plates. In a small bowl, whisk remaining olive oil, butter, lemon juice, and capers, and pour evenly over steaks. Serve warm.

Stuffed Mushrooms

Servings:4
Cooking Time: 10 Minutes
Ingredients:
- 12 baby bella mushrooms, stems removed
- 4 ounces full-fat cream cheese, softened
- ¼ cup grated vegetarian Parmesan cheese
- ¼ cup Italian bread crumbs
- 1 teaspoon crushed red pepper flakes

Directions:
1. Preheat the air fryer to 400°F.
2. Use a spoon to hollow out mushroom caps.
3. In a medium bowl, combine cream cheese, Parmesan, bread crumbs, and red pepper flakes. Scoop approximately 1 tablespoon mixture into each mushroom cap.
4. Place stuffed mushrooms in the air fryer basket and cook 10 minutes until stuffing is brown. Let cool 5 minutes before serving.

Thyme Lentil Patties

Servings: 2
Cooking Time: 35 Minutes
Ingredients:
- ½ cup grated American cheese
- 1 cup cooked lentils
- ¼ tsp dried thyme
- 2 eggs, beaten
- Salt and pepper to taste
- 1 cup bread crumbs

Directions:
1. Preheat air fryer to 350°F. Put the eggs, lentils, and cheese in a bowl and mix to combine. Stir in half the bread crumbs,

thyme, salt, and pepper. Form the mixture into 2 patties and coat them in the remaining bread crumbs. Transfer to the greased frying basket. Air Fry for 14-16 minutes until brown, flipping once. Serve.

Tortilla Pizza Margherita

Servings: 1
Cooking Time: 15 Minutes
Ingredients:
- 1 flour tortilla
- ¼ cup tomato sauce
- 1/3 cup grated mozzarella
- 3 basil leaves

Directions:
1. Preheat air fryer to 350°F. Put the tortilla in the greased basket and pour the sauce in the center. Spread across the whole tortilla. Sprinkle with cheese and Bake for 8-10 minutes or until crisp. Remove carefully and top with basil leaves. Serve hot.

Pepper-pineapple With Butter-sugar Glaze

Servings:2
Cooking Time: 10 Minutes
Ingredients:
- 1 medium-sized pineapple, peeled and sliced
- 1 red bell pepper, seeded and julienned
- 1 teaspoon brown sugar
- 2 teaspoons melted butter
- Salt to taste

Directions:
1. Preheat the air fryer to 390°F.
2. Place the grill pan accessory in the air fryer.
3. Mix all ingredients in a Ziploc bag and give a good shake.
4. Dump onto the grill pan and cook for 10 minutes making sure that you flip the pineapples every 5 minutes.

Bell Peppers Cups

Servings:4
Cooking Time:8 Minutes
Ingredients:
- 8 mini red bell peppers, tops and seeds removed
- 1 teaspoon fresh parsley, chopped
- ¾ cup feta cheese, crumbled
- ½ tablespoon olive oil
- Freshly ground black pepper, to taste

Directions:
1. Preheat the Air fryer to 390°F and grease an Air fryer basket.
2. Mix feta cheese, parsley, olive oil and black pepper in a bowl.
3. Stuff the bell peppers with feta cheese mixture and arrange in the Air fryer basket.
4. Cook for about 8 minutes and dish out to serve hot.

Layered Ravioli Bake

Servings:4
Cooking Time: 20 Minutes
Ingredients:
- 2 cups marinara sauce, divided
- 2 packages fresh cheese ravioli
- 12 slices provolone cheese

- ½ cup Italian bread crumbs
- ½ cup grated vegetarian Parmesan cheese

Directions:
1. Preheat the air fryer to 350°F.
2. In the bottom of a 3-quart baking pan, spread ⅓ cup marinara. Place 6 ravioli on top of the sauce, then add 3 slice provolone on top, then another layer of ⅓ cup marinara. Repea these layers three times to use up remaining ravioli, provolone and sauce.
3. In a small bowl, mix bread crumbs and Parmesan. Sprinkl over the top of dish.
4. Cover pan with foil, being sure to tuck foil under th bottom of the pan to ensure the air fryer fan does not blow it of Place pan in the air fryer basket and cook 15 minutes.
5. Remove foil and cook an additional 5 minutes until the to is brown and bubbling. Serve warm.

Pesto Vegetable Kebabs

Servings:4
Cooking Time: 8 Minutes
Ingredients:
- 12 ounces button mushrooms
- 12 ounces cherry tomatoes
- 2 medium zucchini, cut into ¼" slices
- 1 medium red onion, peeled and cut into 1" cubes
- 1 cup pesto, divided
- ½ teaspoon salt
- ¼ teaspoon ground black pepper

Directions:
1. Soak eight 6" skewers in water 10 minutes to avoi burning. Preheat the air fryer to 350°F.
2. Place a mushroom on a skewer, followed by a tomato zucchini slice, and red onion piece. Repeat to fill up the skewe then follow the same pattern for remaining skewers.
3. Brush each skewer evenly using ½ cup pesto. Sprinkl kebabs with salt and pepper. Place in the air fryer basket an cook 10 minutes, turning halfway through cooking time, unti vegetables are tender. Brush kebabs with remaining ½ cu pesto before serving.

Crispy Eggplant Rounds

Servings:4
Cooking Time: 10 Minutes
Ingredients:
- 1 large eggplant, ends trimmed, cut into ½" slices
- ½ teaspoon salt
- 2 ounces Parmesan 100% cheese crisps, finely ground
- ½ teaspoon paprika
- ¼ teaspoon garlic powder
- 1 large egg

Directions:
1. Sprinkle eggplant rounds with salt. Place rounds on kitchen towel for 30 minutes to draw out excess water. Pa rounds dry.
2. In a medium bowl, mix cheese crisps, paprika, and garli powder. In a separate medium bowl, whisk egg. Dip eac eggplant round in egg, then gently press into cheese crisps t coat both sides.
3. Place eggplant rounds into ungreased air fryer basket Adjust the temperature to 400°F and set the timer for 1 minutes, turning rounds halfway through cooking. Eggplan will be golden and crispy when done. Serve warm.

Sweet Roasted Carrots

Servings: 4
Cooking Time: 25 Minutes
Ingredients:
- 6 carrots, cut into ½-inch pieces
- 2 tbsp butter, melted
- 2 tbsp parsley, chopped
- 1 tsp honey

Directions:
1. Preheat air fryer to 390°F. Add carrots to a baking pan and pour over butter, honey, and 2-3 tbsp of water. Mix well. Transfer the carrots to the greased frying basket and Roast for 12 minutes, shaking the basket once. Sprinkle with parsley and serve warm.

Curried Eggplant

Servings:2
Cooking Time:10 Minutes
Ingredients:
- 1 large eggplant, cut into ½-inch thick slices
- 1 garlic clove, minced
- ½ fresh red chili, chopped
- 1 tablespoon vegetable oil
- ¼ teaspoon curry powder
- Salt, to taste

Directions:
1. Preheat the Air fryer to 300°F and grease an Air fryer basket.
2. Mix all the ingredients in a bowl and toss to coat well.
3. Arrange the eggplant slices in the Air fryer basket and cook for about 10 minutes, tossing once in between.
4. Dish out onto serving plates and serve hot.

Black Bean And Rice Burrito Filling

Servings:4
Cooking Time: 20 Minutes
Ingredients:
- 1 cup uncooked instant long-grain white rice
- 1 cup salsa
- ½ cup vegetable broth
- 1 cup black beans
- ½ cup corn

Directions:
1. Preheat the air fryer to 400°F.
2. Mix all ingredients in a 3-quart baking dish until well combined.
3. Cover with foil, being sure to tuck foil under the bottom of the pan to ensure the air fryer fan does not blow it off.
4. Cook 20 minutes, stirring twice during cooking. Serve warm.

Caramelized Carrots

Servings:3
Cooking Time:15 Minutes
Ingredients:
- 1 small bag baby carrots
- ½ cup butter, melted
- ½ cup brown sugar

Directions:
1. Preheat the Air fryer to 400°F and grease an Air fryer basket.
2. Mix the butter and brown sugar in a bowl.

3. Add the carrots and toss to coat well.
4. Arrange the carrots in the Air fryer basket and cook for about 15 minutes.
5. Dish out and serve warm.

Effortless Mac `n´ Cheese

Servings: 4
Cooking Time: 15 Minutes
Ingredients:
- 1 cup heavy cream
- 1 cup milk
- ½ cup mozzarella cheese
- 2 tsp grated Parmesan cheese
- 16 oz cooked elbow macaroni

Directions:
1. Preheat air fryer to 400°F. Whisk the heavy cream, milk, mozzarella cheese, and Parmesan cheese until smooth in a bowl. Stir in the macaroni and pour into a baking dish. Cover with foil and Bake in the air fryer for 6 minutes. Remove foil and Bake until cooked through and bubbly, 3-5 minutes. Serve warm.

Spinach Pesto Flatbread

Servings:4
Cooking Time: 8 Minutes Per Batch
Ingredients:
- 1 cup basil pesto
- 4 round flatbreads
- ½ cup chopped frozen spinach, thawed and drained
- 8 ounces fresh mozzarella cheese, sliced
- 1 teaspoon crushed red pepper flakes

Directions:
1. Preheat the air fryer to 350°F.
2. For each flatbread, spread ¼ cup pesto across flatbread, then scatter 2 tablespoons spinach over pesto. Top with 2 ounces mozzarella slices and ¼ teaspoon red pepper flakes. Repeat with remaining flatbread and toppings.
3. Place in the air fryer basket, working in batches as necessary, and cook 8 minutes until cheese is brown and bubbling. Serve warm.

Stuffed Portobellos

Servings:4
Cooking Time: 8 Minutes
Ingredients:
- 3 ounces cream cheese, softened
- ½ medium zucchini, trimmed and chopped
- ¼ cup seeded and chopped red bell pepper
- 1½ cups chopped fresh spinach leaves
- 4 large portobello mushrooms, stems removed
- 2 tablespoons coconut oil, melted
- ½ teaspoon salt

Directions:
1. In a medium bowl, mix cream cheese, zucchini, pepper, and spinach.
2. Drizzle mushrooms with coconut oil and sprinkle with salt. Scoop ¼ zucchini mixture into each mushroom.
3. Place mushrooms into ungreased air fryer basket. Adjust the temperature to 400°F and set the timer for 8 minutes. Portobellos will be tender and tops will be browned when done. Serve warm.

Basil Tomatoes

Servings:2
Cooking Time:10 Minutes
Ingredients:

- 2 tomatoes, halved
- 1 tablespoon fresh basil, chopped
- Olive oil cooking spray
- Salt and black pepper, as required

Directions:

1. Preheat the Air fryer to 320°F and grease an Air fryer basket.
2. Spray the tomato halves evenly with olive oil cooking spray and season with salt, black pepper and basil.
3. Arrange the tomato halves into the Air fryer basket, cut sides up.
4. Cook for about 10 minutes and dish out onto serving plates.

Eggplant Parmesan

Servings:4
Cooking Time: 17 Minutes
Ingredients:

- 1 medium eggplant, ends trimmed, sliced into ½" rounds
- ¼ teaspoon salt
- 2 tablespoons coconut oil
- ½ cup grated Parmesan cheese
- 1 ounce 100% cheese crisps, finely crushed
- ½ cup low-carb marinara sauce
- ½ cup shredded mozzarella cheese

Directions:

1. Sprinkle eggplant rounds with salt on both sides and wrap in a kitchen towel for 30 minutes. Press to remove excess water, then drizzle rounds with coconut oil on both sides.
2. In a medium bowl, mix Parmesan and cheese crisps. Press each eggplant slice into mixture to coat both sides.
3. Place rounds into ungreased air fryer basket. Adjust the temperature to 350°F and set the timer for 15 minutes, turning rounds halfway through cooking. They will be crispy around the edges when done.
4. When timer beeps, spoon marinara over rounds and sprinkle with mozzarella. Continue cooking an additional 2 minutes at 350°F until cheese is melted. Serve warm.

Cool Mini Zucchini's

Servings:4
Cooking Time: 25 Minutes
Ingredients:

- 4 large eggs, beaten
- 1 medium zucchini, sliced
- 4 ounces feta cheese, drained and crumbled
- 2 tbsp fresh dill, chopped
- Cooking spray
- Salt and pepper as needed

Directions:

1. Preheat the air fryer to 360°F, and un a bowl, add the beaten eggs and season with salt and pepper.
2. Stir in zucchini, dill and feta cheese. Grease 8 muffin tins with cooking spray. Roll pastry and arrange them to cover the sides of the muffin tins. Divide the egg mixture evenly between the holes. Place the prepared tins in your air fryer and cook for 15 minutes. Serve and enjoy!

Alfredo Eggplant Stacks

Servings:6
Cooking Time: 12 Minutes
Ingredients:

- 1 large eggplant, ends trimmed, cut into ¼" slices
- 1 medium beefsteak tomato, cored and cut into ¼" slices
- 1 cup Alfredo sauce
- 8 ounces fresh mozzarella cheese, cut into 18 slices
- 2 tablespoons fresh parsley leaves

Directions:

1. Place 6 slices eggplant in bottom of an ungreased 6" roun nonstick baking dish. Place 1 slice tomato on top of eac eggplant round, followed by 1 tablespoon Alfredo and 1 slic mozzarella. Repeat with remaining ingredients, about thre repetitions.
2. Cover dish with aluminum foil and place dish into air frye basket. Adjust the temperature to 350°F and set the timer for 1 minutes. Eggplant will be tender when done.
3. Sprinkle parsley evenly over each stack. Serve warm.

Broccoli & Parmesan Dish

Servings:4
Cooking Time: 25 Minutes
Ingredients:

- 1 tbsp olive oil
- 1 lemon, Juiced
- Salt and pepper to taste
- 1-ounce Parmesan cheese, grated

Directions:

1. In a bowl, mix all ingredients. Add the mixture to your ai fryer and cook for 20 minutes at 360°F. Serve.

Falafels

Servings: 12
Cooking Time: 10 Minutes
Ingredients:

- 1 pouch falafel mix
- 2–3 tablespoons plain breadcrumbs
- oil for misting or cooking spray

Directions:

1. Prepare falafel mix according to package directions.
2. Preheat air fryer to 390°F.
3. Place breadcrumbs in shallow dish or on wax paper.
4. Shape falafel mixture into 12 balls and flatten slightly. Ro in breadcrumbs to coat all sides and mist with oil or cookin spray.
5. Place falafels in air fryer basket in single layer and coo for 5 minutes. Shake basket, and continue cooking for minutes, until they brown and are crispy.

Cottage And Mayonnaise Stuffed Peppers

Servings: 2
Cooking Time: 20 Minutes
Ingredients:

- 1 red bell pepper, top and seeds removed
- 1 yellow bell pepper, top and seeds removed
- Salt and pepper, to taste
- 1 cup Cottage cheese
- 4 tablespoons mayonnaise
- 2 pickles, chopped

Directions:

1. Arrange the peppers in the lightly greased cooking basket. Cook in the preheated Air Fryer at 400°F for 15 minutes, turning them over halfway through the cooking time.
2. Season with salt and pepper.
3. Then, in a mixing bowl, combine the cream cheese with the mayonnaise and chopped pickles. Stuff the pepper with the cream cheese mixture and serve. Enjoy!

Roasted Spaghetti Squash

Servings:6
Cooking Time: 45 Minutes
Ingredients:
- 1 spaghetti squash, halved and seeded
- 2 tablespoons coconut oil
- 4 tablespoons salted butter, melted
- 1 teaspoon garlic powder
- 2 teaspoons dried parsley

Directions:
1. Brush shell of spaghetti squash with coconut oil. Brush inside with butter. Sprinkle inside with garlic powder and parsley.
2. Place squash skin side down into ungreased air fryer basket, working in batches if needed. Adjust the temperature to 350°F and set the timer for 30 minutes. When the timer beeps, flip squash and cook an additional 15 minutes until fork-tender.
3. Use a fork to remove spaghetti strands from shell and serve warm.

Toasted Ravioli

Servings:4
Cooking Time: 8 Minutes
Ingredients:
- 1 cup Italian bread crumbs
- 2 tablespoons grated vegetarian Parmesan cheese
- 1 large egg
- ¼ cup whole milk
- 1 package fresh cheese ravioli
- Cooking spray

Directions:
1. Preheat the air fryer to 400°F.
2. In a large bowl, whisk together bread crumbs and Parmesan.
3. In a medium bowl, whisk together egg and milk.
4. Dip each ravioli into egg mixture, shaking off the excess, then press into bread crumb mixture until well coated. Spritz each side with cooking spray.
5. Place in the air fryer basket and cook 8 minutes, turning halfway through cooking time, until ravioli is brown at the edges and crispy. Serve warm.

Broccoli Salad

Servings: 2
Cooking Time: 15 Minutes
Ingredients:
- 3 cups fresh broccoli florets
- 2 tbsp. coconut oil, melted
- ¼ cup sliced s
- ½ medium lemon, juiced

Directions:
1. Take a six-inch baking dish and fill with the broccoli florets. Pour the melted coconut oil over the broccoli and add in the sliced s. Toss together. Put the dish in the air fryer.

2. Cook at 380°F for seven minutes, stirring at the halfway point.
3. Place the broccoli in a bowl and drizzle the lemon juice over it.

Gourmet Wasabi Popcorn

Servings: 2
Cooking Time: 30 Minutes
Ingredients:
- 1/2 teaspoon brown sugar
- 1 teaspoon salt
- 1/2 teaspoon wasabi powder, sifted
- 1 tablespoon avocado oil
- 3 tablespoons popcorn kernels

Directions:
1. Add the dried corn kernels to the Air Fryer basket; toss with the remaining ingredients.
2. Cook at 395°F for 15 minutes, shaking the basket every 5 minutes. Work in two batches.
3. Taste, adjust the seasonings and serve immediately. Bon appétit!

Easy Glazed Carrots

Servings:4
Cooking Time:12 Minutes
Ingredients:
- 3 cups carrots, peeled and cut into large chunks
- 1 tablespoon olive oil
- 1 tablespoon honey
- Salt and black pepper, to taste

Directions:
1. Preheat the Air fryer to 390°F and grease an Air fryer basket.
2. Mix all the ingredients in a bowl and toss to coat well.
3. Transfer into the Air fryer basket and cook for about 12 minutes.
4. Dish out and serve hot.

Roasted Cauliflower

Servings: 2
Cooking Time: 20 Minutes
Ingredients:
- medium head cauliflower
- 2 tbsp. salted butter, melted
- 1 medium lemon
- 1 tsp. dried parsley
- ½ tsp. garlic powder

Directions:
1. Having removed the leaves from the cauliflower head, brush it with the melted butter. Grate the rind of the lemon over it and then drizzle some juice. Finally add the parsley and garlic powder on top.
2. Transfer the cauliflower to the basket of the fryer.
3. Cook for fifteen minutes at 350°F, checking regularly to ensure it doesn't overcook. The cauliflower is ready when it is hot and fork tender.
4. Take care when removing it from the fryer, cut up and serve.

Grilled 'n Glazed Strawberries

Servings:2
Cooking Time: 20 Minutes

Ingredients:
- 1 tbsp honey
- 1 tsp lemon zest
- 1-lb large strawberries
- 3 tbsp melted butter
- Lemon wedges
- Pinch kosher salt

Directions:
1. Thread strawberries in 4 skewers.
2. In a small bowl, mix well remaining ingredients except for lemon wedges. Brush all over strawberries.
3. Place skewer on air fryer skewer rack.
4. For 10 minutes, cook on 360°F. Halfway through cooking time, brush with honey mixture and turnover skewer.
5. Serve and enjoy with a squeeze of lemon.

Spicy Roasted Cashew Nuts

Servings: 4
Cooking Time: 20 Minutes
Ingredients:
- 1 cup whole cashews
- 1 teaspoon olive oil
- Salt and ground black pepper, to taste
- 1/2 teaspoon smoked paprika
- 1/2 teaspoon ancho chili powder

Directions:
1. Toss all ingredients in the mixing bowl.
2. Line the Air Fryer basket with baking parchment. Spread out the spiced cashews in a single layer in the basket.
3. Roast at 350°F for 6 to 8 minutes, shaking the basket once or twice. Work in batches. Enjoy!

Cauliflower Rice–stuffed Peppers

Servings:4
Cooking Time: 15 Minutes
Ingredients:
- 2 cups uncooked cauliflower rice
- ¾ cup drained canned petite diced tomatoes
- 2 tablespoons olive oil
- 1 cup shredded mozzarella cheese
- ¼ teaspoon salt
- ¼ teaspoon ground black pepper
- 4 medium green bell peppers, tops removed, seeded

Directions:
1. In a large bowl, mix all ingredients except bell peppers. Scoop mixture evenly into peppers.
2. Place peppers into ungreased air fryer basket. Adjust the temperature to 350°F and set the timer for 15 minutes. Peppers will be tender and cheese will be melted when done. Serve warm.

Cheesy Cauliflower Crust Pizza

Servings:2
Cooking Time: 12 Minutes Per Batch
Ingredients:
- 2 steamer bags cauliflower florets
- 1 large egg
- 1 cup grated vegetarian Parmesan cheese
- 3 cups shredded mozzarella cheese, divided
- 1 cup pizza sauce

Directions:

1. Preheat the air fryer to 375°F. Cut two pieces of parchment paper to fit the air fryer basket, one for each crust.
2. Cook cauliflower in the microwave according to package instructions, then drain in a colander. Run under cold water until cool to the touch. Use a cheesecloth to squeeze the excess water from cauliflower, removing as much as possible.
3. In a food processor, combine cauliflower, egg, Parmesan, and 1 cup mozzarella. Process on low about 15 seconds until a sticky ball forms.
4. Separate dough into two pieces. Working with damp hands to prevent dough from sticking, press each dough ball into a 6" round.
5. Place crust on parchment in the air fryer basket, working in batches as necessary. Cook 6 minutes, then flip over with a spatula and top the crust with ½ cup pizza sauce and 1 cup mozzarella. Cook an additional 6 minutes until edges are dark brown and cheese is brown and bubbling. Let cool at least 5 minutes before serving. The crust firms up as it cools.

Home-style Cinnamon Rolls

Servings: 4
Cooking Time: 40 Minutes
Ingredients:
- ½ pizza dough
- 1/3 cup dark brown sugar
- ¼ cup butter, softened
- ½ tsp ground cinnamon

Directions:
1. Preheat air fryer to 360°F. Roll out the dough into a rectangle. Using a knife, spread the brown sugar and butter, covering all the edges, and sprinkle with cinnamon. Fold the long side of the dough into a log, then cut it into 8 equal pieces, avoiding compression. Place the rolls, spiral-side up, onto a parchment-lined sheet. Let rise for 20 minutes. Grease the rolls with cooking spray and Bake for 8 minutes until golden brown. Serve right away.

Gorgeous Jalapeño Poppers

Servings: 6
Cooking Time: 25 Minutes
Ingredients:
- 6 center-cut bacon slices, halved
- 6 jalapeños, halved lengthwise
- 4 oz cream cheese
- ¼ cup grated Gruyere cheese
- 2 tbsp chives, chopped

Directions:
1. Scoop out seeds and membranes of the jalapeño halves, discard. Combine cream cheese, Gruyere cheese, and chives in a bowl. Fill the jalapeño halves with the cream cheese filling using a small spoon. Wrap each pepper with a slice of bacon and secure with a toothpick.
2. Preheat air fryer to 325°F. Put the stuffed peppers in a single layer on the greased frying basket and Bake until the peppers are tender, cheese is melted, and the bacon is brown, 11-13 minutes. Serve warm and enjoy!

Cauliflower Pizza Crust

Servings:2
Cooking Time: 7 Minutes
Ingredients:
- 1 steamer bag cauliflower, cooked according to package instructions

- ½ cup shredded sharp Cheddar cheese
- 1 large egg
- 2 tablespoons blanched finely ground almond flour
- 1 teaspoon Italian seasoning

Directions:

1. Let cooked cauliflower cool for 10 minutes. Using a kitchen towel, wring out excess moisture from cauliflower and place into food processor.
2. Add Cheddar, egg, flour, and Italian seasoning to processor and pulse ten times until cauliflower is smooth and all ingredients are combined.
3. Cut two pieces of parchment paper to fit air fryer basket. Divide cauliflower mixture into two equal portions and press each into a 6" round on ungreased parchment.
4. Place crusts on parchment into air fryer basket. Adjust the temperature to 360°F and set the timer for 7 minutes, gently turning crusts halfway through cooking.
5. Store crusts in refrigerator in an airtight container up to 4 days or freeze between sheets of parchment in a sealable storage bag for up to 2 months.

Mediterranean Pan Pizza

Servings:2
Cooking Time: 8 Minutes

Ingredients:

- 1 cup shredded mozzarella cheese
- ¼ medium red bell pepper, seeded and chopped
- ½ cup chopped fresh spinach leaves
- 2 tablespoons chopped black olives
- 2 tablespoons crumbled feta cheese

Directions:

1. Sprinkle mozzarella into an ungreased 6" round nonstick baking dish in an even layer. Add remaining ingredients on top.
2. Place dish into air fryer basket. Adjust the temperature to 350°F and set the timer for 8 minutes, checking halfway through to avoid burning. Top of pizza will be golden brown and the cheese melted when done.
3. Remove dish from fryer and let cool 5 minutes before slicing and serving.

Garlicky Roasted Mushrooms

Servings: 4
Cooking Time: 30 Minutes

Ingredients:

- 16 garlic cloves, peeled
- 2 tsp olive oil
- 16 button mushrooms
- 2 tbsp fresh chives, snipped
- Salt and pepper to taste
- 1 tbsp white wine

Directions:

1. Preheat air fryer to 350°F. Coat the garlic with some olive oil in a baking pan, then Roast in the air fryer for 12 minutes. When done, take the pan out and stir in the mushrooms, salt, and pepper. Then add the remaining olive oil and white wine. Put the pan back into the fryer and Bake for 10-15 minutes until the mushrooms and garlic soften. Sprinkle with chives and serve warm.

Sesame Seeds Bok Choy

Servings:4
Cooking Time: 6 Minutes

Ingredients:

- 4 bunches baby bok choy, bottoms removed and leaves separated
- Olive oil cooking spray
- 1 teaspoon garlic powder
- 1 teaspoon sesame seeds

Directions:

1. Set the temperature of air fryer to 325°F.
2. Arrange bok choy leaves into the air fryer basket in a single layer.
3. Spray with the cooking spray and sprinkle with garlic powder.
4. Air fry for about 5-6 minutes, shaking after every 2 minutes.
5. Remove from air fryer and transfer the bok choy onto serving plates.
6. Garnish with sesame seeds and serve hot.

Honey Pear Chips

Servings: 4
Cooking Time: 30 Minutes

Ingredients:

- 2 firm pears, thinly sliced
- 1 tbsp lemon juice
- ½ tsp ground cinnamon
- 1 tsp honey

Directions:

1. Preheat air fryer to 380°F. Arrange the pear slices on the parchment-lined cooking basket. Drizzle with lemon juice and honey and sprinkle with cinnamon. Air Fry for 6-8 minutes, shaking the basket once, until golden. Leave to cool. Serve immediately or save for later in an airtight container. Good for 2 days.

Zucchini Fritters

Servings:4
Cooking Time: 12 Minutes

Ingredients:

- 1½ medium zucchini, trimmed and grated
- ½ teaspoon salt, divided
- 1 large egg, whisked
- ¼ teaspoon garlic powder
- ¼ cup grated Parmesan cheese

Directions:

1. Place grated zucchini on a kitchen towel and sprinkle with ¼ teaspoon salt. Wrap in towel and let sit 30 minutes, then wring out as much excess moisture as possible.
2. Place zucchini into a large bowl and mix with egg, remaining salt, garlic powder, and Parmesan. Cut a piece of parchment to fit air fryer basket. Divide mixture into four mounds, about ⅓ cup each, and press out into 4" rounds on ungreased parchment.
3. Place parchment with rounds into air fryer basket. Adjust the temperature to 400°F and set the timer for 12 minutes, turning fritters halfway through cooking. Fritters will be crispy on the edges and tender but firm in the center when done. Serve warm.

133

Italian Seasoned Easy Pasta Chips

Servings:2
Cooking Time:10 Minutes
Ingredients:
- ½ teaspoon salt
- 1 ½ teaspoon Italian seasoning blend
- 1 tablespoon nutritional yeast
- 1 tablespoon olive oil
- 2 cups whole wheat bowtie pasta

Directions:
1. Place the baking dish accessory in the air fryer.
2. Give a good stir.
3. Close the air fryer and cook for 10 minutes at 390°F.

Sweet And Spicy Barbecue Tofu

Servings:4
Cooking Time: 1 Hour 15 Minutes
Ingredients:
- 1 package extra-firm tofu, drained
- ½ cup barbecue sauce
- ½ cup brown sugar
- 1 teaspoon liquid smoke
- 1 teaspoon crushed red pepper flakes
- ½ teaspoon salt
- Cooking spray

Directions:
1. Press tofu block to remove excess moisture. If you don't have a tofu press, line a baking sheet with paper towels and set tofu on top. Set a second baking sheet on top of tofu and weight it with a heavy item such as a skillet. Let tofu sit at least 30 minutes, changing paper towels if necessary.
2. Cut pressed tofu into twenty-four equal pieces. Set aside.
3. In a large bowl, combine barbecue sauce, brown sugar, liquid smoke, red pepper flakes, and salt. Mix well and add tofu, coating completely. Cover and let marinate at least 30 minutes on the counter.
4. Preheat the air fryer to 400°F.
5. Spray the air fryer basket with cooking spray and add marinated tofu. Cook 15 minutes, shaking the basket twice during cooking.
6. Let cool 10 minutes before serving warm.

Spinach And Feta Pinwheels

Servings:4
Cooking Time: 15 Minutes
Ingredients:
- 1 sheet frozen puff pastry, thawed
- 3 ounces full-fat cream cheese, softened
- 1 bag frozen spinach, thawed and drained
- ¼ teaspoon salt
- ⅓ cup crumbled feta cheese
- 1 large egg, whisked

Directions:
1. Preheat the air fryer to 320°F. Unroll puff pastry into a flat rectangle.
2. In a medium bowl, mix cream cheese, spinach, and salt until well combined.
3. Spoon cream cheese mixture onto pastry in an even layer, leaving a ½" border around the edges.
4. Sprinkle feta evenly across dough and gently press into filling to secure. Roll lengthwise to form a log shape.

5. Cut the roll into twelve 1" pieces. Brush with egg. Place in the air fryer basket and cook 15 minutes, turning halfway through cooking time.
6. Let cool 5 minutes before serving.

Spinach And Artichoke–stuffed Peppers

Servings:4
Cooking Time: 15 Minutes
Ingredients:
- 2 ounces cream cheese, softened
- ½ cup shredded mozzarella cheese
- ½ cup chopped fresh spinach leaves
- ¼ cup chopped canned artichoke hearts
- 2 medium green bell peppers, halved and seeded

Directions:
1. In a medium bowl, mix cream cheese, mozzarella, spinach, and artichokes. Spoon ¼ cheese mixture into each pepper half.
2. Place peppers into ungreased air fryer basket. Adjust the temperature to 320°F and set the timer for 15 minutes. Peppers will be tender and cheese will be bubbling and brown when done. Serve warm.

Cauliflower Steak With Thick Sauce

Servings:2
Cooking Time: 15 Minutes
Ingredients:
- ¼ cup almond milk
- ¼ teaspoon vegetable stock powder
- 1 cauliflower, sliced into two
- 1 tablespoon olive oil
- 2 tablespoons onion, chopped
- salt and pepper to taste

Directions:
1. Soak the cauliflower in salted water or brine for at least 2 hours.
2. Preheat the air fryer to 400°F.
3. Rinse the cauliflower and place inside the air fryer and cook for 15 minutes.
4. Meanwhile, heat oil in a skillet over medium flame. Sauté the onions and stir until translucent. Add the vegetable stock powder and milk.
5. Bring to boil and adjust the heat to low.
6. Allow the sauce to reduce and season with salt and pepper.
7. Place cauliflower steak on a plate and pour over sauce.

Sautéed Spinach

Servings:2
Cooking Time:9 Minutes
Ingredients:
- 1 small onion, chopped
- 6 ounces fresh spinach
- 2 tablespoons olive oil
- 1 teaspoon ginger, minced
- Salt and black pepper, to taste

Directions:
1. Preheat the Air fryer to 360°F and grease an Air fryer pan.
2. Put olive oil, onions and ginger in the Air fryer pan and place in the Air fryer basket.
3. Cook for about 4 minutes and add spinach, salt, and black pepper.
4. Cook for about 4 more minutes and dish out in a bowl to serve.

Zucchini Gratin

Servings: 2
Cooking Time: 15 Minutes
Ingredients:
- 5 oz. parmesan cheese, shredded
- 1 tbsp. coconut flour
- 1 tbsp. dried parsley
- 2 zucchinis
- 1 tsp. butter, melted

Directions:
1. Mix the parmesan and coconut flour together in a bowl, seasoning with parsley to taste.
2. Cut the zucchini in half lengthwise and chop the halves into four slices.
3. Pre-heat the fryer at 400°F.
4. Pour the melted butter over the zucchini and then dip the zucchini into the parmesan-flour mixture, coating it all over. Cook the zucchini in the fryer for thirteen minutes.

Baked Polenta With Chili-cheese

Servings:3
Cooking Time: 10 Minutes
Ingredients:
- 1 commercial polenta roll, sliced
- 1 cup cheddar cheese sauce
- 1 tablespoon chili powder

Directions:
1. Place the baking dish accessory in the air fryer.
2. Arrange the polenta slices in the baking dish.
3. Add the chili powder and cheddar cheese sauce.
4. Close the air fryer and cook for 10 minutes at 390°F.

Pesto Vegetable Skewers

Servings:8
Cooking Time: 8 Minutes
Ingredients:
- 1 medium zucchini, trimmed and cut into ½" slices
- ½ medium yellow onion, peeled and cut into 1" squares
- 1 medium red bell pepper, seeded and cut into 1" squares
- 16 whole cremini mushrooms
- ⅓ cup basil pesto
- ½ teaspoon salt
- ¼ teaspoon ground black pepper

Directions:
1. Divide zucchini slices, onion, and bell pepper into eight even portions. Place on 6" skewers for a total of eight kebabs. Add 2 mushrooms to each skewer and brush kebabs generously with pesto.
2. Sprinkle each kebab with salt and black pepper on all sides, then place into ungreased air fryer basket. Adjust the temperature to 375°F and set the timer for 8 minutes, turning kebabs halfway through cooking. Vegetables will be browned at the edges and tender-crisp when done. Serve warm.

Cinnamon Sugar Tortilla Chips

Servings: 4
Cooking Time: 20 Minutes
Ingredients:
- 4 flour tortillas
- 1/4 cup vegan margarine, melted
- 1 ½ tablespoons ground cinnamon

- 1/4 cup caster sugar

Directions:
1. Slice each tortilla into eight slices. Brush the tortilla pieces with the melted margarine.
2. In a mixing bowl, thoroughly combine the cinnamon and sugar. Toss the cinnamon mixture with the tortillas.
3. Transfer to the cooking basket and cook at 360°F for 8 minutes or until lightly golden. Work in batches.
4. They will crisp up as they cool. Serve and enjoy!

Healthy Apple-licious Chips

Servings:1
Cooking Time: 6 Minutes
Ingredients:
- ½ teaspoon ground cumin
- 1 apple, cored and sliced thinly
- 1 tablespoon sugar
- A pinch of salt

Directions:
1. Place all ingredients in a bowl and toss to coat everything.
2. Put the grill pan accessory in the air fryer and place the sliced apples on the grill pan.
3. Close the air fryer and cook for 6 minutes at 390°F.

White Cheddar And Mushroom Soufflés

Servings:4
Cooking Time: 12 Minutes
Ingredients:
- 3 large eggs, whites and yolks separated
- ½ cup sharp white Cheddar cheese
- 3 ounces cream cheese, softened
- ¼ teaspoon cream of tartar
- ¼ teaspoon salt
- ¼ teaspoon ground black pepper
- ½ cup cremini mushrooms, sliced

Directions:
1. In a large bowl, whip egg whites until stiff peaks form, about 2 minutes. In a separate large bowl, beat Cheddar, egg yolks, cream cheese, cream of tartar, salt, and pepper together until combined.
2. Fold egg whites into cheese mixture, being careful not to stir. Fold in mushrooms, then pour mixture evenly into four ungreased 4" ramekins.
3. Place ramekins into air fryer basket. Adjust the temperature to 350°F and set the timer for 12 minutes. Eggs will be browned on the top and firm in the center when done. Serve warm.

Caramelized Brussels Sprout

Servings:4
Cooking Time:35 Minutes
Ingredients:
- 1 pound Brussels sprouts, trimmed and halved
- 4 teaspoons butter, melted
- Salt and black pepper, to taste

Directions:
1. Preheat the Air fryer to 400°F and grease an Air fryer basket.
2. Mix all the ingredients in a bowl and toss to coat well.
3. Arrange the Brussels sprouts in the Air fryer basket and cook for about 35 minutes.
4. Dish out and serve warm.

Skewered Corn In Air Fryer

Servings:2
Cooking Time: 25 Minutes
Ingredients:
- 1-pound apricot, halved
- 2 ears of corn
- 2 medium green peppers, cut into large chunks
- 2 teaspoons prepared mustard
- Salt and pepper to taste

Directions:
1. Preheat the air fryer to 330°F.
2. Place the grill pan accessory in the air fryer.
3. On the double layer rack with the skewer accessories, skewer the corn, green peppers, and apricot. Season with salt and pepper to taste.
4. Place skewered corn on the double layer rack and cook for 25 minutes.
5. Once cooked, brush with prepared mustard.

Vegetable Burgers

Servings:4
Cooking Time: 12 Minutes
Ingredients:
- 8 ounces cremini mushrooms
- 2 large egg yolks
- ½ medium zucchini, trimmed and chopped
- ¼ cup peeled and chopped yellow onion
- 1 clove garlic, peeled and finely minced
- ½ teaspoon salt
- ¼ teaspoon ground black pepper

Directions:
1. Place all ingredients into a food processor and pulse twenty times until finely chopped and combined.
2. Separate mixture into four equal sections and press each into a burger shape. Place burgers into ungreased air fryer basket. Adjust the temperature to 375°F and set the timer for 12 minutes, turning burgers halfway through cooking. Burgers will be browned and firm when done.
3. Place burgers on a large plate and let cool 5 minutes before serving.

Zucchini Topped With Coconut Cream 'n Bacon

Servings:3
Cooking Time: 20 Minutes
Ingredients:
- 1 tablespoon lemon juice
- 3 slices bacon, fried and crumbled
- 3 tablespoons olive oil
- 3 zucchini squashes
- 4 tablespoons coconut cream
- Salt and pepper to taste

Directions:
1. Preheat the air fryer for 5 minutes.
2. Line up chopsticks on both sides of the zucchini and slice thinly until you hit the stick. Brush the zucchinis with olive oil. Set aside.
3. Place the zucchini in the air fryer. Bake for 20 minutes at 350°F.
4. Meanwhile, combine the coconut cream and lemon juice in a mixing bowl. Season with salt and pepper to taste.

5. Once the zucchini is cooked, scoop the coconut cream mixture and drizzle on top.
6. Sprinkle with bacon bits.

Turmeric Crispy Chickpeas

Servings:4
Cooking Time: 22 Minutes
Ingredients:
- 1 tbsp butter, melted
- ½ tsp dried rosemary
- ¼ tsp turmeric
- Salt to taste

Directions:
1. Preheat the Air fryer to 380°F.
2. In a bowl, combine together chickpeas, butter, rosemary, turmeric, and salt; toss to coat. Place the prepared chickpeas in your Air Fryer's cooking basket and cook for 6 minutes. Slide out the basket and shake; cook for another 6 minutes until crispy.

Tacos

Servings: 24
Cooking Time: 8 Minutes Per Batch
Ingredients:
- 1 24-count package 4-inch corn tortillas
- 1½ cups refried beans
- 4 ounces sharp Cheddar cheese, grated
- ½ cup salsa
- oil for misting or cooking spray

Directions:
1. Preheat air fryer to 390°F.
2. Wrap refrigerated tortillas in damp paper towels and microwave for 30 to 60 seconds to warm. If necessary, rewarm tortillas as you go to keep them soft enough to fold without breaking.
3. Working with one tortilla at a time, top with 1 tablespoon of beans, 1 tablespoon of grated cheese, and 1 teaspoon of salsa Fold over and press down very gently on the center. Press edges firmly all around to seal. Spray both sides with oil or cooking spray.
4. Cooking in two batches, place half the tacos in the air fryer basket. To cook 12 at a time, you may need to stand them upright and lean some against the sides of basket. It's okay if they're crowded as long as you leave a little room for air to circulate around them.
5. Cook for 8 minutes or until golden brown and crispy.
6. Repeat steps 4 and 5 to cook remaining tacos.

Crustless Spinach And Cheese Frittata

Servings:4
Cooking Time: 20 Minutes
Ingredients:
- 6 large eggs
- ½ cup heavy whipping cream
- 1 cup frozen chopped spinach, drained
- 1 cup shredded sharp Cheddar cheese
- ¼ cup peeled and diced yellow onion
- ½ teaspoon salt
- ¼ teaspoon ground black pepper

Directions:
1. In a large bowl, whisk eggs and cream together. Whisk in spinach, Cheddar, onion, salt, and pepper.

2. Pour mixture into an ungreased 6" round nonstick baking dish. Place dish into air fryer basket. Adjust the temperature to 320°F and set the timer for 20 minutes. Eggs will be firm and slightly browned when done. Serve immediately.

Colorful Vegetable Medley

Servings: 4
Cooking Time: 20 Minutes
Ingredients:
- 1 lb green beans, chopped
- 2 carrots, cubed
- Salt and pepper to taste
- 1 zucchini, cut into chunks
- 1 red bell pepper, sliced
- Cooking spray

Directions:
1. Preheat air fryer to 390°F. Combine green beans, carrots, salt and pepper in a large bowl. Spray with cooking oil and transfer to the frying basket. Roast for 6 minutes.

2. Combine zucchini and red pepper in a bowl. Season to taste and spray with cooking oil; set aside. When the cooking time is up, add the zucchini and red pepper to the basket. Cook for another 6 minutes. Serve and enjoy.

Crispy Shawarma Broccoli

Servings: 4
Cooking Time: 25 Minutes
Ingredients:
- 1 pound broccoli, steamed and drained
- 2 tablespoons canola oil
- 1 teaspoon cayenne pepper
- 1 teaspoon sea salt
- 1 tablespoon Shawarma spice blend

Directions:
1. Toss all ingredients in a mixing bowl.
2. Roast in the preheated Air Fryer at 380°F for 10 minutes, shaking the basket halfway through the cooking time.
3. Work in batches. Bon appétit!

Chapter 9. Desserts And Sweets

Apple Pie

Servings: 7
Cooking Time: 25 Minutes
Ingredients:
- 2 large apples
- ½ cup flour
- 2 tbsp. unsalted butter
- 1 tbsp. sugar
- ½ tsp. cinnamon

Directions:
1. Pre-heat the Air Fryer to 360°F
2. In a large bowl, combine the flour and butter. Pour in the sugar, continuing to mix.
3. Add in a few tablespoons of water and combine everything to create a smooth dough.
4. Grease the insides of a few small pastry tins with butter. Divide the dough between each tin and lay each portion flat inside.
5. Peel, core and dice up the apples. Put the diced apples on top of the pastry and top with a sprinkling of sugar and cinnamon.
6. Place the pastry tins in your Air Fryer and cook for 15 - 17 minutes.
7. Serve.

Fried Cannoli Wontons

Servings: 10
Cooking Time: 8 Minutes
Ingredients:
- 8 ounces Neufchâtel cream cheese
- ¼ cup powdered sugar
- 1 teaspoon vanilla extract

- ¼ teaspoon salt
- ¼ cup mini chocolate chips
- 2 tablespoons chopped pecans (optional)
- 20 wonton wrappers
- ¼ cup filtered water

Directions:
1. Preheat the air fryer to 370°F.
2. In a large bowl, use a hand mixer to combine the cream cheese with the powdered sugar, vanilla, and salt. Fold in the chocolate chips and pecans. Set aside.
3. Lay the wonton wrappers out on a flat, smooth surface and place a bowl with the filtered water next to them.
4. Use a teaspoon to evenly divide the cream cheese mixture among the 20 wonton wrappers, placing the batter in the center of the wontons.
5. Wet the tip of your index finger, and gently moisten the outer edges of the wrapper. Then fold each wrapper until it creates a secure pocket.
6. Liberally spray the air fryer basket with olive oil mist.
7. Place the wontons into the basket, and cook for 5 to 8 minutes. When the outer edges begin to brown, remove the wontons from the air fryer basket. Repeat cooking with remaining wontons.
8. Serve warm.

Apple Dumplings

Servings: 4
Cooking Time: 10 Minutes
Ingredients:
- 4 Small tart apples, preferably McIntosh, peeled and cored
- ¼ cup Granulated white sugar
- 1½ tablespoons Ground cinnamon

- 1 sheet, thawed and cut into four quarters A 17.25-ounce box frozen puff pastry (vegetarian, if a concern)

Directions:

1. Set the apples stem side up on a microwave-safe plate, preferably a glass pie plate. Microwave on high for 3 minutes, or until somewhat tender when poked with the point of a knife. Cool to room temperature, about 30 minutes.
2. Preheat the air fryer to 400°F.
3. Combine the sugar and cinnamon in a small bowl. Roll the apples in this mixture, coating them completely on their outsides. Also sprinkle this cinnamon sugar into each hole where the core was.
4. Roll the puff pastry squares into 6 x 6-inch squares. Slice the corners off each rolled square so that it's sort of like a circle. Place an apple in the center of one of these squares and fold it up and all around the apple, sealing it at the top by pressing the pastry together. The apple must be completely sealed in the pastry. Repeat for the remaining apples.
5. Set the pastry-covered apples in the basket with at least ½ inch between them. Air-fry undisturbed for 10 minutes, or until puffed and golden brown.
6. Use a nonstick-safe spatula, and maybe a flatware tablespoon for balance, to transfer the apples to a wire rack. Cool for at least 5 minutes or up to 15 minutes before serving warm.

Pineapple Sticks

Servings: 4
Cooking Time: 20 Minutes

Ingredients:

- ½ fresh pineapple, cut into sticks
- ¼ cup desiccated coconut

Directions:

1. Pre-heat the Air Fryer to 400°F.
2. Coat the pineapple sticks in the desiccated coconut and put each one in the Air Fryer basket.
3. Air fry for 10 minutes.

Shortbread Fingers

Servings: 10
Cooking Time: 20 Minutes

Ingredients:

- 1 ½ cups butter
- 1 cup flour
- ¾ cup sugar
- Cooking spray

Directions:

1. Pre-heat your Air Fryer to 350°F.
2. In a bowl. combine the flour and sugar.
3. Cut each stick of butter into small chunks. Add the chunks into the flour and the sugar.
4. Blend the butter into the mixture to combine everything well.
5. Use your hands to knead the mixture, forming a smooth consistency.
6. Shape the mixture into 10 equal-sized finger shapes, marking them with the tines of a fork for decoration if desired.
7. Lightly spritz the Air Fryer basket with the cooking spray. Place the cookies inside, spacing them out well.
8. Bake the cookies for 12 minutes.
9. Let cool slightly before serving. Alternatively, you can store the cookies in an airtight container for up to 3 days.

Dark Chocolate Cake

Servings:4
Cooking Time:10 Minutes

Ingredients:

- 1½ tablespoons almond flour
- 3½ oz. unsalted butter
- 3½ oz. sugar free dark chocolate, chopped
- 2 eggs
- 3½ tablespoons swerve

Directions:

1. Preheat the Air fryer to 375°F and grease 4 regular sized ramekins.
2. Microwave all chocolate bits with butter in a bowl for about 3 minutes.
3. Remove from the microwave and whisk in the eggs and swerve.
4. Stir in the flour and mix well until smooth.
5. Transfer the mixture into the ramekins and arrange in the Air fryer basket.
6. Cook for about 10 minutes and dish out to serve.

Chocolate Brownie

Servings: 4
Cooking Time: 16 Minutes

Ingredients:

- 1 cup bananas, overripe
- 1 scoop protein powder
- 2 tbsp unsweetened cocoa powder
- 1/2 cup almond butter, melted

Directions:

1. Preheat the air fryer to 325°F.
2. Spray air fryer baking pan with cooking spray.
3. Add all ingredients into the blender and blend until smooth.
4. Pour batter into the prepared pan and place in the air fryer basket.
5. Cook brownie for 16 minutes.
6. Serve and enjoy.

Brown Sugar Baked Apples

Servings: 4
Cooking Time: 15 Minutes

Ingredients:

- 3 Small tart apples, preferably McIntosh
- 4 tablespoons (¼ cup/½ stick) Butter
- 6 tablespoons Light brown sugar
- Ground cinnamon
- Table salt

Directions:

1. Preheat the air fryer to 400°F.
2. Stem the apples, then cut them in half through their "equators". Use a melon baller to core the apples, taking care not to break through the flesh and skin at any point but creating a little well in the center of each half.
3. When the machine is at temperature, remove the basket and set it on a heat-safe work surface. Set the apple halves cut side up in the basket with as much air space between them as possible. Even a fraction of an inch will work. Drop 2 teaspoons of butter into the well in the center of each apple half. Sprinkle each half with 1 tablespoon brown sugar and a pinch each ground cinnamon and table salt.

4. Return the basket to the machine. Air-fry undisturbed for 15 minutes, or until the apple halves have softened and the brown sugar has caramelized.

5. Use a nonstick-safe spatula to transfer the apple halves cut side up to a wire rack. Cool for at least 10 minutes before serving, or serve at room temperature.

Cherry Cheesecake Rolls

Servings: 6
Cooking Time: 30 Minutes
Ingredients:
- 1 can crescent rolls
- 4 oz cream cheese
- 1 tbsp cherry preserves
- 1/3 cup sliced fresh cherries
- Cooking spray

Directions:
1. Roll out the dough into a large rectangle on a flat work surface. Cut the dough into 12 rectangles by cutting 3 cuts across and 2 cuts down. In a microwave-safe bowl, soften cream cheese for 15 seconds. Stir together with cherry preserves. Mound 2 tsp of the cherries-cheese mix on each piece of dough. Carefully spread the mixture but not on the edges. Top with 2 tsp of cherries each. Roll each triangle to make a cylinder.

2. Preheat air fryer to 350°F. Place the first batch of the rolls in the greased air fryer. Spray the rolls with cooking oil and Bake for 8 minutes. Let cool in the air fryer for 2-3 minutes before removing. Serve.

Easy Mug Brownie

Servings: 1
Cooking Time: 10 Minutes
Ingredients:
- 1 scoop chocolate protein powder
- 1 tbsp cocoa powder
- 1/2 tsp baking powder
- 1/4 cup unsweetened almond milk

Directions:
1. Add baking powder, protein powder, and cocoa powder in a mug and mix well.
2. Add milk in a mug and stir well.
3. Place the mug in the air fryer and cook at 390°F for 10 minutes.
4. Serve and enjoy.

Easy Keto Danish

Servings:6
Cooking Time: 12 Minutes
Ingredients:
- 1½ cups shredded mozzarella cheese
- ½ cup blanched finely ground almond flour
- 3 ounces cream cheese, divided
- ¼ cup confectioners' erythritol
- 1 tablespoon lemon juice

Directions:
1. Place mozzarella, flour, and 1 ounce cream cheese in a large microwave-safe bowl. Microwave on high 45 seconds, then stir with a fork until a soft dough forms.

2. Separate dough into six equal sections and press each in a single layer into an ungreased 4" × 4" square nonstick baking dish to form six even squares that touch.

3. In a small bowl, mix remaining cream cheese, erythritol, and lemon juice. Place 1 tablespoon mixture in center of each piece of dough in baking dish. Fold all four corners of each dough piece halfway to center to reach cream cheese mixture.

4. Place dish into air fryer. Adjust the temperature to 320°F and set the timer for 12 minutes. The center and edges will be browned when done. Let cool 10 minutes before serving.

Fried Banana S'mores

Servings: 4
Cooking Time: 6 Minutes
Ingredients:
- 4 bananas
- 3 tablespoons mini semi-sweet chocolate chips
- 3 tablespoons mini peanut butter chips
- 3 tablespoons mini marshmallows
- 3 tablespoons graham cracker cereal

Directions:
1. Preheat the air fryer to 400°F.
2. Slice into the un-peeled bananas lengthwise along the inside of the curve, but do not slice through the bottom of the peel. Open the banana slightly to form a pocket.
3. Fill each pocket with chocolate chips, peanut butter chips and marshmallows. Poke the graham cracker cereal into the filling.
4. Place the bananas in the air fryer basket, resting them on the side of the basket and each other to keep them upright with the filling facing up. Air-fry for 6 minutes, or until the bananas are soft to the touch, the peels have blackened and the chocolate and marshmallows have melted and toasted.
5. Let them cool for a couple of minutes and then simply serve with a spoon to scoop out the filling.

Grilled Banana Boats

Servings: 3
Cooking Time: 15 Minutes
Ingredients:
- 3 large bananas
- 1 tablespoon ginger snaps
- 2 tablespoons mini chocolate chips
- 3 tablespoons mini marshmallows
- 3 tablespoons crushed vanilla wafers

Directions:
1. In the peel, slice your banana lengthwise; make sure not to slice all the way through the banana. Divide the remaining ingredients between the banana pockets.
2. Place in the Air Fryer grill pan. Cook at 395°F for 7 minutes.
3. Let the banana boats cool for 5 to 6 minutes, and then eat with a spoon. Bon appétit!

Cranberries Pudding

Servings: 6
Cooking Time: 20 Minutes
Ingredients:
- 1 cup cauliflower rice
- 2 cups almond milk
- ½ cup cranberries
- 1 teaspoon vanilla extract

Directions:

1. In a pan that fits your air fryer, mix all the ingredients, whisk a bit, put the pan in the fryer and cook at 360°F for 20 minutes. Stir the pudding, divide into bowls and serve cold.

Cinnamon Canned Biscuit Donuts

Servings: 4
Cooking Time: 25 Minutes
Ingredients:
- 1 can jumbo biscuits
- 1 cup cinnamon sugar

Directions:
1. Preheat air fryer to 360°F. Divide biscuit dough into 8 biscuits and place on a flat work surface. Cut a small circle in the center of the biscuit with a small cookie cutter. Place a batch of 4 donuts in the air fryer. Spray with oil and Bake for 8 minutes, flipping once. Drizzle the cinnamon sugar over the donuts and serve.

Banana And Rice Pudding

Servings: 6
Cooking Time: 20 Minutes
Ingredients:
- 1 cup brown rice
- 3 cups milk
- 2 bananas, peeled and mashed
- ½ cup maple syrup
- 1 teaspoon vanilla extract

Directions:
1. Place all the ingredients in a pan that fits your air fryer; stir well.
2. Put the pan in the fryer and cook at 360°F for 20 minutes.
3. Stir the pudding, divide into cups, refrigerate, and serve cold.

Orange Marmalade

Servings: 4
Cooking Time: 20 Minutes
Ingredients:
- 4 oranges, peeled and chopped
- 3 cups sugar
- 1½ cups water

Directions:
1. In a pan that fits your air fryer, mix the oranges with the sugar and the water; stir.
2. Place the pan in the fryer and cook at 340°F for 20 minutes.
3. Stir well, divide into cups, refrigerate, and serve cold.

Toasted Coconut Flakes

Servings: 1
Cooking Time: 5 Minutes
Ingredients:
- 1 cup unsweetened coconut flakes
- 2 tsp. coconut oil, melted
- ¼ cup granular erythritol
- Salt

Directions:
1. In a large bowl, combine the coconut flakes, oil, granular erythritol, and a pinch of salt, ensuring that the flakes are coated completely.
2. Place the coconut flakes in your fryer and cook at 300°F for three minutes, giving the basket a good shake a few times throughout the cooking time. Fry until golden and serve.

Grape Stew

Servings: 4
Cooking Time: 14 Minutes
Ingredients:
- 1 pound red grapes
- Juice and zest of 1 lemon
- 26 ounces grape juice

Directions:
1. In a pan that fits your air fryer, add all ingredients and toss.
2. Place the pan in the fryer and cook at 320°F for 14 minutes.
3. Divide into cups, refrigerate, and serve cold.

Fruit Turnovers

Servings: 6
Cooking Time: 25 Minutes
Ingredients:
- 1 sheet puff pastry dough
- 6 tsp peach preserves
- 3 kiwi, sliced
- 1 large egg, beaten
- 1 tbsp icing sugar

Directions:
1. Prepare puff pastry by cutting it into 6 rectangles. Roll out the pastry with a rolling pin into 5-inch squares. On your workspace, position one square so that it looks like a diamond with points to the top and bottom. Spoon 1 tsp of the preserves on the bottom half and spread it, leaving a ½-inch border from the edge. Place half of one kiwi on top of the preserves. Brush the clean edges with the egg, then fold the top corner over the filling to make a triangle. Crimp with a fork to seal the pastry. Brush the top of the pastry with egg. Preheat air fryer to 350°F. Put the pastries in the greased frying basket. Air Fry for 10 minutes, flipping once until golden and puffy. Remove from the fryer, let cool and dush with icing sugar. Serve.

Keto Butter Balls

Servings: 4
Cooking Time: 10 Minutes
Ingredients:
- 1 tablespoon butter, softened1 tablespoon Erythritol
- ½ teaspoon ground cinnamon
- 1 tablespoon coconut flour
- 1 teaspoon coconut flakes
- Cooking spray

Directions:
1. Put the butter, Erythritol, ground cinnamon, coconut flour, and coconut flakes. Then stir the mixture with the help of the fork until homogenous. Make 4 balls. Preheat the air fryer to 375°F. Spray the air fryer basket with cooking spray and place the balls inside. Cook the dessert for 10 minutes.

Brownies For Two

Servings: 2
Cooking Time: 15 Minutes
Ingredients:
- ½ cup blanched finely ground almond flour
- 3 tablespoons granular erythritol
- 3 tablespoons unsweetened cocoa powder
- ½ teaspoon baking powder
- 1 teaspoon vanilla extract
- 2 large eggs, whisked
- 2 tablespoons salted butter, melted

Directions:
1. In a medium bowl, combine flour, erythritol, cocoa powder, and baking powder.
2. Add in vanilla, eggs, and butter, and stir until a thick batter forms.
3. Pour batter into two 4" ramekins greased with cooking spray and place ramekins into air fryer basket. Adjust the temperature to 325°F and set the timer for 15 minutes. Centers will be firm when done. Let ramekins cool 5 minutes before serving.

Fiesta Pastries

Servings:8
Cooking Time:20 Minutes
Ingredients:
- ½ of apple, peeled, cored and chopped
- 1 teaspoon fresh orange zest, grated finely
- 7.05-ounce prepared frozen puff pastry, cut into 16 squares
- ½ tablespoon white sugar
- ½ teaspoon ground cinnamon

Directions:
1. Preheat the Air fryer to 390°F and grease an Air fryer basket.
2. Mix all ingredients in a bowl except puff pastry.
3. Arrange about 1 teaspoon of this mixture in the center of each square.
4. Fold each square into a triangle and slightly press the edges with a fork.
5. Arrange the pastries in the Air fryer basket and cook for about 10 minutes.
6. Dish out and serve immediately.

Glazed Donuts

Servings: 2 – 4
Cooking Time: 25 Minutes
Ingredients:
- 1 can [8 oz.] refrigerated croissant dough
- Cooking spray
- 1 can [16 oz.] vanilla frosting

Directions:
1. Cut the croissant dough into 1-inch-round slices. Make a hole in the center of each one to create a donut.
2. Put the donuts in the Air Fryer basket, taking care not to overlap any, and spritz with cooking spray. You may need to cook everything in multiple batches.
3. Cook at 400°F for 2 minutes. Turn the donuts over and cook for another 3 minutes.
4. Place the rolls on a paper plate.
5. Microwave a half-cup of frosting for 30 seconds and pour a drizzling of the frosting over the donuts before serving.

Chilled Strawberry Pie

Servings:6
Cooking Time: 10 Minutes
Ingredients:
- 1½ cups whole shelled pecans
- 1 tablespoon unsalted butter, softened
- 1 cup heavy whipping cream
- 12 medium fresh strawberries, hulled
- 2 tablespoons sour cream

Directions:

1. Place pecans and butter into a food processor and pulse ten times until a dough forms. Press dough into the bottom of an ungreased 6" round nonstick baking dish.
2. Place dish into air fryer basket. Adjust the temperature to 320°F and set the timer for 10 minutes. Crust will be firm and golden when done. Let cool 20 minutes.
3. In a large bowl, whisk cream until fluffy and doubled in size, about 2 minutes.
4. In a separate large bowl, mash strawberries until mostly liquid. Fold strawberries and sour cream into whipped cream.
5. Spoon mixture into cooled crust, cover, and place into refrigerator for at least 30 minutes to set. Serve chilled.

Lemon Iced Donut Balls

Servings: 6
Cooking Time: 25 Minutes
Ingredients:
- 1 can jumbo biscuit dough
- 2 tsp lemon juice
- ½ cup icing sugar, sifted

Directions:
1. Preheat air fryer to 360°F. Divide the biscuit dough into 16 equal portions. Roll the dough into balls of 1½ inches thickness. Place the donut holes in the greased frying basket and Air Fry for 8 minutes, flipping once. Mix the icing sugar and lemon juice until smooth. Spread the icing over the top of the donuts. Leave to set a bit. Serve.

Chocolate-covered Maple Bacon

Servings: 4
Cooking Time: 25 Minutes
Ingredients:
- 8 slices sugar-free bacon
- 1 tbsp. granular erythritol
- 1/3 cup low-carb sugar-free chocolate chips
- 1 tsp. coconut oil
- ½ tsp. maple extract

Directions:
1. Place the bacon in the fryer's basket and add the erythritol on top. Cook for six minutes at 350°F and turn the bacon over. Leave to cook another six minutes or until the bacon is sufficiently crispy.
2. Take the bacon out of the fryer and leave it to cool.
3. Microwave the chocolate chips and coconut oil together for half a minute. Remove from the microwave and mix together before stirring in the maple extract.
4. Set the bacon flat on a piece of parchment paper and pour the mixture over. Allow to harden in the refrigerator for roughly five minutes before serving.

Pumpkin Cake

Servings:8
Cooking Time: 25 Minutes
Ingredients:
- 4 tablespoons salted butter, melted
- ½ cup granular brown erythritol
- ¼ cup pure pumpkin puree
- 1 cup blanched finely ground almond flour
- ½ teaspoon baking powder
- ⅛ teaspoon salt
- 1 teaspoon pumpkin pie spice

Directions:

1. Mix all ingredients in a large bowl. Pour batter into an ungreased 6" round nonstick baking dish.
2. Place dish into air fryer basket. Adjust the temperature to 300°F and set the timer for 25 minutes. The top will be dark brown, and a toothpick inserted in the center should come out clean when done. Let cool 30 minutes before serving.

Cocoa Bombs

Servings: 12
Cooking Time: 8 Minutes
Ingredients:
- 2 cups macadamia nuts, chopped
- 4 tablespoons coconut oil, melted
- 1 teaspoon vanilla extract
- ¼ cup cocoa powder
- 1/3 cup swerve

Directions:
1. In a bowl, mix all the ingredients and whisk well. Shape medium balls out of this mix, place them in your air fryer and cook at 300°F for 8 minutes. Serve cold.

Monkey Bread

Servings:6
Cooking Time: 20 Minutes
Ingredients:
- 1 can refrigerated biscuit dough
- ½ cup granulated sugar
- 1 tablespoon ground cinnamon
- ¼ cup salted butter, melted
- ¼ cup brown sugar
- Cooking spray

Directions:
1. Preheat the air fryer to 325°F. Spray a 6" round cake pan with cooking spray. Separate biscuits and cut each into four pieces.
2. In a large bowl, stir granulated sugar with cinnamon. Toss biscuit pieces in the cinnamon and sugar mixture until well coated. Place each biscuit piece in prepared pan.
3. In a medium bowl, stir together butter and brown sugar. Pour mixture evenly over the biscuit pieces.
4. Place pan in the air fryer basket and cook 20 minutes until brown. Let cool 10 minutes before flipping bread out of the pan and serving.

Roasted Pecan Clusters

Servings:8
Cooking Time: 8 Minutes
Ingredients:
- 3 ounces whole shelled pecans
- 1 tablespoon salted butter, melted
- 2 teaspoons confectioners' erythritol
- ½ teaspoon ground cinnamon
- ½ cup low-carb chocolate chips

Directions:
1. In a medium bowl, toss pecans with butter, then sprinkle with erythritol and cinnamon.
2. Place pecans into ungreased air fryer basket. Adjust the temperature to 350°F and set the timer for 8 minutes, shaking the basket two times during cooking. They will feel soft initially but get crunchy as they cool.
3. Line a large baking sheet with parchment paper.

4. Place chocolate in a medium microwave-safe bowl. Microwave on high, heating in 20-second increments and stirring until melted. Place 1 teaspoon chocolate in a rounded mound on ungreased parchment-lined baking sheet, then press 1 pecan into top, repeating with remaining chocolate and pecans.
5. Place baking sheet into refrigerator to cool at least 30 minutes. Once cooled, store clusters in a large sealed container in refrigerator up to 5 days.

Raspberry Empanada

Servings: 6
Cooking Time: 35 Minutes
Ingredients:
- 1 can raspberry pie filling
- 1 puff pastry dough
- 1 egg white, beaten
- Cooking spray

Directions:
1. Preheat air fryer to 370°F. Unroll the two sheets of dough and cut into 4 squares each, or 8 squares total. Scoop ½ to 1 tbsp of the raspberry pie filling in the center of each square. Brush the edges with egg white. Fold diagonally to form a triangle and close the turnover. Press the edges with the back of a fork to seal. Arrange the turnovers in a single layer in the greased basket. Spray the empanadas with cooking oil and Bake for 8 minutes. Let them sit in the air fryer for 3-4 minutes to cool before removing. Repeat for the other batch. Serve and enjoy!

Fried Snickers Bars

Servings:8
Cooking Time: 4 Minutes
Ingredients:
- ⅓ cup All-purpose flour
- 1 Large egg white(s), beaten until foamy
- 1½ cups Vanilla wafer cookie crumbs
- 8 Fun-size Snickers bars, frozen
- Vegetable oil spray

Directions:
1. Preheat the air fryer to 400°F.
2. Set up and fill three shallow soup plates or small pie plates on your counter: one for the flour, one for the beaten egg white(s), and one for the cookie crumbs.
3. Unwrap the frozen candy bars. Dip one in the flour, turning it to coat on all sides. Gently shake off any excess, then set it in the beaten egg white(s). Turn it to coat all sides, even the ends, then let any excess egg white slip back into the rest. Set the candy bar in the cookie crumbs. Turn to coat on all sides, even the ends. Dip the candy bar back in the egg white(s) a second time, then into the cookie crumbs a second time, making sure you have an even coating all around. Coat the covered candy bar all over with vegetable oil spray. Set aside so you can dip and coat the remaining candy bars.
4. Set the coated candy bars in the basket with as much air space between them as possible. Air-fry undisturbed for 4 minutes, or until golden brown.
5. Remove the basket from the machine and let the candy bars cool in the basket for 10 minutes. Use a nonstick-safe spatula to transfer them to a wire rack and cool for 5 minutes more before chowing down.

S'mores Pockets

Servings: 6
Cooking Time: 5 Minutes
Ingredients:
- 12 sheets phyllo dough, thawed
- 1½ cups butter, melted
- ¾ cup graham cracker crumbs
- 1 Giant Hershey's milk chocolate bar
- 12 marshmallows, cut in half

Directions:
1. Place one sheet of the phyllo on a large cutting board. Keep the rest of the phyllo sheets covered with a slightly damp, clean kitchen towel. Brush the phyllo sheet generously with some melted butter. Place a second phyllo sheet on top of the first and brush it with more butter. Repeat with one more phyllo sheet until you have a stack of 3 phyllo sheets with butter brushed between the layers. Cover the phyllo sheets with one quarter of the graham cracker crumbs leaving a 1-inch border on one of the short ends of the rectangle. Cut the phyllo sheets lengthwise into 3 strips.
2. Take 2 of the strips and crisscross them to form a cross with the empty borders at the top and to the left. Place 2 of the chocolate rectangles in the center of the cross. Place 4 of the marshmallow halves on top of the chocolate. Now fold the pocket together by folding the bottom phyllo strip up over the chocolate and marshmallows. Then fold the right side over, then the top strip down and finally the left side over. Brush all the edges generously with melted butter to seal shut. Repeat with the next three sheets of phyllo, until all the sheets have been used. You will be able to make 2 pockets with every second batch because you will have an extra graham cracker crumb strip from the previous set of sheets.
3. Preheat the air fryer to 350°F.
4. Transfer 3 pockets at a time to the air fryer basket. Air-fry at 350°F for 4 to 5 minutes, until the phyllo dough is light brown in color. Flip the pockets over halfway through the cooking process. Repeat with the remaining 3 pockets.
5. Serve warm.

Brownies

Servings: 8
Cooking Time: 20 Minutes
Ingredients:
- ½ cup all-purpose flour
- 1 cup granulated sugar
- ¼ cup cocoa powder
- ½ teaspoon baking powder
- 6 tablespoons salted butter, melted
- 1 large egg
- ½ cup semisweet chocolate chips

Directions:
1. Preheat the air fryer to 350°F. Generously grease two 6" round cake pans.
2. In a large bowl, combine flour, sugar, cocoa powder, and baking powder.
3. Add butter, egg, and chocolate chips to dry ingredients. Stir until well combined.
4. Divide batter between prepared pans. Place in the air fryer basket and cook 20 minutes until a toothpick inserted into the center comes out clean. Cool 5 minutes before serving.

Coconut Macaroons

Servings: 12
Cooking Time: 8 Minutes
Ingredients:
- 1⅓ cups shredded, sweetened coconut
- 4½ teaspoons flour
- 2 tablespoons sugar
- 1 egg white
- ½ teaspoon almond extract

Directions:
1. Preheat air fryer to 330°F.
2. Mix all ingredients together.
3. Shape coconut mixture into 12 balls.
4. Place all 12 macaroons in air fryer basket. They won't expand, so you can place them close together, but they shouldn't touch.
5. Cook at 330°F for 8 minutes, until golden.

Brown Sugar Cookies

Servings:9
Cooking Time: 27 Minutes
Ingredients:
- 4 tablespoons salted butter, melted
- ⅓ cup granular brown erythritol
- 1 large egg
- ½ teaspoon vanilla extract
- 1 cup blanched finely ground almond flour
- ½ teaspoon baking powder

Directions:
1. In a large bowl, whisk together butter, erythritol, egg, and vanilla. Add flour and baking powder, and stir until combined.
2. Separate dough into nine pieces and roll into balls, about 2 tablespoons each.
3. Cut three pieces of parchment paper to fit your air fryer basket and place three cookies on each ungreased piece. Place one piece of parchment into air fryer basket. Adjust the temperature to 300°F and set the timer for 9 minutes. Edges of cookies will be browned when done. Repeat with remaining cookies. Serve warm.

Honey-roasted Mixed Nuts

Servings: 8
Cooking Time: 15 Minutes
Ingredients:
- ½ cup raw, shelled pistachios
- ½ cup raw almonds
- 1 cup raw walnuts
- 2 tablespoons filtered water
- 2 tablespoons honey
- 1 tablespoon vegetable oil
- 2 tablespoons sugar
- ½ teaspoon salt

Directions:
1. Preheat the air fryer to 300°F.
2. Lightly spray an air-fryer-safe pan with olive oil; then place the pistachios, almonds, and walnuts inside the pan and place the pan inside the air fryer basket.
3. Cook for 15 minutes, shaking the basket every 5 minutes to rotate the nuts.
4. While the nuts are roasting, boil the water in a small pan and stir in the honey and oil. Continue to stir while cooking

until the water begins to evaporate and a thick sauce is formed. Note: The sauce should stick to the back of a wooden spoon when mixed. Turn off the heat.

5. Remove the nuts from the air fryer and spoon the nuts into the stovetop pan. Use a spatula to coat the nuts with the honey syrup.

6. Line a baking sheet with parchment paper and spoon the nuts onto the sheet. Lightly sprinkle the sugar and salt over the nuts and let cool in the refrigerator for at least 2 hours.

7. When the honey and sugar have hardened, store the nuts in an airtight container in the refrigerator.

Cocoa Spread

Servings: 4
Cooking Time: 5 Minutes
Ingredients:
- 2 oz walnuts, chopped
- 5 teaspoons coconut oil
- ½ teaspoon vanilla extract
- 1 tablespoon Erythritol
- 1 teaspoon of cocoa powder

Directions:
1. Preheat the air fryer to 350°F. Put the walnuts in the mason jar. Add coconut oil, vanilla extract, Erythritol, and cocoa powder. Stir the mixture until smooth with the help of the spoon. Then place the mason jar with Nutella in the preheated air fryer and cook it for 5 minutes. Stir Nutella before serving.

Dark Chocolate Peanut Butter S'mores

Servings: 4
Cooking Time: 6 Minutes
Ingredients:
- 4 graham cracker sheets
- 4 marshmallows
- 4 teaspoons chunky peanut butter
- 4 ounces dark chocolate
- ½ teaspoon ground cinnamon

Directions:
1. Preheat the air fryer to 390°F. Break the graham crackers in half so you have 8 pieces.
2. Place 4 pieces of graham cracker on the bottom of the air fryer. Top each with one of the marshmallows and bake for 6 or 7 minutes, or until the marshmallows have a golden brown center.
3. While cooking, slather each of the remaining graham crackers with 1 teaspoon peanut butter.
4. When baking completes, carefully remove each of the graham crackers, add 1 ounce of dark chocolate on top of the marshmallow, and lightly sprinkle with cinnamon. Top with the remaining peanut butter graham cracker to make the sandwich. Serve immediately.

Baked Apple

Servings: 6
Cooking Time: 20 Minutes
Ingredients:
- 3 small Honey Crisp or other baking apples
- 3 tablespoons maple syrup
- 3 tablespoons chopped pecans
- 1 tablespoon firm butter, cut into 6 pieces

Directions:
1. Put ½ cup water in the drawer of the air fryer.

2. Wash apples well and dry them.
3. Split apples in half. Remove core and a little of the flesh to make a cavity for the pecans.
4. Place apple halves in air fryer basket, cut side up.
5. Spoon 1½ teaspoons pecans into each cavity.
6. Spoon ½ tablespoon maple syrup over pecans in each apple.
7. Top each apple with ½ teaspoon butter.
8. Cook at 360°F for 20 minutes, until apples are tender.

Pumpkin Pie

Servings:6
Cooking Time: 2 Hours 25 Minutes
Ingredients:
- 1 can pumpkin pie mix
- 1 large egg
- 1 teaspoon vanilla extract
- ⅓ cup sweetened condensed milk
- 1 premade graham cracker piecrust

Directions:
1. Preheat the air fryer to 325°F.
2. In a large bowl, whisk together pumpkin pie mix, egg, vanilla, and sweetened condensed milk until well combined. Pour mixture into piecrust.
3. Place in the air fryer basket and cook 25 minutes until pie is brown, firm, and a toothpick inserted into the center comes out clean.
4. Chill in the refrigerator until set, at least 2 hours, before serving.

No Flour Lime Muffins

Servings:6
Cooking Time: 30 Minutes
Ingredients:
- Juice and zest of 2 limes
- 1 cup yogurt
- ¼ cup superfine sugar
- 8 oz cream cheese
- 1 tsp vanilla extract

Directions:
1. Preheat the air fryer to 330°F, and with a spatula, gently combine the yogurt and cheese. In another bowl, beat together the rest of the ingredients. Gently fold the lime with the cheese mixture. Divide the batter between 6 lined muffin tins. Cook in the air fryer for 10 minutes.

Party S'mores

Servings: 6
Cooking Time: 15 Minutes
Ingredients:
- 2 dark chocolate bars, cut into 12 pieces
- 12 buttermilk biscuits
- 12 marshmallows

Directions:
1. Preheat air fryer to 350°F. Place 6 biscuits in the air fryer. Top each square with a piece of dark chocolate. Bake for 2 minutes. Add a marshmallow to each piece of chocolate. Cook for another minute. Remove and top with another piece of biscuit. Serve warm.

Sweet Potato Pie Rolls

Servings:3
Cooking Time: 8 Minutes
Ingredients:
- 6 Spring roll wrappers
- 1½ cups Canned yams in syrup, drained
- 2 tablespoons Light brown sugar
- ¼ teaspoon Ground cinnamon
- 1 Large egg(s), well beaten
- Vegetable oil spray

Directions:
1. Preheat the air fryer to 400°F.
2. Set a spring roll wrapper on a clean, dry work surface. Scoop up ¼ cup of the pulpy yams and set along one edge of the wrapper, leaving 2 inches on each side of the yams. Top the yams with about 1 teaspoon brown sugar and a pinch of ground cinnamon. Fold the sides of the wrapper perpendicular to the yam filling up and over the filling, partially covering it. Brush beaten egg(s) over the side of the wrapper farthest from the yam. Starting with the yam end, roll the wrapper closed, ending at the part with the beaten egg that you can press gently to seal. Lightly coat the roll on all sides with vegetable oil spray. Set it aside seam side down and continue filling, rolling, and spraying the remaining wrappers in the same way.
3. Set the rolls seam side down in the basket with as much air space between them as possible. Air-fry undisturbed for 8 minutes, or until crisp and golden brown.
4. Use a nonstick-safe spatula and perhaps kitchen tongs for balance to gently transfer the rolls to a wire rack. Cool for at least 5 minutes or up to 30 minutes before serving.

Marshmallow Pastries

Servings:8
Cooking Time:5 Minutes
Ingredients:
- 4-ounce butter, melted
- 8 phyllo pastry sheets, thawed
- ½ cup chunky peanut butter
- 8 teaspoons marshmallow fluff
- Pinch of salt

Directions:
1. Preheat the Air fryer to 360°F and grease an Air fryer basket.
2. Brush butter over 1 filo pastry sheet and top with a second filo sheet.
3. Brush butter over second filo pastry sheet and repeat with all the remaining sheets.
4. Cut the phyllo layers in 8 strips and put 1 tablespoon of peanut butter and 1 teaspoon of marshmallow fluff on the underside of a filo strip.
5. Fold the tip of the sheet over the filling to form a triangle and fold repeatedly in a zigzag manner.
6. Arrange the pastries into the Air fryer basket and cook for about 5 minutes.
7. Season with a pinch of salt and serve warm.

Merengues

Servings: 6
Cooking Time: 65 Minutes
Ingredients:
- 2 egg whites
- 1 teaspoon lime zest, grated
- 1 teaspoon lime juice
- 4 tablespoons Erythritol

Directions:
1. Whisk the egg whites until soft peaks. Then add Erythritol and lime juice and whisk the egg whites until you get strong peaks. After this, add lime zest and carefully stir the egg white mixture. Preheat the air fryer to 275°F. Line the air fryer basket with baking paper. With the help of the spoon make the small merengues and put them in the air fryer in one layer. Cook the dessert for 65 minutes.

Almond Shortbread Cookies

Servings:8
Cooking Time: 1 Hour 10 Minutes
Ingredients:
- ½ cup salted butter, softened
- ¼ cup granulated sugar
- 1 teaspoon almond extract
- 1 teaspoon vanilla extract
- 2 cups all-purpose flour

Directions:
1. In a large bowl, cream butter, sugar, and extracts. Gradually add flour, mixing until well combined.
2. Roll dough into a 12" x 2" log and wrap in plastic. Chill in refrigerator at least 1 hour.
3. Preheat the air fryer to 300°F.
4. Slice dough into ¼"-thick cookies. Place in the air fryer basket 2" apart, working in batches as needed, and cook 10 minutes until the edges start to brown. Let cool completely before serving.

Molten Lava Cakes

Servings:3
Cooking Time: 10 Minutes
Ingredients:
- 2 large eggs
- 1 teaspoon vanilla extract
- ¼ teaspoon salt
- 3 tablespoons unsalted butter
- ¾ cup milk chocolate chips
- ¼ cup all-purpose flour
- Cooking spray

Directions:
1. Preheat the air fryer to 350°F. Spray three 4" ramekins with cooking spray.
2. In a medium bowl, whisk eggs, vanilla, and salt until well combined.
3. In a large microwave-safe bowl, microwave butter and chocolate chips in 20-second intervals, stirring after each interval, until mixture is fully melted, smooth, and pourable.
4. Whisk chocolate and slowly add egg mixture. Whisk until fully combined.
5. Sprinkle flour into bowl and whisk into chocolate mixture. It should be easily pourable.
6. Divide batter evenly among prepared ramekins. Place in the air fryer basket and cook 5 minutes until the edges and top are set.
7. Let cool 5 minutes and use a butter knife to loosen the edges from ramekins.
8. To serve, place a small dessert plate upside down on top of each ramekin. Quickly flip ramekin and plate upside down so lava cake drops to the plate. Let cool 5 minutes. Serve.

Crème Brulee

Servings:3
Cooking Time: 60 Minutes
Ingredients:
- 1 cup milk
- 2 vanilla pods
- 10 egg yolks
- 4 tbsp sugar + extra for topping

Directions:
1. In a pan, add the milk and cream. Cut the vanilla pods open and scrape the seeds into the pan with the vanilla pods also. Place the pan over medium heat on a stovetop until almost boiled while stirring regularly. Turn off the heat. Add the egg yolks to a bowl and beat it. Add the sugar and mix well but not too bubbly.
2. Remove the vanilla pods from the milk mixture; pour the mixture onto the eggs mixture while stirring constantly. Let it sit for 25 minutes. Fill 2 to 3 ramekins with the mixture. Place the ramekins in the fryer basket and cook them at 190°F for 50 minutes. Once ready, remove the ramekins and let sit to cool. Sprinkle the remaining sugar over and use a torch to melt the sugar, so it browns at the top.

Nutty Fudge Muffins

Servings:10
Cooking Time:10 Minutes
Ingredients:
- 1 package fudge brownie mix
- 1 egg
- 2 teaspoons water
- ¼ cup walnuts, chopped
- 1/3 cup vegetable oil

Directions:
1. Preheat the Air fryer to 300°F and grease 10 muffin tins lightly.
2. Mix brownie mix, egg, oil and water in a bowl.
3. Fold in the walnuts and pour the mixture in the muffin cups.
4. Transfer the muffin tins in the Air fryer basket and cook for about 10 minutes.
5. Dish out and serve immediately.

Ricotta Lemon Cake

Servings: 8
Cooking Time: 40 Minutes
Ingredients:
- 1 lb ricotta
- 4 eggs
- 1 lemon juice
- 1 lemon zest
- ¼ cup erythritol

Directions:
1. Preheat the air fryer to 325°F.
2. Spray air fryer baking dish with cooking spray.
3. In a bowl, beat ricotta cheese until smooth.
4. Whisk in the eggs one by one.
5. Whisk in lemon juice and zest.
6. Pour batter into the prepared baking dish and place into the air fryer.
7. Cook for 40 minutes.
8. Allow to cool completely then slice and serve.

Creamy Pudding

Servings: 6
Cooking Time: 25 Minutes
Ingredients:
- 2 cups fresh cream
- 6 egg yolks, whisked
- 6 tablespoons white sugar
- Zest of 1 orange

Directions:
1. Combine all ingredients in a bowl and whisk well.
2. Divide the mixture between 6 small ramekins.
3. Place the ramekins in your air fryer and cook at 340°F for 25 minutes.
4. Place in the fridge for 1 hour before serving.

Chocolate Chip Cookie Cake

Servings:8
Cooking Time: 15 Minutes
Ingredients:
- 4 tablespoons salted butter, melted
- ⅓ cup granular brown erythritol
- 1 large egg
- ½ teaspoon vanilla extract
- 1 cup blanched finely ground almond flour
- ½ teaspoon baking powder
- ¼ cup low-carb chocolate chips

Directions:
1. In a large bowl, whisk together butter, erythritol, egg, and vanilla. Add flour and baking powder, and stir until combined.
2. Fold in chocolate chips, then spoon batter into an ungreased 6" round nonstick baking dish.
3. Place dish into air fryer basket. Adjust the temperature to 300°F and set the timer for 15 minutes. When edges are browned, cookie cake will be done.
4. Slice and serve warm.

Oreo-coated Peanut Butter Cups

Servings:8
Cooking Time: 4 Minutes
Ingredients:
- 8 Standard ¾-ounce peanut butter cups, frozen
- ⅓ cup All-purpose flour
- 2 Large egg white(s), beaten until foamy
- 16 Oreos or other creme-filled chocolate sandwich cookies ground to crumbs in a food processor
- Vegetable oil spray

Directions:
1. Set up and fill three shallow soup plates or small pie plates on your counter: one for the flour, one for the beaten egg white(s), and one for the cookie crumbs.
2. Dip a frozen peanut butter cup in the flour, turning it to coat all sides. Shake off any excess, then set it in the beaten egg white(s). Turn it to coat all sides, then let any excess egg white slip back into the rest. Set the candy bar in the cookie crumbs. Turn to coat on all parts, even the sides. Dip the peanut butter cup back in the egg white(s) as before, then into the cookie crumbs as before, making sure you have a solid, even coating all around the cup. Set aside while you dip and coat the remaining cups.
3. When all the peanut butter cups are dipped and coated, lightly coat them on all sides with the vegetable oil spray. Set them on a plate and freeze while the air fryer heats.

4. Preheat the air fryer to 400°F.

5. Set the dipped cups wider side up in the basket with as much air space between them as possible. Air-fry undisturbed for 4 minutes, or until they feel soft but the coating is set.

6. Turn off the machine and remove the basket from it. Set aside the basket with the fried cups for 10 minutes. Use a nonstick-safe spatula to transfer the fried cups to a wire rack. Cool for at least another 5 minutes before serving.

Moon Pie

Servings:4
Cooking Time: 10 Minutes
Ingredients:

- 8 large marshmallows
- 8 squares each of dark, milk and white chocolate

Directions:

1. Arrange the cracker halves on a cutting board. Put 2 marshmallows onto half of the graham cracker halves. Place 2 squares of chocolate onto the cracker with the marshmallows. Put the remaining crackers on top to create 4 sandwiches. Wrap each one in the baking paper so it resembles a parcel. Cook in the fryer for 5 minutes at 340°F.

Tortilla Fried Pies

Servings: 12
Cooking Time: 5 Minutes
Ingredients:

- 12 small flour tortillas
- ½ cup fig preserves
- ¼ cup sliced almonds
- 2 tablespoons shredded, unsweetened coconut
- oil for misting or cooking spray

Directions:

1. Wrap refrigerated tortillas in damp paper towels and heat in microwave 30 seconds to warm.

2. Working with one tortilla at a time, place 2 teaspoons fig preserves, 1 teaspoon sliced almonds, and ½ teaspoon coconut in the center of each.

3. Moisten outer edges of tortilla all around.

4. Fold one side of tortilla over filling to make a half-moon shape and press down lightly on center. Using the tines of a fork, press down firmly on edges of tortilla to seal in filling.

5. Mist both sides with oil or cooking spray.

6. Place hand pies in air fryer basket close but not overlapping. It's fine to lean some against the sides and corners of the basket. You may need to cook in 2 batches.

7. Cook at 390°F for 5 minutes or until lightly browned. Serve hot.

8. Refrigerate any leftover pies in a closed container. To serve later, toss them back in the air fryer basket and cook for 2 or 3 minutes to reheat.

Ricotta Stuffed Apples

Servings: 4
Cooking Time: 25 Minutes
Ingredients:

- ½ cup cheddar cheese
- ¼ cup raisins
- 2 apples
- ½ tsp ground cinnamon

Directions:

1. Preheat air fryer to 350°F. Combine cheddar cheese and raisins in a bowl and set aside. Chop apples lengthwise and discard the core and stem. Sprinkle each half with cinnamon and stuff each half with 1/4 of the cheddar mixture. Bake for 7 minutes, turn, and Bake for 13 minutes more until the apples are soft. Serve immediately.

Lemon Berries Stew

Servings: 4
Cooking Time: 20 Minutes
Ingredients:

- 1 pound strawberries, halved
- 4 tablespoons stevia
- 1 tablespoon lemon juice
- 1 and ½ cups water

Directions:

1. In a pan that fits your air fryer, mix all the ingredients, toss, put it in the fryer and cook at 340°F for 20 minutes. Divide the stew into cups and serve cold.

Cream Cheese Shortbread Cookies

Servings:12
Cooking Time: 20 Minutes
Ingredients:

- ¼ cup coconut oil, melted
- 2 ounces cream cheese, softened
- ½ cup granular erythritol
- 1 large egg, whisked
- 2 cups blanched finely ground almond flour
- 1 teaspoon almond extract

Directions:

1. Combine all ingredients in a large bowl to form a firm ball.

2. Place dough on a sheet of plastic wrap and roll into a 12"-long log shape. Roll log in plastic wrap and place in refrigerator 30 minutes to chill.

3. Remove log from plastic and slice into twelve equal cookies. Cut two sheets of parchment paper to fit air fryer basket. Place six cookies on each ungreased sheet. Place one sheet with cookies into air fryer basket. Adjust the temperature to 320°F and set the timer for 10 minutes, turning cookies halfway through cooking. They will be lightly golden when done. Repeat with remaining cookies.

4. Let cool 15 minutes before serving to avoid crumbling.

Hearty Banana Pastry

Servings:2
Cooking Time: 15 Minutes
Ingredients:

- 3 tbsp honey
- 2 puff pastry sheets, cut into thin strips
- fresh berries to serve

Directions:

1. Preheat your air fryer up to 340°F.

2. Place the banana slices into the cooking basket. Cover with the pastry strips and top with honey. Cook for 10 minutes. Serve with fresh berries.

Chocolate Doughnut Holes

Servings:20
Cooking Time: 6 Minutes
Ingredients:

- 1 cup blanched finely ground almond flour
- ½ cup low-carb vanilla protein powder
- ½ cup granular erythritol

- ¼ cup unsweetened cocoa powder
- ½ teaspoon baking powder
- 2 large eggs, whisked
- ½ teaspoon vanilla extract

Directions:

1. Mix all ingredients in a large bowl until a soft dough forms. Separate and roll dough into twenty balls, about 2 tablespoons each.

2. Cut a piece of parchment to fit your air fryer basket. Working in batches if needed, place doughnut holes into air fryer basket on ungreased parchment. Adjust the temperature to 380°F and set the timer for 6 minutes, flipping doughnut holes halfway through cooking. Doughnut holes will be golden and firm when done. Let cool completely before serving, about 10 minutes.

Cinnamon Pretzels

Servings:6
Cooking Time: 10 Minutes

Ingredients:

- 1½ cups shredded mozzarella cheese
- 1 cup blanched finely ground almond flour
- 2 tablespoons salted butter, melted, divided
- ¼ cup granular erythritol, divided
- 1 teaspoon ground cinnamon

Directions:

1. Place mozzarella, flour, 1 tablespoon butter, and 2 tablespoons erythritol in a large microwave-safe bowl. Microwave on high 45 seconds, then stir with a fork until a smooth dough ball forms.

2. Separate dough into six equal sections. Gently roll each section into a 12" rope, then fold into a pretzel shape.

3. Place pretzels into ungreased air fryer basket. Adjust the temperature to 370°F and set the timer for 8 minutes, turning pretzels halfway through cooking.

4. In a small bowl, combine remaining butter, remaining erythritol, and cinnamon. Brush ½ mixture on both sides of pretzels.

5. Place pretzels back into air fryer and cook an additional 2 minutes at 370°F.

6. Transfer pretzels to a large plate. Brush on both sides with remaining butter mixture, then let cool 5 minutes before serving.

Mini Crustless Peanut Butter Cheesecake

Servings:2
Cooking Time: 10 Minutes

Ingredients:

- 4 ounces cream cheese, softened
- 2 tablespoons confectioners' erythritol
- 1 tablespoon all-natural, no-sugar-added peanut butter
- ½ teaspoon vanilla extract
- 1 large egg, whisked

Directions:

1. In a medium bowl, mix cream cheese and erythritol until smooth. Add peanut butter and vanilla, mixing until smooth. Add egg and stir just until combined.

2. Spoon mixture into an ungreased 4" springform nonstick pan and place into air fryer basket. Adjust the temperature to 300°F and set the timer for 10 minutes. Edges will be firm, but center will be mostly set with only a small amount of jiggle when done.

3. Let pan cool at room temperature 30 minutes, cover with plastic wrap, then place into refrigerator at least 2 hours. Serve chilled.

Cranberry Jam

Servings: 8
Cooking Time: 20 Minutes

Ingredients:

- 2 pounds cranberries
- 4 ounces black currant
- 2 pounds sugar
- Zest of 1 lime
- 3 tablespoons water

Directions:

1. In a pan that fits your air fryer, add all the ingredients and stir.

2. Place the pan in the fryer and cook at 360°F for 20 minutes.

3. Stir the jam well, divide into cups, refrigerate, and serve cold.

Lemon Mousse

Servings:6
Cooking Time:10 Minutes

Ingredients:

- 12-ounces cream cheese, softened
- ¼ teaspoon salt
- 1 teaspoon lemon liquid stevia
- 1/3 cup fresh lemon juice
- 1½ cups heavy cream

Directions:

1. Preheat the Air fryer to 345°F and grease a large ramekin lightly.

2. Mix all the ingredients in a large bowl until well combined.

3. Pour into the ramekin and transfer into the Air fryer.

4. Cook for about 10 minutes and pour into the serving glasses.

5. Refrigerate to cool for about 3 hours and serve chilled.

Peanut Butter S'mores

Servings:10
Cooking Time: 1 Minute

Ingredients:

- 10 Graham crackers (full, double-square cookies as they come out of the package)
- 5 tablespoons Natural-style creamy or crunchy peanut butter
- ½ cup Milk chocolate chips
- 10 Standard-size marshmallows (not minis and not jumbo campfire ones)

Directions:

1. Preheat the air fryer to 350°F .

2. Break the graham crackers in half widthwise at the marked place, so the rectangle is now in two squares. Set half of the squares flat side up on your work surface. Spread each with about 1½ teaspoons peanut butter, then set 10 to 12 chocolate chips point side up into the peanut butter on each, pressing gently so the chips stick.

3. Flatten a marshmallow between your clean, dry hands and set it atop the chips. Do the same with the remaining marshmallows on the other coated graham crackers. Do not set the other half of the graham crackers on top of these coated graham crackers.

4. When the machine is at temperature, set the treats graham cracker side down in a single layer in the basket. They may touch, but even a fraction of an inch between them will provide better air flow. Air-fry undisturbed for 45 seconds.
5. Use a nonstick-safe spatula to transfer the topped graham crackers to a wire rack. Set the other graham cracker squares flat side down over the marshmallows. Cool for a couple of minutes before serving.

Custard

Servings: 4
Cooking Time: 45 Minutes
Ingredients:
- 2 cups whole milk
- 2 eggs
- ¼ cup sugar
- ⅛ teaspoon salt
- ¼ teaspoon vanilla
- cooking spray
- ⅛ teaspoon nutmeg

Directions:
1. In a blender, process milk, egg, sugar, salt, and vanilla until smooth.
2. Spray a 6 x 6-inch baking pan with nonstick spray and pour the custard into it.
3. Cook at 300°F for 45 minutes. Custard is done when the center sets.
4. Sprinkle top with the nutmeg.
5. Allow custard to cool slightly.
6. Serve it warm, at room temperature, or chilled.

Chocolate Soufflés

Servings:2
Cooking Time: 15 Minutes
Ingredients:
- 2 large eggs, whites and yolks separated
- 1 teaspoon vanilla extract
- 2 ounces low-carb chocolate chips
- 2 teaspoons coconut oil, melted

Directions:
1. In a medium bowl, beat egg whites until stiff peaks form, about 2 minutes. Set aside. In a separate medium bowl, whisk egg yolks and vanilla together. Set aside.
2. In a separate medium microwave-safe bowl, place chocolate chips and drizzle with coconut oil. Microwave on high 20 seconds, then stir and continue cooking in 10-second increments until melted, being careful not to overheat chocolate. Let cool 1 minute.
3. Slowly pour melted chocolate into egg yolks and whisk until smooth. Then, slowly begin adding egg white mixture to chocolate mixture, about ¼ cup at a time, folding in gently.
4. Pour mixture into two 4" ramekins greased with cooking spray. Place ramekins into air fryer basket. Adjust the temperature to 400°F and set the timer for 15 minutes. Soufflés will puff up while cooking and deflate a little once cooled. The center will be set when done. Let cool 10 minutes, then serve warm.

Sage Cream

Servings: 4
Cooking Time: 30 Minutes
Ingredients:
- 7 cups red currants

- 1 cup swerve
- 1 cup water
- 6 sage leaves

Directions:
1. In a pan that fits your air fryer, mix all the ingredients, toss, put the pan in the fryer and cook at 330°F for 30 minutes. Discard sage leaves, divide into cups and serve cold.

Hot Coconut 'n Cocoa Buns

Servings:8
Cooking Time: 15 Minutes
Ingredients:
- ¼ cup cacao nibs
- 1 cup coconut milk
- 1/3 cup coconut flour
- 3 tablespoons cacao powder
- 4 eggs, beaten

Directions:
1. Preheat the air fryer for 5 minutes.
2. Combine all ingredients in a mixing bowl.
3. Form buns using your hands and place in a baking dish that will fit in the air fryer.
4. Bake for 15 minutes for 375°F.
5. Once air fryer turns off, leave the buns in the air fryer until it cools completely.

Cinnamon-sugar Pretzel Bites

Servings:4
Cooking Time: 1 Hour 10 Minutes
Ingredients:
- 1 cup all-purpose flour
- 1 teaspoon quick-rise yeast
- 2 tablespoons granulated sugar, divided
- ¼ teaspoon salt
- 1 tablespoon olive oil
- ⅓ cup warm water
- 2 teaspoons baking soda
- 1 teaspoon ground cinnamon
- Cooking spray

Directions:
1. In a large bowl, mix flour, yeast, 2 teaspoons sugar, and salt until combined.
2. Pour in oil and water and stir until a dough begins to form and pull away from the edges of the bowl. Remove dough from the bowl and transfer to a lightly floured surface. Knead 10 minutes until dough is mostly smooth.
3. Spritz dough with cooking spray and place into a large clean bowl. Cover with plastic wrap and let rise 1 hour.
4. Preheat the air fryer to 400°F.
5. Press dough into a 6" × 4" rectangle. Cut dough into twenty-four even pieces.
6. Fill a medium saucepan over medium-high heat halfway with water and bring to a boil. Add baking soda and let it boil 1 minute, then add pretzel bites. You may need to work in batches. Cook 45 seconds, then remove from water and drain. They will be puffy but should have mostly maintained their shape.
7. Spritz pretzel bites with cooking spray. Place in the air fryer basket and cook 5 minutes until golden brown.
8. In a small bowl, mix remaining sugar and cinnamon. When pretzel bites are done cooking, immediately toss in cinnamon and sugar mixture and serve.

Nutella And Banana Pastries

Servings:4
Cooking Time:12 Minutes
Ingredients:
- 1 puff pastry sheet, cut into 4 equal squares
- ½ cup Nutella
- 2 bananas, sliced
- 2 tablespoons icing sugar

Directions:
1. Preheat the Air fryer to 375°F and grease an Air fryer basket.
2. Spread Nutella on each pastry square and top with banana slices and icing sugar.
3. Fold each square into a triangle and slightly press the edges with a fork.
4. Arrange the pastries in the Air fryer basket and cook for about 12 minutes.
5. Dish out and serve immediately.

Fried Oreos

Servings: 12
Cooking Time: 6 Minutes Per Batch
Ingredients:
- oil for misting or nonstick spray
- 1 cup complete pancake and waffle mix
- 1 teaspoon vanilla extract
- ½ cup water, plus 2 tablespoons
- 12 Oreos or other chocolate sandwich cookies
- 1 tablespoon confectioners' sugar

Directions:
1. Spray baking pan with oil or nonstick spray and place in basket.
2. Preheat air fryer to 390°F.
3. In a medium bowl, mix together the pancake mix, vanilla, and water.
4. Dip 4 cookies in batter and place in baking pan.
5. Cook for 6minutes, until browned.
6. Repeat steps 4 and 5 for the remaining cookies.
7. Sift sugar over warm cookies.

Lime Bars

Servings:12
Cooking Time: 33 Minutes
Ingredients:
- 1½ cups blanched finely ground almond flour, divided
- ¾ cup confectioners' erythritol, divided
- 4 tablespoons salted butter, melted
- ½ cup fresh lime juice
- 2 large eggs, whisked

Directions:
1. In a medium bowl, mix together 1 cup flour, ¼ cup erythritol, and butter. Press mixture into bottom of an ungreased 6" round nonstick cake pan.
2. Place pan into air fryer basket. Adjust the temperature to 300°F and set the timer for 13 minutes. Crust will be brown and set in the middle when done.
3. Allow to cool in pan 10 minutes.
4. In a medium bowl, combine remaining flour, remaining erythritol, lime juice, and eggs. Pour mixture over cooled crust and return to air fryer for 20 minutes at 300°F. Top will be browned and firm when done.

5. Let cool completely in pan, about 30 minutes, then chill covered in the refrigerator 1 hour. Serve chilled.

Easy Churros

Servings: 12
Cooking Time: 10 Minutes
Ingredients:
- ½ cup Water
- 4 tablespoons (¼ cup/½ stick) Butter
- ¼ teaspoon Table salt
- ½ cup All-purpose flour
- 2 Large egg(s)
- ¼ cup Granulated white sugar
- 2 teaspoons Ground cinnamon

Directions:
1. Bring the water, butter, and salt to a boil in a small saucepan set over high heat, stirring occasionally.
2. When the butter has fully melted, reduce the heat to medium and stir in the flour to form a dough. Continue cooking, stirring constantly, to dry out the dough until it coats the bottom and sides of the pan with a film, even a crust. Remove the pan from the heat, scrape the dough into a bowl, and cool for 15 minutes.
3. Using an electric hand mixer at medium speed, beat in the egg, or eggs one at a time, until the dough is smooth and firm enough to hold its shape.
4. Mix the sugar and cinnamon in a small bowl. Scoop up 1 tablespoon of the dough and roll it in the sugar mixture to form a small, coated tube about ½ inch in diameter and 2 inches long. Set it aside and make 5 more tubes for the small batch or 11 more for the large one.
5. Set the tubes on a plate and freeze for 20 minutes. Meanwhile, Preheat the air fryer to 375°F .
6. Set 3 frozen tubes in the basket for a small batch or 6 for a large one with as much air space between them as possible. Air-fry undisturbed for 10 minutes, or until puffed, brown, and set.
7. Use kitchen tongs to transfer the churros to a wire rack to cool for at least 5 minutes. Meanwhile, air-fry and cool the second batch of churros in the same way.

Glazed Chocolate Doughnut Holes

Servings: 5
Cooking Time: 22 Minutes
Ingredients:
- 1 cup self-rising flour
- 1 ¼ cups plain full-fat Greek yogurt
- ¼ cup cocoa powder
- ½ cup granulated sugar
- 1 cup confectioners' sugar
- ¼ cup heavy cream
- 1 teaspoon vanilla extract

Directions:
1. Preheat the air fryer to 350°F. Spray the inside of the air fryer basket with cooking spray.
2. In a large bowl, combine flour, yogurt, cocoa powder, and granulated sugar. Knead by hand 5 minutes until a large, sticky ball of dough is formed.
3. Roll mixture into balls, about 2 tablespoons each, to make twenty doughnut holes. Place doughnut holes in the air fryer basket and cook 12 minutes, working in batches as necessary.

4. While doughnut holes are cooking, in a medium bowl, mix confectioners' sugar, cream, and vanilla. Allow doughnut holes 5 minutes to cool before rolling each in the glaze. Chill in the refrigerator 5 minutes to allow glaze to set before serving.

Coconut Rice Cake

Servings: 8
Cooking Time: 30 Minutes
Ingredients:
- 1 cup all-natural coconut water
- 1 cup unsweetened coconut milk
- 1 teaspoon almond extract
- ¼ teaspoon salt
- 4 tablespoons honey
- cooking spray
- ¾ cup raw jasmine rice
- 2 cups sliced or cubed fruit

Directions:
1. In a medium bowl, mix together the coconut water, coconut milk, almond extract, salt, and honey.
2. Spray air fryer baking pan with cooking spray and add the rice.
3. Pour liquid mixture over rice.
4. Cook at 360°F for 15minutes. Stir and cook for 15 minutes longer or until rice grains are tender.
5. Allow cake to cool slightly. Run a dull knife around edge of cake, inside the pan. Turn the cake out onto a platter and garnish with fruit.

Pumpkin Pie–spiced Pork Rinds

Servings:4
Cooking Time: 5 Minutes
Ingredients:
- 3 ounces plain pork rinds
- 2 tablespoons salted butter, melted
- 1 teaspoon pumpkin pie spice
- ¼ cup confectioners' erythritol

Directions:
1. In a large bowl, toss pork rinds in butter. Sprinkle with pumpkin pie spice, then toss to evenly coat.
2. Place pork rinds into ungreased air fryer basket. Adjust the temperature to 400°F and set the timer for 5 minutes. Pork rinds will be golden when done.
3. Transfer rinds to a medium serving bowl and sprinkle with erythritol. Serve immediately.

Peanut Butter Cookies

Servings:9
Cooking Time: 27 Minutes
Ingredients:
- 2 tablespoons salted butter, melted
- 2 tablespoons all-natural, no-sugar-added peanut butter
- ⅓ cup granular brown erythritol
- 1 large egg
- ½ teaspoon vanilla extract
- 1 cup blanched finely ground almond flour
- ½ teaspoon baking powder

Directions:
1. In a large bowl, whisk together butter, peanut butter, erythritol, egg, and vanilla. Add flour and baking powder, and stir until combined.

2. Separate dough into nine equal pieces and roll each into a ball, about 2 tablespoons each.
3. Cut three pieces of parchment to fit your air fryer basket and place three cookies on each ungreased piece.
4. Place one piece of parchment with cookies into air fryer basket. Adjust the temperature to 300°F and set the timer for 9 minutes. Edges of cookies will be browned when done. Repeat with remaining cookies. Serve warm.

Olive Oil Cake

Servings:8
Cooking Time: 30 Minutes
Ingredients:
- 2 cups blanched finely ground almond flour
- 5 large eggs, whisked
- ¾ cup extra-virgin olive oil
- ⅓ cup granular erythritol
- 1 teaspoon vanilla extract
- 1 teaspoon baking powder

Directions:
1. In a large bowl, mix all ingredients. Pour batter into an ungreased 6" round nonstick baking dish.
2. Place dish into air fryer basket. Adjust the temperature to 300°F and set the timer for 30 minutes. The cake will be golden on top and firm in the center when done.
3. Let cake cool in dish 30 minutes before slicing and serving.

Delicious Vanilla Custard

Servings: 2
Cooking Time: 20 Minutes
Ingredients:
- 5 eggs
- 2 tbsp swerve
- 1 tsp vanilla
- ½ cup unsweetened almond milk
- ½ cup cream cheese

Directions:
1. Add eggs in a bowl and beat using a hand mixer.
2. Add cream cheese, sweetener, vanilla, and almond milk and beat for 2 minutes more.
3. Spray two ramekins with cooking spray.
4. Pour batter into the prepared ramekins.
5. Preheat the air fryer to 350°F.
6. Place ramekins into the air fryer and cook for 20 minutes.
7. Serve and enjoy.

Fried Pineapple Chunks

Servings: 3
Cooking Time: 10 Minutes
Ingredients:
- 3 tablespoons Cornstarch
- 1 Large egg white, beaten until foamy
- 1 cup Ground vanilla wafer cookies (not low-fat cookies)
- ¼ teaspoon Ground dried ginger
- 18 Fresh 1-inch chunks peeled and cored pineapple

Directions:
1. Preheat the air fryer to 400°F.
2. Put the cornstarch in a medium or large bowl. Put the beaten egg white in a small bowl. Pour the cookie crumbs and ground dried ginger into a large zip-closed plastic bag, shaking it a bit to combine them.

3. Dump the pineapple chunks into the bowl with the cornstarch. Toss and stir until well coated. Use your cleaned fingers or a large fork like a shovel to pick up a few pineapple chunks, shake off any excess cornstarch, and put them in the bowl with the egg white. Stir gently, then pick them up and let any excess egg white slip back into the rest. Put them in the bag with the crumb mixture. Repeat the cornstarch-then-egg process until all the pineapple chunks are in the bag. Seal the bag and shake gently, turning the bag this way and that, to coat the pieces well.

4. Set the coated pineapple chunks in the basket with as much air space between them as possible. Even a fraction of an inch will work, but they should not touch. Air-fry undisturbed for 10 minutes, or until golden brown and crisp.

5. Gently dump the contents of the basket onto a wire rack. Cool for at least 5 minutes or up to 15 minutes before serving.

Delicious Spiced Apples

Servings: 6
Cooking Time: 10 Minutes
Ingredients:
- 4 small apples, sliced
- 1 tsp apple pie spice
- 1/2 cup erythritol
- 2 tbsp coconut oil, melted

Directions:
1. Add apple slices in a mixing bowl and sprinkle sweetener, apple pie spice, and coconut oil over apple and toss to coat.
2. Transfer apple slices in air fryer dish. Place dish in air fryer basket and cook at 350°F for 10 minutes.
3. Serve and enjoy.

Peanut Cookies

Servings: 4
Cooking Time: 5 Minutes
Ingredients:
- 4 tablespoons peanut butter
- 4 teaspoons Erythritol
- 1 egg, beaten
- ¼ teaspoon vanilla extract

Directions:
1. In the mixing bowl mix up peanut butter, Erythritol, egg, and vanilla extract. Stir the mixture with the help of the fork. Then make 4 cookies. Preheat the air fryer to 355°F. Place the cookies in the air fryer and cook them for 5 minutes.

Midnight Nutella Banana Sandwich

Servings: 2
Cooking Time: 8 Minutes
Ingredients:
- butter, softened
- 4 slices white bread
- ¼ cup chocolate hazelnut spread
- 1 banana

Directions:
1. Preheat the air fryer to 370°F.
2. Spread the softened butter on one side of all the slices of bread and place the slices buttered side down on the counter. Spread the chocolate hazelnut spread on the other side of the bread slices. Cut the banana in half and then slice each half into three slices lengthwise. Place the banana slices on two slices of bread and top with the remaining slices of bread to make two sandwiches. Cut the sandwiches in half – this will help them all

fit in the air fryer at once. Transfer the sandwiches to the air fryer.

3. Air-fry at 370°F for 5 minutes. Flip the sandwiches over and air-fry for another 2 to 3 minutes, or until the top bread slices are nicely browned. Pour yourself a glass of milk or a midnight nightcap while the sandwiches cool slightly and enjoy!

Fried Twinkies

Servings: 6
Cooking Time: 5 Minutes
Ingredients:
- 2 Large egg white(s)
- 2 tablespoons Water
- 1½ cups Ground gingersnap cookie crumbs
- 6 Twinkies
- Vegetable oil spray

Directions:
1. Preheat the air fryer to 400°F.
2. Set up and fill two shallow soup plates or small pie plates on your counter: one for the egg white(s), whisked with the water until foamy; and one for the gingersnap crumbs.
3. Dip a Twinkie in the egg white(s), turning it to coat on all sides, even the ends. Let the excess egg white mixture slip back into the rest, then set the Twinkie in the crumbs. Roll it to coat on all sides, even the ends, pressing gently to get an even coating. Then repeat this process: egg white(s), followed by crumbs. Lightly coat the prepared Twinkie on all sides with vegetable oil spray. Set aside and coat each of the remaining Twinkies with the same double-dipping technique, followed by spraying.
4. Set the Twinkies flat side up in the basket with as much air space between them as possible. Air-fry for 5 minutes, or until browned and crunchy.
5. Use a nonstick-safe spatula to gently transfer the Twinkies to a wire rack. Cool for at least 10 minutes before serving.

Kiwi Pastry Bites

Servings: 6
Cooking Time: 45 Minutes
Ingredients:
- 3 kiwi fruits, cut into 12 pieces
- 12 wonton wrappers
- ½ cup peanut butter

Directions:
1. Lay out wonton wrappers on a flat, clean surface. Place a kiwi piece on each wrapper, then with 1 tsp of peanut butter. Fold each wrapper from one corner to another to create a triangle. Bring the 2 bottom corners together, but do not seal. Gently press out any air, then press the open edges to seal. Preheat air fryer to 370°F. Bake the wontons in the greased frying basket for 15-18 minutes, flipping once halfway through cooking, until golden and crisp. Let cool for a few minutes.

Pecan Snowball Cookies

Servings: 12
Cooking Time: 24 Minutes
Ingredients:
- 1 cup chopped pecans
- ½ cup salted butter, melted
- ½ cup coconut flour
- ¾ cup confectioners' erythritol, divided
- 1 teaspoon vanilla extract

Directions:

1. In a food processor, blend together pecans, butter, flour, ½ cup erythritol, and vanilla 1 minute until a dough forms.
2. Form dough into twelve individual cookie balls, about 1 tablespoon each.
3. Cut three pieces of parchment to fit air fryer basket. Place four cookies on each ungreased parchment and place one piece parchment with cookies into air fryer basket. Adjust air fryer temperature to 325°F and set the timer for 8 minutes. Repeat cooking with remaining batches.
4. When the timer goes off, allow cookies to cool 5 minutes on a large serving plate until cool enough to handle. While still warm, dust cookies with remaining erythritol. Allow to cool completely, about 15 minutes, before serving.

Strawberry Shortcake

Servings:6
Cooking Time: 25 Minutes
Ingredients:
- 2 tablespoons coconut oil
- 1 cup blanched finely ground almond flour
- 2 large eggs, whisked
- ½ cup granular erythritol
- 1 teaspoon baking powder
- 1 teaspoon vanilla extract
- 2 cups sugar-free whipped cream
- 6 medium fresh strawberries, hulled and sliced

Directions:
1. In a large bowl, combine coconut oil, flour, eggs, erythritol, baking powder, and vanilla. Pour batter into an ungreased 6" round nonstick baking dish.
2. Place dish into air fryer basket. Adjust the temperature to 300°F and set the timer for 25 minutes. When done, shortcake should be golden and a toothpick inserted in the middle will come out clean.
3. Remove dish from fryer and let cool 1 hour.
4. Once cooled, top cake with whipped cream and strawberries to serve.

Strawberry Cups

Servings: 8
Cooking Time: 10 Minutes
Ingredients:
- 16 strawberries, halved
- 2 tablespoons coconut oil
- 2 cups chocolate chips, melted

Directions:
1. In a pan that fits your air fryer, mix the strawberries with the oil and the melted chocolate chips, toss gently, put the pan in the air fryer and cook at 340°F for 10 minutes. Divide into cups and serve cold.

Coconut Flour Cake

Servings:6
Cooking Time: 25 Minutes
Ingredients:
- 2 tablespoons salted butter, melted
- ⅓ cup coconut flour
- 2 large eggs, whisked
- ½ cup granular erythritol
- 1 teaspoon baking powder
- 1 teaspoon vanilla extract
- ½ cup sour cream

Directions:
1. Mix all ingredients in a large bowl. Pour batter into an ungreased 6" round nonstick baking dish.
2. Place baking dish into air fryer basket. Adjust the temperature to 300°F and set the timer for 25 minutes. The cake will be dark golden on top, and a toothpick inserted in the center should come out clean when done.
3. Let cool in dish 15 minutes before slicing and serving.

Chocolate Macaroons

Servings: 16
Cooking Time: 8 Minutes
Ingredients:
- 2 Large egg white(s), at room temperature
- ⅛ teaspoon Table salt
- ½ cup Granulated white sugar
- 1½ cups Unsweetened shredded coconut
- 3 tablespoons Unsweetened cocoa powder

Directions:
1. Preheat the air fryer to 375°F.
2. Using an electric mixer at high speed, beat the egg white(s) and salt in a medium or large bowl until stiff peaks can be formed when the turned-off beaters are dipped into the mixture.
3. Still working with the mixer at high speed, beat in the sugar in a slow stream until the meringue is shiny and thick.
4. Scrape down and remove the beaters. Fold in the coconut and cocoa with a rubber spatula until well combined, working carefully to deflate the meringue as little as possible.
5. Scoop up 2 tablespoons of the mixture. Wet your clean hands and roll that little bit of coconut bliss into a ball. Set it aside and continue making more balls: 7 more for a small batch, 15 more for a medium batch, or 23 more for a large one.
6. Line the bottom of the machine's basket or the basket attachment with parchment paper. Set the balls on the parchment with as much air space between them as possible. Air-fry undisturbed for 8 minutes, or until dry, set, and lightly browned.
7. Use a nonstick-safe spatula to transfer the macaroons to a wire rack. Cool for at least 10 minutes before serving. Or cool to room temperature, about 30 minutes, then store in a sealed container at room temperature for up to 3 days.

Coconut And Berries Cream

Servings: 6
Cooking Time: 30 Minutes
Ingredients:
- 12 ounces blackberries
- 6 ounces raspberries
- 12 ounces blueberries
- ¾ cup swerve
- 2 ounces coconut cream

Directions:
1. In a bowl, mix all the ingredients and whisk well. Divide this into 6 ramekins, put them in your air fryer and cook at 320°F for 30 minutes. Cool down and serve it.

Apple Pie Crumble

Servings:4
Cooking Time:25 Minutes
Ingredients:
- 1 can apple pie
- ¼ cup butter, softened

- 9 tablespoons self-rising flour
- 7 tablespoons caster sugar
- Pinch of salt

Directions:
1. Preheat the Air fryer to 320°F and grease a baking dish.
2. Mix all the ingredients in a bowl until a crumbly mixture is formed.
3. Arrange the apple pie in the baking dish and top with the mixture.
4. Transfer the baking dish into the Air fryer basket and cook for about 25 minutes.
5. Dish out in a platter and serve.

Roasted Pumpkin Seeds & Cinnamon

Servings: 2
Cooking Time: 35 Minutes
Ingredients:
- 1 cup pumpkin raw seeds
- 1 tbsp. ground cinnamon
- 2 tbsp. sugar
- 1 cup water
- 1 tbsp. olive oil

Directions:
1. In a frying pan, combine the pumpkin seeds, cinnamon and water.
2. Boil the mixture over a high heat for 2 - 3 minutes.
3. Pour out the water and place the seeds on a clean kitchen towel, allowing them to dry for 20 - 30 minutes.
4. In a bowl, mix together the sugar, dried seeds, a pinch of cinnamon and one tablespoon of olive oil.
5. Pre-heat the Air Fryer to 340°F.
6. Place the seed mixture in the fryer basket and allow to cook for 15 minutes, shaking the basket periodically throughout.

Cream Cups

Servings: 6
Cooking Time: 10 Minutes
Ingredients:
- 2 tablespoons butter, melted
- 8 ounces cream cheese, soft
- 3 tablespoons coconut, shredded and unsweetened
- 3 eggs
- 4 tablespoons swerve

Directions:
1. In a bowl, mix all the ingredients and whisk really well. Divide into small ramekins, put them in the fryer and cook at 320°F and bake for 10 minutes. Serve cold.

Banana Chips With Chocolate Glaze

Servings: 2
Cooking Time: 20 Minutes
Ingredients:
- 2 banana, cut into slices
- 1/4 teaspoon lemon zest
- 1 tablespoon agave syrup
- 1 tablespoon cocoa powder
- 1 tablespoon coconut oil, melted

Directions:
1. Toss the bananas with the lemon zest and agave syrup. Transfer your bananas to the parchment-lined cooking basket.
2. Bake in the preheated Air Fryer at 370°F for 12 minutes, turning them over halfway through the cooking time.
3. In the meantime, melt the coconut oil in your microwave; add the cocoa powder and whisk to combine well.
4. Serve the baked banana chips. Enjoy!

Chocolate Lava Cakes

Servings: 2
Cooking Time: 15 Minutes
Ingredients:
- 2 large eggs, whisked
- ¼ cup blanched finely ground almond flour
- ½ teaspoon vanilla extract
- 2 ounces low-carb chocolate chips, melted

Directions:
1. In a medium bowl, mix eggs with flour and vanilla. Fold in chocolate until fully combined.
2. Pour batter into two 4" ramekins greased with cooking spray. Place ramekins into air fryer basket. Adjust the temperature to 320°F and set the timer for 15 minutes. Cakes will be set at the edges and firm in the center when done. Let cool 5 minutes before serving.

Cinnamon Apple Chips

Servings: 6
Cooking Time: 8 Minutes
Ingredients:
- 3 Granny Smith apples, wash, core and thinly slice
- 1 tsp ground cinnamon
- Pinch of salt

Directions:
1. Rub apple slices with cinnamon and salt and place into the air fryer basket.
2. Cook at 390°F for 8 minutes. Turn halfway through.
3. Serve and enjoy.

INDEX

A

All-Purpose Flour

Banana-nut Muffins   28

Blueberry Muffins   33

Chocolate Chip Scones   27

Pigs In A Blanket   23

Mini Pita Breads   23

Green Onion Pancakes   28

Parmesan Pizza Nuggets   35

Crispy Cajun Fried Chicken   70

Coconut Shrimp   99

Fish-in-chips   89

Pizza Dough   125

Almond Shortbread Cookies   145

Cinnamon-sugar Pretzel Bites   149

Fried Dill Pickle Chips   48

Crispy Ravioli Bites   37

Fried Dill Pickle Chips   48

Fried Olives   42

Buttermilk Biscuits   115

Almond

Chocolate Almond Crescent Rolls   20

Almond And Sun-dried Tomato   65

Almond Asparagus   124

Almond Shortbread Cookies   145

Honey-roasted Mixed Nuts   143

Tortilla Fried Pies   147

Almond Green Beans   119

Shallots Almonds Green Beans   120

Almond Flour

Bacon, Egg, And Cheese Calzones   30

Chocolate Chip Muffins   33

Southern-style Catfish   101

Dinner Rolls   108

Pesto Spinach Flatbread   126

Almond Flour Battered Wings   124

Cinnamon Pretzels   148

Cream Cheese Shortbread Cookies   147

Olive Oil Cake   151

Peanut Butter Cookies   151

Pumpkin Cake   141

Chocolate Chip Cookie Cake   146

Strawberry Shortcake   146

Lime Bars   150

Chocolate Doughnut Holes   147

Brown Sugar Cookies   143

Mini Bagels   23

Apple

Apple Rollups   39

Sweet Apple Fries   40

Crispy Apple Fries With Caramel Sauce   121

Healthy Apple-licious Chips   135

Apple Dumplings   137

Delicious Spiced Apples   152

Ricotta Stuffed Apples   147

Apple Pie   137

Baked Apple   144

Brown Sugar Baked Apples   138

Cinnamon Apple Chips   154

Artichoke Heart

Lemon And Butter Artichokes   106

Roman Artichokes   114

Asparagus

Easy Parmesan Asparagus   116

Perfect Asparagus   107

Foil Packet Lemon Butter Asparagus   113

Asparagus Wrapped In Pancetta   111

Cheesy Baked Asparagus   110

Almond Asparagus   124

Asparagus Fries   114

Honey-mustard Asparagus Puffs   104

Parmesan Asparagus   116

Avocado

Bunless Breakfast Turkey Burgers   17

Avocado Tempura   22

Avocado Fries   44

Crab-stuffed Avocado Boats   89

Avocado Rolls   123

B

Baby Carrot

Glazed Carrots   120

Caramelized Carrots   129

Savory Roasted Carrots   104

Roasted Carrots   45

Baby Spinach

Not-so-english Muffins   17

Mediterranean Egg Sandwich   17

Eggs Salad   22

Green Scramble   19

Bacon

Bacon Puff Pastry Pinwheels   23

Bacon Eggs   29

Bacon, Egg, And Cheese Calzones   30

Bacon Cups   34

Peppered Maple Bacon Knots   28

Jalapeño And Bacon Breakfast Pizza   27

Maple-bacon Doughnuts   32

Not-so-english Muffins   17

Bacon-wrapped Mozzarella Sticks   46

Fiery Bacon-wrapped Dates   46

Bacon-wrapped Goat Cheese Poppers   39

Bacon-wrapped Jalapeño Poppers   41

Bacon-y Cauliflower Skewers   50

Bacon And Blue Cheese Burgers   63

Bacon With Shallot And Greens   58

Bacon-wrapped Chicken   71

Butter And Bacon Chicken   75

Hasselback Alfredo Chicken   80

Bacon Chicken Mix   79

Bacon-balsamic Brussels Sprouts   104

Hasselbacks   109

Gorgeous Jalapeño Poppers   132

Chocolate-covered Maple Bacon   141

Cheddar Bacon Ranch Pinwheels   59

Zucchini Topped With Coconut Cream 'n Bacon   136

Air Fry Bacon   47

Bacon-wrapped Onion Rings 49

Chocolate Bacon Bites 46

Bacon-wrapped Cabbage Bites 37

Bacon Butter 38

Bacon-wrapped Pork Tenderloin 63

Bacon Wrapped Filets Mignons 59

Egg Muffins 18

Bacon & Hot Dogs Omelet 17

Spinach-bacon Rollups 21

Bacon And Cheese Quiche 25

Breakfast Quiche 19

Sausage Bacon Fandango 25

Mini Bacon Egg Quiches 25

Roasted Brussels Sprouts With Bacon 120

Green Beans And Potatoes Recipe 118

Cheesy Loaded Broccoli 119

Fried Mashed Potato Balls 106

Bacon Strip

English Breakfast 29

Meaty Omelet 27

Fiery Bacon-wrapped Dates 42

Wrapped Smokies In Bacon 42

Wrapped Shrimp Bites 35

Bacon-wrapped Scallops 99

Steakhouse Filets Mignons 67

Bacon Candy 37

Banana

Banana Baked Oatmeal 20

Banana-nut Muffins 28

Banana Chips With Chocolate Glaze 154

Chocolate Brownie 138

Nutella And Banana Pastries 150

Midnight Nutella Banana Sandwich 152

Fried Banana S'mores 139

Hearty Banana Pastry 147

Grilled Banana Boats 139

Banana And Rice Pudding 140

Beef

Perfect Burgers 22

Inside-out Cheeseburgers 20

Mexican Muffins 44

Ground Beef 61

Stress-free Beef Patties 63

Beef & Mushrooms 56

Meatloaf 62

Friday Night Cheeseburgers 61

Cheeseburgers 55

Bacon And Blue Cheese Burgers 63

Jumbo Italian Meatballs 69

Mexican-style Shredded Beef 58

Roast Beef 60

Beef Short Ribs 67

Bourbon-bbq Sauce Marinated Beef Bbq 54

Smokehouse-style Beef Ribs 66

Bourbon-bbq Sauce Marinated Beef Bbq 54

Chicken-fried Steak 53

Barbecue-style Beef Cube Steak 53

Mustard Beef Mix 62

Garlic Fillets 69

Perfect Strip Steaks 66

Mexican-style Shredded Beef 58

Chives Meatballs 47

Empanadas 60

Delicious Cheeseburgers 53

Simple Beef 64

Mozzarella-stuffed Meatloaf 62

Beet

Veggie Chips 38

Beet Fries 107

Bell Pepper

Cheesy Bell Pepper Eggs 33

Roasted Peppers 40

Fajita Flank Steak Rolls 65

Stuffed Peppers 54

Bell Peppers Cups 128

Cauliflower Rice–stuffed Peppers 132

Spinach And Artichoke–stuffed Peppers 134

Roasted Red Pepper Dip 41

Biscuit Dough

Maple-bacon Doughnuts 32

Lemon Iced Donut Balls 141

Monkey Bread 142

Black Bean

Mexican-style Frittata 118

Black Bean And Rice Burrito Filling 129

Cheese & Bean Burgers 125

Blue Cheese

Bacon & Blue Cheese Tartlets 46

Bacon And Blue Cheese Burgers 63

Blueberry

Blueberry Muffins 33

Bread

Cheesy Mustard Toasts 29

Tuscan Toast 32

French Toast Sticks 27

Strawberry Toast 29

Hole In One 25

Mini Pita Breads 23

Garlic Bread Knots 25

Croutons 42

Apple Rollups 39

Grilled Cheese Sandwich Deluxe 35

Pita Chips 37

Cheesy Garlic Bread 116

Roasted Vegetable Grilled Cheese 125

Roasted Vegetable Pita Pizza 121

Midnight Nutella Banana Sandwich 152

Monkey Bread 142

Pepperoni Pockets 62

Bread crumbs

Italian-style Fried Olives 44

Eggplant Fries 51

City "chicken" 55

Chicken Nuggets 70

Crispy Italian Chicken Thighs 81

Popcorn Chicken 74

Parmesan Chicken Tenders 73

Chicken Cordon Bleu 85

Crispy Sweet-and-sour Cod Fillets 89

Super Crunchy Flounder Fillets 95

Fish Sticks 98

Toasted Ravioli 131

Thyme Lentil Patties 127

Cheese & Bean Burgers 125

Brie Cheese

Yummy Stuffed Chicken Breast 80

Grilled Cheese Sandwich Deluxe 35

Brioche

Smoked Halibut And Eggs In Brioche 100

Broccoli

Pork Egg Rolls 48

Roasted Broccoli Salad 112

Roasted Broccoli

Perfect Broccoli 105

Twice-baked Broccoli-cheddar Potatoes 124

Broccoli Salad 131

Buttered Broccoli 124

Cheesy Broccoli Sticks 123

Broccoli & Parmesan Dish 130

Broccoli With Olives 123

Crispy Shawarma Broccoli 137

Broccoli With Cauliflower 126

Vegetable Nuggets 122

Broccoli And Carrot Bites 47

Perfect Broccoli 105

Broccoli And Carrot Bites 47

Brussels Sprout

Bacon-balsamic Brussels Sprouts 104

Roasted Brussels Sprouts 114

Brussels Sprouts 118

Brussels Sprouts With Balsamic Oil 127

Sweet And Sour Brussel Sprouts 125

Caramelized Brussels Sprout 135

Crispy Brussels Sprouts 119

Brussels Sprout And Ham Salad 106

Buttered Brussels Sprouts 116

Savory Brussels Sprouts 115

Roasted Brussels Sprouts With Bacon 120

Bun

Perfect Burgers 22

Inside-out Cheeseburgers 20

Friday Night Cheeseburgers 61

Cheeseburgers 55

Hot Dogs

Fish Fillet Sandwich 103

Shrimp Burgers 88

Buttermilk

Chocolate Chip Scones 27

Buttermilk-fried Drumsticks 84

Corn Muffins 113

Buttermilk-fried Drumsticks 84

Yellow Squash 117

Corn Muffins 113

Buttermilk Brined Turkey Breast 83

Butternut Squash

Sweet Butternut Squash 114

Shoestring Butternut Squash Fries 119

C

Cabbage

Dijon Roast Cabbage 117

Crispy Cabbage Steaks 121

Bacon-wrapped Cabbage Bites 37

Turmeric Cabbage Mix 116

Carrot

Veggie Chips 38

Carrot Chips 36

Glazed Carrots 120

Yellow Squash And Zucchinis Dish 113

Caramelized Carrots 129

Easy Baked Root Veggies 122

Colorful Vegetable Medley 137

Easy Glazed Carrots 131

Roasted Carrots 45

Savory Roasted Carrots 104

Simple Peppared Carrot Chips 120

Sweet Roasted Carrots 129

Cashew

Spicy Roasted Cashew Nuts 132

Catfish Fillet

Fried Catfish Fillets 92

Catfish Nuggets 100

Southern-style Catfish 101

Air Fried Catfish 100

Cauliflower

Cauliflower "tater" Tots 39

Buffalo Cauliflower Wings 51

Bacon-y Cauliflower Skewers 50

Lemon Caper Cauliflower Steaks 127

Cauliflower Pizza Crust 132

Cheesy Cauliflower Crust Pizza 132

Roasted Cauliflower 131

Cauliflower Steak With Thick Sauce 134

Cauliflower Steaks Gratin 126

Broccoli With Cauliflower 126

Buffalo Cauliflower Bites 40

Cauliflower 107

Cauliflower Rice

Coconut Pudding 29

Turmeric Cauliflower Rice 114

Cauliflower Rice Balls 117

Cauliflower Rice–stuffed Peppers 132

Cranberries Pudding 139

Center Cut Pork Chop

Honey Mesquite Pork Chops 63

Cheddar Cheese

English Muffin Sandwiches 19

Garlic-cheese Biscuits 24

Ham And Egg Toast Cups 31

Cheesy Pigs In A Blanket 49

Friday Night Cheeseburgers 61

Cheese-stuffed Steak Burgers 57

Macaroni And Cheese 110

Twice-baked Broccoli-cheddar Potatoes 124

Cauliflower Pizza Crust 132

Tacos 136

Baked Polenta With Chili-cheese 135

Two-cheese Grilled Sandwiches 126

Cheddar Cheese Lumpia Rolls 42

Cheese Crackers 34

Cherry Tomato

Tomato & Garlic Roasted Potatoes 50

Mediterranean-style Cod 92

Green Beans And Tomatoes Recipe 116

Simple Zucchini Ribbons 118

Tomato Salad 113

Pesto Vegetable Kebabs 128

Tomatoes Frittata 17

Chicken Breast

Savory Ranch Chicken Bites 44

Buffalo Chicken Dip 46

Chicken Nuggets 70

Crunchy Chicken Strips 74

Chicken Gruyere 83

Basic Chicken Breasts. 78

Sweet Nutty Chicken Breasts 83

Buffalo Chicken Meatballs 73

Pretzel-crusted Chicken 76

Cajun-breaded Chicken Bites 70

Popcorn Chicken 74

Family Chicken Fingers 76

Spinach And Feta Stuffed Chicken Breasts 73

Yummy Shredded Chicken 86

Breaded Chicken Patties 85

Parmesan Chicken Tenders 73

Peppery Lemon-chicken Breast 83

Tuscan Stuffed Chicken 71

Bacon-wrapped Chicken 71

Chicken Parmesan Casserole 77

Chicken Cordon Bleu 85

Baked Chicken Nachos 84

Crispy Tender Parmesan Chicken 72

Spicy Pork Rind Fried Chicken 84

Hasselback Alfredo Chicken 80

Basic Chicken Breasts 78

15-minute Chicken 76

Herb-marinated Chicken 71

Savory Ranch Chicken Bites 44

Buffalo Chicken Dip 46

Chicken Nuggets 70

Mustardy Chicken Bites 72

Perfect Grill Chicken Breast 81

Broccoli And Cheese–stuffed Chicken 81

Sweet Lime 'n Chili Chicken Barbecue 77

Chicken Drumstick

Gingered Chicken Drumsticks 72

Sticky Drumsticks 77

Barbecue Chicken Drumsticks 79

Buttermilk-fried Drumsticks 84

Garlic Parmesan Drumsticks 79

Za'atar Chicken Drumsticks 86

Chipotle Drumsticks 75

Zesty Ranch Chicken Drumsticks 82

Chicken Leg

Bacon Chicken Mix 79

Teriyaki Chicken Legs 80

Chicken Tender

Pecan-crusted Chicken Tenders 77

Creamy Chicken Tenders 75

Chicken Chunks 76

Quick Chicken For Filling 81

Chicken Tenders With Basil-strawberry Glaze 79

Air Fried Chicken Tenderloin 79

Blackened Chicken Tenders 75

Chicken Thighs

Chicken Thighs In Salsa Verde 84

Italian Roasted Chicken Thighs 85

Chicken Fajita Poppers 77

Crispy Italian Chicken Thighs 81

Grilled Chicken Pesto 73

Chicken Adobo 86

Cinnamon Chicken Thighs 75

Pickle-brined Fried Chicken 72

Italian Chicken Thighs 74

Jerk Chicken Kebabs 72

Crispy Cajun Fried Chicken 70

Chicken Pesto Pizzas 82

Spice-rubbed Chicken Thighs 81

Ginger Turmeric Chicken Thighs 82

Simple Salsa Chicken Thighs 83

Garlic Ginger Chicken 86

Chicken Wing

Korean-style Wings 44

Buffalo Chicken Wings 80

Shishito Pepper Rubbed Wings 78

Jerk Chicken Wings 86

Dill Pickle–ranch Wings 74

Easy & Crispy Chicken Wings 79

Quick 'n Easy Garlic Herb Wings 84

Salt And Pepper Wings 78

Tangy Mustard Wings 86

Lemon Pepper Chicken Wings 82

Chicken Wings 72

Chipotle Aioli Wings 76

Garlic Dill Wings 77

Harissa Chicken Wings 85

Crispy Wings With Lemony Old Bay Spice 123

Almond Flour Battered Wings 124

Bbq Chicken Wings 42

Fried Herbed Chicken Wings 80

Chickpea

Crunchy Falafel Balls 29

Roasted Chickpeas 39

Chipotle Chickpea Tacos 118

Turmeric Crispy Chickpeas 136

Chocolate

Chocolate Chip Scones 27

Chocolate Chip Muffins 33

Chocolate Almond Crescent Rolls 20

Chocolate-covered Maple Bacon 141

Chocolate Chip Cookie Cake 146

Strawberry Cups 153

Moon Pie 147

Chocolate Lava Cakes 154

Dark Chocolate Cake 138

Chocolate Soufflés 149

Roasted Pecan Clusters 142

Party S'mores 144

Dark Chocolate Peanut Butter S'mores 144

Molten Lava Cakes 145

Coconut Cream

Coconut Eggs Mix 25

Coconut And Berries Cream 153

Coconut Flake

Coconut Shrimp 99

Toasted Coconut Flakes 140

Coconut Flour

Salty Lamb Chops 56

Crunchy Coconut Shrimp 88

Coconut Flour Cake 153

Pecan Snowball Cookies 152

Coconut Milk

Coconut Pudding 29

Gingered Chicken Drumsticks 72

Snapper Fillets With Thai Sauce 94

Hot Coconut 'n Cocoa Buns 149

Coconut Rice Cake 151

Cod Fillet

Air Fried Cod With Basil Vinaigrette 93

Crispy Sweet-and-sour Cod Fillets 89

Fish Fillet Sandwich 103

Lemon-basil On Cod Filet 96

Italian Baked Cod 95

Lemon Butter Cod 92

Cod Nuggets 92

Beer-battered Cod 97

Stevia Cod 103

Better Fish Sticks 93

Panko-breaded Cod Fillets 101

Fish-in-chips 89

Mediterranean-style Cod 92

Coriander Cod And Green Beans 96

Crunchy And Buttery Cod With Ritz Cracker Crust 89

Corn Tortilla

Taquito Quesadillas 43

Tacos 136

Cornmeal

Whole-grain Cornbread 22

Fantasy Sweet Chili Chicken Strips 74

Fried Oysters 101

Air Fried Calamari 104

Corn Muffins 113

Cremini Mushroom

Buttery Mushrooms 106

Pesto Vegetable Skewers 135

Vegetable Burgers 136

Crescent Roll Dough

Chocolate Almond Crescent Rolls 20

D

Dark Chocolate

Dark Chocolate Cake 138

Party S'mores 144

Dark Chocolate Peanut Butter S'mores 144

Dates

Fiery Bacon-wrapped Dates 42

Deli Turkey

Turkey-hummus Wraps 80

Dill Pickle

Fried Ranch Pickles 38

Fried Pickles 36

Two-cheese Grilled Sandwiches 126

Fried Dill Pickle Chips 48

Duck Breast

Balsamic Duck And Cranberry Sauce 79

E

Edamame

Warm And Salty Edamame 48

Egg

Parsley Egg Scramble With Cottage Cheese 32

Spinach Omelet 24

Puffed Egg Tarts 19

Strawberry Pastry 24

Cheesy Mustard Toasts 29

Zucchini And Spring Onions Cakes 19

Bacon Eggs 29

Bacon, Egg, And Cheese Calzones 30

Crust-less Quiche 32

Easy Egg Bites 18

Coconut Eggs Mix 25

Bacon Cups 34

Banana-nut Muffins 28

Blueberry Muffins 33

Cheddar Soufflés 22

Sausage Egg Muffins 30

Jalapeño Egg Cups 26

English Breakfast 29

Whole-grain Cornbread 22

Meaty Omelet 27

French Toast Sticks 27

Creamy Parsley Soufflé 19

Breakfast Bake 25

Sausage Solo 17

Chocolate Chip Muffins 33

Black's Bangin' Casserole 30

Ham And Egg Toast Cups 31

Eggs Salad 22

Cheesy Bell Pepper Eggs 33

Green Scramble 19

Spinach Eggs And Cheese 31

Simple Egg Soufflé 18

Cauliflower "tater" Tots 39

Pork Egg Rolls 48

Venison Backstrap 58

Crispy Ham And Eggs 68

Chicken Nuggets 70

Crunchy Chicken Strips 74

Chicken Gruyere 83

Family Chicken Fingers 76

Chicken Chunks 76

Spinach 'n Bacon Egg Cups 75

Crispy "fried" Chicken 82

Smoked Halibut And Eggs In Brioche 100

Herbed Cheese Brittle 49

Pickled Chips 50

Cheese Eggs And Leeks 27

Egg Muffins 18

Egg In A Hole 30

Mini Bagels 23

Bacon & Hot Dogs Omelet 17

Baked Eggs 31

Smoked Salmon Croissant Sandwich

159

21
Hard-"boiled" Eggs 26
Mini Tomato Quiche 28
Tomatoes Frittata 17
Oregano And Coconut Scramble 32
Bacon And Cheese Quiche 25
Cheese Pie 30

Eggplant
Eggplant Fries 51
Caprese Eggplant Stacks 125
Crispy Eggplant Rounds 128
Curried Eggplant 129
Alfredo Eggplant Stacks 130
Eggplant Parmesan 130

Elbow Macaroni
Macaroni And Cheese 110
Effortless Mac 'n' Cheese 129

English Muffin
English Muffin Sandwiches 19
Not-so-english Muffins 17
Mediterranean Egg Sandwich 17
Egg Muffins 18

F

Feta Cheese
Greek-style Frittata 32
Creamy Chicken Tenders 75
Spinach And Feta Stuffed Chicken Breasts 73
Bell Peppers Cups 128
Cool Mini Zucchini's 130

Firm Tofu
Taj Tofu 18
Sweet And Spicy Barbecue Tofu 134

Flank Steak
Fajita Flank Steak Rolls 65
Spinach And Mushroom Steak Rolls 70
Spinach And Provolone Steak Rolls 58

Flour Tortilla
Breakfast Chimichangas 33
Greek Street Tacos 34

Chipotle Chickpea Tacos 118
Cheese And Bean Enchiladas 122
Tortilla Fried Pies 147
Spinach-bacon Rollups 21
Barbecue Chicken Enchiladas 76

Goat Cheese
Bacon-wrapped Goat Cheese Poppers 39
Fried Goat Cheese 47

Graham Cracker
Peanut Butter S'mores 148
Dark Chocolate Peanut Butter S'mores 144

Grape Tomato
Chicken Pesto Pizzas 82
Mediterranean Zucchini Boats 112

Greek Yogurt
Parmesan Garlic Naan 18
Bagels 34
Cheesy Garlic Bread 116
Glazed Chocolate Doughnut Holes 150

Green Bean
Coriander Cod And Green Beans 96
Green Beans And Tomatoes Recipe 116
Balsamic Green Beans With Bacon 108
Spicy Fried Green Beans 119
Garden Fresh Green Beans 123
Green Bean Sautée 124
Lemony Green Beans 126
Colorful Vegetable Medley 137
Almond Green Beans 119
Shallots Almonds Green Beans 120
Blistered Green Beans 108
Green Beans And Potatoes Recipe 118
Crunchy Green Beans 114
Crispy Green Beans 120

Green Cabbage
Crispy Cabbage Steaks 121
Turmeric Cabbage Mix 116

Ground Turkey
Bunless Breakfast Turkey Burgers 17
Spicy Turkey Meatballs 43
Mini Greek Meatballs 43

H

Halibut Fillet
Lime Flaming Halibut 91

Hamburger Bun
Perfect Burgers 22
Inside-out Cheeseburgers 20

Heavy Cream
Effortless Mac 'n' Cheese 129

I

Italian Sausage
Sausage Egg Muffins 30
Stuffed Peppers 54

J

Jack Cheese
Apple Rollups 39
Fajita Flank Steak Rolls 65

Jumbo Shrimp
Crunchy Coconut Shrimp 88
Wrapped Shrimp Bites 35

K

Kale
Tuscan Stuffed Chicken 71
Kale Chips 43
Garlic Parmesan Kale Chips 48
Chili Kale Chips 41

Kiwi
Fruit Turnovers 140
Kiwi Pastry Bites 152

L

Lamb Chop
Garlic And Oregano Lamb Chops 55
Air Fried Thyme Garlic Lamb Chops 60
Rosemary Lamb Chops 52
Lamb Chops 59

Lemon

Charred Shishito Peppers 42

Chicken Gruyere 83

Lemon Sage Roast Chicken 78

Peppery Lemon-chicken Breast 83

Za'atar Chicken Drumsticks 86

Chicken Wings 72

Lemon-basil On Cod Filet 96

Garlic-lemon Scallops 87

Lemon Butter Scallops 100

Lemon Butter Cod 92

Sardinas Fritas 92

Lobster Tail

Buttery Lobster Tails 103

Easy Lobster Tail With Salted Butetr 88

Cajun Lobster Tails 88

Crispy Parmesan Lobster Tails 102

M

Macadamia Nut

Cocoa Bombs 142

Mozzarella Cheese

Bacon, Egg, And Cheese Calzones 30

Jalapeño And Bacon Breakfast Pizza 27

Pizza Eggs 31

Corn Dogs 67

Air Fried Cheese Chicken 84

Dinner Rolls 108

Portobello Mini Pizzas 122

Mediterranean Pan Pizza 133

Cheesy Cauliflower Crust Pizza 132

Caprese Eggplant Stacks 125

Spinach Pesto Flatbread 129

Alfredo Eggplant Stacks 130

Cinnamon Pretzels 148

Mozzarella-stuffed Meatloaf 62

O

Okra

Hot Okra Wedges 120

Okra 113

Taco Okra 107

Garlic Okra Chips 127

Okra Chips 41

Taco Okra 107

Onion

Zucchini And Spring Onions Cakes 19

Onion Marinated Skirt Steak 30

Green Onion Pancakes 28

Roasted Peppers 40

Onion Ring Nachos 50

Party Buffalo Chicken Drumettes 74

Pulled Turkey Quesadillas 78

Roasted Yellow Squash And Onions 111

Pancetta Mushroom & Onion Sautée 120

Sautéed Spinach 134

Bacon-wrapped Onion Rings 49

Beer-battered Onion Rings 40

Potato Skins 34

Pork Belly Marinated In Onion-coconut Cream 52

Bacon & Hot Dogs Omelet 17

Hashbrown Potatoes Lyonnaise 21

Onions 111

Tilapia Teriyaki 99

Orange

Orange And Brown Sugar–glazed Ham 56

Orange Marmalade 140

Creamy Pudding 146

P

Parsnip

Chewy Glazed Parsnips 124

Veggie Chips 38

Honey-roasted Parsnips 112

Pear

Honey Pear Chips 133

Pecan

Pecan-crusted Chicken Tenders 77

Chilled Strawberry Pie 141

Buttery Spiced Pecans 36

Pepperoni

English Muffin Sandwiches 19

Pizza Eggs 31

Thick-crust Pepperoni Pizza 46

Chicken & Pepperoni Pizza 81

Pepperoni Chips 51

Pepperoni Rolls 47

Pepperoni Pockets 62

Phyllo Dough

S'mores Pockets 143

Pineapple

Pepper-pineapple With Butter-sugar Glaze 128

Pineapple Sticks 138

Fried Pineapple Chunks 151

Pita Bread

Pita Chips 37

Roasted Vegetable Pita Pizza 121

Pizza Dough

Thick-crust Pepperoni Pizza 46

Home-style Cinnamon Rolls 132

Calzones

Plantain

Plantain Chips 36

Caribbean-style Fried Plantains 126

Pork Belly

Crispy Five-spice Pork Belly 66

Pork Belly Marinated In Onion-coconut Cream 52

Pork Chop

Honey Mesquite Pork Chops 63

Crouton-breaded Pork Chops 60

Buttery Pork Chops 61

Simple Pork Chops 55

Almond And Sun-dried Tomato Crusted Pork Chops 65

Mccornick Pork Chops 66

Pork Loin Chop

Wasabi-coated Pork Loin Chops 57

Tonkatsu 67

Pork Loin Steak

Crispy Pork Pork Escalopes 53

Pork Rib

Sweet Potato–crusted Pork Rib Chops 64

Teriyaki Country-style Pork Ribs 56

Extra Crispy Country-style Pork Riblets 61

Pork Sausage

Country Gravy 26

Pork Tenderloin

City "chicken" 55

Mustard And Rosemary Pork Tenderloin With Fried Apples 54

Mustard Herb Pork Tenderloin 64

Bacon-wrapped Pork Tenderloin 63

Mustard Pork 53

Portobello Mushroom

Stuffed Portobellos 129

Portobello Mini Pizzas 122

Potato

Sweet Potato-cinnamon Toast 31

Tomato & Garlic Roasted Potatoes 50

Skinny Fries 48

Potato Chips 49

Homemade French Fries 35

Veggie Chips 38

Crispy Pierogi With Kielbasa And Onions 69

Potato-wrapped Salmon Fillets 90

Sweet Potato–wrapped Shrimp 104

Rich Baked Sweet Potatoes 115

Prawn

Crispy Prawns 44

Spicy Prawns 102

Provolone Cheese

Not-so-english Muffins 17

Spinach And Mushroom Steak Rolls 70

Turkey-hummus Wraps 80

Roasted Vegetable Grilled Cheese 125

Layered Ravioli Bake 128

Spinach And Provolone Steak Rolls 58

Pumpkin

Sweet Roasted Pumpkin Rounds 109

R

Radish

Parmesan Herb Radishes 107

Sea Salt Radishes 118

Red Bell Pepper

Fajita Flank Steak Rolls 65

Steak Kebabs 68

Jerk Chicken Kebabs 72

Bell Peppers Cups 128

Pesto Vegetable Skewers 135

Cottage And Mayonnaise Stuffed Peppers 130

Mediterranean Pan Pizza 133

Pepper-pineapple With Butter-sugar Glaze 128

Roasted Vegetable Pita Pizza 121

Colorful Vegetable Medley 137

Roasted Red Pepper Dip 41

Red Onion

Onion Marinated Skirt Steak 30

Pulled Turkey Quesadillas 78

Rice

Coconut Pudding 29

Ricotta Cheese

Tuscan Stuffed Chicken 71

Portobello Mini Pizzas 122

Roma Tomato

Roasted Red Salsa 45

S

Salmon

Garlic And Dill Salmon 91

Simple Salmon 98

Simple Salmon Fillets 92

Teriyaki Salmon 87

Salmon Patties 96

Potato-wrapped Salmon Fillets 90

Horseradish-crusted Salmon Fillets 95

Salmon Patties 96

Potato-wrapped Salmon Fillets 90

Horseradish-crusted Salmon Fillets 95

Lemon-roasted Salmon Fillets 93

Miso-rubbed Salmon Fillets 103

Outrageous Crispy Fried Salmon Skin 102

Garlic And Dill Salmon 91

Simple Salmon 98

Simple Salmon Fillets 92

Teriyaki Salmon 87

Maple Balsamic Glazed Salmon 102

Smoked Salmon Croissant Sandwich 21

Lemon Butter–dill Salmon 97

Maple Butter Salmon 96

Honey-glazed Salmon 90

Scallop

Buttery Scallops 33

Lemon Butter Scallops 100

Sea Scallop

Garlic-lemon Scallops 87

Timeless Garlic-lemon Scallops 89

Seared Scallops In Beurre Blanc 93

Super-simple Scallops 90

Sea Scallops 94

Garlic Lemon Scallops 87

Self-Rising Flour

Bagels 34

Garlic-cheese Biscuits 24

Scones 21

Buttermilk-fried Drumsticks 84

Cheesy Garlic Bread 116

Glazed Chocolate Doughnut Holes 150

Garlic Knots 110

Shishito Pepper

Charred Shishito Peppers 42

Shishito Pepper Rubbed Wings 78

Shrimp

Wrapped Shrimp Bites 35

Coconut Jerk Shrimp 100

Shrimp Al Pesto 92

Italian Shrimp 98

Chili Blackened Shrimp 96

Shrimp Burgers 88

Easy-peasy Shrimp 98
Quick And Easy Shrimp 98
Chili-lime Shrimp 93
Coconut Shrimp 99
Sweet Potato–wrapped Shrimp 104
Very Easy Lime-garlic Shrimps 93
Crunchy Coconut Shrimp 88
Lemon Shrimp And Zucchinis 96

Sirloin Steak

Air Fried Grilled Steak 59
Beef Al Carbon (street Taco Meat) 63
Steak Kebabs 68
Peppered Steak Bites 55
Air Fried Steak 58
Steak Bites And Spicy Dipping Sauce 64

Skirt Steak

Medium Rare Simple Salt And Pepper Steak 24
Onion Marinated Skirt Steak 30
Champagne-vinegar Marinated Skirt Steak 56

Smoked Sausage

Cheesy Pigs In A Blanket 49

Spaghetti Squash

Roasted Spaghetti Squash 131
Spaghetti Squash 122

Spinach

Spinach Omelet 24
Greek-style Frittata 32
Mediterranean Egg Sandwich 17
Eggs Salad 22
Egg White Frittata 29
Green Scramble 19
Spinach Eggs And Cheese 31
Spinach And Mushroom Steak Rolls 70
Spinach And Feta Stuffed Chicken Breasts 73
Spinach 'n Bacon Egg Cups 75
Sautéed Spinach 134
Pesto Spinach Flatbread 126

Squash

Yellow Squash 117
Sweet Butternut Squash 114
Roasted Yellow Squash And Onions 111
Yellow Squash And Zucchinis Dish 113
Spaghetti Squash 122
Roasted Spaghetti Squash 131
Shoestring Butternut Squash Fries 119

Sweet Potato

Veggie Chips 38
Sweet Potato–crusted Pork Rib Chops 64
Sweet Potato–wrapped Shrimp 104
Rich Baked Sweet Potatoes 115
Simple Roasted Sweet Potatoes 111
Easy Baked Root Veggies 122
Sweet Potato Fries 117
Sweet Potato Chips 41
Thyme Sweet Potato Chips 38

T

Tapioca Flour

Eggplant Fries 51
Crunchy Veal Cutlets 68
City "chicken" 55
Extra Crispy Country-style Pork Riblets 61
Super Crunchy Flounder Fillets 95
Fried Dill Pickle Chips 48
Fried Olives 42

Tiger Shrimp

Quick And Easy Shrimp 98

Top Sirloin Steak

Air Fried Grilled Steak 59

Tuna

Tuna Cakes 91
Italian Tuna Roast 94
Tuna-stuffed Tomatoes 97

Tuna Steak

Ahi Tuna Steaks 88
Sesame Tuna Steak 88

Turkey

Turkey-hummus Wraps 80
Herb Seasoned Turkey Breast 83
Pulled Turkey Quesadillas 78
Buttermilk Brined Turkey Breast 83
Mini Greek Meatballs 43
Spicy Turkey Meatballs 43

Turkey Bacon

Not-so-english Muffins 17
Hasselbacks 109
Spinach-bacon Rollups 21

Turkey Breast

Herb Seasoned Turkey Breast 83
Pulled Turkey Quesadillas 78
Buttermilk Brined Turkey Breast 83

Turnip

Veggie Chips 38

W

White Bean

English Breakfast 29
Avocado Tempura 22

White Bread

Midnight Nutella Banana Sandwich 152
Grilled Cheese Sandwiches 46

White Chocolate

Moon Pie 147

White Fish Fillet

Tortilla-crusted With Lemon Filets 96

Y

Yellow Cornmeal

Fried Oysters 101

Yellow Squash

Yellow Squash 117
Yellow Squash And Zucchinis Dish 113

Yukon Gold Potato

Smashed Fried Baby Potatoes 111
Mini Hasselback Potatoes 107
Blue Cheesy Potato Wedges 38

Z

Zucchini

Zucchini And Spring Onions Cakes 19

Parmesan Zucchini Fries 38

Simple Zucchini Ribbons 118

Yellow Squash And Zucchinis Dish 113

Pesto Vegetable Skewers 135

Stuffed Portobellos 129

Zucchini Gratin 135

Pesto Vegetable Kebabs 128

Easy Baked Root Veggies 122

Zucchini Fritters 133

Cool Mini Zucchini's 130

Colorful Vegetable Medley 137

Lemon Shrimp And Zucchinis 96

Zucchini Chips 51

Mediterranean Zucchini Boats 112

Zucchini Bites 105